Praxis and Revolution

NEW DIRECTIONS IN CRITICAL THEORY

Amy Allen, General Editor

New Directions in Critical Theory presents outstanding classic and contemporary texts in the tradition of critical social theory, broadly construed. The series aims to renew and advance the program of critical social theory, with a particular focus on theorizing contemporary struggles around gender, race, sexuality, class, and globalization and their complex interconnections.

For a complete list of titles, see page 277.

Praxis and Revolution

A Theory of Social Transformation

Eva von Redecker

Translated by Lucy Duggan

Columbia University Press

New York

Columbia University Press
Publishers Since 1893
New York   Chichester, West Sussex
cup.columbia.edu

Library of Congress Cataloging-in-Publication Data
Names: Redecker, Eva von, author. | Duggan, Lucy, 1986– translator.
Title: Praxis and revolution : a theory of social transformation / Eva von Redecker ;
translated by Lucy Duggan.
Other titles: Praxis und Revolution. English.
Description: New York : Columbia University Press, [2021] | Translation of:
Praxis und Revolution : eine Sozialtheorie radikalen Wandels. | Includes bibliographical
references and index.
Identifiers: LCCN 2020053549 (print) | LCCN 2020053550 (ebook) |
ISBN 9780231198226 (hardback) | ISBN 9780231198233 (trade paperback) |
ISBN 9780231552547 (ebook)
Subjects: LCSH: Revolutions. | Social action. | Social change.
Classification: LCC HM876 .R425 2021 (print) | LCC HM876 (ebook) |
DDC 361.2—dc23
LC record available at https://lccn.loc.gov/2020053549
LC ebook record available at https://lccn.loc.gov/2020053550

Columbia University Press books are printed
on permanent and durable acid-free paper.
Printed in the United States of America

Cover image: iStock.com/duncan1890

Contents

Preface to the American Edition

Societies change. If they did not, they would be unable to confront challenges, solve crises, and handle confrontations. They would be unable to survive. Among those changes, the label "revolution" is reserved for the most radical and profound type of transformation. Reforms may address parts of a society, but revolutions affect the whole. Speaking of "revolution" also transports the hope that such change is not just happening to people, but driven by them, and for the better. Like coups and elections, revolutions can result in new governments. But their aim is normally larger: it is to bring about entirely new forms of government, with institutions that increase self-determination. Constitutional assemblies, parliaments, and councils were all "made by revolution." But revolutions can also directly target social structures. While political revolutions locate the domination they aim to overthrow between governments and people, social ones attack the oppressive relations between groups brought into hierarchy by material distribution and identity formation. Social revolutions can challenge not just how we are ruled, but who we are, who owns what, how we relate to one another, and how we reproduce our material life.

Despite the much-desired scope and ambition that the concept of revolution evokes, its received form is at odds with the contemporary landscape of struggles. Neither a "big bang" nor a "core contradiction" approach to revolution fits the multiple sites of organizing, occupying, and rebelling that social movements pursue at present.

However, revolution need not be understood as sudden and unified—this is at least what *Praxis and Revolution* argues. The book sets out to show that even the prototypical revolution in France 1789 is better reconstructed as processual and as driven from various peripheries. The reader will spend more time in prison cells, knitting circles, affinity groups, and antechambers than at the Bastille, and they will have ample opportunity to meet the revolution there.

In order to construct a theoretical model of an expanded understanding of revolution, *Praxis and Revolution* adds two specific terms to our thinking about radical change: the notion of interstices and the concept of metalepsis. Those terms are not exactly self-explanatory. In the book itself, they are laid out within a framework of social theory, a framework that synthesizes and updates philosophical debates on practice, on structures, on rules and agency. Here, in the opening, I simply want to introduce "interstices" and "metalepsis" by way of illustration. I start in reverse order, with the more obscure term. "Metalepsis"—like "dialectics"—is a term of ancient rhetoric. And like dialectics, when borrowed to theorize history, this term addresses the question of how we get from here to there. Dialectics, as the basis of left-Hegelian or Marxist philosophy of history, asserts that the force of contradictions can move us to the place of their resolution. Metalepsis is concerned with a similar passage, but gives it a different flavor: How do we get from this total mess to a place where things make sense?[1] How indeed, if the mess won't even fit into the mold of one supercharged contradiction? Metalepsis, as a figure of speech, is on the surface utterly absurd and unintelligible. Not the kind of neat metaphorical stand-in of one word for a recognizably similar other. Not "sail" or "vessel" for "ship." More something like "a specimen of what the rats would desert first." That is, you need to know a whole different play on words to provide the context that allows you to decode the first. It makes one's brain hurt a bit, but revolutions, as history can tell, are not easy or straightforward either. Nor are they always possible, since history is not set up as a riddle. The idea of metalepsis is rather that sometimes, through partly contingent circumstances, structural conjunctures ensue that allow for the replacement of old with new. Not every unintelligible sentence is a play on words. But whether or not a given sequence might be one is never fully determined by its given form. It depends on what kinds of clues are brought up in the course of guessing. This guessing, in historical struggles, is not a linguistic activity, at least not one detached from material practice. Metaleptic replacement is when one of the ultimate tools of fossil-gadget-powered petty masculinity—the leaf blower—was used during the Portland protests to blow back teargas onto the police. Metaleptic replacement is when, for a precious period of two weeks, the Share-a-ton opens in insurrectionary Minneapolis. Its name and its practice fuse in double metonymy the riches of a hitherto privately owned hotel chain, the Sheraton, with an economy of abundance: share a ton. Taken over by activists, though apparently with a certain level of consent by the former management, the hotel opened its doors to the unhoused in the city and those who needed shelter in the midst of uprising. Its operations amazed observers:

> While no one seemed to be in charge, somehow, overnight, the operation provided not just the services of a hotel—complete with volunteers pushing carts of linens down the halls for housekeeping—but a health clinic and a donation drop-off site. What had been a conference room now bore hand-drawn signs saying "HARM REDUCTION," with condoms for the taking and Narcan at the ready. Residents were encouraged to participate in tasks and decision making, and, together with the volunteers, they had nightly meetings to discuss things like the name and security of the sanctuary.[2]

This sanctuary, a place hardly intelligible in the existing order of things, is one example for what is meant by interstices. It is a short-lived anomaly, yet it forms a crack through which a possible different future illuminates the present. The Share-a-ton did not last, facing eviction as well as internal collapse, which goes to show that revolution in one interstice is impossible. The dots need to be joined. Yet for that to happen, nothing "else," no recourse to a totally different order is required. What is needed is more of those breaks with the same. More interstices that cultivate abundant relationality and counter oppression, more metaleptic sites of refunctioning what is already there, more footholds from which to push back against reaction. This commitment to the interstitial might come as a disappointment for pumped-up dreams of revolutionary militancy and discipline, but those are bound to be disappointed anyway.

Interstitial activism is antiheroic. Its attitude is captured in one North American moment of this otherwise terribly European book, when a gender-queer diva from the ranks of ACT UP is promoting siding with failure. Siding with failure is something entirely different than failure alone. To occupy the site of failure is to refuse abandonment, to persist in struggle, and to nourish concrete hope. And not to abandon the weak, in times of a pandemic affirmed by neoliberal autocrats as deadly selection, can amount to an encompassing revolutionary program. "No one is sacrificed. Everyone is essential" is the motto of a sketched revolution that the Black Lives Matter cofounder Opal Tometi and the filmmaker Avi Lewis narrated in October 2020.[3] Metaleptically reviewing the bleak present from the future, they formulate an interstitial focus: "What was needed was a spark. That spark was us."

I only started studying the Black Radical Tradition after completing this book, in the context of a subsequent project on property and capitalist domination. I realized that I had been ignorant of a wellspring of theorizing on interstitial change while writing a book on it. Many of the motifs I originally encountered in German Jewish anarchists like Gustav Landauer and Martin Buber have been constitutive for Black Liberation for centuries, since the practice of marooning as exodus from slavery. Those enclaves of freedom were essential for organizing the escape routes for enslaved people from the South to the North, and in the Caribbean they formed partisan bases for the Haitian Revolution.[4] In the twentieth century, it is especially in Black Feminist engagement with the Black Panther Party that the insistence on sustained interstitial politics was formulated—most famously perhaps in Audre Lorde's reflections on Malcolm X's legacy, which contain the crucial slogan "Revolution is not a one-time event."[5] In "Retelling Black Radicalism for the 21st Century," Kehinde Andrews also equates Black Liberation with a "concrete politics" starting "in your home, you community, your school."[6]

One effect of the interstitial extension of revolutionary politics is an overcoming of the private vs. public divide. This overcoming surpasses and reverses bourgeois feminist logics. Not "the personal is political," but "the revolution is interstitial." No longer detached from the reproduction of everyday life, radical politics can be seen as arising from the labor of care and from the concrete concern for freedom and survival in oppressed communities. In this vein, Alexis Pauline Gumbs powerfully demonstrates how we might open the concept of mothering onto politics. "Mothering," she writes, is "a queer collaboration with the future" and "a technology of transformation."[7] But it is not just that the political dimension of reproduction comes to the fore in the interstitial perspective. It is also that radical politics can articulate their dependency on sustenance. Caring for the revolution equals making it. Siding with the precarious side of failure, if done in the spirit of radical reproduction, reaches beyond failure. The Black Lives Matter facilitator maree adrienne brown grounds the detached Beckettian mantra "fail, fail again, fail better" in a Black ecofeminist spirit. Discussing nonlinear and iterative movement practice, she claims: "In that paradigm there is no failure. Everything we attempt, everything we do, is either growing up as its roots go deeper, or it's decomposing, leaving its lessons in the soil for the next attempt."[8]

This book provides a long argument for interstitial revolution, and a detailed model of it. That model integrates the mechanism of metalepsis to overcome the most obvious rejoinder to prefigurative politics: that the transition from the small-scale to the whole is unaccounted for. Of course, the notion of metaleptic transfer, of refunctioning messy sequences in the light of hitherto interstitial alternatives, has drawn rejoinders of its own. I will briefly touch on the two most salient ones. The first critique, which my colleagues Frieder Vogelmann and Martin Nonhoff raised and helped me think through, is concern with the lack of "struggle" in my approach. I of course retort that care can be a hell of a struggle, but it is true: this is not a model of agonistic politics. I believe that much bolder transformation is made in contamination and refunctioning than in confrontation. I see little radical potential in the left seizing hegemony with the correctly configured antagonism. Revolution must be more than counter-counter-revolution. But this is not an argument against barricades; in itself it is not even one against violence. Riots in the line of Vicky Osterweil's reasoning can be seen as a perfectly prefigurative practice, a form of "queer birth" as she describes them: "riots struggle in the sphere of social reproduction: looting makes day-to-day life easier by changing the price of goods to zero, relieves pressure by spreading wealth in the community, and reinforces bonds of solidarity and kinship through mutual struggle and action."[9]

Now that we are in a supermarket, the second line of critique is immediately at hand. Is this a model to tackle capitalism? Isn't the recourse to the French Revolution, and the neat fit with antiracist and feminist articulations, an indication that processual, interstitial change only works for overcoming status-orders or personal domination? I sometimes want to say, "Dude, if you think that feminism is so much easier to solve than anticapitalism, then what are you still doing there in my way?" but I nevertheless share the concern. This book doesn't theorize capitalism, but it commits me to the claim that capitalist domination, even of the impersonal kind, can be reconstructed in practice-theoretical terms. In my new book *Revolution for Life*, I sketch capitalism as the order that is anchored in the modern property form and has resulted in alignments that perpetuate the practice of investment and emission.[10] I have never been convinced by the claim that capital, as self-valorization of value, was altogether disseevered from human agency, yet prone to produce crises that opened it up for intervention. Isn't that just a slightly hyperbolic way to say that it is aggregated yet not entirely beyond disaggregation?

Today, we are confronted not only with the wealth of capitalists to reappropriate but also with the debris of past production to deal with. We face not only the material interests of the ruling class but also a wave of neofascist phantom-owners siding with them.[11] In this situation, a narrowly workerist model of revolutionary agency—even if that agency were to actualize—is impotent. We need not only to expropriate the expropriators but also to abolish propertized oppression, not only to overcome alienation but also to repair catastrophic damage and bear lasting loss. This book does not invoke the concept of revolution in order to show that the task itself is easy. How could it, after so many defeats and failures? And yet, the interstitial lens may help to see what has already begun.

This text, in its journey from German PhD to book, is already wrapped in many layers of gratitude spelled out at the end of the German preface. The extraordinary privilege and joy of seeing it translated into English require further additions. I am very grateful to Lowell Frye at Columbia University Press for shepherding the production of the book through a pandemic, to two anonymous reviewers for their extremely helpful reports, and to my wonderful editors, Wendy Lochner and Amy Allen, for their support and enthusiasm. I also want to thank Raymond Geuss and Judith Butler for their generous words of encouragement at the outset. All of my amazing students from fall 2015 at the New School helped open my eyes to North American politics, and Mithra Lehn, Mariam Matar, and Marianna Poyares have remained indispensable interlocutors ever since.

At the center of this book, and my gratitude, is the person who actually translated it, Lucy Duggan, my friend and my favorite novelist. Putting the original text into the hands of someone who, I have to admit, is better with words than I myself was an extraordinary fortune. It also was a lot of fun, leading to long linguistic discussions and mutual challenges in scrutiny and inventiveness. Funding for the translation was thankfully provided by the Börsenverein des deutschen Buchhandels. I am obliged to Raymond Geuss for double-checking that the translation of the Greek background literature on metalepsis was correct. In the tedious effort of translating the references while libraries were in lockdown, Ann Copestake provided me with additional PDFs and with moral support, and Lynn Hunt was unbelievably helpful when her English page numbers were the last ones left that I could not track down. Fulvia Modica then lifted my own page numbers and magically transformed them into that condensed version of a book known as its index.

Throughout and all over again, Aurélie Herbelot helped me to say what I had to say and to cut the crap.

Preface to the German Edition

In revolutions, everything changes, but that doesn't mean that everything is new. Change arises from the existing state of affairs, through the refunctioning of existing structures, subject to practices that are anticipated and learned in the interstices of society. This constant underground work provides a stable footing that is necessary to ensure that the continuation doesn't simply preserve traditions, that the breakdown doesn't simply leave emptiness, and that crises do not simply cause paralysis.

However, this does not mean declaring that interstitial praxis is the new subject of the revolution—that is, that it makes revolutions. Revolutions are not "made" at all—unlike books, for which a particular author admits responsibility, in spite of all polyphony and collective work. Revolutions emerge from constellations of conditions that are not steered by anyone.

Even if we do not steer something, we can still understand it (better). This book devotes a good 250 pages to determining constellations of radical change from the perspective of social theory, and finally to encapsulating them with the term "metalepsis," borrowed from ancient Greek rhetoric. Metalepsis is a reversed interlocking—in this case, the interlocking of strange praxis and the structures that enable it to take place—that makes the transition possible.

For those who write them, doctoral dissertations are the transition into the academic community. The traditional rituals that are still connected with them—despite all neoliberal homogenization—create remarkable relationships: the adoption by dissertation advisors (known in German as "doctor-mothers"

and "doctor-fathers") is followed by the emergence of a scholarly work. Just as nuns, after completing their novitiate, are admitted to the convent community in a symbolic ceremony of marriage, the doctoral candidate becomes, when she defends her thesis, part of the academic congregation. As a member of that community, she ultimately has the task of making her work fit for the world again and transforming her dissertation into a book—not least in order to separate herself from her journeyman's piece, so that she can turn to new fields of research.

I am still amazed that this was possible. And this amazement leads me to something that is quite simple and certainly not new: gratitude.

In order to do justice to all the help, encouragement, and kindness that has carried me through the last years, it would be easy to fill another 250 pages. I hope that I will be able to express my gratitude in many ways that go beyond the next paragraphs, and I will limit myself here to naming the contributions without which this book would never have been written at all.

I am grateful to Rahel Jaeggi, my doctoral advisor for the dissertation on which this book is based: for the brilliant mixture of unreserved enthusiasm for the project in general and justified skepticism toward almost all of its specific hypotheses. The very experience that completely overwhelmed me for long periods during the writing of the dissertation—being addressed already as a philosophical partner in conversation, something that I could only expect to become gradually through the work on this text—seems, in retrospect, to be the most generous gift. So there is such a thing as a learning process.

Rahel offered me an inspiring and constantly enriching context, both at the Humboldt University and, temporarily, at the New School, New York, in which I was able to find cooperations, challenges, and friendships that would not be found in such abundance in many intellectual centers—I am therefore also grateful to my wonderful colleagues at the Lehrstuhl.

Finally, I would like to thank Rahel for the great personal trust that she placed in me and for filling the ivory tower with so much life that I was never forced to waste precious time brooding over whether I was in the right place.

My thanks go to Raymond Geuss for being my second advisor, and for even agreeing in the first place to take this project on so shortly before retirement. The semester that I spent writing in Cambridge secured the backbone of the entire project. The thoroughness and integrity with which Raymond engaged with my ideas were an invaluable help; I must also thank him for an unforgettable tutorial in ancient Greek, which enabled me to trust in my own fundamental terminology, as well as for advice and encouragement while I was reworking the manuscript for the book.

Several people helped with the enormous task of reading almost the entire manuscript: Daniel Loick read the dissertation, Lukas Kübler the book manuscript, and Lea-Riccarda Prix was there for the precarious steps in between. As partners in discussion, all three are irreplaceable fixtures in my philosophical constellation.

For reading, critiquing, and improving individual parts, I am grateful to Judith Butler, Robin Celikates, Lucy Duggan, Antke Engel, Sophia Ermert, Aurélie Herbelot, Leonie Hunter, Matthias Mader, Tobias Matzner, Judith Mohrmann, Johanna M. Müller, Katrin Pahl, Sophie von Redecker, Isette Schuhmacher, Margarete Stokowski, and Selana Tzschiesche.

Individual chapters and their earlier drafts benefited from being discussed in the following contexts: in several workshops with Nancy Fraser's Einstein Group; in the series of events on forms of life that Estelle Ferrarese organized in Paris and at the CMB Berlin; at Antke Engel's ten-year anniversary celebration of the Institute of Queer Theory; once in the colloquium for feminist philosophy at the HU (Mikkola); twice in the social theory colloquium in Jena (Rosa/Strecker, Rosa/Reitz); and once in the political theory colloquium in Bremen (Nonhoff/Vogelmann).

I am grateful to the social philosophy colloquium at the HU for much more than the two meetings at which I was able to present my work: for a constant intellectual base.

For invitations to colloquia and lecture series where I discussed this work, my thanks go to Sarah Bufkin (Oxford), Alice Crary (New York), Christine Hauskeller (Exeter), Hilge Landweer and Christine Kley (FU Berlin), Christian Thies (Passau), Adriana Zaharijević (Belgrade), and the Philosoph*innengruppe (Frankfurt a. M.).

I also received helpful feedback at conferences in Prague, New York, Nisyros, Erlangen, Hannover, Geneva, Zürich, and Dresden. A special role was played by the very first talk I gave on revolution, at the Frankfurt graduate conference in 2010. I thank my lucky stars that I ended up on a panel with Bini Adamczak and Daniel Loick—and I thank Bini and Daniel for everything else.

It was a pleasure to work with Campus (the publisher), and Isabell Trommer as a fantastic editor, despite the editing having to happen in a fragmentary way.

For good advice and support at crucial moments—or all the way through—as well as for useful editorial and institutional insights, I am grateful to Elisabeth Bonsen, Antke Engel, Estelle Ferrarese, Iwona Janicka, Patricia Purtschert, Martin Saar, Margarete Stokowski, Sabine Lammers, and Sidonia Blättler.

Working closely with Isette Schuhmacher, Johanna M. Müller, Lea-Riccarda Prix, and Hilkje Hänel was crucial for me. It is astonishing that you managed not only to look after my intellectual needs better than anyone else but also to keep all the other needs in mind.

The enormous demand for teaching in practical philosophy and critical theory at the Humboldt University—with seminars of up to one hundred participants—often seemed to be a hindrance to my work on this book. But dialectical contextualization, as I would try to explain in one of these seminars, means that something can be true without excluding the opposite truth: I also would not have been able to write this book without my students. With their thirst for knowledge, they continually reminded me of the point of theoretical work, and at the same time made sure I questioned its results. This book would be much less interesting if I hadn't also written it with and for you.

At the point where one can thank people for intellectual and editorial support, crucial preconditions must already have been met. It is an immense luxury and a great stroke of luck that I can live in a household that allows me to write. My deepest gratitude to the ones I love, to my friends and to my sister, who share my life with me, and also to all the guests who had patience with a host who was busy writing.

And at the same time, sometimes it is necessary to retreat to a place that has central heating and fewer rooms. Thank you, Ann, for shelter at 346 (and everywhere else) and thank you for the peaceful paradise of Richardstraße, Lea. A big thank you also to the Zeckendorf-Tower-WG and to Hof Schoolbek.

Pingu, I know you distrust any ritual acknowledgments. I will simply remain grateful to you forever.

I have talked so much here about persistent supportive work, and there is only one person who has really carried me through all transitions: my mother. She taught me and continues to show me what is important along the way: love of freedom, presence of mind, taking action, and honesty.

Susanne von Redecker, née Steffen, I thank you with all my heart and dedicate this book to you.

Introduction

". . . It Is a Revolution"

On the occasion of the storming of the Bastille on July 14, 1789, Louis XVI is said to have asked one of his courtiers, the Duke de La Rochefoucauld-Liancourt, whether the events in Paris were a revolt. "Non, Sire, c'est une révolution"—"No, Sire, it is a revolution" was his answer.

And with that, we might think, revolution was defined once and for all. Nevertheless, this book will make the case that we should disentangle "revolution" from the inevitable associations with the storming of the Bastille, and understand it from a new perspective. It will present revolution as a form of radical change that is initiated in the interstitial spaces of a social order and that leads, through lengthy processes of transfer, to a new constellation. New, because the unthinkable comes to be taken for granted. For this process, rehearsing the future and repurposing the present are more vital than uprisings and rupture. To distinguish revolutions as a specific mode over and above "mere change," what becomes definitive is then not the moment of violent culmination, but the shape of the new praxis that emerges: Is it anchored in historical moments that have so far been understood as revolutionary? Does it carry forward the richest possible legacy of emancipatory hopes and promises?

A concept of revolution in terms of praxis and process is established in three ways in this book. The introduction traces the history of the term, showing which dilemmas and desiderata arise from existing theories of revolution and require a response from any new attempt at definition. The four main sections of the book then make use of social theory to develop the approach to transformation that underpins the "extended" concept of revolution. Precisely because so many hopes and so many drastic historical experiences are concentrated in the term, the *theory* of revolution should link back to an idea of how social change actually works and thus ground the concept in social philosophy. This second and most detailed layer of argumentation will be enriched by four reflections on the experience of revolution, in the form of literary examples. Mary Wollstonecraft's novella *Maria: or, The Wrongs of Woman*, Charles Dickens's *A Tale of Two Cities*, a video installation by Matt Ebert and Bryan Landry, and Isak Dinesen's short story "The Proud Lady" will take a third, somewhat subterranean route to argue that our understanding of revolution should be reconfigured. Instead of focusing on the events to which Louis XVI and Rochefoucauld-Liancourt were referring, they invite us to see decisive social struggle in everyday practices, exemplified by a relationship constellation in a prison, a gathering of knitting women, a militant drag queen, and a runaway granddaughter.

THE CONCEPT OF REVOLUTION

Even if the quick-witted remark "Non, Sire, c'est une révolution" really was heard at the time of the storming of the Bastille, in the vocabulary of the day, this would initially only have meant that, in the vicissitudes of world history, another turning point had been reached in the eternal ups and downs. This meaning of "revolution" goes back to what was originally the language of astronomy, in which the "revolutions of the celestial bodies" described their unvarying orbits. Starting from the Renaissance, the apexes of these orbits were thought to parallel extreme historical situations. As its Latin root suggests, "revolutio" actually referred to a re-turn to the starting point, the initial constellation.[1] Thus, the "Glorious Revolution" in England—the only modern political event that was awarded the title of "revolution" before the American and French Revolutions—was not Cromwell's founding of a republic after the execution of Charles I, but the successful, constitutional transfer of the throne to William III of Orange.

Uprisings and rebellions, on the other hand, were already a ubiquitous political phenomenon in the early modern period. In France, for example, they occur repeatedly throughout the seventeenth and eighteenth centuries; prisons are generally stormed as part of the standard repertoire, even though we now only connect this with the Bastille.[2] However, these revolts never described themselves as "revolutionary." And even during the revolution itself, the representatives of the third estate did not make use of this term at first. In the writings of Voltaire and Jean-Jacques Rousseau, the philosophers most widely read by opponents of the court, the idea does play a role insofar as they considered history to be changeable and described a whole variety of upheavals as revolutions. Still, their hopes for political renewal were precisely *not* pinned to the concept of revolution. If anything was politically innovative and charged with meaning, it was the constitution—which was to be created by the newly instituted National Constituent Assembly. In July 1789, the Assembly still met in Versailles, and was in no way amenable to the idea that the rabble-rousers of the Bastille should be seen as part of its endeavors.[3]

References to a revolution only began to prevail when the mobilization of the masses became more pressing, in the course of the Revolutionary Wars and the internal escalation of the First Republic. Even then, personified allegories such as Reason and Freedom, and later the republican figure of Hercules, remained far more important.[4] Furthermore, those who talked of revolution were still not making an unambiguous claim to the newness of their own society. "Revolution" continued to mean "rolling back into position," even if it was the rolling back of counterrevolutionary forces. Later, such disparate theorists of revolution as Karl Marx and Hannah Arendt grappled with the fact that the participants of the French Revolution hid the unprecedented nature of their own actions from themselves by drawing on historical examples. But in the terms of the time, it made sense for these participants to see themselves as revolutionary in those very moments when they were reestablishing a more fundamental order—whether it was that of nature, which was retrospectively supposed to have brought forth innovations as significant as human rights, or that of the Roman Republic, whose insignia were adopted by Robespierre's Republic in a downright cultish fashion.

Nevertheless, such imitations can also be read according to the modern sense of revolution, as signs that something unprecedented really had occurred. It may be that people took refuge in historical costumes and cosmic laws in order to escape the very bottomlessness of the new—that which Hannah Arendt called "the abyss of freedom" and Marx "new scenes in world history."[5] But in the current modern understanding, revolution means exactly that—radical change that is not a "return," but a new beginning. In this understanding, the three elements that were just distinguished are mixed for the first time: efforts at transformation across the whole of society like the National Constituent Assembly, practices of collective resistance like the storming of the prison, and the sensation of having passed an apex, pushed by forces that seem almost physical.

Although the French Revolution was to remain paradigmatic for the Western European imagination, its contours came to be defined not only by this combination of elements but also by the grouping of further events. Both the American Revolution and the Polish-Lithuanian constitutional transformation underlined the central role of constitutions, which subsequently also became the object of revolutionary desire in almost all the small German states. And only the "Black Jacobins" of Haiti achieved, in 1791, the liberation that all other revolutions had invoked as a metaphor: the transition from slavery to self-governance.

It is in this enriched and newly constructed interpretation of "revolution" that the courtier's reply becomes a punch line. With his comment—"Non, Sire, c'est une révolution"—he not only corrects his ruler, but predicts his fall.

The new view that revolutions did not strive for the old starting point but for a new, higher state was also made more plausible by other tendencies that made themselves felt in Western Europe. In the philosophy of the Enlightenment, world history may have been interpreted as a cycle by Moses Mendelssohn and most of the French encyclopedists, but the notion of continuous historical progress also emerged. Gotthold Ephraim Lessing's *The Education of the Human Race* put forward this idea, as did Nicolas de Condorcet's *Sketch for a Historical Picture of the Progress of the Human Spirit*, which was written during the chaos of the revolution.

The events of the eighteenth and nineteenth centuries gave strong grounds to believe that there really were new things to be found in the world, and that all in all, history was moving in a particular direction. Colonial expansion, the development of new technology and techniques of production, population growth, and the beginnings of urbanization were all signs, in Western European eyes, of forceful strides forward, not mechanical cycles. Increasingly, they were viewed as having secular sources either in nature or in human activity itself. On a phenomenological level, the steam engine and the revolutions, which Marx later called the "locomotives of history," are really not so distant from each other: both were "patented" at the end of the eighteenth century, and both laid the foundations for the mobility of the nineteenth century.

Yet on the other hand, it is precisely the experience of revolution, the supposed culmination of progress, that shattered the enlightened picture of continuous development. Critics of the revolution see its decline into terror as chaotic and barbaric; its proponents find themselves confronted with the fact that it is not the flourishing sovereignty of the people that awaits at "the end," but a reenthronement of the Bourbons, already anticipated by Napoleon's blatant imitation of their insignia. Thus, from the beginning, there was disagreement both over whether the new was better and over whether the old had been overcome at all.

HISTORICAL MATERIALISM AS A THEORY OF REVOLUTION

If Karl Marx is the most influential philosopher of revolution, this is not least because he succeeded in bringing these conflicting moments together not just in a concept, but in a whole theory of revolution. This theory encompasses the role of continuous development as well as shocking events, the role of rebellious participants as well as processes taking place over their heads, and the role of innovation as well as continuity.

As a fundamental historical factor, Marx singled out the gradual increase in productive forces. As technology, knowledge, and the organization of work make it possible to produce goods for the satisfaction of human needs ever more effectively and in ever greater complexity, Marx argues, this progress compels the rest of society (and human needs themselves) to develop as well. Forming the basis for any society and a criterion for distinguishing different forms of society from one another, the relations of production—the way in which productivity is organized—do not in fact develop continuously, according to Marx, but through dialectical turning points. These, the actual revolutions, take place when contradictions mesh together on two levels. On the one hand, the relations of production—that is, the institutional order—have to prevent the full use of the increased productive forces, and on the other hand, a group of participants is needed whose material interests lie in overcoming the existing order and who succeed in presenting this as a general interest.

Thus, for Marx, revolutions have a driving force and a mechanism. They are fed by underlying technological progress, and succeed due to the dialectical nature of history—that is, due to the fact that history as a whole is a structure formed by contradictions. Productivity grows continuously, as does the working class; in dialectical terms, just as the working class negates its bourgeois exploiters, so technological growth negates the functionality of the existing conditions of production.

These two levels, the dynamics of productive forces and class struggle, are often cited as an inconsistency between a developmental model of change and a focus on collective agency in Marx's view of history, especially as Marx himself could never explain in a satisfactory way how it was that the objective conditions actually translated themselves into the actions of individual and collective subjects.[6] Even so, this tension can also be foregrounded as the crux of the materialistic theory of revolution. The core point of that theory would then consist in the very requirement that certain disposable and certain indisposable conditions must come together in order for revolutions to succeed. Seen in this light, revolutions—and history in general—contain a "passive element."[7] Recognizing this safeguards a materialist theory of transformation from deterministic and voluntaristic simplifications—such as vulgar Marxism or Blanquism—and establishes what is possibly the most promising element of historical materialism.[8]

Although the orthodox Marxist interpretation of the French Revolution has by now been refuted in almost all its particulars by historians,[9] it is still clear that

the course taken by the revolution suggests the materialistic schema of dialectical progress.[10] Against the backdrop of the long process of the Industrial Revolution, the political revolution represents the point of culmination, at which the
power of the aristocracy, rooted in feudal agriculture, is transferred to the rising
capitalist bourgeoisie. The liberal legal system, so important for the triumph of
capitalism, is hailed as universal moral progress by the bourgeoisie, with reference
to supposedly natural human rights. The lower classes, having fought together
against the crown and the nobility, are now divided into those who own capital
and those who can only bring their own labor to the market. This produces the
next contradiction.

As a *theory* of revolution, however, historical materialism always demands more
than just a convincing interpretation of what happened in the past—the real focus
is understanding the future. Another reason that the Marxist model became so
influential was the fact that it offered answers to urgent practical questions about
revolution. If we imagine revolutions as processes with a beginning, a moment
of transition, and a result—that is, as events that have to break out, take over, and
stabilize themselves—the Marxist theory of revolution can show that progress and
dialectics are decisive factors at each of these points. Revolutions break out, for
Marx, not only because material contradictions become increasingly extreme, but
because at the same time a group of participants—a class—also emerges, which
has both an interest in overcoming the existing order, and the power to do so.
The moment of transition from one social order to another occurs in revolutions
because the sphere in which contradictions force a dialectic change also defines
the form of society as a whole—progress does not take place in fragments. At the
same time, the transition is not presented as a total break with the past or a complete scene change. The new society "is born from the old one."[11] This continuity
in the midst of discontinuity forms a foundation for stabilization, because what
grew before remains preserved in dialectic form. Moreover, the new order is lasting because of its progressive nature: after every revolution, the world is more productive and freer, and after the last, the socialist revolution, it is even peaceful
and free of alienation. The Marxist view may never have entirely exhausted the
field of interpretations of revolution, but it does mark out the dimensions of how
much would have to be offered in order to match it: beyond simply talking about
revolution, a new theory of revolution would have to provide a philosophical justification for its own concept of the driving force and mechanism of change.

And so, it is not so much other theories whose arguments have refuted Marx's
monumental concept of revolution, but particular historical tendencies and
experiences—that is, precisely the stuff of which historical materialism is made—
that have rendered it problematic. These challenges, which have provoked

theorists to amend the Marxist corpus or to distance themselves from it, can be illustrated by a cursory run-through of the historical experiences of unsuccessful revolutionary outbreaks, transitions, and stabilizations.

THE DILEMMA OF OUTBREAK

In the course of the "long nineteenth century," it was the breaking out of revolution that initially presented a dilemma. Although industrial progress proceeded inexorably, the most organized work forces in Western Europe were not initiating revolutions; this wore down the belief in a reliable link between progress and dialectics. German social democracy formulated two conflicting dogmatic responses to this dilemma. Seen with hindsight, these answers probably tended to exacerbate the problem. Karl Kautsky's variant of scientific socialism insisted that a dialectical logic of history was necessary, and remained rigidly attached to the tactic of waiting for the right moment. Dialectics would take effect, perhaps even when progress was unexpectedly slow. Eduard Bernstein's revisionism, on the other hand, openly dissented from the view that saw technical progress as being inseparable from dialectical intensification and suggested seeking progress through parliamentary elections rather than open class struggle. In a sense, this meant taking the side of progress rather than dialectics. When, in the run-up to the First World War, broad swathes of the working class were mobilized successfully, but under the chauvinist banner of national warfare rather than in the name of international solidarity, both variants were rejected. Evidently a longer wait could also lead to dramatic losses—and parliamentary symbiosis with the nation could lead people to abandon their own class interests entirely.

This set the seal on the "outbreak dilemma," which drew (diametrically opposed) responses from both Lenin and the first generation of the Frankfurt School. Much as Lenin claimed to have his roots in Marx's concept of history, his understanding of revolution actually follows from the disintegration of that concept.[12] The avant-garde party takes over, as it were, the work of the faltering historically progressive tendencies. Class struggle for Lenin is primarily a question of power politics: a concern that may be interpreted dialectically, but that is in fact solved on an organizational and martial level.

Where Lenin pursues a kind of forced dialectics, the first generation of the Frankfurt School theorizes a deferred or "negative" dialectics. Revolution is still conceptualized in the mode of progress and via the mechanism of dialectics, but both aspects become ambivalent. With the rise of European fascism in mind, and ultimately the Shoah, it seemed that social progress could no longer be connected with the formidable growth of productive forces unless the immense possibilities for regression were also taken into account. The pacification of the consumption-orientated working class in the postwar West finalized the diagnosis of the outbreak dilemma: from the point of view of critical theory, ideology was the decisive element explaining what was now an unbridgeable gulf between objective social contradictions and the absence of a subjective will to rise up. On the one hand, the theoretical work that followed was "only" directed at the condition for the possibility of revolutions. However, as a critique of ideology, it did take on an extremely far-reaching task. Once we no longer assume that revolution is brought about by people who are predestined for the task by their class status, working on ideology promises to have revolutionary consequences in two ways: it erodes an important pillar of the existing order, and it also works directly to release its addressees for revolutionary praxis.

THE DILEMMA OF TRANSITION

However, without a solid anchoring in broader historical tendencies, revolutionary praxis itself ran into a further dilemma, namely, that of the transition. It was in the second half of the twentieth century that this dilemma became difficult to avoid: It seemed to become clear that the transition to something truly new and truly better, which had always been difficult, placed human society before a paradoxical—if not impossible—task. Given that the communist revolution had evidently failed even in the places where its enemies had not defeated it—failed especially measured against its own ideals[13]—the question seriously arose of whether it was at all possible for a form of life to change radically for the better.

This doubt, which had always attended the modern notion of revolution from the conservative side,[14] was already expressed in the first half of the twentieth century by antiauthoritarian criticism of Lenin from among socialists. Rosa Luxemburg, for instance, made the clear-sighted prediction that authoritarian organization would ultimately see the triumph of the old, internalized "knut" over revolutionary goals.[15] Martin Buber, who was accustomed to demanding the congruence of revolutionary means and ends from an anarchist and utopian socialist perspective, summarized the transition dilemma as a "tragedy of revolutions": "Their tragedy is that as regards their *positive* goal they will always result in the exact opposite of what the most honest and passionate revolutionaries strive for, unless and until this [deep social reform] has so far taken shape *before* the revolution that the revolutionary act has only to wrest the space for it in which it can develop unimpeded."[16] If the new is not already there, Buber suggests, the old will always retain the upper hand. This paradoxical diagnosis threatens to erode the possibility of transition entirely, and simultaneously presents this book with the challenge of reimagining it.

In the development of theory in the second half of the twentieth century, three partly overlapping strands can be roughly identified, which could justify Buber's pessimistic assessment. Since the milieu of French theory had retained particularly deep roots in the communist party, the Stalin shock had a strong effect there and led, in many intellectual biographies, to drastic breaks with Marxist approaches. Structuralism, which regards society as being reproduced in a stable manner in practices and orders of signification, is the clearest example of a shift in philosophical focus toward the forces of persistence.

Secondly, the theory of subjectivity that developed in response to Louis Althusser and Michel Foucault asserts that the experiences and formation of oppressed subjects precisely do not make them into the bearers of revolution. Rather, the theory of subjectivity explains the permanence of existing forces through their extension into the subjects themselves, subjects that are only formed at all through that extension. Without the basic dialectical assumption of necessary and productive contradictions, there is no feasible way out of these conditions.

The notion that the existing conditions are rooted not just in the particular system of production but in various societal arrangements that have emerged in the course of history and been psychologically internalized is also a basic insight of feminist and antiracist theory. Already before this idea became more widely established, thinkers such as Simone de Beauvoir and Frantz Fanon documented it thoroughly. That racism, patriarchy, and heteronormativity would all be resolved with a change in economic system now not only appeared implausible in the light of real existing socialism but also seemed to be refuted on a theoretical level, where they were recognized as having their own logics inherent in their historical genesis and psychological anchoring. But if there are multiple forms of oppression that cannot be collapsed into one another (at least not entirely)—that is, if we view society as "intersectional"—this undermines, in an even more fundamental way, the concept of transformation found in historical materialism. After all, revolutions can only prove themselves unambiguously to be turning points on the way to a higher, better form of society if we can locate them on a line of dialectical progress that traces an overall development. If this line frays into different aspects, countercurrents suddenly become perceptible—for instance, the fact that the civic freedom that was achieved by the French Revolution did not endow women with formal rights, and forced them into a compensatory role outside the public and economic sphere. While their class had attained dominance, bourgeois women in Western Europe in the nineteenth century were more exposed to patri-archal domination and restriction than they had been in the eighteenth century. At the same time, when we multiply the arenas of struggle, the model of dialecti-cal intensification does not stand firm either. Instead, diverse possibilities open up, allowing contradictions to be shifted or obscured, as when the Western Euro-pean working class loses sight of its conflict with capitalist exploiters because it becomes mired in colonial-racist and national-chauvinist feelings of superior-ity. And even if we apply the categories of intersectionality theory, which are in any case sometimes defined too directly by social identities, it will be very diffi-cult to establish which tendencies and phenomena actually relate to which "contradictions."

Even without the factors outlined, which gave scant hope for change, the con-cept of revolution could not simply "grow" along with the multiplicity of oppres-sion in order to get it under control. If structuralism can no longer conceive of a dynamic driving force such as progress, and the theory of subjectivity makes it seem improbable that the contradictions on the side of the participants will come to fruition, then intersectional multiplication changes the whole landscape. The prevailing conditions now come to appear as a kind of knot that can be neither untangled—because all starting points are tied up in it—nor cut. For in fact there is not even *one* knot that could be severed. Something that looks like a knot from one perspective may be a social bond when seen from another point of view.

In the face of such paradoxes, it is not so surprising—and is also a result not of quietist ideology but of real problems in the classic concept of revolution—that if the social philosophy of the late twentieth century ever talked of transforma-tion rather than just about persistent forces, an actual notion of revolution no lon-ger even came into consideration. Both in approaches that focus on subversion and variability and in contexts where revolution is eclipsed by a downright apoc-alyptic concept of "events,"[17] the project of a *theory* of revolution is abandoned. The interpretative bracket of dialectical progress just does not stretch enough to hold together struggles for change on the part of individual social groups, grass-roots resistance practices, and historical turning points. Even in critical theory, which had come to see itself if not as a direct advocate then as the placeholder for a revolution that had failed to arrive, the concept tended to fade into the back-ground. When historical lines of progress remained dominant—as in the early work of Jürgen Habermas and in Axel Honneth's reflections on the realization of freedom—these lines are evolutionary, without dialectical points of culmina-tion. However, in Axel Honneth's recent work *The Idea of Socialism*, the revolutionary legacy has returned to the foreground.[18] He envisages processes of learning and experimentation that unfold pragmatically. Still, these remain evolutionary in themselves, insofar as there is no question of going beyond the normative horizon represented by the notion of social freedom.[19] In a certain sense, then, Honneth is concerned not with the next turning point, but with completing a transition—albeit a very far-reaching one—that has already been demarcated.

Not without regret, Raymond Geuss summarizes the theoretical rejection of the term "revolution" as follows:

> If the prospects for a traditional revolution, a radical change in the political structure in the direction of increasing substantive rationality, were grim in the 1930s or the 1950s, they are, if anything, much worse at the start of the twenty-first century. We also lack a belief in a unitary, teleologically structured history and the consolation of the "dialectic." It is understandable under these circumstances that attempts to appropriate the Frankfurt School might concentrate on what might seem the only viable portion of their legacy, their cultural criticism in the narrow sense. This is perfectly understandable, but it is a mistake.[20]

While Geuss advocates that the theory of revolution be pursued beyond the premises of progressive dialectics, Wendy Brown emphasizes that with the end of a teleological notion of history and of the "consolation of dialectics," we must also admit that we have lost the classic notion of revolution. She suggests that we examine its legacy and give up what cannot be salvaged.[21] From this "left-wing grieving process," she expects at least to regain a utopian horizon, though without a mechanism to reach it: "To recuperate a utopian imaginary in the absence of a revolutionary mechanism for its realization."[22] However, relinquishing the realization mechanism of revolutionary efforts does not solve the transition dilemma, but only underlines it. In order to circumvent it, we would need entirely new forms of praxis. And indeed, Brown has recently pointed to signs of such new forms:

> I think there are many many forms of political action today that actually are making efforts in this direction. I think there's all kinds of experiments going on in prefigurative politics—that is, politics that is trying to anticipate another world, a different order. I think there are all kinds of oppositional efforts that are coalitional, that are multi-dimensional, and open, and pluralistic. . . .
>
> A lot of especially the youth-oriented or youth-built Left projects today are extremely promising, extremely exciting, and full of the kind of energies we need

that link alertness to race, to sexuality, to gender, to sustainability, to the survival of the planet, to indigeneity . . . *and* to capitalism, without reifying one of
those, without fetishizing any one of those. And I think it's still very difficult to
figure out how to mount a serious challenge to a regime of globally integrated,
finance-dominated capitalism that will take seriously that that existing regime
will literally bring life to an end as we know it within a century if we don't replace
it with something else.[23]

THE DILEMMA OF STABILIZATION

At the start of the twenty-first century, some genuine elements of revolutionary
protest action have actually shifted back into focus. The "fight for the squares"—
Tahrir, Zuccotti Park, Gezi—confronted those in power with fundamental
demands for transformation. These occupations seemed to come about spontaneously, but were often meticulously prepared: the participants coordinated with
one another in a range of ways beforehand. One effect of these movements was
that the outbreak dilemma, which had become so unassailable, suddenly melted
away like mist. Protest and resistance are back. In diverse settings, people tested
out a radical form of grass-roots democracy and pluralist organization, and a strategy emerged that was also able to counter the paradox of transition. The methods used here already embodied the principles underpinning the demands for the
future, and therefore did not threaten to extend the wrongs of the past over the
heads of the revolutionaries. Rather than fighting out social contradictions along
paths already prescribed by dialectics, the assemblies on the squares started from
scratch, beginning by creating a forum in which questions of collective life could
be negotiated and decided—if it grew strong enough. Hannah Arendt, who analyzed the ways in which power is constituted from basic political action, showed
in her essay "The Tradition and Spirit of Revolution" how in all modern revolutionary moments such councils were temporarily formed. However, Arendt's portrayal itself leads to the diagnosis of a painful dilemma. For after the outbreak
and the transition, the stabilization of the new system proves to be elusive.
According to Arendt, "the failure of the revolution" was that it did not provide
the "revolutionary spirit" with a "lasting institution."[24] Contrary to Arendt's diagnosis, which blames the antipolitical urgency of compassion for the failure of the
French Revolution, Judith Mohrmann recently pointed out the essential role of
emotion in politics, particularly revolutionary politics.[25] Still, this obviously does

not overcome the concern over the long-term safeguarding of particular revolutionary achievements.

Recent theories of radical democracy take the motif of constitutive power as the starting point for a differentiation between politics and "the political," which emerges, they argue, when the whole of an order is called into question and the object of social conflict is renegotiated. When the interplay between existing institutions and new, constitutive power is perpetuated, these approaches seem able to make a virtue of the instability evoked by Arendt. This is appealing from the point of view of a theory of democracy. However, it shifts us so far from a notion of transformation that actually sets its sights on an entirely new institutional fabric, including the realm of the social, that revolution as such moves out of reach—what Arendt meant was that existing political organs of rule should be replaced by councils, and not that the latter should keep the former on their toes.

But the inadequacy of mere interventions is also revealed from another perspective, when we consider the fact that they assume a level of solidity on the side of existing institutions that we can seemingly no longer take for granted, even in Western parliamentary democracies. The question seems less about getting things to move at all than about making them move effectively in the right direction. With unparalleled global synchronicity, counterrevolutionary and conservative-revolutionary projects are currently creating authoritarian alternatives to the legacy of the revolutionary tradition, of 1968 and feminism.

The desire to separate revolutionary forms of politics from revolutionary demands for transformation is also strangely in tension with the fact that the expectation of radical change has, in a way, intensified into a prevailing mood in today's world. A kind of "background certainty" has emerged: We are aware that our form of life is running out of resources and that we are caught up in the catastrophic dynamic of climate change. However, this is more often articulated in the form of an apocalyptic expectation of doom than in revolutionary hope. Where the end of the world seems more likely than world revolution, we could be tempted to imagine, like Walter Benjamin, that we can no longer do anything better with the locomotive of history than pull the emergency brake and make it stop.[26] But after almost one hundred years of additional historical experience, the fear arises that we might stop the train over an abyss, which could be one factor leading today's critical theory to make new attempts at mapping out revolution.

The question of how a revolutionary transformation—or, to use Arendt's phrase, a "new beginning"—can be safeguarded in the long term can also be understood as a question about constitutions. Along these lines, Hauke Brunkhorst has declared progress in the medium of law—as a learning process inscribed in constitutions—to be a revolutionary motor.[27] Meanwhile, Christoph Menke argues that revolution is best understood precisely as the excess of the supposed stabilization dilemma, so that the instability itself safeguards rather than threatens change. Revolution for him does not coincide with instituting a legal order, but could be seen as perpetuating the moment "before" this act: the reaching of a verdict through collective political means.[28] This picture emerges—in a negatively dialectical vein—from an analysis of the given frame of domination, which is anchored in the form of rights. In an expanded politics no longer foreclosed by the privative nature of individual subjective rights, stability or "peace and quiet" would then be granted by a new and sole form of human right: the right to retreat—"permanent revolution with holiday entitlement," if you will.

In a certain sense, Menke's comprehensive account still remains true to Brown's demand that we delay the question of transformation mechanisms, as his argumentation does not specify revolutionary actors and historical dynamics.

It is the integration of this social theoretical level that defines the project of Rahel Jaeggi. Taking the dynamic of immanent critique as her starting point, she views forms of life as problem-solving arrays of practice, which are kept in motion by various crises or contradictions. She restates a philosophy of history that again brackets progress and dialectics, yet in inverted order. Here, the drive behind progressive change is not a given, self-perpetuating tendency toward progress, but the dialectics of crisis-induced learning processes, which can emerge in all areas of a form of life. The mechanism whereby crises can therefore be overcome successfully, i.e., nonregressively, is then progress, in which previous learning experiences are enriched by new ones. Solutions to problems coagulate into forms of life as robust bundles of practices, taking on a stability that promises to be sustained in future learning progress.

However, in order to be fully realized, this model requires either a sufficiently integrated and conscious subject, able to react to crises by learning from them, or a very strong concept of objectively existing practical contradictions. The former recalls Menke's notion of complete revolutionary politicization. Yet that would mean that we would first need a revolution in order to create such a subject capable of learning—at least the drive and mechanism of *this* change would then have to be described by other means than learning. The latter, the assumption that there are objective contradictions (and not just differences, discontinuities, ambivalences, anomalies) pointing the way ahead, faces the challenge of dispelling the doubts about dialectical premises that have been illustrated through the outbreak and transition dilemmas. If the contradictions are there, why do they not take effect reliably? And if additional contingent factors are necessary in order to reveal and intensify such contradictions, what is driving these factors? Dogmatically dialectical positions declare these processes to be automatic.

Undogmatic historical materialists such as Jaeggi—and also Marx, in certain interpretations and in certain phases of his work—remain reliant, at this point, on conceptions of radical change that treat its form as an open question.

In *Praxis and Revolution*, therefore, the question of the drive and mechanism of change will be isolated from that of progress and dialectics. For the time being, it is "only" necessary to understand the dynamics of transformation—and thus to focus on a subject that is certain to exist.

DISASSEMBLING THE LOCOMOTIVE

The way in which we understand what is required of a concept of revolution is partly determined by our assumptions about the "track bed" of history. The majority of this book will be concerned with defending a particular view of the "making of the social" and using it as a basis to explain how change happens at all. This will eventually allow us to delineate how revolutionary change must firstly be radical, and must secondly be anchored in practices that are connected with the revolutionary legacy. The latter already implies that revolutionary change cannot remain entirely unconscious. It may take place behind the backs of the actors to the extent that they cannot predict the consequences of their actions and rarely have their aims clearly in mind—let alone having the realization of those aims firmly "in hand." But somebody has to have trusted in an alternative praxis rather than what already exists, and somebody must have seen this alternative as innovative in a broader sense. Moreover, the structural transformation has to be connected with human actions. Revolutions are not natural disasters. They do not engulf society from the outside. Nor are they comparable with climate change, which can be traced back to human actions but was not promoted in advance as a good alternative by any group of people.

We could say that relating revolutions to human actions via a notion of praxis means getting rid of the "track bed"—as if Marx's "passive elements" were simply cleared away, and as if revolutions were ultimately only dependent on our deliberate actions. There are those who might welcome this move, given that Marx's "track bed" is so saturated with a teleological philosophy of history and with an economistic social theory. However, this book opts for a "rematerialization." For when, as here, actions are subordinated to the notion of praxis, they themselves become partly inaccessible, unconscious, taking on their own logic— and thus, in a sense, they become "material." The point is then not to clear away the track bed and invent a floating locomotive, but to switch to a picture in which the conditions and the driving force of revolution are not two clearly separate things, but are ultimately made of the same substance. The whole first half of this book is dedicated to the task of developing and defending this interpretation of the social. Understood as praxis, the human ability to act forms a rigid track bed; understood as praxis, the material conditions are themselves in motion.

This approach does justice to Wendy Brown's plea that the classic concept of revolution should be subject to a fundamental renegotiation, while also endeavoring to go one step further beyond the initial goal marked by her argument. I develop new terms for transformation mechanisms alongside the minimum of utopian hope. This does not mean rolling the notion of revolution back into its Hegelian-Marxist orbit. The movement that this account of revolution takes could instead be described as obeying a centrifugal force; it is concerned with expanding the radius of positions consulted, not eliding those arising from the lessons of the revolutionary dilemmas. Nor will that be the only expansion.

We have already touched on various positions that focus on what holds back transformation (critique of ideology, structuralism, theory of subjectivity, radical democracy), and my revision of revolution is geared to take them into account. All of these positions make reference to failed revolutionary dynamics. They do so not only because of the unquestionable fact that humanity has not yet been emancipated but also because it was above all those events that found expression in Western academic philosophy. Moments that partly encouraged greater optimism, such as the self-liberation of colonized peoples and the women's movement, only occasionally entered the canon of theory, and then only in a rudimentary form. Not that there was no reflection on these subjects—it just belongs to a legacy that is barely recorded in any will or testament. When Réné Char states in a phrase repeatedly quoted by Arendt—"notre héritage n'est pas précédé d'aucun testament"—that the rules governing the appropriation of cultural inheritance have generally been suspended, this is even more the case for potential discourses of revolution.[29] The critical examination of the inheritance—to stay with Wendy Brown's image—thus requires us first to ask what sort of legacy we are dealing with—and what sort of "we."

INTERSTITIAL HERITAGE

In the spirit of a "pearl-diving" criticism that undertakes to bring up fragments from the past,[30] I would like to illustrate the two decisive conceptual suggestions of this book, which will capture afresh the drive and mechanism of social change, through two quotations from the context of the early second wave of the women's movement.

The *Black Women's Manifesto* is a photocopied typewritten anthology that appeared in 1969 in New York. It contains a piece of social analysis by Frances Beal, titled "Double Jeopardy: On Being Black and Female." The text was also included the following year in the volume *Sisterhood Is Powerful*, and is a groundbreaking example of what later became known as the theory of intersectionality, which reflects on the possibilities for a radical victory over multiple power relations that interlock while remaining distinct. In her text, Beal also discusses her understanding of revolution, and demands: "We must begin to understand that a revolution entails not only the willingness to lay our lives on the firing line and get killed. In some ways, this is an easy commitment to make. To die for the revolution is a one-shot deal; to live for the revolution means taking on the more difficult commitment of changing our day-to-day life patterns."[31]

Prioritizing living rather than dying for the revolution requires a fundamentally changed understanding of what a revolution is. Not a one-off, martial event but a continuous process. As encapsulated in the title of a recent anthology of feminists of color, *Revolutionary Mothering*, it is something that needs long-term care.[32]

Beal's vision of "living for the revolution" connects with a passage in the speech given by Helke Sanders in 1968 in Frankfurt am Main. Sanders represented the Free University of Berlin at the conference of Socialist German Student Union (SDS) delegates, which is mainly remembered for the tomato thrown in protest against the dominant behavior of men during the discussions. Sanders formulated the position of the "Council for Action to Free Women" as follows: "we cannot solve the oppression of women throughout society at an individual level. so we cannot wait for a time after the revolution. . . . we want to try, already within the existing society, to develop models for a utopian society. but in this countersociety, there finally has to be space for our own needs."[33]

These two beacons of a feminism that saw itself as revolutionary—the first from the context of the Black Panthers, and the second from the New Left in the Federal Republic of Germany—throw an illuminating light on strategies of transformation. From the multiplicity of emancipatory goals, the question immediately arises of how all these hopes can be brought into the revolutionary scenario. The answer points in the direction of a revolutionary politics of forms of life.[34] Two themes stand out in this context: everyday praxis, and anticipation. These urgent reminders that we must take account of everyday praxis as a setting for revolution do not refer to the individual level or what is seen as psychological—as is otherwise often the case in the movement of

1968—but relate to shared practices. "Day-to-day life patterns," "countersocieties" within the existing order, thus become arenas of a transformation that is more far-reaching than the notion of a struggle. This leads to a change in perspective. Rather than looking out for the grandiose event of revolution, these thinkers seem to make a sweeping gesture around themselves, and to say that if we approach it in the right way, then this very moment, this ordinary day, is fit to be called a revolution—a veritable "Non Sire. . . ."

In this book, I use the term "interstitial" to argue that the success of revolution is entrusted neither to overarching historical processes nor to singular events, but to that which takes place in the emancipatory in-between spaces within society. According to the *Oxford English Dictionary*, "interstitial" means both "located in spaces in between" and "extending the spaces in between." Complete or radical interstitial change would then consist in making spaces that were once interstices into a new core—which does not yet say anything about how this should be achieved.

The interstitial structure of transformation processes opens up an alternative understanding of the temporal aspect of revolution, breaking with the usual instrumental sequence that positions the revolution as a means between past and future. A single effort for such a revolution, Beal says, is simple and trivial when compared with a continuous effort. And Sanders suggests that in this continuous effort, the order of past and future is reversed. The postrevolutionary work has to be done now, before the revolution. That in itself would then be the revolution.

METALEPTIC TRANSFER

Interstitial change is a process that moves in a certain direction, but that gets its direction neither from steering toward a goal located in the future—the telos—nor from an internal law of dynamic motion. The mechanism of progress is replaced with path-breaking persistence. Enclaves of the future in the present open up a new perspective on choosing the right methods to deal with existing antagonisms. They demand skill and care in the transfer that would ultimately bring the whole present to the desired future.

Understanding such mechanisms of transfer is the core concern of *Praxis and Revolution*. It introduces a new term that promises to bring together diverse facets of the revolutionary dynamic: "metalepsis." In rhetoric, this ancient Greek term describes a fairly rare rhetorical figure requiring a double transfer. One of its typical forms involves switching the end for the means or the cause for the effect. The temporality just described, in which the relationship between past and future is reversed, is "metaleptic" in this sense. However, as we will see, metalepsis can also include more refined conceptions of transfer and reversal such as performative critique or paradigm shift.

While it will only really be possible to take stock at the end of the book, a relationship is already beginning to emerge between the interstitial-metaleptic perspective and the three dilemmas discussed earlier. Viewed more broadly in terms of an extended process—described by Juliet Mitchell in 1965 as the "longest revolution"[35]—the question of how to begin does not call for a decisive opening shot, but rests on the moments or practices in the existing context that prove to be those with a potentially "postrevolutionary" quality. Beginning would then mean strengthening and expanding those moments or practices—"living for the revolution." In the metaleptic reversal of before and after, the paradox of the impossible transition is also dissolved. It is a question not of an abrupt scene-change, but of the structures that make it possible to elevate an underground praxis, turning it into a new paradigm. It would then be the institutionalization and routinization of those paradigms that promised stability. The new—as something that had been persistently rehearsed—would lose its transience.

PREFIGURATION

The image of an interstitial, metaleptic revolution, drawn from Beal and Sanders, corresponds in many ways to the strategy of "prefiguration," which was already discernible in the quotation from Brown. This term has recently become the basis for renewed discussions on the left, which have returned with fresh intensity to a concept of transformation that has long been discredited as "utopian socialism" and preserved only by communitarian anarchism. In post-Marxism, the idea comes up in debates about the commons and about commonization, and is adopted as an exodus strategy in a post-operaistic context.[36] In radical Black Studies, the tradition of "marooning," the enclave of escaped slaves, is reactivated in the term "undercommons."[37] Today's anarchism, as portrayed by Uri Gordon, follows the tactic of "prefigurative politics."[38] Iwona Janicka, meanwhile, has expressed this as a mimetic solidarity with singularity.[39] In Queer Theory, José Muñoz and J. J. Halberstam are prominent voices for a future encapsulated in concrete utopias or "queer times and spaces."[40] The radical democratic form of organization seen in Occupy and other public square movements, which fits particularly well into Isabell Lorey's theory of exodus,[41] is, as we have seen, also designed as an anticipation of the future. Likewise, the last massive wave of feminist mobilization made explicit reference, in its calls for a strike on International Women's Day 2017, to the motto of the Argentinian group "Ni Una Menos": "Ponemos en practica el mundo en el que queremos vivir"—"Let us put into practice the world in which we want to live."

However, this perspective on change remains one-sided, at least as a theory, as long as it ignores the element introduced by Marx as "passive conditions," which was then translated into rigid material praxis. It does not take a particularly sharp mind to make accusations of "naïvity" or "voluntarism" against the notion that we can change the world through isolated jumps forward. But such accusations only hit home if the jump forward is always supposed to promise success (that would be naïve), or if it was supposed only to depend on the will of the actors (that would be voluntaristic).

If the transformation at which prefigurative politics aims is interstitial, then the task for theory is to gain a better understanding of its driving force and its mechanism. Is it at all possible to develop a plausible understanding of radical change—ultimately, a historical perspective—that is mobilized from the interstitial spaces and structured in "jumps forward that work backward"? When does metalepsis succeed? The focus is then not on whether prefigurative politics is "right or wrong," but on the structural conditions needed for its success.

PERFORMATIVE PARADIGM SHIFTS (AND MOLEHILLS)

This book will develop a model of transformation from fundamental terms that seem rather to be inclined toward "skepticism" of revolution: that is, from a notion of praxis which is rooted in repetition, and a notion of structure on which future action depends. On that basis, the task will be to ascertain how change works at all—which is also a prerequisite for potentially revealing the turning points at which human efforts can have an effect. Revolution will eventually come back into focus, when social tendencies toward change coincide with human striving for emancipation.

At its heart, the social theory of radical change that unfolds in the second half of this book draws on a synthesis of Thomas S. Kuhn's idea of paradigm shifts and Judith Butler's concept of performative critique.[42] Both, I would like to show, share an interstitial orientation and a metaleptic dynamic. Furthermore, they can be incorporated into the materialistic theory of praxis proposed in the first half of the book. It may seem surprising that Kuhn, of all people, can be invoked as the thinker behind a processual concept of revolution. This is made possible by a specific reading for which Margaret Masterman prepared the way.[43] This reading introduces a Wittgensteinian, praxis-theoretical motif into the very core of Kuhn's idea—that is, into the term "paradigm" itself. The paradigm will be formed from what are initially concrete, crude, and provisional approaches, which only emerge at all because the usual processes fall into a state of crisis and are blurred by recurring anomalies—among them, not least, the embryonic new paradigm. New practices that stand the test of time are then, according to Masterman, both expanded and sedimented through transference or the creation of analogies; they become the foundations—or, as I call them, "anchors"—for ever broader realms of society.

Performative critique enters the picture of a processual Kuhn as the moment that is actually interstitial. It provides the anomaly (or, as Butler says, "trouble"), and at the same time offers potential starting points for alternative continuations of praxis. My understanding of performative critique is based on a more radical interpretation than the usual one. Already in terms of Butler's own approach, the diagnosis of a "mere subversion" seems to me to be a misreading. In fact, Butler describes in a range of cases—the most prominent of which is her analysis of drag—a mechanism that has drastic consequences, namely, the breaking up of a fundamental structure through an emerging praxis that had hitherto been unintelligible. If we call that subversion, we must mean more than variation or flexibility—something closer to the subversive hollowing-out of a structure from beneath, which can then collapse entirely. After all, one of Marx's names for the revolution is "Old Mole."[44]

Butler's own theoretical framework does not help to illuminate the conditions for success. We can make up for this by means of structuration theory. As the starting point, I describe a situation of structural layering, which is made possible by the fact that practices are ambivalent or multifunctional. Variation is therefore made possible not by a deviation within "a" structure, but by the situation that emerges from the collision of different structures. If a praxis that would normally only be intelligible in a special—or, in my terms, subcollective—context is found in a mixture with the elements of a generally legible structure, then it is possible to follow on from it in two directions. We can continue to repeat it in a hegemonic sense; but it can also be adopted into the subcollective codes and continued according to them. If the latter takes place, then that which really ought to be unintelligible is articulated. It becomes an exception, and for a structure that claims to be entirely consistent, this is so intolerable that its status as an irreducible foundation begins to crumble. Through this, the scope for opposing connections is once again increased.

The pattern that begins to emerge here is metaleptic in the literal sense of the ancient Greek term. From a collection of similar elements, one is grasped, but proves to be false. "Meta-" in this context means "from between similar ones"; "-lepsis" is "taking hold" or "picking out," which might mean choosing wrongly. Metalepsis is therefore not just a *lapsus*, which could happen at any time, but a reversed interlocking that relies on the right structures.

In the rhetorical figure of metalepsis, a double transfer takes place—from one play on words through another to the referent. Performative critique follows the same logic: an unintelligible practice is incorporated into an articulated structure and is then drawn from there and wielded against the overarching order. In interstitial change, there is a sense in which the Mole says, "I'm already here."

Having the "Mole" say "I'm already here" at this point is also a form of rhetorical metalepsis: First, one needs to enter the context of the German fairytale about a race between hare and hedgehog. In this story, the hedgehog "wins" the race against the odds, because he has asked his identical-looking hedgehog spouse to hide at the finish line and greet the hare by saying, "I am already here." Then, second, the mole replaces the hedgehog in the formulation in question and brings in the metaphor for revolution. Thus, the reference shifts onto this book's topic. That is to say, even if we cannot see the unintelligible revolutionary praxis in advance, it will become clear, after it has articulated itself and eroded the prevailing paradigm, that it must always already have been there. If that is so, then prefigurative interstitial practices really do form the necessary condition for all radical social change. However, they are only sufficient for a revolution if metaleptically layered structures enable their transition into an anchoring structure—a new paradigm.

ARCHITECTURE, DECORATION, AND SHORTCUTS

In order to unfold the concept of metalepsis fully, this book is arranged in four systematic parts that each explore one fundamental term. Praxis, structure, performative critique, and paradigm shifts are the motifs that determine this structure. The first part defines the concept of praxis, sets out the normativity of practices, and all in all establishes a praxeological understanding of the social. The second, taken by itself, sketches out a dynamic concept of structure that can be connected with the theory of praxis, on the basis of which social formations can be analyzed as disparate constructs of varying density. The third part revises performative critique so that it allows us to explain interstitial structural upheavals. And the fourth part finally reinterprets the concept of the paradigm shift, applying it to recent histories of revolution and bringing it into line with the figure of metalepsis.

Each of the four systematic parts is developed against the backdrop of a literary example. Apart from the video installation that illustrates the third part, these examples are all literary and follow Mary Wollstonecraft, Charles Dickens, and Isak Dinesen into their portrayals of the French Revolution. However, especially as they tend to move outside the canonical settings, they can also all be understood as moments in a women's movement that is not split into waves or generations.

Those readers who are not so interested in the conceptual work of (academic) philosophy, or who do not like to spoil a good question with too quick an answer, are advised to concentrate on each of the ten-page sections that present this material briefly at the beginning of each part. In response to just one key philosopher, theoretical puzzles are drawn from the example scenarios that the four chapters then seek to solve: With the help of Foucault's "ascending analysis," we can ask what led to the break-up of the ménage that Wollstonecraft describes so progressively. From Dickens's knitters, who foster new structures despite being trapped in a feudal society, we will learn about the conditions of agency, which Marx explored as man-made yet unfree. With her antiheroic activism, the drag queen Marta, from Matt Ebert's film, offers a clue to those collective contexts that Gustav Landauer saw as "revolutionary beginnings" and as possibilities for far-reaching change. And the ambivalent position of the petitioners portrayed by Isak Dinesen, who do not want to prevent the execution of the last marquise but to mitigate it, presents an unstable picture that allows us to ask, with Walter Benjamin, what sort of constellation would let us decide whether the change that has taken place has really turned out to be radical.

However, grounding revolutions in terms of social theory as a form of radical change does not mean in turn that any radical change is also revolutionary. Radical change is just one of the elements of the notion of revolution introduced at the beginning—relating to what it means to have passed a historical turning point. The two other factors also have to be involved: historical actors have to strive for transformation, and collective practices of resistance have to play a role. The praxeological account of agency has both delimited and expanded these elements: intentions and actions do not directly translate themselves into the goals being pursued. Revolutions do not just happen and succeed because someone wants something to change and certain groups rebel. But if in doubt, it is this that makes processes of transformation into revolutions. That was the limitation. But the interstitial-metaleptic position also proposes an expansion—that is, an expansion of what is understood as the striving for transformation and the practice of resistance.

BUT WILL IT REALLY GET BETTER?

The expansion of what comes to count as revolutionary has consequences not only in terms of social theory and phenomenology but also at a normative level. Whether we really want to bestow the name "revolution" on the transition to a new social paradigm depends—at least in the more emphatic use of the term—on whether the innovation aims at something better. Whereas Liancourt was only alerting Louis XVI to the drastic nature of the change, after over two hundred years of further attempts and the emancipatory hopes invested in them, the term "revolution" has come to be densely inscribed with normative expectations. When we emphatically use the term "revolution," we are not just referring to any old efforts at transformation or to some arbitrary practices of resistance. In the Marxist theory of revolution, these normative expectations are contained in supposed dialectical progress. Interstitial metalepsis does not yet say anything about the quality of a change—after all, this is exactly what decontaminates it in terms of the philosophy of history. Interstitial spaces can produce both the good and the bad; a new social paradigm, even one that is keenly anticipated by the action of some groups, can still be horrifying—or can become so in the process of transfer.

Nevertheless, if we take up the immanent position that is implied by the metaleptic-interstitial perspective, the following portrayal of revolution does present a normative orientation, although this generally remains implicit. For it is precisely in the central practices of resistance and in the efforts at transformation that a measure for the evaluation of revolutions would be tested out and established. "True" revolutions would be those with normative aims that are most substantially anchored in the norms of previous revolutionary praxis—or that, to use Jaeggi's terms, can be reconstructed as a story of the enrichment of revolutionary experience,[45] albeit one that remained marginal. The normative requirements applied to revolutions are therefore partly set by themselves, without the need for a notion of actual progress in terms of universal history—such notions have rightly been criticized by Amy Allen as Eurocentric.[46] But the question of which elements become decisive and gain precedence, pointing the way to the future, is dependent on how previous praxis can be combined with current praxis.

This orientation is newly adjusted by practices that can only be accessed at all through the expansion of the term "revolution." "True" revolutions are redefined as soon as we group previous revolutionary practices differently. This is a fragile set of connections, especially if we measure it against the supposed stability of ultimate justifications, normative foundations, or philosophies of history, but it is one that can direct situated judgments and therefore transcend contexts. In the conclusion, examples will show how the classic revolutionary normativity of liberty, equality, and fraternity is expanded and recentered if we confront it with the demands of the literary examples as they relate to one another. However, this will do no more than illustrate an approach that can only be fully validated through philosophical justification (in the sense, for instance, of Linda Zerilli's renewal of Arendt's theory of judgment) and through richer material (such as Peter Weiss's *Aesthetics of Resistance*).[47]

Thus, on every level—social theory, phenomenology, normativity—the examples have the function of carrying forward an objection to Liancourt's definition of revolution that was already raised by Marx in some sense: the assertion that change was not decided "at the Bastille." This point can be derived from philosophical analysis of the conditions for transformation, but it can also be learned by redirecting our gaze to other scenarios. I have chosen these examples and embedded them in historical findings in order to imply that the revolutionary could be found in temporary liaisons in a prison, in knitting circles in a poor Parisian district, in queer affinity groups, and in the petitions made by female households. A sideshow? Non, sire, c'est une revolution.

PART I

Maria's *Ménage* and the Transience of Heterotopian Praxis

The first quarter of this book aims to develop a notion of praxis that will enable us to think further about interstitial change and serve as a fundamental concept of social theory. The literary scenario that will enhance our understanding of practices marks out one of those "in-between spaces" implied by interstitial change. However, "Maria's *ménage*" shows first and foremost how transient and unstable such practices of revolutionary novelty can prove to be, so that the example draws particular attention to the counterforces, and to the sometimes insurmountable rigidity of the prevailing circumstances. Thus, the theory of praxis developed in the subsequent three chapters actually takes its cue from an example in which the anticipatory rehearsal of postrevolutionary practices is unsuccessful. For if the analytical vocabulary is to be workable for further discussion, it must be capable of encompassing not only the characteristics of the interstitial but also what they might be up against. Otherwise, success—the mere possibility of which is challenging enough to demonstrate—would be built in from the start.

The "*ménage-à-trois*" in question—which is as much a set of intertwined relationships as a household—has its setting in the eighteenth century and forms part of a fragmentary novel by the abolitionist and feminist Mary Wollstonecraft. The text was published as *Maria: or, The Wrongs of Woman* by Wollstonecraft's spouse,

William Godwin, in 1798, one year after she died in childbirth.[1] Although far
lesser known than Wollstonecraft's popular theoretical treatise, *A Vindication of
the Rights of Women*, and initially entirely without success at the time,[2] the fictional text was explicitly designed by the author as a continuation of the *Vindication*, testing out its ideals in a concrete everyday setting. The constellation
involves three central characters, very different in status and background, who
meet in a mental institution. Jemima is a hardened guard, whose story of exploitation begins practically at birth: she was an illegitimate child. Darnford is a
failed adventurer and political freethinker, and Maria is a bourgeois housewife
whose fortune-hunting husband deceived her, robbed her of her child, and
locked her away. The three come to love one another, reveal their biographies and
their political beliefs to one another, and devise, at the climax of the plot, a daring escape plan: Jemima is to begin by kidnapping Maria's daughter, and is then
to free Darnford and Maria, whereupon they will all make their way together to
postrevolutionary France and set up home together, with Jemima explicitly playing the role of second mother to the child.[3] At the same time, this plan fades oddly
into the background for a while, as the characters are occupied with their lively
exchange and with the togetherness that they manage to carve out of the institutional routines. Or alternatively, to describe the situation from another perspective: the characters get a good way toward realizing the plan within the
institution, in which the illegitimate ("bastard") worker, thief, and ex-prostitute
Jemima holds the keys to the freedom of the educated, bourgeois Maria and
Darnford, who in turn each have exactly the same level of freedom within their
everyday life as inmates, regardless of gender—they are equally able to observe
each other when walking in the courtyard, to exchange books with marginalia,
and to meet each other secretly under Jemima's protection.

Within this clearly demarcated setting, the novel offers a perfect example of
interstitial praxis, a praxis located in the in-between spaces, beyond the generally
established patterns of action. The constellation of the three characters, the shape
taken by their relationships and activities, differs drastically from the expectations
of the surrounding society, as well as from their own previous experiences in that
society. It is, however, not "utopian" in the sense of an ideal sociality that has yet
to be reached. The alternative has already been realized in concrete terms, but
without being institutionally or structurally anchored: instead, it is fleetingly
located in the interstices. Unlike the concept of the marginal, the topography of
the interstitial does not immediately fit into an image of periphery and center. It
also does not presuppose that the interstices remain local and temporary as a result
of oppression or exclusion, although we might reach this diagnosis after analyzing them more closely.

As distinctive enclaves, or scattered particles contrasting with their surroundings, interstitial spaces correspond most closely to what Michel Foucault described in a lecture from 1967 as a heterotopia. Foucault's neologism is, however, far more specific than its excessive uptake would imply. Heterotopias are defined as places within a society in which the usual principles of that society's order are reversed in a complex way: "Counter-sites, a kind of effectively enacted utopia in which the real sites, all the other real sites that can be found within the culture, are simultaneously represented, contested, and inverted."[4] Thus, contrary to the implications of the prefix "hetero-," it is not mere difference that plays a role here but a reversal of the usual patterns of order, which must, however, remain recognizable in this reversal. With a chain of examples ranging from Persian gardens through brothels and cemeteries to pirate ships, Foucault demonstrates that the common thread is not that something is different, but that normality is turned upside down. This reversal, however, is far from being a marker of promising nests of resistance. Rather, Foucault underlines the fact that countersites or "other"-sites support the surrounding system and relegate opposing tendencies to a place where they are fenced in. Heterotopias are therefore a special case of the interstitial, but they do help to illustrate that if our discussion of main strands and interstices is to have real substance, then we must at least take a significant difference as our starting point. There must be a reason that the practices in question are not absorbed into the ordinary, although this reason need not necessarily be elaborated to the same extent as Foucault's image of inverted mirroring. Nevertheless, if we demonstrate that there is a deviation or a heterotopia, this certainly does not yet allow us to predict whether it calls the fundamental order into question by way of expansion, or whether it actually protects the current order by absorbing disruptive factors. If something is located in the interstices, this can also mean that it will stay there without widening them. Foucault's concept of heterotopia thus also intervenes against wishful thinking that the "other places" always anticipate the actual future.

It certainly seems that the case described by Wollstonecraft, at least, is intended to have precisely such an optimistic, forward-looking dimension. *The Wrongs of Woman* belongs to the genre of the Jacobin novel, which emerges at the end of the eighteenth century.[5] The work not only features a progressive political narrative, in which the ideals of the French Revolution are realized, but also probes the potential for expanding and transposing those ideals. In the existential attempt to take the demands of the French Revolution seriously in a radical way, a new, reworked picture of revolutionary praxis also emerges.[6] In collective work on everyday relationships, the point is not to storm the ruling institutions, but to leave them behind.

Wollstonecraft's characters embody the demand that liberty, equality, and fraternity be understood beyond the political sphere (defined in narrow terms), as organizing principles in family life and the workplace. When it comes to intimate relationships, *The Wrongs of Woman* actually demonstrates a complete reversal of the paradigms common at the time. Within the walls of the prison, a free, egalitarian union temporarily unfolds, in which friendly, fraternal, and romantic affection mingle in a form of utopian solidarity. Through these relationships, Jemima also emancipates herself from her harsh working conditions and begins to approach the cases entrusted to her according to her own, much more accurate judgment, going as far as open sabotage. In the new shared household that the protagonists plan to establish, class boundaries will also lose their force, beginning with reproductive work.

Through their experience of one concrete negation of the usual order, the characters gain the points of reference needed to describe the fundamental wrongness of this order, a task that Maria undertakes in a letter to the daughter who was stolen from her. Only on the basis of deviating interstitial praxis can the suffering or discomfort caused by the original contexts be converted into emphatic rejection and criticism. Measured against the free relationships that the characters ironically experience in prison, now the institutions of ordinary life appear to deprive people of freedom—above all, marriage under the coverture law according to which men own all property. Maria encapsulates this diagnosis when she equates the married state with the Parisian fortress: "Marriage had bastilled me for life."[7] The alternative to the confinement in such relationships is found in the patterns of the *ménage*. In the interstices, the revolutionary discourse can be lived out in a groundbreaking way. In Wollstonecraft's story, one might say that the Bastille is to be stormed from within.

The perspective in which radical change is based on a departure rather than a decisive battle corresponds to the exodus model of revolution. It is subject to the same idea of successive transformation as interstitial change, except that here the interstices from which change is supposed to emerge are imagined as being consciously thought out and actively upheld from the start. Where objective social dynamics are at play in interstitial change, subjectively reflected striving takes their place in the exodus model. When other forms of relationship arise in the heterotopian interstices, the aim is to expand these spaces, a departure from the existing order, which hopes to take that whole order with it.

Wollstonecraft's narrative marks an interesting pivotal point that allows us to trace a temporalization of the seemingly spatial exodus metaphor. Somewhat analogously to the shifting of the utopia concept from an image of faraway islands to a vision of the future,[8] the stations of the exodus can also be plotted on a time line. The biblical narrative of the departure from slavery in Egypt, with long wanderings in the desert, the covenant, and the final arrival in the promised land, saw a revival in the eighteenth century in the ideas of the pioneers and in the Declaration of Independence of the United States, and is present in Wollstonecraft's text in reports of Darnford's ventures as a settler. Seen from the institution, as Maria demonstrates in her long letter to her daughter, the phase of servitude would be her time in the normal institutions of society, and the longed-for place of the future is France. However, the actual exodus taking place here is not the political migration but the social transformation. The aim is not to go to a different place, but to make the world into a different place. "France" effectively stands for the principles that the characters find to be realized in their *ménage* and that, in their socially critical thinking, they vehemently recommend to society as a whole.

In Foucault's work in particular, the focus on concrete, situated praxis as the starting point for potential transformation comes to form a method that can be summarized as "ascending analysis." As Foucault sets out in *The Will to Knowledge*, this approach does not take overarching units or central institutions as its starting point, but as the object requiring explanation: "The analysis, made in terms of power, must not assume that the sovereignty of the state, the form of the law, or the over-all unity of a domination are given at the outset; rather, these are only the terminal forms power takes."[9] Foucault envisaged that the investigation should initially register much smaller individual phenomena, and should work its way up from them to the larger formations. This perspective can also be applied to the concept of change as such. From this, an idea emerges that Foucault only sketches out in general terms at a few points in his work, the idea of "ascending" or, in fact, interstitial transformation, which takes the form of a temporalized, gradual exodus of "walking on the spot":

> Hence there is no single locus of great Refusal, no soul of revolt, source of all rebellions, or pure law of the revolutionary. Instead there is a plurality of resistances. . . . But this does not mean that they are only a reaction or rebound, forming with respect to the basic domination an underside that is in the end always passive, doomed to perpetual defeat. . . . At times [they mobilize] groups or individuals in a definitive way, inflaming certain points of the body, certain moments in life, certain types of behavior. Are there no great radical ruptures, massive binary divisions, then? Occasionally, yes. But more often one is dealing with mobile and transitory points of resistance, producing cleavages in a society that shift about, fracturing unities and effecting regroupings. . . . And it is doubtless the strategic codifications of these points of resistance that makes a

revolution possible, somewhat similar to the way in which the state relies on the institutional integration of power relationships.[10]

This image is the objective side, an outline showing the progress of what exodus envisages as successful change. If this expansion indicates the maximum perspective of that change, it is nonetheless important not to measure it only against this. The minimum demand of the exodus endeavor is radical in itself: it requires that its direct context, at least, should be made available not for the continuation of the existing order, but for the testing of alternative orders. This form of breaking out, as a moment of what Herbert Marcuse described as "Great Refusal" (which—contrary the implications of Foucault's allusion—could well be local and marginally situated), nevertheless does not present itself initially as a self-aware avant-garde act in the case of the *ménage*. The ensemble finds itself in a dilemma. Life so far seems—especially for the main character, Maria—entirely unlivable, and it is only through the experience of the newly emerging forms of relationship that the characters gradually come to hope that they could dare to break out, in order to let those forms of relationship break through entirely.

But the forging of friendship, the preparations, and the escape are not the whole story. In any case, because Wollstonecraft never finished her novel, we do not possess its definitive ending. However, there are five sketches for alternative versions of the ending, all of which are printed in the published edition. All are marked by great disillusionment. Where there should have been a grandiose emigration, only the escape from the institution is successful, with the director of the institution disappearing in order to avoid being called to account for irregularities. However, the egalitarian household is not realized. Maria and Darnford are tried for adultery and both convicted. Maria is financially and socially bankrupt; Darnford returns to his restless way of life and leaves Maria for other women; the child is dead. There are several variations on this course of events, of which the fourth and shortest simply reads: "Divorced by her husband—Her lover unfaithful—Pregnancy—Miscarriage—Suicide."[11] In all of these endings, Jemima disappears completely from the scene, only to reappear abruptly in the final sketch: she comes to Maria's bedside, leading by the hand the daughter who in this case has survived, when Maria has just taken laudanum.[12] Thus, *The Wrongs of Woman* is certainly not a story of how the anticipation of alternative practices fosters structural change.

Furthermore, the failure of Maria's *ménage* after the escape also extends back into the heterotopia, if we look more closely. As remarkable as the constellation in the institution might seem, it is still infused with condescension and prejudice. When Jemima clear-sightedly explains the material conditions that left her only the choice between sex work and the poor house, Darnford and Maria react with a rambling lament over the lack of moral education among the lower classes.[13] And in order to lay claim to a continuum of female oppression through economic dependency and vulnerability to sexual violence that would include both herself and Jemima, Maria continually makes use of the metaphor of slavery, even though the fate of the black people who really suffer from this form of exploitation is never reflected elsewhere in her socially critically remarks, let alone in her interstitial praxis.[14]

Nevertheless, this example does not refute the possibility of exodus per se. It is just that the efforts of those who embark on the departure are not enough to ensure that their movement coincides with a process of interstitial change. Ironically, the example of our prison co-op also offers a particularly good demonstration of interstitial change—but the "successful" transformation does not relate to those aspects of the interstitial praxis that the protagonists were counting on.

Already in his heterotopia lecture, Foucault identified institutions of imprisonment as the typical modern form of heterotopia—"those in which individuals whose behavior is deviant in relation to the required mean or norm are placed. Cases of this are rest homes and psychiatric hospitals, and of course prisons."[15] Although it was still important to him within the heterotopia discussion not to allow "counter-sites" any fundamental explosive power, Foucault analyzed those very institutions in *Discipline and Punish* as the epitome of the modern disciplinary society, which had been emerging since the beginning of the eighteenth century.[16] He takes several routes through the subject, drawing on an abundance of material to demonstrate that the growing importance of imprisonment should not simply be interpreted as a shift in the system of punishment toward a less cruel form of justice. Instead, the fact that almost all forms of punishment have been replaced with imprisonment shows that a new form of power and rule is operating.[17] This new form of power does not take hold of its subjects' lives in order to set up an example of sovereignty, as was the case with premodern rituals of torture. As a disciplinary power, it aims instead to use control and training to ensure that members of society are taught to be productive and to restrain themselves.[18] Thus, when Jemima is caught stealing, her arm is not chopped off, but is trained instead in the workhouse, from which she is then recruited for her employment in the asylum.[19]

In fact, the institution in which Wollstonecraft's three main characters find themselves not only exemplifies, as a prison, a form of institution in the process of expansion but also typifies a capitalist enterprise. Described as being privately run, it offers Jemima opportunities that she did not possess in traditional or domestic work contexts. The horrendous business model—imprisoning people who are brought in by their relatives, without any detailed checks—is profitable. In a sense, Jemima is the exponentially exploitable subject. Beyond Marx's classic characterization of the doubly free worker, who can freely sell his labor but is also "freed" of the means of reproduction, she also lacks all recognition and sense of belonging. As an illegitimate child and a prostitute, she is free in the sense that only an outlaw is free. Meanwhile, the very fact that she can move freely at all represents a great achievement for her, compared with her experience of forced labor in the house of correction. The "Sanatorium" business offers her a new, more anonymous mode of social integration. The inmates in her care, meanwhile, can also be described from the vantage point of the marketization story. They are the ones who obstruct capitalist socialization: Maria blocks her husband, whose business has run into debt, from accessing money as capital, and Darnford is active as a social revolutionary.

We can therefore retrospectively describe the institution in Wollstonecraft's novel as a laboratory for the future, in which mechanisms can be found that were to reconfigure a whole formation of society over the next two hundred years. However, it is not these isolated "origins" alone, as Foucault puts it, which have explanatory value. It is not the interstitial contexts alone but the conditions for their expansion that have to be brought to light: "There can be no doubt about the importance of these models. But it is precisely these models that, before providing a solution, themselves pose problems: The problem of their existence and the problem of their diffusion."[20]

The question of the diffusion of interstitial models of praxis will occupy the rest of this book, while the next three chapters will begin by theorizing their existence. The attempted escape described by Wollstonecraft, in which the protagonists succeed in storming out of the fortress but the new praxis of solidarity in relationships still does not prove to be resilient or gain acceptance, raises the question of the persistent strength of the given. In order to capture the powerlessness of the struggle for exodus not just against the forces of opposition, but also against the protagonists' own patterns of behavior, the praxis-theoretical vocabulary will prove advantageous.

Throughout the first section, a notion of praxis will be developed that is useful as a fundamental term in social theory, and that is able to capture the interstitial scenario sketched out here.

In the first chapter, praxis will be introduced via the characteristics of practical normativity and practical knowledge. Already on this basis, we can reach the proposition that all agency is dependent on the presence of a corresponding, preexisting pattern of praxis, and action is therefore not just rule-governed but also structured by repetitions.

However, this makes it sound as if genuinely new practices cannot possibly emerge. To deny the success of the *ménage* on this level seems wrong; we would be misunderstanding the egalitarian love-cooperative between three people if we did not describe it as a new praxis, albeit a fleeting one. Some more recent praxis-theoretical approaches solve the problem of innovation by interpreting practices themselves as "molecular"—but this undermines the potential of praxis to be a fundamental term. A more detailed analysis of the materiality of practices will develop an alternative to this strategy in the second chapter, and show that practices are indivisible in their normative, symbolic, and material aspects. Variability is still not ruled out if we take account of the fact that practices are open to interpretation. Innovation emerges from the overlapping of ambivalent practices.

Subsequently, in the third chapter, the question returns as to the forces that help some interstitial practices expand and make others fail. As we have seen, Wollstonecraft's scenario certainly contains elements that later came to shape society as a whole. If the *ménage* of solidarity achieves less success than marketization and discipline, then it should be possible to capture the reasons for this in a first approach by focusing on the connections between practices. Two relationships are decisive in this process, namely, the constellative and regulatory role on the one hand, which can be taken on by a series of practices fixing another in place ("alignment"), and on the other hand, the mimetic and constitutive function of one praxis grounding a range of others ("anchoring").

Reflecting on the tracks followed by certain practices repeating themselves while others are suspended, we already begin to approach the next section, which will take us a step further: just as temporary instances of deviant praxis can be understood as dynamic, so can the structuring of society as a whole.

I

The Rules of Praxis

T he theory of praxis can be summarized as the approach that takes as its starting point a fundamental "priority of praxis." This is the assumption that "praxis," understood as the realm of action and activity in contrast with, for instance, mere contemplation,[1] has a particular precedence and a specific irreducibility. In order to reconstruct whether this basic assumption can be substantiated, it is first necessary to clarify what is meant by praxis. Particularly when this term is understood so broadly that the entire realm of the social can be absorbed into it—Maria's cell and the whole of English society, the flight from the institution and the French Revolution—it has to be enriched terminologically, so that we are not left with an entirely empty category. To that end, this chapter concentrates particularly on the normativity of praxis. I distinguish between three types of rule (which define, constitute, and evaluate praxis) and the corresponding ways in which these rules are conveyed. If we then go on to determine the "repeatability" of practices, then we will have reached an initial idea of what characterizes the peculiar rigidity and indisposability that confronts Maria's *ménage*.

THE PRIORITY OF THE PRACTICAL

In his "Theses on Feuerbach" of 1845, the young Marx emphatically proclaimed that the false alternative of objective materialism versus the idealistic emphasis on free activity was to be overcome in the concept of praxis. On the one hand, perceptible matter was to be understood philosophically as "human sensuous activity," while practical action was in turn to be regarded as "objective activity."[2] In Marx's philosophy, this concept of praxis corresponds with the fundamental assumption that social circumstances form an organism structured and propelled by contradictions. His own work devoted far more attention to the task of determining these basic contradictions than to spelling out the social ontology of activity that is both "sensuous" and "objective." However, the concept of praxis was adopted in the subsequent Marxist tradition and developed further, precisely where the dialectic theory of society was seen as untenable or at least in need of revision.[3] Praxis is central to the work of Jean-Paul Sartre, although his strict distinction between passive, inert "series" and active, consciously creative "praxis" threatens to fall back into the opposition between objective materialism and activist idealism.[4] Some of the formulations of the praxis concept that are inspired by historical materialism, such as those of Pierre Bourdieu, Anthony Giddens, and Rahel Jaeggi, will be consulted in more detail in the course of this discussion. At this point, we will first look to Louis Althusser for the core idea of the priority of the practical, which will emerge as the point of convergence with non-Marxist theories of praxis.

Treating praxis as a fundamental term does not just mean saying something about what constitutes the social world—that is, conducting what philosophers call social ontology—but also coincides with social theory's interest in explaining particular social phenomena. If we are interested here in why an egalitarian romantic constellation was able to survive for a while in an institution organized in a certain way, then we are hoping for insight not only into the making of the social but also into its way of functioning. Praxis theory prioritizes practices as causal factors when explaining specific social phenomena. Louis Althusser encapsulates this perspective by referring to a dictum of Blaise Pascal, in words that have since been cited many times: "Pascal says more or less: 'Kneel down, move your lips in prayer, and you will believe.'"[5] Althusser invokes this "great formulation," as he calls it, in the course of his theory of ideology, which is materialist in the sense that it explains the ideological formation of individuals (that is, the way in which their formation reproduces the structures of power) not through the transfer of values, but through the rehearsal of concrete modes of behavior, which are the prerequisite—as with Pascal's believer—for certain convictions and identities to emerge. Even if we do not share Althusser's opinion that these formative rituals ultimately all merge together in the ideological state apparatus, we can still reassert the priority of practical behavior as a formulation of what could be meant by the determination of consciousness through Being.

But why should praxis be so irreducible? It is the phenomenological tradition of thought that has formulated answers to this question. For instance, in his early work, Martin Heidegger demonstrates in his analyses of existence that our entire access to the world is prestructured by the relationships that we maintain, through a range of practices, with the various things that appear in it. Those relations in their entirety make up our day-to-day life, or, as Heidegger calls it, our "Dasein as care."[6] For Heidegger, these phenomenological studies were a mere way station before what he called the "fundamental ontological" investigation of being as such. Nevertheless, the structure they present, in which we are conditionally embedded in a world that is preformed and perpetuated through practice, still became a starting point for subsequent theories of praxis, as well as being one of the sources instigating Foucault to advance a radical historicization of philosophical ontology.[7]

The other particularly influential expression of the priority of the practical comes from the late work of Ludwig Wittgenstein. Charles Taylor refers to Heidegger's and Wittgenstein's philosophies as the fundamental "double attacks on the disengaged picture of the mind," arguing that each of them has shown that there is a background knowledge that is constitutive for our theoretical relationship to the world, and that is only conveyed by "engaged agency," that is, by involvement in praxis.[8] It is his interest in the philosophy of language that leads Wittgenstein to the notion that such everyday agency deserves explanatory priority. After giving up on the idea of considering words according to correspondence theory, or in analogy to rules, he demonstrates in his *Philosophical Investigations* that linguistic meaning is dependent on the use of words in context in the world and thus suggests a new basis of semantics. According to the new, pragmatist view of language, it is the particular practical context and the implicit knowledge gained by sharing a form of life that ensure communication in specific "language games." As soon as the use of a word is removed from such practical contexts, its meaningfulness collapses—bringing us back to the priority of the practical.

For social philosophy, the arguments sketched out here lead us to the insight that we would be misconstruing the things that happen in the realm of the social if we tried to trace them back to something "outside the practical." Both the idea that actions could be explained entirely with reference to individual intentions or values, and the notion that particular, invariable structures determine all activities in advance, would be examples of such misinterpretations.[9] However, unlike other forms of criticism, the theory of praxis can sometimes show us how such mistakes arise—for instance, from the specific distortions to which the praxis of philosophizing exposes its own objects. There can be few practices, other than that of sitting motionless during the night in bad light, alone (albeit neither too cold nor too hungry), lost in thought, hunched over a desk, that would be likely to bring forth that doubt, so influential in the history of philosophy, as to whether a piece of wax on the tabletop—measured against the certainty of one's own thinking—"really" exists.[10]

THREE TYPES OF RULE

Although praxis-theoretical approaches in philosophy often react against an "intellectualism" that is supposedly specific to theory, when we look at the recent social sciences, we certainly cannot claim that praxis has been forgotten about. In anthropology, praxis-theoretical approaches began to assert themselves already in the late sixties,[11] and from there, they took on a strong influence over the development of theory across the social sciences. In sociology, praxis theory has become a paradigm in itself[12]—and some have even declared a praxis-theoretical turn across the entire discipline.[13]

All theories of practice are united by the fact that they start from the assumption of the "priority of the practical" and conceive of practices as fundamental units of the social. At the same time, however, it can be observed that praxis theories are, to some extent, divided by a common basic term. The meaning of praxis is anything but consistent across the theories: practices can be consciously shaped by humans,[14] or they can be interactions between objects;[15] they can be recombinable according to the situation,[16] or they can be held captive in a strictly structured field;[17] praxis can be activity with meaning and purpose,[18] or virtually blind routine.[19]

Nevertheless, there are points of convergence. In an article surveying the disparate field of praxis theory, Andreas Reckwitz identifies two such core elements, namely, materiality and the "'implicit,' non-rationalist logic" of the practical.[20] Formulated rather more broadly, this results, for him, in an understanding of practices as "a routinized type of behaviour which consists of several elements, interconnected to one other: Forms of bodily activities, forms of mental activities, 'things' and their use, a background knowledge in the form of understanding, know-how, states of emotion and motivational knowledge."[21] While Reckwitz explores the theories of praxis as part of his project of building a social and cultural theory motivated by poststructuralism, Rahel Jaeggi works from a pragmatist Hegelian concept of praxis to develop a theory of forms of life, in which the desiderata of critical theory and historical materialism can be newly formulated. Among the aspects of practices that are decisive for this project, the characteristics of materiality and routinization once again come to the fore,[22] but the picture is also enriched by a teleological index and by the question of how practices relate to one another: "Practices are habitual, rule-governed, socially significant complexes of interlinked actions that have an enabling character and through which purposes are pursued."[23]

From this, four characteristics of practices emerge that are critical for my argument, namely, that practices are rule-governed, repeatable, material, and open to interpretation. In my view, the first of these requires the most clarification. Existing theories of praxis often place one-sided emphasis on a particular type of normativity, attempting to bring praxis into line with either implicit, teleological, or schematic normativity. However, it is only possible to trace *both* the reproduction *and* the transformation of the practical if we regard it as "rule-saturated" across its whole breadth. My discussion will only touch on the other three characteristics in order to give them further nuance—compared with Reckwitz, for instance, I give precedence to the iterability of practices over the aspect of routine; compared with Jaeggi, I propose that practices are not so strongly goal-orientated, and emphasize their ambivalence and constitutive openness to interpretation.

By defining practices as a pattern of action, we already imply a normative index. Practices are designed for continuation, and they form a template—in Latin, "norma"—for the shape of that continuation. If practices can be taken as patterns and thus become instructions, then we can ascribe to them the character of rules. This resemblance to rules can be unfolded in different variants, giving us a clearer picture of normativity in the specific context of praxis theory. As I will try to show later on, practices can both follow rules and set them, and ultimately they can themselves serve as rules in a certain sense.

However, by suggesting that the normativity of practices covers such a broad field, I am in no way arguing that we should imagine them as an especially detailed catalog of rules. Rather, we should note that the rules of praxis are not spelled out as in a handbook, but are implicit; in fact, this is an important conviction of praxis theory. That, at least, is how Reckwitz summarizes this point, when he indicates that "the 'normativity' of action . . . is not to be understood praxeologically as 'instructions providing rules for how to act,' " before outlining the alternative: "Only within the practical knowledge that goes far beyond norms can implicit normative criteria in the sense of a socially 'appropriate' practice become effective. These implicit normative criteria of appropriateness within a complex of practices must be distinguished from the explicit and perhaps formalized catalogs of norms that may be present, which cannot represent the whole field of the implicit and may even contradict it."[24]

Already in this short statement, at least three uses of normativity appear ("implicit normative criteria of appropriateness"; "formalized catalogs of norms";

"the field of the implicit") that praxis theory supplies as replacements for the image of a *homo sociologicus* doggedly following "instructions providing rules for how to act."[25]

It therefore seems helpful to differentiate between different levels on which praxis is rule-governed, so that we can then go to each level in turn to consider the potential implicitness of normative knowledge. I will distinguish and discuss three forms of rules: those that define praxis, those that are internal to praxis, and those that generate praxis. I will then explore how each of these is propagated. Besides the much-vaunted notion of "learning by doing," which can only be facilitated by the last of the three types of rules, two other types of norm-transmission will take shape: norms internal to praxis correspond to "learning by talking," and the schemas that define practices to a kind of "learning by seeing."

The most fundamental rule of all seems to be the one that lets us recognize a certain praxis in the first place. If I did not know that musical instruments existed, I would not be able to decode the action of playing the piano. I have to possess what the social historian and theoretician William R. Sewell calls a "schema" for the relevant praxis in order to recognize it. This is even more the case for more ambiguous practices. At a decisive turning point in Wollstonecraft's novel, when Maria plans to escape from her tyrannical husband, Mr. Venables, it becomes clear that he is entirely ignorant of the sentimentalist practices for handling emotions. Maria was induced to make a final break from her spouse when she became aware that he had planned to prostitute her to a business partner. When she then, after an argument about the continuation of the marriage, goes to the piano and begins to play expressively—"the cadence was probably wild and impassioned,"[26] her spouse is satisfied to see that she has calmed down and will not go on pestering him with "romantic stuff, well enough in a miss just come from boarding school." Here, Maria's husband lacks the schema for a certain bourgeois form of controlling and cultivating one's feelings: it is not just that he has not mastered this praxis himself; he is not even able to recognize it and see that far from calming down, Maria is enacting a dramatic affective turning point. This misunderstanding already points to the fundamental role of schemas for any interaction. It is always possible to make a mistake about which defining rule applies, but behavior that seems to fall outside the entire set of possible schemas is thereby rendered unintelligible. Only when engaged in recognizable practices can actors be "known by seeing" by others. Indeed, Maria's case exemplifies the danger of falling beyond the reach of all intelligible schemas. Upon learning that she left him, her husband can successfully declare her mad. After all, there hadn't been any sign that she might resolve to do so—or so it seemed to him.

Schemas or "praxis-defining norms" guide us in recognizing which practice we are dealing with, be it the straight-forward practice of piano-playing as piano-playing, or the more ambiguous one of piano-playing to harness one's emotional upheaval. Beyond or rather "inside" those rules about what is going on in the first place, we can situate another type of normativity, which is set by the praxis itself. Praxis-internal or praxis-evaluating rules are familiar to those who are well versed in the praxis. Thus, in her arguments with her husband, Maria accuses him of having transgressed the basic norms surrounding marriage. He, meanwhile, suggests that they should interpret these norms differently and: "Like many other married people, who were above vulgar prejudices, tacitly consent to let each other follow their own inclination."[27] While the schema is shared—both know that they are arguing about the practice of marriage—they differ on its internal normative code. Internal norms do not only become obvious in dramatic disagreements. They are conveyed by any evaluative description that actors give of their practice, as when Maria comments on her piano-playing, with reference to the internal norms of sonata performance: "Turning to a sprightly lesson, I executed it with uncommon vivacity."

The idea that a sprightly lesson should be played with vivacity might easily be familiar even to someone who cannot play the piano. To have a praxis truly at one's disposal requires more than simply recognizing its schema and being informed about its internal norms. When it comes to the actual ability to do something—the know-how—emphasis is often placed on the implicit knowledge on which practices are said to be based. Implicitness does not mean that the relevant knowledge cannot be transferred—it just means that the transfer takes place through imitation, experimentation, and rehearsal. The rules generating praxis can only be acquired in the praxis itself. Piano-playing is a particularly pertinent example of this, because it requires very sophisticated physical abilities. However, if we assume that practices are always upheld by embodied actors and often also imply a specific relationship with objects, then all of them have a dimension of praxis-generating rules, which we can only access "by doing." Not only piano-playing but also the praxis of talking shop about a musical performance thus require not only a level of "knowledgeability" but also a specific "ability."[28]

THREE FORMS OF PRACTICAL KNOWLEDGE

If we distinguish in this way between the three realms of recognition, knowledgeability, and ability, we can demonstrate that specific theories of praxis often prioritize one of these realms. Teleological concepts of praxis, such as Alasdair MacIntyre's Aristotelian approach, accentuate the claim that practices are always connected with purposes, which can only be pursued through them, and from which their internal criteria of evaluation are derived. It is only based on these purposes that MacIntyre reaches his definition of praxis as "any coherent and complex form of socially established cooperative human activity through which goods internal to that form of activity are realized in the course of trying to achieve those standards of excellence which are appropriate to, and partially definitive of, that form of activity."[29] Thus, for MacIntyre, if we lack insight into the purpose and with it the evaluation criteria of a praxis, then we cannot recognize it properly at all; even ability itself ultimately means being able to orientate oneself fluently according to the criteria of excellence of a particular praxis. For Michel de Certeau, too, the setting of goals is the focus, albeit from the opposite point of view. Unlike MacIntyre, he does not see the praxis-internal rules as being fixed; instead, they can be tinkered with, repurposed, and tricked with "makeshift creativity." Here, it is knowledgeability that forms the foundations of a delicate "antidiscipline" and that is foregrounded in response to Foucault's diagnosis of an all-too-seamless enforcement of the disciplinary society.[30] Still, the type of norms in the foreground here are those internal to practices. Actors do not redefine schemas or follow embodied implicit rules, but are guided by the internal standards of the practices they carry out.

A different strand of praxis theory regards the praxis-evaluating norms, which can be acquired, as it were, "by talking," as little more than a decorative addition on the top of the rules that actually generate praxis, which it considers to be conveyed only "by doing," through a training process. On this question, Bourdieu converges with Wittgensteinian authors such as Giddens. Seen from the perspective of "know-how," the rules that are explicitly made and articulated in praxis are merely "a second-best" designed to "counter the failures or hesitations of the habitus"[31] and can only reflect retrospectively on a structure presumed already to exist. But here, even the existence of a practical pattern of action is due to its successful expression in praxis, in an "enterprise of inculcation tending to produce habitus that are capable of generating practices regulated without express regulation or any institutionalized call to order."[32] As this formulation already suggests, the approach that prioritizes the rules which I call "praxis-generating" partly entails that they cannot even be called "rules" anymore. Rather, as dispositions that are to be mastered within a field or within a form of life, it is they that are supposed to explain why actors are ever able to follow rules in the first place.[33]

If, instead of accentuating the praxis-evaluating or praxis-generating rules, we foreground those that define praxis, we find ourselves, so to speak, on the level of transferring praxis "by seeing." Thus, Sewell explains practices as a conglomerate of material resources and mental "schemas." In Butler's performativity theory, too, the accent seems to be placed on the ability to recognize practices. Norms, as Butler understands them, set conditions for intelligibility. They determine which actions fall under which schemas—a child whose mother is unmarried is seen in the society portrayed by Wollstonecraft as a "bastard," and sex between a married woman and a man who is not her husband is seen as "adultery."[34] The pressure of this normativity then arises not only from the sanctions that correspond to such categories but also from the fact that rejecting the existing social forms is scarcely possible.[35] The inmates of a mental institution are united by the fact that they have, through their practices, disregarded particular schemas that are fundamental to their society—whether exemplified by Maria's attempt to take the dissolution of her marriage into her own hands, or by the drastic behavior of some of the other inmates, which causes Maria herself to question their status as fellow human beings.[36]

Unlike the rules of habitual know-how, there is no reason in principle why these rules of seeing should have to remain implicit. It is rather that, as the constitutive background of the practices within which the actors then orientate themselves, they generally go unnoticed. Any explication usually has an educational purpose, or comes about in reaction to a disruption[37]—as, for example, when the presiding judge at the end of *The Wrongs of Woman* reasserts the prevailing definition of marriage in opposition to Maria's attempts to reinterpret it ("the institution which fraternizes the world"):[38]

> For his part, he had always determined to oppose all innovation, and the new-fangled notions which incroached on the good old rules of conduct. We did not want French principles in public or private life—and, if women were allowed to plead their feelings, as an excuse or palliation of infidelity, it was opening a floodgate for immorality. . . . Too many restrictions could not be thrown in the way of divorces, if we wished to maintain the sanctity of marriage; and, though they might bear a little hard on a few, very few individuals, it was evidently for the good of the whole.[39]

The limits on such explanations of the rules defining praxis seem to be of a quantitative, rather than of a qualitative, nature. If too many were called into question at the same time, interaction and communication would collapse.

When the norms for recognizing praxis are prioritized in this way, much of the content of the internal norms can be captured by dividing the schemas into ever-smaller elements. The norm for the appropriate performance of a sonata, which internally evaluates the practice of piano-playing, can also be described as the defining norm of a successful piano-sonata-performance, which can of course also be seen as a praxis in itself. However, this thins out the rich vocabulary with which norms are negotiated within practices, so that the focus is only on whether a certain schema is fulfilled or not.

REPEATABILITY

It follows from this discussion of the normativity of practices that the "priority of the practical" takes the following shape: Although practices fundamentally rely on rules, at the same time they always precede the rules. The schemas that classify what we are doing in the first place are informed by the praxis that came before them. We can recognize what we have seen before. The criteria for whether we are doing what we are doing correctly are only set with the particular practices—in their absence, nothing could be located "internally" to them. And the know-how that generates practices can only be acquired in the practical action itself, not "by doing" just anything, but by doing this particular thing, that is, practicing the piano.[40] Furthermore, practices never repeat themselves in isolation, but always appear together with their contexts of sanction or gratification. This conditional relationship between normativity and repeatability is not one-sided. The rules of praxis are, on the one hand, dependent on the previous instantiations of a pattern of action; but vice versa, it is the (praxis-defining, praxis-evaluating, and praxis-generating) rules that keep the repetitions on a recognizable, familiar, and feasible path.

That the constituent ingredients of praxis are not found in practices in a "raw" state, so to speak, also becomes clearer when viewed as an effect of the structure of repetition. A praxis cannot be constituted by any random ordering of material, but only by one that can also be deciphered as a repeatable pattern of action. Practices are, to move on to their second general characteristic, always part of a chain of repetition with spatial and temporal dimensions.

Interestingly, even in this respect, Wollstonecraft's text fits into a reconstruction of the social in terms of praxis theory. As she explains at the outset, she was concerned not with creating a narrative portrayal of one woman's fate, but with revealing how certain fates are structured by social patterns. In her words: "In many instances I could have made the incidents more dramatic, would I have sacrificed my main object, the desire of exhibiting the misery and oppression, peculiar to women, that arise out of the partial laws and customs of society. In the invention of this story, this view restrained my fancy; and the history ought rather to be considered, as of woman, than of an individual."[41]

Just as Wollstonecraft presents her story as being "of women" rather than one individual, praxis does not relate to singular instances. A practice, as Rahel Jaeggi says, "is not only not a single action; above all, it is especially not an action performed just once."[42] This emerges already from the concept of a "pattern" of action: for any pattern to be recognizable, it must be possible to identify recurring, regular elements in it.

Repeatability is also a key to the question of why, via practices, the social realm as a whole can be gradually reconstructed, and not only individual occurrences. As Reckwitz concludes: "From the point of view of praxis theory, the social aspect of a practice consists . . . in the repetitiveness—made possible by a collectively incorporated practical knowledge—of the same sorts of activities across temporal and spatial boundaries."[43] Repeatability functions here as "repetitiveness of the same sorts of activities," rather than, for instance, "repetition of the same activity," drawing attention to an important point: Because they take place in different times and spaces, practices necessarily take on additional differences. Every particular point in time and space is also a specific, historical, and material context, which influences the praxis itself. Following Derrida, this structure of deviating repetition can be called "iterability."[44] However, here praxis theory has to resist the poststructuralist elevation of iterability into an absolute. Iterability is not a self-propelled mechanism. Difference does not arise magically from the dynamic of repetition, but is instilled by the specific practical contexts within which the practice takes place.

Thus, if practices form repetitions, this does not apply only to routines. Not only activities that take place almost constantly and almost unconsciously fall under the heading of praxis; less common occurrences also take their form from templates and make further repetition possible.[45]

With regard to the "priority of practices" discussed here, we can first of all make the quite banal observation implied by iterability, that analyzing something as a praxis always means taking account of some kind of previous praxis and regarding it as constitutive. In a certain way this equates to the imperative to historicize, but additionally determines the units of analysis. Furthermore, the dynamics of processual repetition give us quite a different picture of social action than that of singular acts brought about intentionally by individual (or collective) actors. As Hans Joas and Wolfgang Knöbl show with reference to Giddens, the influence of phenomenologists such as Henri Bergson and Maurice Merleau-Ponty is discernible here.[46] Thus, Giddens writes, " 'actions' as such are only constituted through a discursive moment of attention to the *durée* of lived experience."[47] Recognizing the priority of praxis therefore also means not isolating actions from the flow of repeatable patterns of action, but instead interpreting the fact that they can be recognized at all as an indication that they must have precursors that they are following.

Undoubtedly, this confronts revolutionary impatience with a strong counter-current in the direction of the existing order. Looking back on our romantic cell through the lens of practice theory, some factors in its unsustainability gain sharper contours. The instability of the newly envisioned relationship and in particular Darnford's unreliability after the escape point to the fact that the generative rules, the know-how for the new practices, were not sufficiently available to the protagonists—unsurprising, given that what they were trying to enact in their egalitarian triangle really was something new. They had not had much chance to rehearse. Moreover, the scope for misunderstanding was vastly increased by the fact that the presumed schemas inspired by the French Revolution—"liberté, egalité, fraternité"—had rarely been put into practice across class and gender boundaries, and thus the internal evaluation of how it might best be implemented became almost impossible. Darnford might well have thought that he was following the rules of liberty when temporarily ignoring Maria and pursuing other relationships. However, the habits and interpretations of the actors involved only form a small part of the explanation of the course of events. Clearly, a role is also played by the practices pursued in society at large, as well as by the walls of the prison. It is to the latter that we will turn in the next chapter, as one must when wanting to storm a bastille, be it from within or from without.

2

The Materiality of Praxis

P raxis theory was supposed to help analyze the transformative potential of Maria's *ménage*. However, even the first tentative definition of the basic term "praxis" has implications that throw a problematic light not only on abrupt revolutionary changes but also on the small details of heterotopian patterns of action. If the ability to act always relies on existing patterns of action, it seems unclear how anything new—for example, the radical solidarity that arises within the walls of the asylum—could ever be possible. Even at an episodic, local level, how were Maria, Jemima, and Darnford ever able at all to bring about a reordering of class, rank, and gender in line with revolutionary ideals?

The fact that praxis theory has a certain "conservative tendency" has been observed many times.[1] However, this is particularly noticeable in the context of a broader chiasmus in the history of ideas. Directly following the French Revolution, it was conservative opponents of the revolution such as Edmund Burke and Friedrich von Gentz who pointed out the persistence of existing social forms.[2] With the terms of modern politics only just coined—the spectrum from "left" to "right" derives from the seating order in the National Constituent Assembly of 1789—the conservatives discarded the left option as self-defeating. To them, it seemed that attempting a fundamental reorganization of society was not just wrong, since they did not share its aims, but also impossible, because it failed to recognize the way in which human praxis was constituted. They saw revolutions, at least on the French model, as a doomed experiment.[3]

Since at least the second half of the twentieth century, however, it has been the other side that has endeavored to theorize the forces of inertia in society. Much as they differ at the level of detail, the most significant projects of Western

European left-wing social philosophy can be summarized as attempts to explain social stability. Critique of ideology, structuralist social and cultural theory, Bourdieu's praxeology, as well as the subjectivation theories that follow Althusser and Foucault are all designed, in some cases explicitly, as contributions to the question of why social change does *not* take place. At least a certain "state of the art" therefore defines the social ontologically as being tied to repetition, echoing the normative approach of Gentz and Burke.

This is the challenge that motivates this book: to take account of the tenacity of the social that emerges from praxis theory, and nevertheless to outline a plausible theory of radical change. The present chapter is concerned only with rejecting a solution that is, in a sense, "too easy." That solution would be to recombine the isolated elements of praxis in order to make change and repetition consistent with each other. In response to this, I will present my own understanding of the material side of practices (which precisely cannot be separated from their symbolic side) and then explain how "indivisible" practices can remain malleable, thanks to their ambivalence and their contextual overlaps.

MOVING MATTER

Can the praxis-theoretical perspective followed here be turned into a theory of transformation, despite its proximity to "conservatism"? In fact, a few recent approaches have quite literally opened up the concept of praxis in order to capture social change: by isolating the individual parts of practices, they make it possible to describe change as the recombination of those elements. According to this position, it is precisely praxeology that allows us to incorporate a diachronic and dynamic perspective into social theory. Thus, for instance, Elizabeth Shove announces in the monograph on which she collaborated with Mika Pantzar and Matt Watson, *The Dynamics of Social Practice*: "Our opening contention is that theories of practice have as yet untapped potential for understanding change."[4] Meanwhile, William R. Sewell, in his remarkable attempt to mediate between culturalist historians, on the one hand, and structure-oriented historical sociologists on the other, even presents a praxeological interpretation of the storming of the Bastille.[5] He also highlights Giddens's praxeological concept of structure as "particularly congenial" when it comes to integrating the vicissitudes of history into the often rather static vocabulary of social theory.[6]

Here, I would like to demonstrate that these approaches are only able to dynamize practices at the cost of undermining the basic premise of praxis theory, which prioritizes the practical. That is to say, the idea of recombination is ultimately based on the notion that the symbolic elements of practices can be separated from the material components. In contrast with this, I will show that a properly praxeological understanding of materiality not only refuses to disconnect the rules from their implementation but also refuses to detach interpretation from its objects.

Shove et al. assume that practices always rest on a connection between "material, competence and meaning."[7] They understand material as the things that are used in a practice, including "objects, infrastructures, tools, hardware and the body."[8] Competence, in this case, means not only being able to evaluate the execution of a practice but also possessing the practical knowledge necessary to execute it—two things that are evidently different, but that combine to allow actors to become participants in a practice, or, as Shove et al. express it, to become "carriers" of a practice. Finally, the element of "meaning" is understood as all the aims that the participants follow in their practice, and how they explain their actions. The emergence and disappearance of practices can then be described as the establishment and dissolution of this connection between the three elements. Building on this, the authors take the view that changes in practices, and therefore ultimately social change as a whole, can be explained as the exchange or adoption of such elements. Shove et al. explicitly claim that their model requires that the material, competence, and meaning of particular practices can be separated from one another: "This ... approach ... supposes that elements, however they might be defined, are somehow 'out there' in the world, waiting to be linked together. If we go along with the idea that practices exist when elements are integrated, we need to recognize two related possibilities: One is that relevant elements exist without being linked (proto-practice); the second is that practices disintegrate when links are no longer sustained."[9]

This assumption seems untenable to me. If competences and things were combined in practices in a contingent manner, then "the practical" nature of practices would be meaningless. In fact, praxis theory starts precisely from the insight that free-floating competences and things "out there ... waiting to be linked" do not exist. Jemima's temporary work as a laundress is not a combination of elements such as a washtub, the ability to wash clothes, and the aim of earning money or promoting cleanliness, elements that previously existed in isolation from one another, perhaps at an earlier point in history. Being able to wash clothes is something that cannot be defined or identified—and above all cannot be learned—without referring to the specific qualities of soap, water, textiles, and washtub. The competence cannot be isolated from the praxis. Similarly, we cannot sensibly understand the meaning and purposefulness of a praxis as something that has a continuous life before, during, and after incorporation into the relevant practice. Of course, we could say that particular meanings or intentions remain in existence, but are connected with different practices. Thus, the meaning of punishment, as shown by Foucault, may have been connected up to classical times with the practice of torture, and from the end of the eighteenth century almost exclusively with imprisonment. However, Foucault's study is a perfect demonstration that torture and imprisonment do not have the same meaning at all. Rather, he seems to show us that we can only understand a "new" praxis if we do not try to slot it into the continuity of the wish to punish, but instead shift it into another context of function and meaning—in this case, at least according to Foucault's suggestion, the context of early capitalist processes that were to form a productive, controllable subjectivity and create a defined, manageable class of delinquents.

But in all this talk of material that has always already been interpreted, are we even starting from the assumption of materiality any longer? In fact, I take the view that it is only through a notion of "material moved by praxis" that it is possible to escape the idealism of free-floating interpretations and speak of materiality as a fundamental characteristic of the practical. In Marx's early work, the definition of all human activity as "living activity" above all means embedding it in the process of the self-reproduction of the species, of society, and of the individual. Without material foundations—without what Marx calls "metabolism between man and nature"—this activity is generally impossible.[10] Equally, when Foucault ascribes discipline, as a specifically modern form of power, not to philosophical ideas or economic necessities, but to the ordering of walls, windows, and lamps in a prison, the material dimension of praxis comes into view.

Practices are material in the first place simply because those who carry them out have bodies—or are bodies. Thus, Maria's lonely brooding in the prison cell is no less embodied and therefore "material" than Darnford's short-lived attempt to settle as a farmer in the pioneer towns of North America. It is the mode of this materiality that is decisive. It differs from that of a pile of boulders on an uninhabited planet and from that of an inanimate object viewed in isolation. In the terminology of early Heidegger, one could say that things in practices are not just "present-at-hand" ("vorhanden"), but "ready-to-hand" ("zuhanden"), meaning that they are already in a certain way directed toward the interaction that will then be maintained in the praxis.[11] It is not as if there is water, a washtub, the laundry, the laundress, and then finally the action of washing: a specific interaction with these things is itself washing. This is why Bruno Latour insists that objects do not only reflect the social, but *are* the social.[12] Their "readiness-to-hand" must not, however, be confused with frictionless preprogrammed execution. Jemima's work as a washerwoman does not just mean that she earns her keep for a while but also that she badly breaks her shin. Objects, bodies, and infrastructures always also imbue a practice with unintended possibilities. They are not simply absorbed into their function in that practice, and they can therefore become the pivot or the turning point into a different practice, as when Jemima, in her later career, uses her access to her customers' pants not only in the praxis of prostitution but also in that of pickpocketing. The contours that things give to a praxis not only offer further latent possibilities, but often also set clear boundaries or conditions. Darnford's restless wish to travel, which caused him to leave his plantation for several months, was incompatible with the material conditions of farming, as he was forced to recognize when he returned. Thus, the priority of praxis also expresses itself in the irreducibility of the material dimension of the social. In terms of methodology, these considerations imply that we must be precise when describing and interpreting the materiality of practices. This precisely does not mean that material things should be elevated to a higher plane, but instead that we should trace as exactly as possible which historical and practical processes of materialization they have undergone.

The notion of inseparability protects against two other possible approaches to the materiality of practices, both of which are overly absolute. Firstly, it is never the case that we can look merely at the material conditions of a situation—once again, in an artificially frozen state—and deduce which practice will unfold in it. While Foucault has demonstrated in detail that imprisonment in solitary confinement is an important moment in the disciplinary process, ensuring that prisoners examine their conscience and internalize guilt in specific ways, Maria uses that same setting in quite a different manner.[13] As if the cell were a "room of one's own" avant la lettre, she makes use of it to draft a long letter to her daughter, justifying her unconventional decisions in a socially critical autobiography. However, from the point of view of praxis theory, we should not conclude that Maria is able to do this because her free will transcends her physical circumstances, but should instead analyze in more detail all the practices that impinge on her situation and overdetermine it. Such practices might include her exchange with Jemima and Darnford, as well as her long-standing experience of having to remain firm in the face of severely limited freedom.

Although the human carriers of a praxis share many characteristics with the objects shaped through praxis, it seems to me that a second fruitless generalization—at least for the questions posed by this book—involves flattening the difference between humans and other material to the extent that objects are ascribed an equal ability to act.[14] We can certainly describe the praxis of washing clothes with a new washtub and an inexperienced washerwoman in such a way that both the tub and the woman find their way into the praxis in parallel. The latter initially does not have the strength or the right technique to scrub the clothes effectively, and the former leaks. However, when the tub later becomes sound and the arm muscles are more developed, our analysis of the cooperation between these "agents" should not obscure the difference between them, which consists in the fact that the washerwoman observes and evaluates her own actions, receiving advice from colleagues and criticism from customers. The washtub, meanwhile, conveniently stops leaking because it follows the natural law whereby wet wood swells up and gradually closes the gaps between the staves. Ignoring the different modes of these processes would ultimately also entail an ignorant approach to the material that is supposedly being prioritized.

INDIVISIBLE PRAXIS

Rather than tracking the fate of elements that can be isolated, and that converge sometimes in one practice, sometimes in another, it seems imperative to recognize the wholeness of practices, and to see that they are at least as essential to the shape of their potential elements as these elements are for them. Competences, meanings, and even "things" are always the dynamic result of a pattern of praxis, and not the stable building blocks of that practice. Or in other words: the relation has precedence over the relata.

However, this does not mean that it is never analytically useful to consider particular dimensions of practices in isolation. In particular, a brief discussion of William R. Sewell's modular notion of praxis will tell us that we are ultimately looking at a subtle difference in emphasis, rather than two incompatible approaches.

In his understanding of praxis, Sewell remains close (though not quite as close as he sometimes claims) to the approach of Anthony Giddens, who will be discussed in more detail in the second half of this book.[15] While Giddens, as will be explained later, defines practices as consisting of rules and resources, Sewell talks of combining schemas and resources—setting a terminological course that he believes does more justice to the material dimension of praxis. Within the dual nature of practices, resources are the material drawn on in the praxis. The more sophisticated description as a resource is justified, in comparison with Shove et al.'s concept of material, by the fact that from the outset, Sewell emphasizes the implications of the interaction with things, infrastructures, and bodies in terms of a theory of power: "Resources are anything that can serve as a source of power in social interactions."[16] Looking more closely, however, this connection can only be upheld if power is understood in a very broad sense as an equivalent to the ability to act. The washtub and washboard as resources in Jemima's daily work do not lend her any direct power over others in social interactions: For the time being, they only allow her to carry out her work as a washerwoman.[17] Heaving extremely heavy washtubs around may mean that washerwomen end up with upper arms that make them particularly intimidating members of the revolutionary mob,[18] but this would then be an effect on an adjacent practice in which countless further resources come into play.[19]

Whatever effects are promised by a particular resource, it is clear that they are only activated indirectly, via certain patterns of interpretation. These are Sewell's schemas, meaning "not only the array of binary oppositions that make up a given society's fundamental tools of thought, but also the various conventions, recipes, scenarios, principles of action, and habits of speech and gestures built up with these fundamental tools."[20] Thus, in the French Revolution, the washerwoman Marquet defends herself from the accusation that she bit and kicked a police officer who wanted to prevent her from stirring up a crowd against a butcher: "The woman . . . responded 'that she was born with an extremely violent character, that she is a laundress and that laundresses in general are not well-behaved people.'"[21] What is decisive for Sewell is the transferability of the pattern of interpretation—in my example, whether it can be transferred from a laundress to a militant sans-culotte.[22] Transferability allows Sewell to define the central moment in social change as a moment in which a different schema than usual is applied to the particular resources involved. However, Sewell resists the idea that schemas are always the decisive factor determining practices. As an argument for the anti-idealistic design of his theory, he points out that nonhuman resources, at least, possess a material reality that cannot be reduced to rules or schemas.[23] Certainly, we cannot interpret everything at will—a washboard cannot be transformed back into a tree. Nevertheless, in spite of all his insights into the reciprocal interdependent relationship between resources and schemas, Sewell's picture of that relationship is ultimately too simple. This emerges precisely at the point where he means to emphasize co-constitution: "If schemas are to be sustained or reproduced over time . . . they must be validated by the accumulation of resources that the enactment engenders. Schemas not empowered or regenerated by resources would eventually be abandoned and forgotten, just as resources without cultural schemas to direct their use would eventually dissipate and decay."[24]

Unlike Elizabeth Shove, Sewell does not assume that interpretative schemas and objects continue to exist unimpeded when they are separated from practices—"out there," as it were. Instead, they apparently dissolve over time or become weathered, much like a house that is no longer inhabited, or an antiquated custom that people have ceased to uphold. However, in his insistence on an independent material element of praxis, Sewell gives up the more promising (historical) materialism which asserts that practices are material through and through, but are also always following particular rules or schemas. That is precisely the processual characteristic that differentiates them from static artifacts, whose metaphysics clearly informs the separation of form and content that can be seen in Sewell's pair of terms.[25] We may be able to make the distinction that a washtub is made of wood but has taken on the form of a tub, but when we look at practices, as phenomena that are carried out, we will not be able to trace a fault line between material and form-idea. We can only recognize an abandoned house at all due to our knowledge of the practices of living; it remains entirely a resource within the same interpretative framework. And if it becomes a different resource—a stone quarry or a barricade—then that does not happen because a detached schema has appeared from somewhere else. Instead, the house is incorporated into the repetition cycle of another intersecting practice—that of building or that of partisan struggle—a praxis that is resource-saturated all along.

The fundamental lack of a clear distinction between resources and schemas becomes especially obvious just when we reach the most essential element of practices, namely, their human carriers. On the one hand, these embodied carriers are the activators of the schemas governing practices. At the same time, they are themselves also a "resource"—one that not only possesses the special ability to make use of schemas, but has also reached its own "form" through the sedimentation of schemas. The knowledge that has become embodied in the process of previous praxis determines our future ability to act. Sometimes this occurs in a very physical sense, as Jemima shows when she lists her possibilities of earning a living. Since she was born out of wedlock, no one will employ her as a servant. After she breaks her leg as a laundress, she cannot return to that heavy work. Her choice is therefore limited to protoindustrial work in textiles, theft, or sex work. But as Jemima explains: "Not having been taught early, and my hands being rendered clumsy by hard work, I did not sufficiently excel to be employed by the ready-made linen shops."[26]

From another perspective, Sewell's suggestion that practices are divisible could also be attributed to his one-sided view of their normativity. If there were only schemas, only praxis-defining rules, then perhaps these could sometimes be detached from one material and applied to another. But then we would not be dealing with practices but with conventional processes of naming. Practices are intrinsically dependent on being embodied in implicit know-how. That know-how cannot simply be reinterpreted—it has to be retrained. In the same way, orientation within practices—being well informed about them—is interdependent with the definitions of those practices.

For the purposes of analysis, there is no reason not to pause the performance of a practice artificially in order to get a cross-section, and then separate resources from schemas. However, in doing so, we must not lose sight of the fact that schemas can only be determined with reference to the goals and material conditions of a praxis; the resources themselves must still be understood throughout as sedimentations of previous practices. If a so-called resource were to be stripped of its interpretative frame, we would not see its naked materiality, but the shape of a previous (or, in the case of overdetermination, an existing alternative) schema of interaction. The instruments of work, including the hand of a laundress, are themselves products of previous work, as Marx elaborates in the *Grundrisse*.[27] The strength of praxis theory seems to consist precisely in its ability to theorize this insight, since by prioritizing practical implementation, it considers practices in their unity—entirely material and entirely dependent on interpretation.

AMBIVALENCE AND OPENNESS TO INTERPRETATION

Our discussion of the priority of praxis already produced a severely conditional picture of human action: It is only feasible and intelligible as a repeating continuation of established patterns. Now that we have also rejected the suggestion that building blocks could be cut from these patterns and replaced, it seems that this conditionality is completely restrictive. In order to claim that practices have any plasticity at all, practices and the transfer of praxis have to be looked at afresh. Through this, we will see that they contain a fundamental residue of ambivalence, which is found both in the element of not quite explicable know-how—praxis-generating rules—and in the chains of repetition in which praxis is ordered. This ambivalence, or openness to interpretation, is the last characteristic of practices that I will discuss here.

Although the process is not always carried out explicitly, every continuation of a praxis rests on a particular interpretation of previous practices and of the material circumstances. The schemas that mediate the repetition of a praxis are the most basic interpretation, performed by the actors themselves (though this is certainly not always conscious). The attempt to make that interpretation explicit is in itself always a further and more thorough process of interpretation and not a simple revelation. Furthermore, it is possible to describe everyday actions in more detail than would be contained in an attempt to explain the schemas involved, and such everyday actions also almost invariably allow for a number of different descriptions. In established practices, in which implicit knowledge is shared, this goes unnoticed; in somewhat more unusual situations, the openness can, however, also be brought to light "openly."[28] For instance, the following scene takes place immediately after Maria is committed to the institution in *The Wrongs of Woman*, and describes her first meeting with Jemima:

> A woman entered in the midst of these reflections, with a firm, deliberate step, strongly marked features, and large black eyes, which she fixed steadily on Maria's, as if designed to intimidate her, saying at the same time—"You had better sit down and eat your dinner, than look at the clouds."
>
> "I have no appetite," replied Maria, who had previously determined to speak mildly; "why then should I eat?... Do you really think me mad?... " "Could any thing but madness produce such disgust for food?" "Yes, grief; you would not ask the question if you knew what it was.... Yet I will take some refreshment: I mean not to die.—No; I will preserve my senses; and convince even you, sooner than you are aware of, that my intellects have never been disturbed...."
>
> Doubt gathered still thicker on the brow of her guard, as she attempted to convict her of mistake [*sic*].
>
> "Have patience!" exclaimed Maria, with a solemnity that inspired awe. "My God! how have I been schooled into the practice!"[29]

By refusing to eat, Maria means to express her grief at being imprisoned on false pretenses and separated from her child. However, Jemima assumes that she is dealing with a mentally confused patient, and interprets this very refusal to eat as a sign of madness. Maria then changes her praxis. The situation teaches her that in the eyes of her guard, rationality is not ascribed according to sentimental expressiveness, but instead according to bodily self-preservation, among other things. Maria takes this as a sign that Jemima has never known grief—to which Jemima could justifiably reply that Maria has never known hunger. The refusal to eat is therefore interpreted in contradictory ways. Its basic features are recognized by both characters on a phenomenological level—but under different schemas, so that the question remains open as to which praxis the food-refusal actually constitutes. An entirely unidentifiable action, meanwhile, indecipherable as any kind of act, would be even more likely to be regarded as one of the signs for which Jemima is on the lookout.

Another striking aspect of this scene is the awareness that in such an interaction, to a certain extent, "praxis has the last word." Maria is perfectly aware that it will ultimately not be what she says, or how reasonably she justifies herself, but her future behavior that determines whether Jemima ascribes her actions to the logic of madness or to that of heart and head. Even if we, like the omniscient narrator, could "look inside Maria's head," we would not find a more revealing algorithm there. After all, the fact that Maria intends to prove her sanity does not in any way have to mean that she is really in possession of her senses—it is not uncommon for the mentally unstable to try to do exactly that. Both Jemima, with her searching look, and Maria, with her patience, are aware that the key to the rules of praxis lies in praxis itself—that is, in what happens next.

It is only in extreme situations that the openness of practices to interpretation means that an actor risks being called insane.[30] However, more everyday activities still always invite multiple interpretations, which may be compatible,[31] or may compete. If the question of what a person is doing can be answered equally well with the claim that he is making a bond for life or with the assertion that he is "bastilling" someone for life,[32] then these descriptions may be directed at the same object, but they already imply contrasting judgments. And ultimately, one and the same praxis can also be covered by two incompatible descriptions—as is shown by the question of whether Maria, when she takes off her ring and takes back her marriage vows, has divorced her husband (her own interpretation, and later that of Darnford), or only temporarily taken on "preposterous airs" (such is the assessment of her husband, which will later be upheld in court).[33]

If we argue that practices are open to interpretation, we imply that phenomenology takes precedence over teleology. Alternatively, we could interpret practices and distinguish between them by looking at their aims.[34] Teleological notions of praxis regard the purpose of a praxis as its defining quality—"This means that a sequence of actions is recognized as a certain practice based on knowledge of their purposes."[35] From this perspective, the fact that an action can clearly serve several purposes is explained by arguing that in that case several practices are coinciding in time and space.[36] However, this solution surrenders the genuine ambivalence of the practical, and to some degree also the priority of praxis. Here, by arguing that practices are open to interpretation, we will instead start from the assumption that patterns of praxis can often be described phenomenologically, and continued practically, before their purpose has been identified. This also means that we can still see many practices as being genuinely "multifunctional," and we can still claim that a practice retains its identity even after its purposes have changed or been lost.

That does not mean that actors do not have any purpose in their practices, or that we can no longer ascribe any purposes—perhaps even purposes contradicting those of their carriers—to practices. In this view, purposefulness simply enters the game one step later, as a possible interpretation of one's own actions or those of others. Though less stable than the more basic, praxis-shaping schemas, this teleological interpretation does describe a praxis more fully and more informatively. In other words, another specific variant of the priority of practices emerges: they appear before they are ascribed a fixed purpose. Interpretations take place from multiple perspectives, vary according to the connecting practices or background practices involved, sediment themselves in descriptions and in the embedding of those descriptions in broader narratives, and can in that process also slide into deep contradictions.

It is not only the goal of a practice that is a question of interpretation but also the scope of the series of actions to which a praxis relates. Practices are "scalable" in the sense that no abstract rule accounts for the extent of their patterns. Depending on the details we focus on and the points of reference we use for comparison, a context with a different "radius" comes into view: for Wollstonecraft, the practice of confinement may be Jemima turning the key on her evening round through the cells, while for Foucault, the practice of confinement covers the development of Western European prisons over two centuries.

However, regardless of how broad the scope is, the definition of a praxis requires that it is material, repeatable, interpretable, and governed by rules. These rules are saturated with practical knowledge and can be further defined as praxis-internal know-how, praxis-generating competence, and praxis-defining recognition. From this perspective, that which we refer to as actions—whether it is imprisonment in a cell or escape from it, the storming of the Bastille or the pursuit of heterotopian ways of living—proves to depend on multiple layers of conditions, and to rely on skill and material collected in previous practices. If we take this further toward a theory of action, the argument that the practical takes priority can therefore be formulated such that it is only possible to act in a social context in and through preexisting patterns of action.

CHANGE THROUGH OVERLAPPING

Both the material weight and repetitiveness of practices seem predestined to illustrate the insistent reproduction of an existing situation, rather than to explain any drastic change. And even their persistent openness to interpretation does not automatically lead to more flexibility. When nothing ever remains quite constant, there is always the possibility of finding a form that will dampen an explosive contradiction, turning it into a tolerable ambivalence. For all its rich facets, the normativity of the practical that was introduced in the previous chapter also tends to cling to existing circumstances. Praxis-defining recognition is learned from previous praxis, praxis-internal know-how orientates itself according to the traditional purposes of an activity, and even praxis-generating competence is always attained in the context of the given. All of this seems likely to mean that the future is only, as Bourdieu formulates it, a continuing "present past."[37] But surely it must still be possible for something genuinely new to happen? Isn't the fascinating aspect of Maria's *ménage* in the asylum the fact that it gives rise to forms of relationship that are actually new, egalitarian, and nonexclusive?[38]

The "exclusion of the future" could be corrected theoretically by arguing against the notion that action is determined by habitual patterns of praxis, and by proposing that people in fact have a greater level of agency in general. However, given all the points we have discussed which suggest that action is conditional on practice, this seems highly implausible. Indeed, we will only arrive at a very unsatisfactory theory of social change if we attribute it to the idea that historical subjects suddenly freed themselves from the very patterns of action that otherwise explained social stability so well, both beforehand and afterward.[39]

In Wollstonecraft's text, it is striking that both the narrator and the characters, in their own reflections, draw a great deal of attention to the fact that their actions are not without precedent. In fact, each of the characters is equipped with a history describing, sometimes meticulously, the experiences that then, under these specific institutional conditions, yield innovation.[40] Thus we hear about the deep friendships with servant girls that Maria cultivated already in her youth, and there is a detailed account of how the influence of a benevolent, unmarried, eccentric uncle familiarized her early on with freethinking positions. In turn, Jemima's relationship with the educated, middle-class Maria and Darnford is anticipated by the fact that she worked for several years as a mistress for a cranky writer. These examples could be multiplied and unfolded further. At the same time, they are augmented by particular life stories that repeat themselves to an exhausting degree, perpetuated by the existing institutions. Alongside Jemima, various other illegitimate half-orphans feature as minor characters. All are abandoned, one by Jemima herself. Maria meets a series of women in unbearable marriages: some trudge numbly on, while others end up in a state that leads them, like Maria, to be committed to the asylum.

Given that the characters themselves describe what they are doing as a recombination of familiar patterns—such as marriage and sisterly or brotherly friendship[41]—it may seem that in rejecting modular conceptions of praxis, we have discarded a useful theoretical motif too hastily. However, it seems to me that there are alternatives which can describe such combinations better than the ones discussed so far. After all, it is not as if the "schemas" of intrafilial relationships are being related to the resource of marriage (or the schema of marriage to the resources of fraternal relations?), thus creating a new praxis. We can still reject boundaries between the different elements of praxis (because, as I have tried to show, they are not separate elements but inseparable aspects), while observing certain transfers taking place.

Like all subjects, the characters in the text find themselves at the intersection of various practices, in cycles of repetition that have quite different frequencies; they move through contexts into which many further practices intrude, in which they may not participate *by doing*, but which they can discover *by seeing*[42]—"borne out as I am by a variety of circumstances" as Maria describes herself toward the end of the text.[43] The practices in which they move in a narrower sense also remain open to interpretation (see chapter 2), meaning that the resources and rules of various practices can overlap within them and change themselves together. Where points of transition emerge between one praxis and another, it is often only a sign that they had already been ambivalent for a while (and that they will probably stay that way). An example would be the transition to a trusting relationship between Jemima and Maria, in the process of which Jemima shifts away from the disciplinary guardedness that is expected to be her attitude to the inmate, gradually beginning to test whether Maria is actually being falsely imprisoned and deserves her trust and affection: "Jemima indeed displayed a strange mixture of interest and suspicion; for she would listen to her with earnestness, and then suddenly interrupt the conversation, as if afraid of resigning, by giving way to her sympathy, her dear-bought knowledge of the world. . . . Jemima's countenance, and dark hints, seemed to say, 'You are an extraordinary woman; but let me consider, this may only be one of your lucid intervals.' "[44]

The practices of interested sympathy and those of mistrustful surveillance take place in roughly the same material setting. We need the cell and the two women and we need Jemima's sharp attention—so far, the overlap is there. That overlap, however, does not only apply to the level of material arrangement; this would in any case be far too little to define the situation. In the description of the scene, with its strange mixture of strictness and sympathy, it is already clear that various schemas are in play simultaneously, and orientation toward one of them will in turn fail to meet the praxis-internal measures of the other. At the same time, Jemima brings a doubling of deeply embodied attitudes into the situation:

affection on the one hand, and bitter experience on the other, from which, respectively, she derives her know-how for sisterliness and surveillance.

In this ambivalence, the possibility for transition from one practice to another emerges—allowing a new variant to form. At least, the way in which the story continues certainly leaves room for the interpretation that this is exactly how Jemima forges her specific, skeptical alliance with Maria. The motif of overlapping can be expanded and defined more generally as a condition for innovation. Precisely the most revolutionary moments of the whole constellation, such as the redefinition of close relationships, can be understood as an overlapping of the practices of marriage, friendship, and *fraternité*, which coincide to allow the sedimentation of new practical knowledge and new patterns of action. Thus, we need not take practices apart, but must instead map them onto one another; we need not recombine elements, but must instead repurpose their contexts, making transformation thinkable on that basis.

3

The Connections Between Practices

I n the heterotopian relationship model exemplified by Jemima, Darnford, and Maria, the Bastille-like walls of early capitalist and patriarchal practices seem, for a while, to be overcome. In their cell, in the overlaps between friendship, comradeship, eroticism, and conspiracy, the three characters really seem to have created new relationship practices of egalitarianism and solidarity. But then, why is it that here, too, the ensemble breaks its revolutionary character after liberation? From this point of view, it seems that the argument formulated so far—that action is conditional on praxis—is not too fixed but too loose. Why don't Jemima, Maria, and Darnford live happily ever after, once their relationship praxis is established? Why not simply continue to repeat "the right thing"?

It is the connections between practices that decide which practices are able to continue. Looking at these connections, we will find that they have two characteristic forms: "alignment," which orders practices, and "anchoring," which provides them with a foundation.

PARTS WITHOUT A WHOLE?

It is clear that the conditions for continuing a praxis do not only lie in a previous history of repetition or in learning the pattern of action in question but also in how the praxis is formed and positioned in connection with other practices. Already, we have seen that the interpretation of practices always refers to the context of further practices. It is only as events continue to develop that we can determine whether Maria's refusal to eat is a sign of madness or an appropriate emotional reaction. But does that mean that practices always become lost among countless others, all equally important? Ann Swidler, whose approach will be discussed in more detail later, points out the problem of an apparent arbitrariness, which would emerge if there were no more to say about the connections between practices: "The question is whether among all these various kinds of practices we can distinguish some that are more central, more controlling, more determinative than others—in given kinds of situations—or whether we are simply awash in practices, each patterned and habitual, each subject to revision as it is transposed or replicated, and none more influential than any other."[1]

Just as Swidler rejects this flood of equally contingent practices, we can add a number of defining conditions to our example. The fact that Maria's mental state is being put to the test at all is due to various factors: she is in an asylum, a modern institution where the guards are charged with intensive pastoral care of the inmates, and her story takes place in the wake of the Enlightenment, when the distinction between reason and irrationality emerged as a defining difference. In other contexts, she might only have been asked whether she disliked the food, or whether she was not hungry.

Since my central question concerns the historical possibilities for transformation, the connections between practices are interesting not only in this sense as an interpretative horizon but also, beyond that, as the basis of precisely those power relations that determine our ability to act. One way to understand such connections between practices would be to see them as being organized such that each is ascribed a fixed place and all of them together form a stable whole. Bourdieu takes a similar approach when he identifies social fields. As has been pointed out many times, this creates extremely static scenery. Bourdieu argues that the habits of actors are fed by experiences (early ones in particular), which they gather in their field.[2] The impressions that shape them then become productive as a generator of appropriate practices—"*habitus*, a product of history, produces individual and collective practices—more history—in accordance with the schemes generated by history."[3] Perfectly adapted to its field, habitus is therefore always in the process of re-creating an identical copy of that field. Practices serve here as keys to the logic of a particular field, but as soon as the logic has been deciphered, they no longer have an irreducible role. If anything new is observed— such as our unusual cell in the asylum—it can no longer be explained by referring back to the field from which it presumably emerged.

A social theory is only "heterotopia-compatible" if, on the "system side" of its terminology, there is no assumption of a closed order—whether that of a field, as in Bourdieu's case, or that of a coherent system of values, as in Talcott Parsons's structural functionalism.[4] Practices, then, are connected not by a part-whole relationship, but by a contingent, constitutive relationship whose specific contours would first have to be reconstructed in an ascending analysis. This means that the reproduction of practices is conditional on such partial connections, and takes place in between two alternatives: between a scenario in which any kind of practice could be continued just as arbitrarily as any other and a scenario in which, by definition, the whole field of all practices is always simultaneously being repeated.[5]

I will now introduce two terms that seem to capture such connections between practices very fittingly. Here, I am already working toward the question of how the structural characteristics of social connections are formed, which will be discussed in the next part of this book. By interrupting the transition from the level of praxis to that of structure with a more minor intermediate step, I aim to avoid implying that in spite of all demands for diagnostic openness, there is really a simple part-whole relationship—but this time between structures and the practices that instantiate them. The first constellation discussed here involves the orientation of different practices toward one another, while the second is an encapsulation or anchoring of practices in one another, expressed in the following terms: *alignment* as a constellative-regulatory connection and *anchoring* as a mimetic-constitutive connection. This does not mean that there are no other ways to relate practices to one another convincingly. These two forms seem, however, to be revealing with regard to the social mechanisms of reproduction— that is, the question of why Maria's *ménage* failed.

ALIGNMENT

The notion of alignment was introduced by the political scientist Thomas E. Wartenberg in the course of the "power debates."[6] Wartenberg introduced the concept in order to capture the extent to which local, dyadic power relations are dependent on a constellation of other actions that are not directly involved, but that are orientated toward the situation in question. According to Wartenberg, the idea of a background that is constitutive for a configuration is taken from gestalt psychology. Transferred to social arrangements, he formulates it as follows: "An entire set of practices have to be coordinated in certain very specific ways in order for such power to be constituted."[7] Wartenberg's focus is only on situations that can be described in terms of "power over," as one actor having another's actions at their disposal. He himself does not take the next step implied by his arguments: although he refers this situation back to the social arrangement that makes it possible, he does not give up the priority of the notion of "power over" in favor of a structural concept of power ("power to").

Jeffrey C. Isaac has demanded this with particular vehemence,[8] but a variety of theories of power taking their cue from Foucault have also taken the step of understanding power as structural.[9] Power then ultimately merges—and this is particularly relevant for my purposes—with the ability to act that a particular social position accords to a particular actor. Amy Allen, for example, defines power in this sense "simply as the ability or capacity of an actor or set of actors to act."[10]

Joseph Rouse, who reads Wartenberg in a manner that is already remarkably close to a social theory of structure, has in turn suggested adopting Wartenberg's notion of alignment for praxis theory.[11] This already points in the direction I want to take, suggesting that we consider the concept of alignments, a concept designed for situations of personal power relations, as a general condition for the practical ability to act. A particular praxis becomes inescapable when other practices are interlinked so as to prevent alternatives or strongly sanction them. It is not (only) the particular "pull" of an individual praxis which ensures that it is repeated but also the "push," as it were, of other established forms of action that sets the course. When Wollstonecraft has Maria describe the horrors of her marriage, she seems to be at pains to avoid the impression that the problem is simply the tyrannical spouse's bad character. Rather, a range of practices come together—that is, practices of property,[12] the impossibility of divorce, the fact that a woman cannot rent a room without being categorized as "fallen" and treated as such. It is the arrangement of these practices that leads to Maria's statement "Marriage had bastilled me for life."[13] It is obviously difficult to decide what takes on the actual regulatory function in each case—an advantage of referring to alignment or interlinking is that a constellation of practices can be given the combined responsibility for a particular effect, so that we need not try to ascribe the decisive function to one specific factor, taking on a burden of proof that is counterfactual and ultimately cannot be satisfied. At any rate, it becomes clear that this series of practices combine to form a background, against which the complex of practices forming marriage becomes dominant—together, as a constellation, they take on the regulatory function of fixing this praxis in its patriarchal form.

Alignments can alternatively also be defined by referring back to Sewell's distinction between the resource side and the schema side of social praxis. They represent connections between practices in which a series of practices becomes a resource for a further praxis. Although my central concern has been analyzing the example of Wollstonecraft's novel, these definitions of relationships can also be illustrated by the methodology of Foucault's *Discipline and Punish*, which acts as a backdrop here. As we have seen, he begins by expressing astonishment at a great transformation, specifically the reorientation of almost the whole realm of punishment toward the praxis of imprisonment. Foucault seeks to show that this change is not explained, as is often assumed, by the internal shift of the judiciary in the time of the Enlightenment toward a more lenient and humane approach. Instead, he suggests that the focus on imprisonment should be interpreted as a key moment in a different development, namely, the emergence of a new, model formation of power: that of the disciplinary society. Practices involving locking people up are interpreted by Foucault as being part of a large-scale alignment. What he describes is the way in which a particular form of subjectivation in a disciplinary society is "fixed" by institutional routines, new methods of survey- ing the population, architecture, techniques for the examination of conscience, and discourses of reform.

Referring to the interlinking of practices allows us to examine how practices specifically become condensed into institutions, such as in marriage, prison, or civil court, as complexes of practices. Institutions can be described as arrange- ments of practices that are coordinated with one another or orientated toward one another.[14] From the point of view of praxis theory, characterizing a structure as an institution does not tell us anything about its effectiveness—the practical arrangements also have to work in order for an institution to develop its effect. Nor is it inevitable that the institutional chains of practices that strike us most obviously are the most lasting structures in a society. In *The Wrongs of Woman*, at least, it becomes clear that the walls of the institution are certainly surmount- able. In the end, it dissolves into chaos when the director makes a sharp exit in the face of accusations of corruption. Rather than doing her duty as a warder, Jemima then carries Maria past the inmates, some of whom have broken out of their cells in a murderous frenzy, and rescues her from the building.

ANCHORING

However, the boundaries of class do not prove to be surmountable in this case. In her letter to her daughter, Maria had described why her first attempt to escape from her husband and go to France failed: her departure was delayed because she was still waiting for suitable servant girl.[15] The one who was recommended to her then turned out to be a spy in the pay of her husband, and gave her a sleeping draught so that she could be separated from her child and committed to the institution. This turn of events conceals as a matter of course the very thing that ought to astonish us: the fact that Maria was at all prepared to risk her own safety and that of her child just because it seemed unthinkable that she, a bourgeois woman, would simply travel without a servant or employ one of the women in the harbor town who did not have any references. These examples show that the regulatory function taken on by practices in a particular constellation cannot be reduced to the level of brute facts. Maria's escape is made more difficult because there is nowhere for her to stay, and at last becomes fatally dependent on the question of whether she finds a reputable servant—this turn of events rests precisely on the question of what she counts as "staying the night" and as "traveling." As we learn from Jemima's biography in all its dramatic detail, it is not factually impossible—despite all the hardship involved—to spend the night somewhere or to travel independently as a woman at the end of the eighteenth century in England. But it is out of the question for Maria, not simply in her own opinion, but due to the way in which the practices in which she moves are socially "anchored."

Ann Swidler uses the term "anchoring" to describe the relationship between practices and a kind of "foundational practice." Foundational or "anchor" practices define what else a particular practice counts as, over and above itself—for instance, whether an activity can be seen as "work" or as a "vice," or whether it can be seen as "human" at all. However, this definition itself remains in the mode of praxis: "Thus a practice encodes the dominant schema—encodes it as a pattern of action that people not only read but enact—a schema that is never explicitly formulated as a rule."[16] How, though, can this connection be captured more precisely? Swidler herself mentions several different aspects in her explanation. She regards anchor practices as playing the role of constitutive rules in John R. Searle's sense. Analogously to the declaration that for Searle creates an institutional fact—that something in a specific context must count as this or that—it is a practice itself that takes on this role. However, practices do not speak for themselves in that way. It is always only when we see how a practice is taken up and continued that we can recognize it as becoming constitutive for a whole area of the social world. Meanwhile, Swidler also emphasizes that it is often the very practices which are at the center of antagonistic confrontations that come to be reinforced all the more strongly. Thus, this seems rather to be a case in which the calling into question of one particular praxis means that another is all the more required to remain in its place.[17] Finally, she underlines the important role played by the public representation of anchor practices as a kind of demonstration of "how things stand."

In order to be able to adopt the idea of anchor practices, I would like to transfer them in a somewhat more detailed way to the concept of praxis developed here so far. We can begin by saying that "anchoring" is evidently primarily concerned with the regulatory side of practices. If one praxis is based on another because they share the same resources, I would refer to this as an ambivalent praxis and not as a relationship of anchoring, which Swidler after all always conceives of as one praxis providing the basis for a whole series of others. Corresponding to the three types of rules taking effect in practices, three variants of anchoring can then be conceptualized, all of which mean that a praxis serves as the schema or paradigm for a series of further practices.[18]

The first variant would then also be the one that seems to dominate for Swidler: a praxis becomes a "schema" for other practices in the narrower sense, in that it defines them. One praxis is therefore anchored in another when its recognizability is dependent on whether it also fulfills that other praxis. If a particular lodging does not allow Maria to uphold certain anchor practices of morality, it cannot even be considered as a possible place to stay.

The second variant would rest on the fact that the norms internal to a particular praxis are extended beyond it and become evaluative criteria for broader areas of the social world—thus, for instance, we can say that in the discourses of the French Revolution, people began to evaluate the political relationship between citizens according to the internal ideals of "fraternity," while in the final scenes of *The Wrongs of Woman* there is a negotiation of whether the practice of marriage could also be anchored in this way.

Thirdly, the function of a particular praxis as an anchoring basis can also be understood such that its praxis-constitutive rules, its know-how, serve as an indispensable prerequisite for entering into other practices. In her biographical letter to her daughter, Maria does reflect critically that the bourgeois education of girls undermines a certain active drive, but this still does not help her to overcome this deeply anchored inability to act—in the decisive moment of the escape, she swoons in Jemima's arms and is dependent on her to be carried through the tumult.

The explanation offered here is necessarily condensed, because unambiguous examples for precisely one of these variants seem rather contrived—in fact, there is usually a mix, in which one praxis becomes the basis for others in several senses, making them recognizable, assessable, and feasible—a set of relationships that I would summarize as being mimetic and constitutive.

Before I come back to Wollstonecraft's text in more detail, I would like to illustrate this mimetic-constitutive moment somewhat more precisely, using *Discipline and Punish*. Both in his own depiction of specific disciplinary practices of imprisonment and in the way in which he traces their proliferation over time, Foucault follows a logic of anchoring. We need only think of the book's rousing overture, in which he discusses a specific process of torture and then contrasts it with the meticulous regulation of the daily routine in a Paris prison for young offenders, three quarters of a century later. The subsequent chapters also tend to start from particular cases or methods in which the constitutive pattern is crystallized which Foucault sees as the signature of the new form of power. Jeremy

Bentham's notorious sketch of the panopticon is ultimately only the definitive example of the series in which the rest of the depiction is anchored. Foucault is not attempting to reconstruct ideal types, but paradigmatic concretions. Precisely because the methods, actions and devices discussed were real, they can play a double role, on the one hand illustrating his claims, but at the same time also being shown to be hypothetical anchor practices, whose real historical function and duplication is up for debate.

When we look again at the scalability of practices, at the way in which they fill gaps of very different sizes, then the relationship of anchoring can also be understood as a kind of encapsulation that makes things more concrete. So that a praxis can be founded in a "broader" context, it must often not simply be a part of that context or connect functionally with other parts, but must call up a very specific and recognizable schema when it is carried out, in order to find almost automatic acceptance: "How could the prison not be immediately accepted when, by locking up, retraining and rendering docile, it merely reproduces, with a little more emphasis, all the mechanisms that are to be found in the social body? The prison is like a rather disciplined barracks, a strict school, a dark workshop, but not qualitatively different."[19]

AMBIVALENT ANCHOR PRACTICES

Wollstonecraft herself explicitly analyzes the breakdown of Maria's *ménage* after she gains her freedom, showing that it is due to the concrete alignment of social and juridical practices of power. The possibility for Jemima, Maria, and Darnford even to enter into a fleeting egalitarian relationship is dependent on the role-reversing constellation of the "heterotopia of imprisonment." However, the "internal" failure of the *ménage* can be understood best by looking back and examining the ambivalent basic schemas of the emancipatory praxis itself.

A particular bourgeois sexual morality that differentiates between the binary genders to an extreme degree, tying legitimate sexuality for women to the married state and equating all other variants with the distorted image of prostitution understood as a dehumanizing praxis—this sexual morality saturates almost all social relationships in Wollstonecraft's text. On the one hand, Maria does try to subvert this picture. She replaces marriage with an ideal community of reciprocal rights and duties, thereby legitimizing her desire for Darnford. On the other hand, she only gains the leeway to do this by transmuting her original marital situation into its supposed opposite: according to her own claims, she only reaches the decision to leave her husband after she discovers that he intends to let a businessman friend of his have her in exchange for money, and thus to prostitute her.

Maria inserts her own desire for freedom into the discourse of bourgeois demands for emancipation. The moral legitimacy of these demands never stemmed purely from an abstract reference to natural rights; it also stemmed from moral superiority and "reason" as demonstrated particularly in family life.[20] In several ways, Maria's husband embodies the iniquities of the ancien régime: deeply in debt and yet addicted to spending, with a hot temper and a weak character, promiscuous and unromantic. During their arguments over the separation, he suggests that they continue the marriage, but "like many other married people, who were above vulgar prejudices, tacitly consent to let each other follow their own inclination"; it is this that definitively places him within the schemas of prerevolutionary aristocratic frivolity.[21] Maria does not answer him, since she already has a concrete escape plan, but instead sits down at the piano to master her feelings. Her description of these feelings leaves us in no doubt. As a self-possessed and cultivated bourgeois woman, she sees and hates her tyrant as, among other things, a "whore"—bringing to mind the Paris bourgeoisie with their hatred of Marie Antoinette: "I . . . began to play a favourite air to restore myself, as it were, to nature and drive the sophisticated sentiments I had just been obliged to listen to, out of my soul. They had excited sensations similar to those I have felt, in viewing the squalid inhabitants of some of the lanes and back streets of the metropolis, mortified at being compelled to consider them as my fellow-creatures, as if an ape had claimed kindred with me."[22]

However, it is this extreme differentiation between the dehumanizing and the respectable forms of sexuality that also hinders the realization of parity in the relationships that constitute Maria's *ménage* within the institution. This leads to the paradoxical situation in which Maria offers Jemima, who as a former sex worker is well aware of the possibilities for freedom afforded by that profession, the role of comother, while at the same time venting about prostitutes as inhuman animals and monsters in the letter she writes to her daughter. There is therefore no need to make use of a field that repeats itself as a simultaneous totality in order to explain the failure of the heterotopia, when we can instead recognize specific anchor practices that become the fault lines in a precarious rearrangement—or that stand in the way of the attempt to claim the practices of liberty, equality, and fraternity postulated in the French Revolution as anchor practices for personal relationships between the classes and the sexes, as Wollstonecraft at least tries to do in her Jacobin novel.

The *ménage* has shown that bourgeois morality forms both the foundation for efforts toward emancipation and the abyss for cross-class solidarity. However, this does not mean that we can establish how far this praxis structures the whole of society—for this, we would need to follow it through countless further contexts. Nor is it necessarily the only crystallization point of the overarching formation— even in the *ménage* itself, other anchor practices intrude, such as the freedom to make contracts. This freedom only features on the margins of Wollstonecraft's fragment, in connection with the contrasting praxis of poorhouses, which is already central in Polanyi's analysis of marketization.[23] Jemima describes such a poorhouse as being filled with more suffering than all the other institutions she has passed through (brothel, prison, asylum). Her way out of this situation is precisely due to the very marketization that has also yielded new forms of exploitation in modern history: the former manager of the poorhouse employs her after becoming a businessman and opening a private asylum.

It has become clear that a praxis-theoretical reconstruction of the social is flexible enough that it can also encapsulate moments that go against the grain. These need not be neutralized as "exceptions," or treated as mysterious and inexplicable, but can be defined as depending on particular alignments. We can also go on to describe the established practices that anchor them. However, this does not mean concealing the fact that heterotopian practices may be transient and fragile. If they are not fixed through stable alignments and if they do not rest on resilient basic practices, their patterns will not continue. Maria's *ménage* remains a heterotopia in the sobering sense of the term: an episodic counterpraxis to the social order, dependent on the institutional context that isolates it.

Although Foucault describes prisons themselves as heterotopias, he still credits them with a whole other career. Their practices of regulating time and optimizing productivity have moved beyond the status of an isolated experiment, becoming a new fundamental anchor practice. Foucault summarizes this at the end of the book, again in hyperbolic form, referring to the prison school in Mettray: "The specific, institutional supports of these methods have proliferated since the founding of the small school at Mettray; their apparatuses have increased, with hospitals, schools, public administrations and private enterprises; their agents have proliferated in number, in power, in technical qualification. . . . In the normalization of the power of normalization, in the arrangement of a power-knowledge over individuals, Mettray and its school marked a new era."[24] Foucault portrays "epoch-making" as a process whereby specific practices are simultaneously extended and intensified. This seems to demand a theoretical vocabulary that would be capable of conceptualizing the formation of structure in line with the "ascending method" from relatively scattered and concrete starting points, without abandoning the priority of praxis. That brings us to the next part of this book.

PART 2

Jacobin Knitters and the Tracks of Structuration

In his novel *A Tale of Two Cities*, Charles Dickens unfurls a complex panorama of the great French Revolution. Like many other authors, he is concerned with the question of how historical conditions combine with human actions to shape events. A few years before Dickens, Karl Marx had immortalized this relationship in "The Eighteenth Brumaire of Louis Bonaparte" with an influential phrase, not so much answering the question as setting a problem: "Men make their own history, but they do not make it just as they please in circumstances they choose for themselves; rather they make it under present circumstances, given and inherited."[1]

The idea that we make our history under unchosen circumstances could mean that there is a sphere in which we are free, and a sphere of predetermined constraints. We would then have to ask which factors are fixed and which are variable. But the notion that people are in some ways tied to circumstances as they make their own history can also be understood to mean that the whole process is inaccessible, but can still be regarded as self-created, because the existing circumstances are themselves the result of human action. Understood in this second way, the "present circumstances, given and inherited" will be discussed in what follows under the heading of "structure." However, this means that we must return to the following questions: What are structures? How do they emerge? Above all, how do they change? How can they be predetermined and at the same time manmade? What does it mean to see actions and even history itself as being mediated by them?

Unlike Wollstonecraft's clearly prorevolutionary position during the "French Revolution Debate," Dickens's attitude is ambivalent, coming with the historical distance of slightly more than half a century.[2] His sympathy with enlightened ideals and the suffering of the oppressed mingles with the horror of prerevolutionary violence. The ending of his novel follows the emplotment of a tragedy, which was also characteristic of the way in which republican actors saw themselves around the turn of the years 1793/1794, the time in which the crucial part of the novel's plot takes place.[3] Still, unlike the conservative critics of revolution, Dickens leaves us in no doubt that the social hierarchy of the ancien régime in its violence, despotism, and irrationality was worse than the high points of Jacobin terror.

Prerevolutionary social stratification is illustrated by Dickens early on in the book, in an encounter on a narrow street corner. On the way to a lavish festivity, the minister and cabinet member Marquis Evrémonde tears through the poverty-stricken Paris quarter of Faubourg Saint-Antoine, mowing down and killing a child playing in the street—an accident that has happened before. While the Marquis curses the delay to his journey and throws a gold coin to the grieving father of the child, a locally respected wine merchant named Defarge remarks that the child is probably better off dead than alive. This remark causes the Marquis to praise Defarge as a philosopher and to donate a further coin. However, as the horses set off, the coin lands once again in the carriage. The Marquis stops the carriage and tries in vain to identify the culprit among the people gathered— the grief-stricken father, a woman knitting, and other bystanders—and then descends into furious insults: " 'You dogs!' said the Marquis,. . . 'I would ride over any of you very willingly, and exterminate you from the earth. If I knew which rascal threw at the carriage, and if that brigand were sufficiently near it, he should be crushed under the wheels.' "[4]

Already at this point, Dickens has drawn a striking picture of the differing conditions for action that apply to different social groups. After he has killed one of them through negligence, Marquis Evrémonde can go on to threaten the other inhabitants of the Faubourg Saint-Antoine with death if they dare to show signs of discontent. Dickens then goes on to capture the whole spectrum of social relationships and their apparently unchangeable nature, but notes a tiny irregularity:

> So cowed was their condition, and so long and hard their experience of what such
> a man could do to them, within the law and beyond it, that not a voice, or a hand,

or even an eye was raised. Among the men, not one. But the woman who stood knitting looked up steadily, and looked the Marquis in the face. It was not for his dignity to notice it; his contemptuous eyes passed over her, and over all the other rats; and he leaned back in his seat again, and gave the word "Go on!" He was driven on, and other carriages came whirling by in quick succession; the Minister, the State-Projector, the Farmer-General, the Doctor, the Lawyer, the Ecclesiastic, the Grand Opera, the Comedy, the whole Fancy Ball in a bright continuous flow, came whirling by. The rats had crept out of their holes to look on, and they remained looking on for hours; soldiers and police often passing between them and the spectacle, and making a barrier behind which they slunk, and through which they peeped. The father had long ago taken up his bundle and hidden himself away with it, when the women who had tended the bundle while it lay on the base of the fountain, sat there watching the running of water and the rolling of the Fancy Ball—when the one woman who had stood conspicuous, knitting, still knitted on with the steadfastness of Fate. The water of the Fountain ran, the day ran into evening, so much life in the city ran into death according to rule, time and tide waited for no man, the rats were sleeping close together in their dark holes again, the Fancy Ball was lighted up at supper, all things ran their course.[5]

The previous part of this book concluded that the inability to act results from the fact that actors have always been embedded in interconnected practices. Implicit knowledge, learned in previous practices, allows their continuation or repetition. However, as a trace of the past, these practices do not only open a path into the future but also confine that path within narrow bounds—there are no available modes of action beyond the learned patterns. In his narrative, Dickens pushes the monotony of such repetition as far as it will go, right into the rhetorical repetition of the same verbs: the *haut volé* flocks to a ball in splendid coaches; one carriage follows close behind another, past the onlookers, whose practices of desperately seeking food and hiding themselves in dark holes seemingly have more in common with the rats in the gutters than with the daily tasks of the social elites. If these different spheres do cross due to an accident, the overlap is used to reinforce the gap between them. The relatives of the dead child only have access to a very limited repertoire of hidden acts of resistance. The Marquis, meanwhile, can threaten them with his lordly right to kill. Everyone knows that this practice is open to him, and they quickly scatter, returning to their own practices of starving, grieving, watching, and knitting. The spheres are separated according to the unchanged structure of social hierarchy. And yet, when the knitter stares unwaveringly at the Marquis's face, this structure is transgressed for a moment.

In the terminology of social theory, the notion of structure serves both to make the social order and power imbalances visible, and to explain how people's ability to act depends on social conditions. "Structures" appear in the form of hierarchical organization and are also expressed in what a particular protagonist is able to do. But this does not yet tell us much about what exactly defines structures, what they can be said to "consist" of, or how they come into the world at all.

At this point in his narrative, Dickens imitates the premodern world-view, according to which the natural order and the social order share the same logic. "All things ran their course"—unalterably. However, if any historical event has given credence to the Enlightenment idea that orders can be changed by human action, then it would have to be the French Revolution, which will also be Dickens's concern for the next few hundred pages. Not for nothing is the carriage brought to a halt in Faubourg Saint-Antoine—this district of eastern Paris later came to be known as the stronghold of the sansculottes; the Bastille stood on the border of the district, and it was from here, on July 14, 1798, that the prison was stormed. Indeed, later on in *A Tale of Two Cities*, we meet the same ensemble of characters with the roles reversed. M. Defarge and the father of the dead child are chairing the revolutionary tribunal; Mme. Defarge, the knitting woman in the opening scene, is one of the main prosecutors, and the nephew of Evrémonde is sentenced to death (the Marquis himself having died when his palace was set on fire).

Such a change of scene is enough to unsettle any concept of an ever-lasting natural order. But even notions of structure that aim to codify stable social laws are often defeated by the reality of such drastic change. If we regard structures as static, or even as a kind of social "natural law,"[6] they cannot contribute anything illuminating to the analysis of processes of change, either at a micro level or at a macro level. Mme. Defarge's stubborn gaze on the street corner, just as much as the revolutionary break from the feudal system of estates, would then represent insurmountable challenges: they accomplish something that they should not be able to achieve under the existing circumstances.

From this we could easily draw the conclusion that it is better not to shift to the vocabulary of structure, and that instead we should stop at the concept of praxis that has already been developed. At least contingent recombinations of individual practices do not present any kind of contradiction to far-reaching changes. However, this would mean losing the opportunity to see the teeming mass of individual local practices from some sort of a bird's-eye view, and bring them together into a picture of social order. It is not only no coincidence that the collision takes place on that street corner; we can also foresee that it would take place in a similar way on many other prerevolutionary corners—precisely because we would be dealing with the same structures. It seems that people's ability to act is determined here by stronger factors than simply which practices they have learned so far. Not only do the inhabitants of Saint-Antoine continue the practices that already represent their main activities—starving, grieving, knitting—their ability to act is also constrained by the fact that almost all forms of interaction are anchored in the institutions and the worldview of a stratified society. This translates itself into patterns of interpretation, and also manifests itself in the material arrangement of practices. After all, in the scene described by Dickens, all the executive organs—soldiers and police—are busy building barriers between the classes. At the very moment when they are directly exposed to the despotism of a superior, the options of the Parisian underclass are reduced to a minimum that Dickens portrays as quasi-animal-like.

Furthermore, in order to give a name to change at all, it is necessary to draw a distinction—for instance, by contrasting old and new structures. Among the speechless onlookers who witness the carriage accident, Dickens includes a traveling road-mender. Later in the novel, when revolution has broken out, this road-mender becomes a political agitator and encounters Evrémonde again, on the Marquis's country estate. When he argues with a post office worker and rent collector who is loyal to the nobility, the scene takes the following turn: "And in a moment of reluctance and hesitation on that functionary's part, the mender of roads, once so submissive to authority, had remarked that carriages were good to make bonfires with, and that post-horses would roast."[7] That first carriage would certainly also have been flammable. Where should we place the theoretical measure that in one case points to the practice of arson and in the other to that of servility? It does seem to be captured particularly well by the notion of structure.

However, the transition from the concept of praxis to that of structure can also be motivated the other way round, by what began to emerge in the previous part: the fact that practices are themselves dependent on the links between them. No analysis that is concerned with how practices change can simply content itself with pointing out their diversity. If the broader arrangement of practices changes such that different alignments and anchorings emerge, some practices are squeezed out while others are perpetuated. Praxis that is continued along such tracks produces a kind of structured matrix in which society reproduces itself. Although the following chapters must first show in detail how this transition takes place, when looking at a panorama like that of *A Tale of Two Cities*, it is already obvious that practices develop contours that can be understood as structures.

However, it is not immediately clear at all that an analysis ascending from the vocabulary of praxis results in the most workable understanding of the social conditions for action. From a more orthodox Marxist perspective, at least, this must seem doubly questionable. The historical-materialist alternative to a "broad" praxis-theoretical concept of structure would first of all insist not only that some areas of society have some kind of shaping influence but also that we can identify one factor that will be fundamentally important across history: the means of production. And this itself is in turn understood in a specific—namely, dialectical—way as being dynamic. This means that Marx himself was operating with a key based on many presuppositions, in order to develop a nuanced view of action and its conditions. Nevertheless, as a sharp political observer, he occasionally bumped into the limits of his own theoretical reach. The "Brumaire" text cited earlier is a very good example of this, especially since it even shows Marx considering motifs that we would rather expect to meet in a performative theory of praxis than in classic historical materialism.

How exactly Marx relates and even defines the two strands—the "objective" development of the productive forces and "subjective" action in class war—varies in the course of his work and according to whom he is addressing. Even in the direct historical context of the Brumaire text, we can look to *The Poverty of Philosophy*, on the one hand, to find the classic historical-materialist conception in which the development of the productive forces has priority, and tensions between this development and the relations of production lead to revolutions.[8] On the other hand, the *Communist Manifesto* makes use of actor-focused formulations, celebrating the proletariat as a revolutionary subject.[9] However, the ability of the proletariat to act is in turn partly conditional on the degree of organization that it has gradually gained in the day-to-day struggle of labor,[10] a claim that Marx negatively confirms in the "Brumaire," when he argues that illiterate farmers, working isolated parcels of land, are unable to represent their collective interests or even to be aware of them.[11]

Quite independently of how strongly this conditional relationship applies and whether the structuring economic development is understood strictly as a quantifiable technological increase in efficiency,[12] or more broadly as the capacity of a society to satisfy needs, this model is distinguished by the fact that the structures that are said to create conditions are themselves thought of as dynamic. For Marx, this means that the discrepancy between a rigid model of structure and the historical change that undermines it does not arise in the first place, because the structures that he sets out as being fundamental are themselves in motion. Thus, in the actual moment of revolutionary action—assuming it relates to these conditions in the right way—there is no theoretical gulf between the actions of a person and the circumstances on which they depend. Marx obviously knew that this "textbook development" could not always fit the actual course of history,[13] and he ended up struggling instead to explain the situation when no dynamic of action could be observed, and even more so when the dynamic went awry. In his essay on the Eighteenth Brumaire, he reflects on these difficulties with particular intensity. From the start of the nineteenth century, French history had already diverged from the step-by-step model leading from feudalism via bourgeois capitalism to socialism, a model that was only really developed on the basis of the French Revolution. First of all (1814–1830), the Bourbons were reinstated and introduced a strict, Catholic-monarchist policy of restoration. When they were removed from power by the "citizen king" Louis Philippe de Orléans, things seemed to be back on track, as was confirmed by the February Revolution of 1848, which was inspired by early socialist ideas. However, already in December of that year, the short-lived Republic fell into the hands of Louis Napoleon, nephew of Napoleon I, who was elected president. Three years later, he abolished the Republic through a coup, and after confirming his dictatorial powers with a plebiscite, he proclaimed himself emperor. Thus, rather than observing a continuation of the laws of motion found in the revolution, Marx is bewildered to find himself confronted with—of all things—a repetition of its failure, which he calls "a farce."

It is not only in Marx's work that we find the uncomfortable idea that the past is being blindly dragged along by an insurmountable force. Remarkably, the most revolutionary roles in Dickens's narrative are often given to those characters who seem to be most effectively trapped in blind repetitive compulsions—but at the same time, according to his diagnosis, this is also why change itself fails to happen. At the core of the novel's plot is Dr. Manette, a sensitive gentleman who is plagued by dramatic "relapses" into his past. As a young doctor on a mission to combat ignorance, he once attempted to bring the aforementioned Marquis Evrémond to justice for the fact that he and his brother raped and murdered a farm girl. As a result of these efforts, instead of the guilty parties, Manette himself disappears into the Bastille for ten years, where he tries to stay sane by working as a shoemaker. After he is freed during the storming of the Bastille, he emigrates to England, where his daughter lives. When the twists and turns of the plot bring him back to France, he suffers from increasingly frequent bouts of insanity, in which he always starts out monotonously mending shoes and ends up at the head of a revolutionary tribunal that is pushing ahead with the execution of political opponents, including members of his own family. Dickens portrays this as a double relapse into the ancien régime. On the one hand, Manette imagines himself back in the Bastille; on the other he works, despite having been an idealistic humanist, to realize the same policy of elimination that he suffered at the hands of the aristocracy. This presents us with a similar mental image to Martin Buber's "tragedy of revolutions": the idea that processes of change fail because the practices for which they strive are not rehearsed enough "before the revolution" in order to structure the future.[14]

In fact, Marx also turns out to be concerned with the problem of a "mad Englishman." The whole French nation, he suspects in 1849, just a few years before Dickens, is doomed to repeat its own history:

> The nation is like the mad Englishman in Bedlam who thinks he is living in the time of the pharaohs and complains every day how hard it is to work in the Ethiopian gold mines, immured in a subterranean prison, a flickering lamp fixed to his head, behind him the overseer with his long whip . . . The Englishman, so long as his mind was working, could not rid himself of his obsession with gold mining. The French, so long as they made revolutions, could not rid themselves of the memory of Napoleon, as was demonstrated by the [presidential] election of 10 December [1848].[15]

While, in the "Exodus" in the previous part of this book, it was the departure that failed due to a lack of "training," here it is the arrival that fails: the protagonists lack the capacity to realize that they have arrived at very different structures. Marx also offers a slightly less fantastical approach to the dilemma of self-undermining in revolutionary action. In his analysis of the political events in France, he emphasizes a further determining factor, which goes beyond his newly "ruined philosophy of history,"[16] a factor that he describes with great bitterness as "a tradition of all dead generations" that weighs "on the brains of the living like a nightmare."[17] The "present circumstances, given and inherited" here are the historically prominent patterns and practices in which, for Marx, revolutionary action seems to be clothed. Not only did the nephew restage the actual coup enacted by his uncle, the Eighteenth Brumaire of Napoleon I, in a comparatively pitiful style; even the heroes of the great French Revolution borrowed their costumes and phrases from Roman history, a tendency that Marx initially highlights as a general inclination of historical actors: "And just when they appear to be revolutionising themselves and their circumstances, in creating something unprecedented, in just such epochs of revolutionary crisis, that is when they nervously summon up the spirits of the past, borrowing from them their names, marching orders, uniforms, in order to enact new scenes in world history."[18]

However, Marx then tries to take back what might seem to be a drastic revision of his notion of history, using two further distinctions. The first is the distinction between the "veiling" but ultimately appropriate "use of uniforms" and the misguided, regressive recourse to old models. He argues that the appropriate variant takes place when actors in transition phases of world history need a kind of mask in order to deceive their contemporaries as to the ultimately profane, unheroic content of their actions.[19] In contrast, actors may resort to the past in an entirely hollow manner that does not even achieve the prosaic "tasks of their time," that is, the adaptation of the relations of production and class organization to the already altered productive forces. Instead, they create mischief as pure repetition, farce, or caricature, exemplified by the coup d'etat of Louis Napoleon and in fact already by the events that preceded it, the struggles of the Second Republic, which from Marx's perspective were led by false early socialist principles and produced an "empty" repetition of the great Revolution. The criterion deciding this distinction therefore does not lie in the form of revolutionary action—costumes and the "cold hand" of the past can be found in both variants—but in the close fit between this imitative action and the first strand of historical conditions, namely, the more fundamental material dynamic of development. This last then forms the basis of Marx's hope that it might be possible to make a second distinction: between the aforementioned bourgeois revolutions, which are reliant on "borrowed language," and for that very reason at first ecstatically accelerated and then followed by the long hangover of disillusionment,[20] and the approaching true socialist revolution that could stand by its own content, would not require any recourse to the past, and would draw only "from the future."[21] For Marx, it is the far more laborious progress of this revolution, interrupted by hindrances and backward steps, which indicates that it remains at the level of actual material developments. Thus, if Marx—himself using borrowed biblical language, oddly enough—speaks of the fact that the revolution of the nineteenth century has to "let the dead bury their dead," then this is not because future revolutionary action will no longer be dependent on conditions, but because it will be conditional in a different way and, he hopes, in a truly resilient way, namely, on a situation that "makes impossible all reversion."[22]

Marx, then, is aware of the "culturalist" notion that action is conditional on continuing past praxis, but uses it only as a supplement in case there is a failure of the structure that for him is actually crucial. However, if that happens too often, this will clearly undermine the supposedly fundamental status of the structure. If the course of events can be explained more often and better with recourse to the "additional structure" of historically rehearsed routines and patterns of reaction than through the dialectic of productive forces, then this single area can no longer be seen as setting the pace independently. But this also means a reshuffle in the combination of dynamic structures that are supposedly fundamental, and disruptive elements that are static and only short-lived. If both come into question as crucial conditions for action, as present circumstances, given and inherited, it seems sensible to find a notion of structure that encompasses both aspects.

We have now outlined from two perspectives what we would need in order to return to our carriage scene equipped with the right terminology. Either we must develop the vocabulary of praxis further, moving from the idea of links between practices to a sufficiently dynamic concept of structure, or we would have to mediate, within the Marxist legacy, between the dynamic basic structure, in its downgraded state, and the insistent repetitions of the past. Embarking on this task is made easier by the fact that the theory of structuration developed mainly by Anthony Giddens, which has been particularly influential in the social sciences, is already determined to achieve both of these things through its notion of "dual structure." Within the framework of a praxis-theoretical social ontology, it offers a toned-down reconstruction of historical materialism. In the first of the following chapters, Giddens's proposal will be translated into the praxis-theoretical vocabulary developed here so far. Through this, I hope to show that several of the central criticisms and countersuggestions directed at Giddens's notion of structure can already be "met halfway," and the theory of structuration—with "alignments" as materialist additions—can, on the whole, be defended.

However, this does not yet mean that it is really plausible at its core. This core is the focus of the second chapter. Giddens's motto of "duality" refers to the "two-track" nature of structures: the dependence between individual actions and patterns of order always goes two ways. There should, Giddens says, be nothing contradictory about the claim that action is dependent on preexisting patterns and that these patterns are likewise dependent on individual actions. But how can that be shown in theoretical detail? The previous part of this book already offered a detailed explanation of one of the two "tracks," showing the dependence of every action on existing patterns. But what about the return ticket, the journey from individual instances to the structure? This route determines whether we can see structures as remaining interdependent with praxis, meaning that they are potentially at our disposal—rather than seeing them as a result of human action that immediately gains autonomy and remains external to further praxis. The theoretical puzzle presented by the "recursiveness" of structures is not sufficiently explained through Giddens's own Wittgensteinian approach. However, it can be solved with an understanding of performativity based on a theory of recognition, as found in the work of Judith Butler. Through this, structures can ultimately be defined as "performatively aggregated praxis" and therefore become compatible with the ideas presented in the first part.

However, if we look again at the prerevolutionary Paris street corner with this understanding of performative structuration or "aggregation," two further challenges emerge. It seems that the "recursive" notion of structure has become all too variable to represent the rigidity of certain aspects of the order described by Dickens. And at the same time, any deviation from that order—the stubborn gaze of the woman knitting—still remains paradoxical. The combination of structures must therefore be differentiated again, through the notion of anchoring, into several grades of stability or "aggregate states." Through this, a heterogeneous image of the social order emerges, including in-between spaces where moments of fleeting structuration can also be observed—the interstitial.

By conceptualizing structure along these lines and making it "fit for transformation," we can finally glimpse how the carriage scene links with the shaken framework of society as a whole, and which hidden preconditions provide new structures to the woman knitting. In this part, the perspective on social change remains altogether "passive." If they are able to accumulate, interstitial spaces can slowly combine into structures. If structures allow gaps, new praxis can build up in those gaps. Only in the next part will we discuss whether and how interstitial praxis can also intervene "actively" in the existing order.

4
The Duality of Social Structures

We require a notion of structure that is both compatible with praxis theory and substantial enough to include the conditional nature of the ability to act, but also still dynamic enough to let us reconstruct historical change with recourse to human praxis. For the most part, this seems to correspond with the concerns of Anthony Giddens's theory of structuration. The basic premise of this theory is that structures are "dual," meaning that they are understood both as a condition and as a result of praxis. This allows social reproduction and transformation to be brought into a unified terminological frame, without one of them becoming paradoxical (and without the whole vocabulary losing its meaning).

In my presentation of Giddens's notion of structure, which follows later, it will still be necessary to make a few modifications, which in each case are due both to convincing challenges from Giddens's critics and to the specific concerns of my project. In this chapter, the first question will be whether Giddens's approach can be defended against objections that could be said to resemble Marx's arguments in the passages from the "Brumaire" cited earlier, in that they bring up the same resistance to the idea that action is globally shaped by previous praxis. It seems to me that such a defense can succeed with the help of the motif of "alignment" introduced in the previous part. From a materialist-structuralist perspective, some have argued that Giddens's attempts at theoretical mediation remain subjectivist "and do not touch base with the material circumstances";[1] these accusations can be parried by my own attempt at mediation, if we emphasize more strongly that the practical reproduction of rules and resources is channeled through existing links between practices—links that themselves still depend on recursive reproduction. To reach this result, I will first introduce Giddens's notion of structure and then outline in detail the extent to which he justifies the formation of structure from recursive praxis through the interplay of rules and resources. I will then defend this conception against the accusation of idealism voiced by Sewell, who generally sympathizes with the theory of structuration. To counter Sewell, I highlight the role of "alignments" in the formation of structure. Enriched in this way, structuration theory can ultimately withstand the more fundamental objections of structuralist Marxists such as Douglas Porpora and can, unlike their understanding of structure as a framework of organization, also encompass a historical perspective on a given order.

STRUCTURATION THEORY

Giddens's approach aims to overcome various dualisms pervading social theory—between subjectivism and objectivism, between phenomenology and structuralism,[2] between determinism and voluntarism, between micro and macro analysis.[3] In each case, Giddens proposes leaving these dualisms behind with the help of a core premise, namely, the duality of structures. We could say that in each instance, this premise allows him to set off on the "return journey," which is also necessary here when it comes to mediating between structure and the ability to act: How should we picture the idea that not only is action dependent on structures, but structures themselves can in turn be traced back to actions? Giddens's central claim is that "the structural properties of social systems are both medium and outcome of the practices they recursively organise."[4] Or, with a slightly different emphasis: "[Social structures] drawn upon in the production and reproduction of social action are at the same time the means of system reproduction."[5]

Structures are therefore simultaneously the effect of actions and the condition for them. As Giddens never tires of emphasizing, this means that they are neither a limitation on the freedom to act that otherwise exists nor a determining script, but always "both constraining and enabling."[6] He defines actors as "knowledgable," in that they are capable of observing and examining their own actions and the actions of others, though this is not interchangeable with the ability to explain their motivation, which he sees as a much greater challenge. The crucial point to which he keeps returning is that a large part of social life involves the day-to-day continuation of routines—and that all social life relies on these routines. Such circuits of repetition form "the material grounding of . . . the recursive nature of social life."[7] When it comes to analyzing a society,

Giddens does not so much recommend looking out for its codified rules and central institutions, but rather makes the following point: "That many seemingly trivial procedures followed in daily life have a more profound influence upon the generality of social conduct."[8] His weighting falls unambiguously on that which Stanley Cavell, another great Wittgensteinian, called "the uneventful."[9] All individual agency is thus based on what has gone before, which structures its particular context. "Every individual is at once positioned in the flow of day-to-day life; in the life-span which is the duration of his or her existence; and in the duration of 'institutional time,' the 'supra-individual' structuration of social institutions. Finally, each person is positioned, in a 'multiple' way, within social relations conferred by specific social identities."[10]

However, it is all these determinants that represent the conditions for the individual ability to act, meaning that an actor continues with a social praxis—"knows how to 'go on'"—and in the process once again reproduces the conditions that made the action possible.[11] The ability to act depends on structures in the same way as speech depends on language,[12] leading Giddens to concede: "To relate the 'I' to agency, it is necessary to follow the detour suggested by structuralists."[13] Thus, on the one hand, the "structuralist detour" is recommended when we are dealing with the theory of action, resulting in the hypothesis that the ability to act is dependent on structures, as we discussed in detail in relation to the pattern of praxis. Meanwhile, on the level of a theory of the social, Giddens's approach promises that this is not a one-way street. The dual notion of structure—its interdependency with its own instantiations—makes Giddens's terminology attractive for conceptualizing social change.[14] Structures that are sensitive toward individual practices would mean not "freezing" the social in a form of structural determinism, and would at least open up the possibility that is our particular concern here: a dynamic of transformation that starts from interstitial praxis.

Nevertheless, this does not yet tell us much about how this magically self-supporting mechanism is supposed to work. How does it happen that a series of practices can be regarded as "more" than the practices themselves, and defined as a structure? I would first like to look at Giddens's own attempts to explain the other side of the reliance of actions on structures—the recursive formation of structures in actions.

One element has already been mentioned. It rests on the change in perspective that Giddens achieves by prioritizing routines and everyday events. By describing the initial situation under analysis in a less dichotomous way, namely, not as a discrepancy between isolated individual activities and their external structures, but as a "durée" or "flow" of practical actions, he substantially shrinks the gap that his theory has to bridge. If we start by understanding action as processual in the first place, we can emphasize either the moment of flow within an action or the individual moments that lead to that flow—something like the relationship between a melody and its notes. Still, it is clearly not enough to define structures simply as a "flow of action"—this may allow us to capture the constitutive relationship of individual actions to structures, but the determining power of those structures would be lost.

Clearly, Giddens does not want his notion of structure to be understood as a purely quantitative phenomenon in which particular ways of acting are accumulated—roughly in keeping with the motto "the wider the river, the stronger the current." If, as he claims, he wants to follow poststructuralist insights into the conditionality of subjectivity without letting subjectivity become meaningless,[15] he has to find a better way of illuminating the perspective of the actors, and incorporate it into his explanation of the structure-forming "effect." He moves in this direction when he emphasizes that actors act under the conditions of copresence and are able to watch their own behavior consciously. Here, the notion of "monitoring" allows him to maintain an elegant vagueness, since it precisely does not imply complete "control," but instead, in the sense of the technical metaphor of early computer screens, means simply the representation of current processes. In a sense, people "track" what they are doing, which does not mean that they also know this and are entirely in charge of it. Giddens uses this claim primarily in order to be able to respond to accusations of determinism, by introducing a certain leeway of freedom to act. However, he does so without showing exactly how this leeway emerges from self-observation—after all, the subjectivation theories of Althusser or Foucault's middle period would turn this finding in precisely the other direction. Be that as it may, Giddens assumes that copresence and monitoring provide building blocks to explain the formation of structures, without going into further detail. I will take up these suggestions in the next chapter and develop them by adding motifs from recognition theory. But first, I will turn to the justification of duality, the part of Giddens's theory that he explains most thoroughly.

RULES, RESOURCES, RECURSIVENESS

The particular direction that Giddens takes in explaining the formation of structures results from his analysis of how structures are constituted. That is, he sees structures, like practices, as consisting of rules and resources.[16] The rules that he particularly has in mind are the ones I classified in the first chapter as "praxis-generating rules." Although Giddens underlines the embodiment and habitualization of actions, he does not follow Bourdieu in his understanding of these rules, but explicitly takes his cue from Wittgenstein.

As Wittgenstein tries to demonstrate in his famous rule-following argument,[17] we misunderstand rules if we regard them as having a defined content, a representation of which is located in the minds of those who apply them. There are always countless different ways of formalizing what someone seems to be following when they do something. Even if there were something like an algorithm that people followed in their actions, we would not be able to look inside the minds of actors and identify it. And even if we could, we would then have to go in search of the rule determining the application of the rule.

Therefore, according to Wittgenstein, we should let go of the idea that it is ever possible to state particular rules that explain actions. However, that certainly does not mean that there is no point in talking about rules. It just means that the question of rules is flipped in a pragmatic direction and always depends on how actors continue in their practices. Rules are "procedures of action, aspects of *praxis*."[18] There is no other criterion for the possession of a rule than that of praxis: it can never be known more definitively than by looking at what happens next.[19] At the same time, every event is an indication that some rules are clearly being followed—without any rules there would be no praxis. Following Wittgenstein, Giddens describes rules in this sense as "techniques or generalizable procedures applied to the enactment/reproduction of social practices."[20]

In the definition of praxis in the previous part, we already saw that praxis-generating know-how can only be transferred *by doing*. There, I stressed the fact that intuitive imitation and physical training cannot entirely be replaced by verbal instructions. With Wittgenstein, Giddens now approaches the argument from the opposite direction, namely, from the notion of rules itself, and concludes that it is not possible to conceive of a set of instructions for action that are spelled out in their entirety. "Most of the rules implicated in the production and reproduction of social practices are only tacitly grasped by actors: They know how to 'go on.'"[21] Such practical "knowing how to go on" can thus be understood as the product of previous practice, which itself has a structuring effect.

However, future practice and past practice do not only depend on the expertise of their carriers. Everything that plays a role in practices, everything needed to form their phenomenology, beyond the rules of how to complete an action, can be regarded as a resource. By viewing resources "from the vantage point of praxis," so to speak, Giddens already describes them as the medium for the power to act. As actors who know the rules come into contact with resources—be they human abilities or things (Giddens distinguishes here between authoritative and allocative resources)—they gain in power.[22]

MATERIALISM THROUGH THE TRANSFER OF PRAXIS

For Giddens, the resources of practices are only ever set in motion by practical rules, which leads William R. Sewell to criticize his account for idealism.[23] Giddens provides further provocation for this accusation by declaring structures themselves to be "fictional," because as "rule-resource sets" they only arise from the combination of "real" resources with virtual rules.[24] Structuring force, it seems, is only ever invested in the rules and therefore remains at the level of ideas; resources are the passive material that is used as needed. In response to this, Sewell suggests a reformulation. Rather than rules, he speaks of schemas, cultural patterns of interpretation, which are then interwoven with the resources in a mutually constitutive relationship (see also chapter 2). These resources themselves are sometimes described by Sewell as "material" or, given that manual dexterity or perfect pitch can also be resources, sometimes only as "actual." Thus, structures should also be understood as "dual" in the sense that they are always both actual and virtual, consisting of schemas and resources.[25] However, it seems questionable to me whether Sewell's projection of the ideal/material opposition onto the terms virtual/actual is helpful. Although he aims to increase the value of the material side, his apparent limitation on the notion of rules could also be understood as a considerable expansion of the side presented as "virtual." For with his more precise understanding of rules as "schemas of interpretation," Sewell gives up the pragmatic aspect of Giddens's rules.[26] For the latter, rules are precisely not a "pattern of thought" but rules for transformation, which are only expressed and perpetuated in praxis.[27] As Giddens understands them, rules are located neither "in the heads" of actors nor in some free-floating realm of cultural ideas, but can always only be read tentatively from the interactions maintained in practices and things. The materialism that Sewell rightly demands therefore stands and falls depending on how well the role of resources in praxis is illuminated, and has little to do with whether we simply decree structures to be supremely "tangible."

For if the praxis-generating rules, as Giddens understands them, can only be acquired and transferred in praxis, then resources always represent an irreducible condition for the formation of structures. Where they are not present, no one can repeat a praxis, or rather a praxis cannot repeat itself, so that the rules that he supposedly overestimates are actually dependent on material conditions in a fundamental way. This does not seem to be the case for Sewell's transferable and explicable schemas.

In short, structures can be defined as links between rules and resources such as to give Giddens's notion of rules priority, without automatically losing the materiality of resources. But how can we define resources more clearly, as Sewell urges us? In their materiality, resources always already introduce certain possibilities to practices; however, that which makes them resources of a specific practice is only accrued within that practice. A part of the "rules" of praxis is therefore always stored within the resources: resources could be seen as a reservoir of possible ways of behaving. In *A Tale of Two Cities*, Dickens describes how the distinguished, older Dr. Manette, at the sight of a workbench and a set of shoemaker's tools, always falls into a trance. With a vacant look, he begins repairing shoes—his constant activity during the decade that he spent in solitary confinement in the Bastille. Shoemaking is regarded as the prototypical trade of the sansculottes, which allows Dickens to associate the delusional political radicalism and merciless advocation of the *terreur*, which likewise only overcomes Dr. Manette in phases, with his experience of deprivation in the Bastille. This exaggerated example nevertheless foregrounds the extent to which things as resources can activate particular practices—even if they usually do not automatically compel them to take place. Resources structure the way in which we deal with them; their qualities cogenerate rules. They possess this power, however, not through characteristics beyond practices. Instead, we could say that it is invested in them in the praxis—though, as the extreme case of Dr. Manette's workbench demonstrates, it can then not simply be removed again. However, this example also illustrates a problem with Giddens's terminology, which is due to the way in which he equates resources with instruments of power. The workbench, the awl, and the last may give Dr. Manette the power to mend shoes, but even if we understand power very broadly, like Giddens, as the ability to act, this description of resources is misleading in suggesting an increase in power. Whether that is the case depends on the individual praxis and its links with other practices. Unlike a real shoemaker, Manette actually gains a greater ability to act after his housekeeper burns the workbench that he has kept hold of.

Starting from the inseparability of rules and resources in the course of a practice, we can now gain quite an extensive view of structuration. Rules and resources are only reproduced in practices but also have a structuring effect, moving beyond an individual praxis to generate further practices. Practices are more than simply moments in a flow of praxis. They (re)produce elements that contour this flow, as structures: rules and resources.

MATERIALISM THROUGH LINKS BETWEEN PRACTICES

Giddens's conception has also fallen under a different suspicion of idealism, one that seems more serious to me than Sewell's reservations. The worry is that Giddens may describe quite well how the rules and resources of practices have a structuring effect when they are repeated, but that he cannot capture why it is that some practices are continuously repeated and others are not. But this was the very question we started out with. If no resistance stirred on Dickens's street corner, can we really explain this best by saying that the practices of meekness were continued? Aren't we really more interested in the question of why some people end up in the carriage and others under the wheels, rather than how tyrannical/aristocratic practices and poor-quarter practices are reproduced? This would be a question not about "structures" in the sense of the continued diachronic flow of the plot as Giddens sees it, but about "structure" as a synchronic fabric or network of organization in a certain society. The notion of structure in the latter sense not only would then achieve a certain task in social theory and explain the ability to act, but would extend into "theory of society" and answer the question of the social order's internal organization.

This approach is exemplified by Douglas V. Porpora, who attacks Giddens's notion of structure and does not simply demand additional work, like Sewell, but dismisses Giddens's attempt to develop a cultural-materialist notion of structure. As the superior alternative, he proposes a definition of structure that he presents as Marxist and critical-realist, as "systems of human relationships among social positions."[28] If we see structures as the actual social relations and positions—class relations, for example—Porpora says, then we can derive interests and causalities from them that would be a first step toward marking out the playing field on which some would then repeat certain practices, while others repeated different ones. We might almost say that it is perhaps better not to do as I did in presenting the example in the first chapter of this section, emphasizing the repetitive verbs (some people starve, stare, and knit, while others celebrate and whizz past in one grand carriage after another); instead, we should emphasize the nouns. It is these that ultimately label the social positions characterizing the ancien régime, and the structuring social relations are arrayed between them: on the one side of the barrier "the rats," and on the other, "the Minister, the State-Projector, the Farmer-General, the Doctor, the Lawyer, the Ecclesiastic, the Grand Opera, the Comedy."[29]

Indeed, it seems that the build-up of repetitions is at first glance a less meaningful reason than the organization of society when it comes to explaining the emergence of structures. At second glance, however, it becomes clear that Porpora can only claim to be able to dismantle Giddens's notion of structure because he reduces practices to "behavior" and allows them to be seen as relational only in the sense of personal interactions, at most.[30] In addition, Giddens's approach allows us to account for the factors determining the build-up of repetitions, so that many of the justifiable materialist questions can be answered. I would like to elaborate on this slightly, before I finally turn the tables and accuse Porpora himself of not being able to fulfill the diachronic conditions of his notion of structure.

Giddens himself tries to use the concept of the social system to capture the synchronic network of the social structure of organization, which I have contrasted here with his structures as a diachronic flow of action. For him, the emergence of this social system is also due to the recursive reproduction of practices. It is when we look at the whole system from a bird's-eye view that a cross-section of structures emerges: "The rules and resources drawn upon in the production and reproduction of social action are at the same time the means of system reproduction."[31] Thus, for Giddens, the social system is and remains dependent on practices; it arrives as an unintended side effect of praxis action and does not precede that action as a basis. Furthermore, he goes against the approach to structure found in German-speaking sociology, refusing to see it as being equipped with an inherent logic. The unintended side effects of practices do not link together into a system that can reproduce itself independently of the actors. For Giddens, then, "system" in fact represents the weaker alternative to the notion of society, and could perhaps be better described as "social formation," since he uses this terminology in order to avoid what he sees as the assumptions of closedness, homogeneity, and an endogenous dynamic of transformation implied by the modern notion of "society."

With this critique, Giddens aligns himself with the historical sociologist Michael Mann, who fought even more vehemently for a departure from the notion of "society" and wanted to see it replaced with the notion of "overlapping organizational networks."[32] Seen in this way, Giddens's "system" does not allow us to draw any instructive conclusions as to its internal relations—it is through the dissemination of practices that the system is created, and it cannot itself be brought in to explain the patterns of this dissemination.

However, if we build on the arguments presented at the end of the last section and allow our theory to include not only the perpetuation of practices but also the links between them, it becomes clear that the factors demanded by Porpora are already in place. The interstitial approach allows us to look separately at the context in which practices repeat themselves, as long as this context is not imputed with a different ontology from that of dual structures. The links between practices can be highlighted in their effect on the reproduction of other practices—nevertheless, they themselves remain dependent on repetition. The lack of resistance shown by the inhabitants of Saint-Antoine is not automatic, but reproduces itself under the conditions of constellative-regulatory alignments, some of which are even named in Dickens's narrative. Thus the Marquis threatens, for instance, that he will also run over the person who threw back the coin: "If I knew which rascal threw at the carriage, and if that brigand were sufficiently near it, he should be crushed under the wheels."[33] Since it seems that the credibility of the threat is only a question of whether the "brigand" can be caught, the people of Saint-Antoine, with their "long and hard . . . experience of what such a man could do to them," take care not to move on to more open practices of resistance.

However, the reproduction of the whole system could also be due to broader links between practices. Thus, the masked ball provides a boost to the Paris dressmaking trade, which in turn contributes taxes that finance "law enforcement," which erects the barriers between the ragged bystanders and the costumed elite, keeping the class differences intact. Such arrangements of practices, mutually supporting one another, can be reconstructed through the theory of structuration and can also explain why certain practices are perpetuated while others are prevented. The social ontology of structures as rule-resource sets (or rather, as the next chapter will show, as aggregated praxis) does not prohibit us from emphasizing their functional dependences on one another in the form of alignments. On the contrary, this is the only way for the tracks of praxis to become a panorama of society in which structures are connected and do not simply run parallel to one another.

Still, the theory of structuration does not thin out its material from the start in such a way that only a skeleton of supposedly "hard," causally effective basic structures remains, as Porpora demands in the name of a critical-realistic approach. Because of this, structuration theory remains able to describe situations in which a series of actions has a different effect from stabilizing the system. They can still be reconstructed as instantiations of rule-resource-dependent, historicizable structures, and do not simply appear as pure "coincidences" or "deviations." As we have seen, the accident on the street corner was observed by a traveling road-builder, who will end up burning down the château of the Marquis Evrémonde. As soon as the practice of burning down castles is in turn widespread enough to shape the structure of other practices, such as the outbreak of the "Great Fear" in the summer of 1789,[34] it can itself be regarded as an alignment and as a condition for the build-up of practices that leads to the formation of structures. Under such changed circumstances, it will then be the road-mender who is able to make effective threats.[35]

In alignment, it is a series of practices that has a crucial effect on the course of others. Meanwhile, at the end of the previous part, I presented anchoring as a second prototypical form of links between practices, in which one particular praxis defines many further practices in a mimetic-constitutive manner. The specific relationship between rules and resources in the "basic practice" or "anchor practice" is repeated in those further practices in a recognizable way. The "offshoots" feed on the legitimacy of the anchor praxis and at the same time stabilize its structure.

Such links between practices can also be brought in to explain particular aspects of an individual social formation based on the recursive concept of structure—in fact, they have more potential here than the sychronic view of structure as an established arrangement of society. For as Porpora shows, that view of structure derives its explanatory power from the interests that actors have due to their social position. Porpora emphasizes that this is not about causal laws working "behind the backs" of the actors, but about actual interests emerging from their position in the structure of society. These interests can be made commensurable and confronted with one another, because they are always understood in material terms. This also means that they cannot then multiply themselves infinitely into the motives accompanying different practices.

Now the objection could be raised that Porpora defines a historically very specific idea of motivation and interests as a fundamental concept of social theory. Already Dickens's street scene does not seem to fit into this logic—after all, the gold coin finally lands again in the carriage. We could follow Karl Polanyi and describe Porpora's idea of interests as the normativity of profit-orientated participation in the market, which is generalized in market societies, having been disembedded from other social relations and priorities. In the late eighteenth and "long" nineteenth century, this normativity itself became the basis of various other practices.[36] As an "anchor praxis," it could be described as a special combination of rules and resources—as specific strategic rules of behavior that maximize benefit, or as resources that are handled as if they were goods. In Dickens's panorama of society, an emerging generalization of these practices begins to be perceptible, although they are still portrayed as special cases—whether in the nefarious profit-driven relationship of the Marquis to his tenants or in the secret trade plied by a grave robber.

But such structured historical developments are exactly what Porpora's vocabulary is unable to capture, unless they follow a causal logic that is internal to the system, but that requires as its *movens*—the material interests of the actors—that which in this case needs to be explained. Porpora willingly admits that he is unable to say more about the genesis of the structural links that he wishes to highlight as the necessary prerequisite for Giddens's structuration processes: "The arrangement of social relationships in the world, however it came about in the first place, is now analytically prior to rules, norms and ideology."[37] Evidently,

Porpora does not start from a deterministic understanding of dialectics, in which the social relations in this arrangement automatically lead to the next arrangement. But unless we are to adopt such a deterministic approach, Porpora's "however it came about" would also be all we could say about social change from the perspective of structuration theory.

If my argumentation is correct, much of that which Porpora is able to explain through the notion of an organizational system could also be captured by analyzing specific links between practices, without having to pay the price of declaring these links to be a larger architecture that itself can no longer be historicized, referred back to structured human praxis, and therefore explained. With a dual notion of structure, we can use the praxis-internal rules of the class system to understand why the coin once again lands in the carriage (see chapter 5) and—this, at least, is the hope, not yet fulfilled—also develop a theory encompassing the overarching processes of radical change.

Structures are therefore not the repeated practices but the expression of these practices in the form of stable rule-resource sets. They are not only the many points but also the line that connects them and at least hints at the course they will take in the future. As to which practices are continued and aggregated into structures in this way—this question can only be answered if we reconstruct the links between the practices that might form structures. These links, which I have outlined here in terms of alignment and anchoring, can nevertheless not be isolated and excluded from the duality of structure, but emerge in turn in a structured way from historical practices.

5

Recognition and Performative Structuration

The dual understanding of structure is based on the premise that structures are both the prerequisite and the result of repeated praxis. What Giddens calls "recursive" structure formation rests on the fact that the elements of structure—rules and resources—are stabilized in repeated praxis and have a structuring effect beyond individual practices. Meanwhile, it is the links between practices that determine which ones can be aggregated into structures—links that can ultimately also be regarded as configurations of practices that are dependent on recursive repetition.

Although we have now begun to outline the parameters for structuration, it seems to me that its actual mechanism is still insufficiently clear—and it is ultimately this that decides whether we will succeed in creating the synthesis that is one of the aims of structuration theory. Andreas Reckwitz has shown very emphatically that structuration theory endeavors, through the duality of structure, not only to reconcile the alternatives of a system-centric and an actor-centric perspective but also to find a way of dissolving the opposition between two fundamentally different concepts of structure, namely, as normative rules and as regularities. Contrary to Reckwitz's pessimistic assessment, I will try to show in this chapter that such a synthesis can succeed—at least more substantially than it does in Giddens's version, which Reckwitz sees as the most successful attempt. However, this means looking more closely at the perspective of the actors than Giddens does in his passing remarks on monitoring and copresence. In the familiar sociological terms, Reckwitz translates the opposition between the paradigms of regularities and of rule-bound normativity into an opposition between a simple hermeneutic of observation and a "double hermeneutic" based on the perspective of the participants.[1] Yet it seems to me that a praxis-theoretical notion of structure would lead us to a kind of "triple" hermeneutic of "observing participants." Basing this on my differentiation between three different levels on which practices follow rules, we could see it as follows: at a praxis-internal level, practices set rules, and at a praxis-generating level, the repetition of practices leads to regularities. The fluctuation between these two levels requires a further additional step. This can be provided by the "praxis-defining" rules or Sewell's schemas, which have to be fulfilled in order for any praxis to be recognizable. Since actors, in perpetuating praxis, orientate themselves toward schemas that they perceive as regular, they "make" these performatively into a rule. "Aggregated" praxis is therefore more than "pure" praxis—namely, structure—because it marks out the space that the actors navigate, given their dependence on intelligibility and their susceptibility to sanctions.

At this point in our thinking, we can finally also take an initial look at the way in which the erosion of structures can be described in the context of structuration theory, and thus get closer to transformation.

NOTHING BUT PRAXIS, BUT STILL MORE THAN PRAXIS

Given the astonishing proximity of Giddens's structuration to Butler's theory of performativity, it seems odd that the two are not often connected. Apart from being a question of different disciplines and different theoretical strategies, this may have terminological reasons, since elements of the two theories that have very similar content are referred to with different vocabulary. Thus, Butler always speaks of "subjects," Giddens of "actors." Butler generally uses "performance" rather than "praxis." Although Giddens does admit in some places that his notion of structure is actually only derived from an analysis of power,[2] for Butler the theme of power is much more pronounced, since she is writing in the wake of Foucault. When Butler speaks of the contours of power, she does not use the term "structure," but "norm." On the one hand, this is due to the fact that she tends to see "structure" as being connected terminologically with ahistoric unchangeability—that is, with a strictly structuralist usage such as that of Claude Lévi-Strauss. At the same time, she has a specific interest in the processes that Foucault describes as "normalization," and is therefore especially orientated toward phenomena where normative expectations are closely connected with the enforcement of norms and even ultimately with the elimination of the "abnormal." However, for the purposes of our analysis, Butler's norms can be brought into line with Giddens's structure, through the common denominator of power. Both serve as a condition for the ability to act, and are in a specific, recursive, interdependent relationship with that ability. At this point, Butler in turn does not speak of "recursivity," like Giddens, but of "performativity," which will be my focus in the following discussion. For Butler allows us to take up the moments of "copresence" and monitoring that are only sketched out in Giddens's approach, and enrich them with insights from the theory of recognition, so that the formation of norms or structures can be understood as a performative effect of the relation to norms in an individual praxis. Butler describes the two-track relationship between structures and their instantiations, which Giddens calls "duality," in the following terms: "In fact, the norm only persists as a norm to the extent that it is acted out in social practice and reidealized and reinstituted in and through the daily social rituals of bodily life. The norm has no independent ontological status, yet it cannot be easily reduced to its instantiations; it is itself (re)produced through its embodiment, through the acts that strive to approximate it, through the idealizations reproduced in and by those acts."[3]

In the first part of the passage cited here, it seems that everything will come down to the irreality of the norms beyond their instantiations. They are described as lacking an ontological status of their own.[4] Regardless of whether they are played out and embodied, structures are—as Giddens also says[5]—nothing but a chain of repeating practices. We could say that structures are aggregated practice, and therefore only an accumulation of actions leading in the same direction, actions in which particular resources are used according to particular rules or schemas. An observer could identify such structures by noting the points where action is concentrated—in a "single hermeneutic," leading to a definition of structure as regularity. Praxis-generating rules would then essentially be transferred "blindly."[6] The role that is played for Bourdieu by early conditioning is taken on in Butler's "learning by doing" by continuous repetition.[7] However, the fact that she understands this as being guided mimetically already suggests that a less blind synthesis can be found, which I will discuss later.

Butler then seems to contradict herself—or rather, she contradicts the picture of the norm as being merely a series of practices. Norms, she continues in the passage cited earlier, cannot be reduced to their occurrences; they owe their existence to a kind of surplus between the patterns of action that reproduce themselves and an accompanying effect of idealization. Invested with a strange intentionality, actions apparently "seek" to "approach" norms. Reckwitz, in his work on the notion of structure as an alternative model to the paradigm of regularity, reconstructs the actor-centered perspective of rule-following, as we saw earlier. This perspective, he says, enters into the actors' process of discovering the world in a double hermeneutic, and adopts from them the meaning and justification of particular actions. Structures are therefore not identified on the level of praxis-generating rules, but accessed through praxis-internal rationalizations.

However, a notion of structure on this basis runs the risk, on the one hand, of losing sight of motivations that the actors may be unaware of, and at the same time risks drawing an excessively rationalist picture of action—as if all everyday actions always had a meaning and good reasons, and as if these meanings and reasons were not often only created in exceptional cases of conflict or questioning by an external observer. Bourdieu describes the problem of dealing scientifically with a speaking object as one that condemns sociologists to an endless vacillation between boundless trust and mistrust in the discourse of that object.[8] His answer as to how that tension should be resolved is clear—the observer has authority. While the "subjects do not, strictly speaking, know what they are doing," their actions reveal their deeper truths: "What they do has more meaning that what they know."[9] Giddens tries to counter this objectivism with his idea of the duality of structure, which continually oscillates between the poles of regularity and rule-following. On the one hand, it is the rules that the actors apply in practice that define the structures, while on the other, it is the existence of a regular chain of action, in which the resources support the transfer of praxis-generating rules, that allows structures to continue existing.

Now, however, the question arises of whether this duality really represents two sides of *the same* coin or in fact tries to patch together two very disparate phenomena: on the one hand, actors follow rules and, on the other, the social sphere contains regularities. Reckwitz's own suggestion is then to replace such attempts at synthesis, which are never entirely smooth (though Giddens, in his opinion, makes the best effort), with a multidimensional model of structural analysis, constantly shifting between partial perspectives. This should lead to a social theory "with a maximum of content."[10] However, once we are not simply concerned with the toolkit for multifaceted empirical analysis, but with the building blocks of an encompassing social theory, this kind of heuristic no longer seems workable. The question of which of the dimensions of structure is then decisive in each case, and how they are related to one another, cannot be left unanswered. But how can we reach an improved version of the synthesis that is being attempted? So far, with Butler, we have only repeated the same oscillation between "structure as a chain of instances" and "structure as a guiding ideal," with a different emphasis, making its paradoxical aspects explicit.

REPETITION, RECOGNIZABILITY, PERFORMATIVITY

In the work of Judith Butler, the recursive effect of practices on the formation of structures is reconstructed as performativity, and explicitly connected with the reflexiveness of subjectivity, which for Butler is always subordinate to intersubjective relationships of recognition. It seems to me that her vocabulary is preferable to Giddens's rather thin and somewhat monadic notion of copresent observing actors, and at the same time makes the process of structuration plausible—while also justifying Butler's own claim, mentioned earlier, that structures are both more than their instantiations and simultaneously nothing but those instantiations. Butler does not only locate the sedimentation of structures at the level of unconscious embodiment—as Bourdieu does, for instance, and to some extent also Foucault—but also in the shared household of evaluative criteria, which are used to preserve intersubjective recognition. We could say that this opens up a new perspective, correcting the problem that led to Giddens's memorable warning about Foucault, namely, that his subjects "do not have faces."[11] In her theoretical perspective, Butler generally remains closer to Foucault than Giddens does himself, but on this point it can still be said that her additions go further than Giddens's own, since his actors never seem to meet a "counterpart" who likewise embodies the structures. Faces, yes, but not facing one another.

It is by prioritizing these counterparts that Butler is able to foreground the fundamental role of praxis-defining rules. Actions have to be intelligible in the social world. Whether that is the case depends on whether an action is compatible with the schemas that others have at their disposal. These schemas represent the framework used by social actors to interpret one another's behavior. At this point, the notion of recognition begins to play its crucial role, and it might be useful to distinguish between a basic and a specific use of recognition as a term.[12] On the basic level, which concerns us here, recognition refers to the question of recognizability as such, or, as Butler also calls it, "intelligibility." This basic recognition is not accorded to praxis activities "unconditionally" or "arbitrarily," but is aligned with the existing shared schemas. This does not make it impossible for something to happen that would be entirely incommensurable with the patterns of recognition—but it would not then count as an "action" or "praxis." Just as actors would not be able to carry out any praxis without having the praxis-generating rules of know-how at their disposal, it would also remain undone if it could not be deciphered in the social context in a more general way, using the existing schemas. These are evidently shared more broadly than other rules of praxis—in order to recognize something, we do not need to be able to do it ourselves, nor must we be well informed about it. Instead, whether we can recognize it depends on the social structures with which we are familiar.

Against this background, it is now possible to further clarify what Butler means by performativity. As a linguistic term, it refers to the ability of certain statements to create that which they refer to.[13] Originally, the term was used by J. L. Austin in his programmatic text *How to Do Things with Words*, as a particularly clear example of the inadequacy of a semantics that only considered the question of truth. Alongside the content of a statement (a "locution"), he argues that it is also necessary to consider its pragmatic, "illocutionary" aspect.[14] Only then does it become clear that a speech act has "more" meaning than we can read simply from a series of words out of context. Here we need only think of the sentence "You are a good philosopher," and the meaning that it takes on in the carriage scene, as a patronizing comment by the Marquis in response to Defarge's bitter remark, which was certainly not meant to be conciliatory. The performative variant is a particularly striking type of pragmatic, illocutionary meaning; here, a statement actually establishes a certain state of affairs in the world.[15] When the Marquis expresses his willingness to kill his adversary if he gets hold of him, a threat takes shape and does not fail to have the desired effect.

In his critique of Austin, Jacques Derrida pointed out that it is not the act of the speaker that is performative.[16] Doing things with words depends, he says, on the conventions connected with words—we could also refer to established practices. Only as a repetition or "iteration" of those conventions can performative acts take place. Butler agrees with this critique, attributes performative effects even more firmly to the social structures that make them possible, and broadens the motif substantially. The Marquis's threat would not be successful if it were not for the coachman and the carriage, a legal system blind to the arbitrary cruelty of the aristocracy,[17] and the previous experience of such draconian praxis. In the same vein, every praxis is ultimately bound to the conditions of iterability, including those that do not establish any "things" or "facts" in the world beyond their own execution. In order to be recognizable, a praxis must repeat previous praxis and be repeatable. In other words, it must be decipherable on the basis of the praxis-defining rules that precede it. If it did not fit into any schemas, it would not come into effect as a social praxis. Thus, in a certain way, we can already interpret any intelligible praxis that is carried out as being due to the success of a small performative act. We only "do" something at all, whether with words or without, if it is connected with existing structures through basic recognition.

So far, however, with the small performative in every praxis, it seems that all we have done is find a very complicated way to reconstruct, once again, a particular feature of actions: they are dependent on structures. But the reverse of this, the dependence of structures on actions, which is our real concern here, can be found within that same feature. To be precise, we could say that Butler locates a double performativity in every intelligible praxis. Alongside (or, rather, *in*) the "effect" of its own success, the praxis also affects the structure in which it is rooted. What emerges as a performative effect is not only a specific successful praxis, carried out by the subject in relation to the schemas of an existing structure, but also a validation and perhaps a slight variation of that same structure.

This could be described formally as a process of simple addition: seen as an iterable chain of repetition, the structure would initially "be" a series of n practices, to which the "+1" of a further instantiation is added. The effect of the praxis in question is to vary the original structure so that it becomes "n+1." However, this would only be the minimal definition of the way in which performativity forms structures, giving us a purely quantitative picture of structure, according to a theory of regularity. Already in the introductory quotation, Butler objected to this, arguing that a norm cannot be reduced to its occurrences and that it is actually "more" than a series of its own instantiations. I will discuss this surplus, layer by layer.

THE TRIPLE HERMENEUTIC

The social relations of recognition allow us to expand on the hypothetical "simple hermeneutic" of observation. First of all, we should note that the pure observation of regularities is in itself a fiction. Repetitions must be individualized in space or in time, in order to be regarded as different instances of the same thing. In the social realm, however, making this distinction inevitably means that a larger discrepancy emerges, since further factors come into effect from the individual context. Conversely, this means that whenever regularities are detected, an interpretative process of construction must already have taken place. Even an external observer would therefore have to make use of basic rules in order to perceive regularities.[18] This not quite so "simple hermeneutic" is already embedded in the process of iterability. The series of repetitions is only created through the imitative response of the subject, whose actions draw on preceding praxis. The "aggregation" of individual instances into a structure could therefore be described as resulting from the imitation of these instances—once again as a performative effect, if you will. This dynamic culminates in Butler's seemingly paradoxical claim that the copy precedes the original:[19] even if that which later represents the original (the structure) was there earlier than the copy (the action), it did not then yet have the status of an original. Thus, only the imitation makes something into a model, and in this sense every instantiation creates the structure *as a structure*—not only by adding to it, as we saw earlier, but also, in a way, by "seeing it as a whole." We can take a similar approach when recalibrating our notion of rules in response to Wittgenstein's rule-following argument. Rules reside in praxis and assume their authority retroactively. For if, according to Wittgenstein, there is no clearer criterion for the existence of a rule than a specific, socially established way of continuing a series of instantiations, meaning that a certain—Wittgenstein calls it a "hardened"[20]—form of praxis becomes the evidence of rule-following, then the rule can only be detached from that praxis at a hypothetical level. Accordingly, Klaus Puhl suggests the following Wittgensteinian analysis of rules: "The rule is only developed in retrospect from the behavior that is then recursively, in a sort of circular movement, interpreted as following the rule. This also retrospectively changes the meaning and identity of the behavior from which the rule is derived."[21] The relationship described here between "behavior" and "rules" can be applied to practices and structures. The shift in the "meaning and identity of the behavior from which the rule is derived" would then be the recursive transition from regularity to rule with which we are concerned here.

There is no exit option from this recursiveness, in the sense that actors are constantly required to follow social schemas in their practices. An "act" can therefore not avoid—as Butler announced—"approximating" the "idealizations" that it always creates when it is carried out.

However, there is still something mechanical about this upgraded "simple hermeneutic." Subjects clearly orientate themselves in a broader, richer way; they are not simply replication mechanisms, continually digesting the examples that they imitate. Here it becomes apparent that in the social realm, there is always more at play than just basic recognition. Actions are guided in a more sophisticated way than simply by the search for recognizability as such—that is, they are not only directed toward intelligibility. Although intelligibility functions as a limit on what counts as a praxis at all, thus creating exclusions, everything that falls "into" its area is additionally overdetermined by more substantial criteria. In the collision in Saint-Antoine, there may be one action that, from the point of view of the Marquis, does not even count as an action at all—Mme. Defarge's stare. However, all the "readable" practices of the Paris mob—such as the practice of lowering one's gaze or the practice of throwing back coins, of meekness or resistance— are immediately connected with a layer of further evaluative criteria and practical consequences. As a praxis is recognized according to a particular schema, the internal rules emerge which are connected with that praxis. Depending on how far the actors are knowledgeable about the practices, these practice-internal rules then guide the action. And even if they are not knowledgeable, they will be judged and recognized in the social realm subject to the rules of the practices in which they take part. This kind of recognition in a narrower sense therefore works on the actors as a "carrot and stick," according to the praxis-internal rules. The course it takes can only be reconstructed through a "double hermeneutic," by interpreting the interpretations of the actors.

If we can now say that particular patterns of action become stable as structures because the actors themselves construct links that work as rules and orientate their actions according to their expectation that these links will be recognized and validated, then we have not defined an entirely new notion of structure, but are still continuing to work with iterable regularities.[22] This is not only because rule-following practices are, of course, also in repetitive relationships. Above all, it is because the image of a participant who is well versed in the rules, on whom the double hermeneutic depends, is excessively simplistic and suggests particularly static situations in which subjects possess extensive knowledge. It seems much more realistic to imagine that the actors may have the ability to master the praxis-internal rules, but also to take the idea seriously that there could be a kind of sliding transition between social regularity and rules. This arises from the fact that subjects often repeat activities and routines with which they identify, even before they have rationalized them any further. Wherever a repetition does not take place entirely unconsciously, it must already involve some praxis-defining schemas or rules being formulated as a guide. In this process, particularly in contexts that keep changing, the observing participants continually make new use of the conditions of recognition, taking account of the sort of interpretations, reactions, and sanctions that can be expected in the existing circumstances.

To continue the conceit, this could be described as requiring a "triple hermeneutic." The social relations of recognition are on the one hand structured by the fact that subjects always find themselves in loops of repetition that are routinized or otherwise "blind." But because, on the other hand, they make their expectations of recognition into a rule, the subjects follow the regularities of praxis in a structured way. It is only their ability to guess the patterns of recognition being followed by other actors ("copresent" actors, in Giddens's phrase) that explains the "pull" generated by reflection that actions follow when they "strive to approximate" the norm, as Butler says. Subjects therefore do not act out their ability to act in the form of a monologue—as if there were only praxis-generating rules. They also do not orientate themselves only through self-reflexive monitoring according to the praxis-evaluating rules that are familiar to them—as if there were only internal rules. Instead, they guide their actions according to supraindividual relationships of recognition, which manifest themselves in a socially shared set of schemas and in a knowledge of the associated reactions and sanctions that can be anticipated. The simple hermeneutic of external observation therefore combines itself with the double hermeneutic that reconstructs the rules of participation to form a triple hermeneutic of observing participants who continually reassess the contours of the social and thus keep structures dynamic. Structures are the performative effect of aggregated praxis, because they provide not only the patterns that are followed by action but also those patterns that are used to recognize the action and that allow the action to orientate itself in expectation of corresponding recognition by social counterparts.

Butler herself mainly focuses on examples where the nonfulfillment of a schema leads to exclusion from human praxis per se, that is, where the practices that are suspended are so fundamental that the choice is between fulfillment of the praxis-defining rules—even if this fulfillment is flawed—and complete unrecognizability. The actors in Dickens's scene are portrayed as resembling rats in various ways, and the accident is decisively influenced by the fact that the Marquis perceives a child of the underclass as being more of an inanimate obstacle than a fellow human—or, less anachronistically, "one of God's creatures." Still, to demonstrate how the use of schemas for orientation becomes visible due to a disruption, a more typical social situation would be one of practical misunderstandings or contradictory interpretations.

As the first part described in detail, practices are open to interpretation in the sense that depending on context and perspective, the same situation can be understood in different ways not only in its nuances but also in terms of which praxis is actually being carried out. At the very least, observing participants cannot always deduce schemas unambiguously—that is why a kind of performative surplus exists, as argued earlier, which works backward from the classification of a praxis to create a structure. On the street corner, the potential for conflict emerges from the fact that the Marquis's behavior contradicts expectations in an offensive manner, in a situation that the bystanders clearly see as warranting an admission of guilt, or at least some kind of expression of condolences. Instead, he makes use of a praxis that follows the schema of alms giving, probably his most established mechanism for avoiding tiresome contact with the poor population. Measured by the internal rules of the relevant practices, donating a gold coin would be a generous gesture in the context of alms giving. However, in the context of expressing condolences, it is so cynical and disrespectful that it is dramatically rejected by its intended recipients, in spite of the risks. The coin therefore ends up back in the carriage. Of course, in a situation of alms giving, this would be an almost unthinkable provocation, which the Marquis accordingly threatens with punishment. Thus, at this point the schemas join together from one point of view to mean that the praxis of alms giving is rejected in an almost inflammatory manner, while from the other perspective, there is an insulting refusal to express even the smallest sympathy, and instead the right to murderous despotism is reasserted. In both cases, this leads something decisive to happen to the structure of class relations. These are, in the eyes of all the participants in the situation, shown in a specific light, which in a certain way reflects the existing situation back onto previous encounters. The "long and hard experience of what such a man could do" hardens further, and is confirmed so definitively as a rule for the practices in which the classes encounter each other that a certain desperate courage, which already expressed itself in this situation, becomes more deeply inscribed. If even a situation that would—in such an extreme way—have required some respect from the Marquis toward his subjects escalates into a ferocious demonstration of his authority, this stabilizes a particular picture that the observing participants have of the social conditions. From the perspective of an external observer, too, the fact that they take this picture as a basis for action makes it more likely that one can count on further instantiations of such a structure. For the Marquis, we can assume more simply that the situation presents itself as yet another irksome encounter with the despicable rabble, whose signs of rebelliousness (that desperate courage from another perspective) confirm his usual draconian mode of conduct as an appropriate pattern of action that should be continued.

The differing perspectives at the level of praxis-internal rules that are especially emphasized here (although they are reduced schematically to two) do not dissolve the notion of structure into subjectivity, because it remains bound to the continuation of praxis. Even in a situation like this one, where we assume a disparity between the schemas being applied, the same actions are being carried out, from which the actors draw conclusions about their social circumstances *by seeing*. However, it is *by doing* that they have to continue those actions, and thus what they have "seen" will inevitably be reproduced so that it continues to structure the social space. It is only because the failed alms giving and the failed expression of condolences can both be registered in the schemas of damaged class relationships that they were intelligible at all, and able to link together—performatively—with a series of related practices, creating a particular configuration of praxis-conditioning rules and resources. This configuration is what we call structure, which we can now define as performatively aggregated praxis.

EROSION

Alongside the focus on more drastic conflicts, where the struggle for recognizability according to specific, praxis-generating rules means that recognizability as such is always also at stake, there is a further form of one-sidedness affecting current research in performativity theory. It results from the fact that Butler mainly examines practices in which the resource side of the praxis amounts to the ability of bodies to fulfill specific schemas. This does not mean, as critics often falsely suppose, that Butler ignores material entirely, but is instead due to a selective choice of examples. At least if performativity theory is to be adopted and generalized for social theory, this means that some further additions need to be made. The conditions of the performative never consist only in schemas that ensure or deny recognizability as praxis-defining rules, but also lie in the resources that must be mobilized for repetition. Unlike in the relatively immaterial linguistic iteration, in practices the corporeal and tangible world is reproduced.

Locating this materiality on the level of structure now allows us not only, as the last chapter showed, to say something about what is required for the performative process whereby practices are aggregated into structures, but also to address the converse process whereby structures are eroded or softened.

A specific and sophisticated version of structural disaggregation, which perfectly fits our requirements for interstitial radical change, will be explored in the second half of this book under the title of "metalepsis." However, we already have various possible perspectives on the question of how the process of forming structures could go into reverse. These possibilities can be divided into processes of erosion that start from the context, and those that start from the structure itself. The first would be present if the alignments were dissolved that had been supporting the continuation of a praxis. If the police officers and soldiers who patrol between the noble carriages and the inhabitants of Saint-Antoine were to desert, as the National Guard later did when it was supposed to be defending the Bastille, perhaps the accident described by Dickens would already lead to a situation in which we could no longer say that "all things ran their course."

The loss of an anchor praxis would be similar. If, for example, the three-estate system is no longer seen as unquestionable and worthy of recognition under all circumstances, then the practices which "repeat" that system lose part of their guarantee of recognition. It may be that the women described by Dickens—"the women who had tended the bundle while it lay on the base of the fountain, sat there watching the running of water and the rolling of the Fancy Ball"—no longer share the perspective at all that the narrator then sets forth, namely, that the things in question—the water, the noble carriages, and the blood on the pavement—are simply following their natural course.

Such contextual factors—with a certain amount of terminological acrobatics, we could call them "disalignment" and "unmooring"—are therefore likely to facilitate an erosion of structures. However, they would have to manifest themselves in the overall arrangement of structures. After all, many practices stubbornly go on repeating themselves, even long after the conditions that supported them have been lost.

The fragility of structures themselves—right up to the point where they actually stop being reproduced—can, first of all, come from the resources side. When the things, abilities, and persons that are mobilized in the praxis become not only unavailable but also irreplaceable, a structure can be forced to suspend itself. Usually, however, such a case would tend to result in various attempts at substitution and modification, if there were not a parallel breakdown on the rules side of the structure. In an extreme case, this breakdown would naturally be compelled by a loss of resources—if the praxis cannot perpetuate itself materially, then the rules of know-how that generate it can no longer be transferred. But often enough, a breakdown of rules already accompanies the loss of resources or even precedes it. For example, at the start of Dickens's novel, the brutal Marquis already finds himself in a situation in which the dynastic structures of his praxis have been eroded. His nephew and sole heir has studied philosophy and law, has absconded to England, and refuses to take over the management of the properties and estates. For the uncle, this means the disappearance of an important resource that would be necessary in order to perpetuate the praxis according to the traditional schema—as a feudal constellation continuing through the generations. At the same time, this case can be described as a breakdown in the rules of the structure. We might say that something has gone wrong for the aesthetic and highly sensitive nephew Darnay in his process of learning the praxis-generating rules—the knowledge of domination—and that the reproduction of practices has therefore failed. Or we might follow the nephew himself in arguing that he regards the praxis-internal norms of tenant farming as being incompatible with his enlightened attitude and that he therefore deliberately refuses to reproduce these practices. Either way, the structure breaks down from the side of the rules. However, as is clear to the reader and certainly to the Marquis, they immediately take the resource side with them. An heir who no longer wants to collect the rent is an unusable resource or even no resource at all in the praxis of feudal rule, just as useless as barren land.

However, even this line of argument, which is supposedly focused on the processes of breakdown within structures, has at various points already had recourse to practices that escape those structures or run counter to them. Whether it is the disobedience of the National Guard, the enlightened sensibility of the recalcitrant heir, or the perspective of the women who observe the contrast between luxurious carriages and dark holes and see not the rule of order but arbitrary despotism, don't they function, once again, as unexplained exceptions to the model of structure discussed here? Doesn't the notion of structure become watered down if these structures suddenly don't have to be continued? In order to be able to reconstruct these problematic practices not only as breakdowns in repetition but as repetitions of *other* structures, a reproduction of *other* practices, I will begin the next chapter by suggesting how we might differentiate between the multiplicity of structures according to their varying range and level of stability, using a model that then allows us to trace the processes of innovation and transformation.

6

Structures in Three States of Aggregate

In the previous chapter, I suggested that we can imagine the structure-forming side of the duality of structures as a performative effect of the fact that observing participants, dependent on recognition, take up and continue previous praxis. In the light of the specific instantiations taking place at that point, the assembly of previous practices can include shifts in emphasis, which might mean that the structure in question is, in a sense, reaggregated.

However, even when the image of dual structures is bolstered in this way, it is still susceptible to Margaret Archer's fierce criticism that Giddens—and by implication also Butler—pays for the advantage of dynamizing structures with the disadvantage of creating an image of the social that is in some ways "euphemistic." For Archer, the dependence of structures on their instantiations makes them seem tepid and flexible, obscuring the fact that many social relations are reinforced coercively.[1] This does not mean that we should follow the orthodox Marxist and critical-realist line of thought and split the field of practices into a more fluid realm of the cultural and a more fundamental basis of "real" social structures. Instead, I suggest dividing the whole practical domain heuristically into three "states of aggregate," in which structures are grouped depending on their "hardness," or on how easy they are to circumvent. This allows us to continue to understand the entire social realm through praxis theory—that is, through a culturalist and Marxist lens—as well as keeping it within the fundamental premises of performative structuration theory. At the same time, we should be better able to capture the disparity of the social realm, providing a further basis to explain its dynamic character. By differentiating between the reach of different structures, we should finally also be able to identify the contexts that give us the unfaltering stare of the woman knitting, and at the same time to explain why this stare remains unintelligible to the Marquis.

PETRIFIED STRUCTURES

I would like to suggest a terminological framework that divides up the continuum of social structures, all of which are generated from recursive praxis. This double insight is important here: all social structures are performative aggregates of social praxis, but they differ crucially with regard to their stability in relation to actors and other structures. Thus, if we agree with Giddens or with the theory of performativity on the level of social ontology, then we can still admit that this does not exhaust the possibilities of an analysis of social structures, and that we have still barely broached the really interesting question of which structures can be changed, and how. Although we cannot anticipate the answer to this before the diagnostic work has been done, it seems sensible to approach it with a nuanced vocabulary.

The metaphor guiding my classification of different types of structure is borrowed from Ludwig Wittgenstein's *On Certainty*. There, Wittgenstein categorizes the differing firmness of our convictions by comparing them with the layers of a riverbed: water, sand, stone. The passage in question is as follows:

> 96. It might be imagined that some propositions, of the form of empirical propositions, were hardened and functioned as channels for such empirical propositions as were not hardened but fluid; and that this relation altered with time, in that fluid propositions hardened, and hard ones became fluid.
>
> 97. The mythology may change back into a state of flux, the river-bed of thoughts may shift. But I distinguish between the movement of the waters on the river-bed and the shift of the bed itself; though there is not a sharp division of the one from the other. . . .
>
> 99. And the bank of that river consists partly of hard rock, subject to no alteration or only to an imperceptible one, partly of sand, which now in one place now in another gets washed away, or deposited.[2]

Wittgenstein introduces this illustration in order to better explain why in the case of some statements—such as his colleague George E. Moore's claim "I know these are my hands"—both a skeptical response and the original statement of knowledge are inappropriate. For Wittgenstein, there is a fundamental level of conviction here that cannot be suspended without causing all praxis to break down. If we can no longer be sure of knowing this, then we no longer know what "knowing" means. However, Wittgenstein does not imagine this "rock bottom of my convictions" as an independent foundation, but says, "one might almost say that these foundation-walls are carried by the whole house."[3] And, as is more intuitive in the case of the riverbed than in that of a foundation, this rock bottom can also be subject to processes of change. It is this definition of relations that I would like to borrow for my map of social structures.

The "stone" layer would therefore stand for indisputable praxis, for the structures that themselves create the tracks on which other actions take place. Depending on the form of life, different things are regarded as being entirely without alternative. However, what is important to note is that it is always only from the perspective in which the alternatives are imaginable that we can gain enough distance to identify the apparently unquestionable bedrock—otherwise, it remains as invisible as the proverbial water is to the fish. That still does not mean that it would be, in a mechanical way, impossible to act against these petrified structures—the action would simply not be an action in its particular context, but a fit of madness, an unintelligible action. It would fall, in the vocabulary of the previous chapter, entirely outside the shared schemas. Following the line of argument presented in the first part of this book, on the links between practices, we can imagine the "riverbed" as those structures in which practices must be anchored in order to count as praxis at all. In the scene described by Dickens, social status forms such a basic aspect of all practices that it would hardly be possible to imagine a practice that would completely disregard it. Instead, it is reiterated as part of almost all further practices; forms of family, employment, and political praxis are anchored in it. If Mme. Defarge had stepped forward and held the Marquis to account in the same way as another aristocrat might have done whose hunting dog had come to grief under the wheels of the carriage, she would have been regarded as utterly mad. And even the potential act of resistance that Dickens does describe—her unfaltering stare at Evrémonde's face—is obscured by the petrified social structure: "It was not for his dignity to notice," as Dickens expresses it. "His contemptuous eyes passed over her, and over all the other rats; and he leaned back in his seat again, and gave the word 'Go on!'"[4] In this social situation, at least, the act of resistance has no structures in which it could be anchored; it falls outside all schemas. The Marquis is able to leave the scene as if his authority had been reinstated, literally with the Wittgensteinian formula of rule-following on his lips: "Go on!" Dickens consistently carries this interpretation to its conclusion when he moves on to the quasi-natural course of events. In terms of social ontology, structures can be analyzed as being generated by individual acts of praxis, but many of them—here the separation of nobility and third estates—demonstrate the phenomenology of reified invariables: things running their course. "The water of the Fountain ran, the day ran into evening, so much life in the city ran into death according to rule, time and tide waited for no man, the rats were sleeping close together in their dark holes again, the Fancy Ball was lighted up at supper, all things ran their course."[5]

In the structures that form the "basis of things" in this way, anchored praxis therefore has a specific status of indisputability. And not only does "the spade" bend against this rock, as Wittgenstein describes it, but in one way or another all further practices have to be moored to that rock, if they are to be recognized. Nevertheless, few structures are so petrified that there is no possible subcontext in which they could be suspended—more on that later. Still, in two senses, their status is unquestionable: their recognizability and their validity are so self-evident that they never need to be articulated.

SOLIDIFIED STRUCTURES

In this, they differ from the broad realm of social praxis that is sanctioned, perhaps contested but generally familiar, which we can regard as tough, sedimented structures—Wittgenstein's "sand." If we return to our street corner in Saint-Antoine, we meet with a great many such practices, some of which are enforced in a draconian manner. The norm of obsequiousness toward the Marquis is crystal clear to the poor Parisians. The Marquis Evrémonde has the right to threaten the person who threw the coin with death, while his own negligent killing of the child remains an unpunished accident. The ability of the inhabitants of Saint-Antoine to act is reduced to almost nothing, but in this tense climate, a tiny desperate gesture has such weight as an act of resistance that it forces the Marquis to assure himself of his own authority in quite a drastic way, without entirely being able to avoid the fact that it has just proved open to dispute. Even if it is embedded in rigid social structures, sedimented social praxis is prominent in comparison with more spontaneous, more local forms of praxis, to the extent that it can appeal to general recognizability. It determines a standard, it can rely on being expected and recognized, and this already gives it sanctioning power. Its schemas may not be an unquestionable basis, but they are reliable, in that they can be assumed to be generally shared. In contrast with the anchor structures, which have become part of the "flesh and blood" of all the actors, and whose internal rules are used to assess much of social praxis, when it comes to articulated structures, only their schemas are quasi-universal—they are recognized by competent actors, even if there is always scope for competing interpretations.

This category is extremely broad. Just as "sand" can range from hard clumps to liquid mud, in any particular case we must analyze the alignments in which articulated practices are linked with one another, from which they then take their structuring potential. This kind of analysis is in fact carried out by the actors themselves—partly through conscious reflection, and partly in their interpretations of situations, which tend to be rather reflexive or intuitive. In contrast with Bourdieu's understanding of habitus, it seems appropriate here that this process should be imagined as continuous and open—experiences can often become pivotal points at which a structure appears in a new way and is then confirmed in connection with a different practice. Solidified structures can therefore rearticulate themselves, and practices can aggregate themselves in a new way, precisely because they exist in a mutually dependent performative relationship with individual actions. But if the tracks along which articulated structures are perpetuated ultimately depend on the existing links between practices, then there certainly could be many structures that are visible to all actors, but that have such inexhaustible resources at their disposal and are supported by such stable alignments that they essentially become just as hard and unchangeable as those structures that are entirely taken for granted. However, they would then probably come to anchor various further practices, for which they would simply seem to be a given, meaning that they would sink toward the bottom.

THE FLEETING INTERSTICES

But where should new experiences and alternative practices come from, if the course of things is determined by the riverbed of anchor-structures, and actions always seek to approach the articulated structures? Doesn't Mme. Defarge's unswerving gaze disprove this conception of social structure? If it were only a deviation from a structure that does not allow any deviations, where could it have come from? If all actions are mediated by structures, and every performance reiterates something, which patterns nurture Mme. Defarge's stare? If we wish to remain true to the social theory that I introduced as performative structuration, her potential for resistance and above all her potential to become a revolutionary leader later on must also be founded on shared recursive praxis.

At this point, I would like to bring in the most transient aggregate state that structures can have, namely, the "fluid" local practices that generate and perpetuate patterns of recognition, rules, and resources that can, in some cases, deviate significantly from the hegemonic patterns, even if they are often derived from them in subtle ways. In order to come together at all and begin something new, actors must make use of shared patterns and routines. Unlike the patterns of articulated structures, these are certainly not intelligible to everyone (yet), but are precariously dependent on the subjects who maintain them. The idea of particular "nests" of praxis, in which praxis that is unintelligible from a hegemonic perspective is nevertheless upheld, has already been sketched out theoretically in various ways. After all, it emerges almost by itself, if we follow the poststructuralist deconstruction of closed systems and the prioritization of "difference" in a particular way. For this difference need not then be located only in central antagonisms, as the school of hegemony theory sees it, but can alternatively also be located in internal heterogeneities or even in scattered particles of incommensurability—in the interstices. Foucault's concept of heterotopias is, as we saw in the introduction to part 1, still tied quite closely to the overarching structures of society of which it is a distorting mirror. In Butler's work, we find the more intensely discontinuous figure of the unintelligible; however, in order not to be paradoxical within Butler's own theoretical framework, this figure requires its own heterodox context of recognition: that which is described here as an interstitial space. A related category would be that of subalternity. The term, borrowed from Antonio Gramsci, was used in the Subaltern Studies Group around Ranajit Guha to investigate the politics of resistance in rural India and South East Asia with a decided focus on the perspective of the colonized.[6] Gayatri C. Spivak analyzed the term in depth, pointing out the extent to which particular practices of resistance, especially those of rural women, can be ignored even in emancipatory Marxist histories, precisely because they did not make use of the patterns that resistance was supposed to take on in order to be imaginable from this perspective.[7]

Such contexts are indispensable in the framework of praxis theory which I require here in order to explain at all how the "interstitial" ability to act emerges. The term "subalternity" is defined as oppression that becomes intensified as it cannot be represented. Despite the examples I have given, which are undoubtedly tendentious, I would like to keep the notion of the interstitial formally open. Practices with a limited reach, which are only intelligible in very specific contexts of recognition, may just as much form the core of an elite culture or "merely" represent eccentric activities. However, it makes a great difference whether the corresponding practices just happen to be interstitial, or whether they are more markedly discontinuous with the general structures, as the concept of unintelligibility implies, and have therefore not only remained hidden, but been kept invisible. The interstitial practices in question could only be continued through learning by seeing, through direct expansion of the contexts of recognition, if they could in some way be located in the schemas of existing anchor practices—otherwise they are unintelligible.

Now, of course, one could ask why we should assume at all that such interstices exist—don't they just shift the question one step further? In order to avoid this objection, we must keep in mind the direction of the deductive process that has fundamentally been set out here, which assumes that heterogeneity, and not unity, represents the "typical case," as it were. In order to be possible, practices do not depend on general recognizability, but only on contextual recognizability. All the more so because even what is regarded as "general" often contains a tacit contextualization, while conversely, every interstitial context could in principle be declared general, and could then become a point of reference from which, perhaps, a more fine-grained analysis could in turn bring heterogeneities to light. Thus, on the one hand, setting the course of "disparity all the way down" is a basic premise of social theory that is not justified any further. On the other hand, it can at least be explained retrospectively by adopting the corresponding praxeological perspective. Given that practices take the form of repetitions through varying contexts—as painstakingly as I have sounded them out so far for signs of standardization and the structure-formation—the converse phenomenon kicks in almost automatically, namely, the splitting off of peculiarities that are dependent on situations. Specific, locally stabilized deviations can then develop further in a direction that ultimately makes them incommensurable with some of the practices from which they stemmed. In view of the fact that situations where there are general, overarching contexts of recognition seem to depend on far more prerequisites than such local contexts, it seems plausible to suppose a certain level of disparity.

Conversely, though, this line of argument in support of disparity makes it obvious that quite a generous heuristic arbitrariness is at work in the distinction between the general and the interstitial reach of structures—it would be easy to claim that the transition between them lapses into vagueness. Still, for my further investigations, it is crucial that a difference exists between structures that one can see at work almost everywhere and those that are reserved for very special contexts, as is surely acceptable from an intuitive point of view. The ideal vision of interstitial transformation, in which practices that were initially interstitial gradually grow into general and articulated structures, rests on precisely such a continuum in the reach of structures. I hope, though, that my discussion of metaleptic change in the next chapters will prove the tripartite differentiation to be useful.

INTERSTITIAL STRUCTURATION

Taking up our original aim after these considerations, we can again return to Dickens's novel, which provides an impressive example of an interstitial context. When we accompany Mme. Defarge to her knitting companions, we are met with an illustration of local, temporary, or "fleeting" praxis:

> In the evening, at which season of all others Saint Antoine turned himself inside out, and sat on door-steps and window-ledges, and came to the corners of vile streets and courts, for a breath of air, Madame Defarge with her work in her hand was accustomed to pass from place to place and from group to group. . . . All the women knitted. They knitted worthless things; but, the mechanical work was a mechanical substitute for eating and drinking; the hands moved for the jaws and the digestive apparatus: if the bony fingers had been still, the stomachs would have been more famine-pinched. But, as the fingers went, the eyes went, and the thoughts. And as Madame Defarge moved on from group to group, all three went quicker and fiercer among every little knot of women that she had spoken with, and left behind. Her husband smoked at his door, looking after her with admiration. "A great woman," said he, "a strong woman, a grand woman, a frightfully grand woman!"[8]

What we see taking place is the entirely everyday activity of knitting. It connects the women in what Jean-Paul Sartre would call a "series," which he would present as an unconscious, quasi-automatic replication of praxis, in contrast with his emphatic understanding of "real" praxis elevating itself beyond its own conditions of action.[9] The women all do the same work, and this seems on many levels to satisfy basic needs, or at least to suppress them. Knitting numbs hunger; it holds the passive women together in some way. But something else is also happening. It seems that Mme. Defarge has a certain key function. The women she speaks to gain in determination; her husband begins to sing her praises.

Already during the French Revolution, and then more strongly in later antirevolutionary and misogynist writings, the figure of the knitter—*la tricoteuse*—stands for radicalized Jacobin women who leave their domestic space but paradoxically bring its trappings with them into the public sphere. They are regarded as bloodthirsty and aggressive, but are also often presented as opportunistic *cla-queuses* who sit at the foot of the guillotine and count the falling heads. Dickens builds on this topos. In *A Tale of Two Cities*, the knitters do not only take part in the storming of the Bastille and follow the court cases in the time of *terreur*. They are the first to create the list of counterrevolutionary enemies—in a cryptographic knitting pattern, over years, their handiwork produces something like wanted posters for all of those who would deserve the guillotine. Circling back to our opening quotation: Mme. Defarge's stare at the Marquis's face came from this praxis and owes its ambiguity to it. She has to look carefully in order to make an accurate portrait of her adversary. But she also acted from a shared praxis in which recognition was distributed according to quite different patterns, and in which it is very much allowed for a woman to meet a man on equal terms; and it goes much further: this praxis anticipates that an ordinary citizen will become the judge of an aristocrat.

If we wish to analyze social change plausibly in a praxis-theoretical register, we must be able to refer to such interstitial, makeshift patterns. They foster social practices that are not already bound together performatively into more general norms or structures, but that, in the case of the knitters, are unquestionably in the process of becoming so:

> Darkness closed around, and then came the ringing of church bells and the dis-
> tant beating of the military drums in the Palace Court-Yard, as the women sat
> knitting, knitting. Darkness encompassed them. Another darkness was closing
> in as surely, when the church bells, then ringing pleasantly in many an airy stee-
> ple over France, should be melted into thundering cannon. . . . [10] So much was
> closing in about the women who sat knitting, knitting, that they their very selves
> were closing in around a structure yet unbuilt, where they were to sit knitting,
> knitting, counting dropping heads.[11]

What we gain here is a picture of the basis for the revolutionary ability to act: structures that have already been established interstitially. At this point, this basis only has the status of a necessary condition for change. When the ancien régime collapses, the knitters can come forward and, instead of composing coded wanted posters, direct the revolutionary beheadings. In the changed practical alignments, the patterns of their interstitial praxis can then articulate themselves through performative aggregation into structures. In his description, Dickens envisions exactly the metaleptic form that is taken on by the formation of structure, as I have argued in this section: "So much was closing in about the women who sat knitting, knitting, that they their very selves were closing in around a structure yet unbuilt, where they were to sit knitting, knitting, counting dropping heads." The women will be able to count falling heads while they knit, because they are already doing so. It is only because they are already anticipating the patterns of the approaching revolutionary jurisdiction as they knit that that jurisdiction will ever be able to articulate itself. Gathered around a structure that is still absent, the knitters form that very structure, assisted by circumstances that can in turn be referred to with the words "so much was closing in about the women." It is those unchosen, given, and inherited circumstances that surround the women. Still, they have already begun, imperceptibly, to make history. Who? Both. The women and their circumstances, which exist already, transmitted from the past. For in their aggregated praxis, they are tied to structures that are never quite accessible, but can still be changed. The course that things run can be the course from a scarf to a wanted poster or from a church bell to a cannon—since "things" are the resources of practices, which can accumulate performatively into structures.

PART 3

Marta's Invisible Affinity Group and Interstitial Upheavals

This book is supposed to be about revolution, but so far we have talked more about stability. At any rate, the first half of the book produced a basic vocabulary of social theory that captures, above all, the persistence of the existing state of affairs. Practices have been defined as ways of interacting with material that can only be perpetuated when carried out according to three different types of rule: practice-generating rules of competence, practice-defining rules of recognition, and practice-evaluating rules of knowledge-ability. Structures have proven to be "aggregated praxis," emerging when social actors assemble practices and actively continue them. With their different degrees of hardness (fleeting, solidified, petrified), structures give the social order its contours. In each instance and overall, this means that repetition and reinforcement shape events. Interstitial forms of political action, isolated attempts at exodus—it really seems that these do not automatically expand to create broader change.

However, it is only as we embark on the second half of the book, having found a way to explain in terms of social theory how existing circumstances are reproduced, that we can begin the search for a plausible interstitial theory of revolution. Before the final part leads us back into the midst of the French Revolution, the reference material for this section will leap forwards in time, into the much more recent past.

"You don't have to be gay" is the slogan plastered on the placards of the counterdemonstrators, alongside the notorious "God hates gays." Marta stumbles between them, confused and interested in equal measure, until she reaches the edge of the ACT UP demo itself, and hesitates between the placards that have been left on the ground.

Since 1987, US queer activist group ACT UP has been campaigning against the homophobic response of the pharma industry and the US government to the AIDS crisis. In 1990, it organized a demonstration against the national Centers for Disease Control (CDC) and Georgia's sodomy laws. The protest lasted two days. First, in the so-called "Sodomy action," the traffic was blocked. The next day, demonstrators marched against the CDC because, among other things, its statistical survey of AIDS deaths excluded many illnesses affecting only HIV-positive women, meaning that the extent and risks of the epidemic were distorted.[1] During this campaign, the performance artists Matt Ebert and Bryan Landry made a twelve-minute video work titled *Marta: Portrait of a Teen Activist*.[2] Marta, named after the acronym of the public transport system in Atlanta and played by Bryan Landry in drag as a schoolgirl, is conceived as a homage to the ACT UP demonstrators. However, according to Douglas Crimp, the portrait actually works against the glorification of its subject and reflects, in its mode of portrayal, an ironic form of self-deprecation that is specifically queer: "The video wonderfully captures how—far from heroic—terribly awkward, how terribly queer it can feel to engage in activism."[3]

When asked about her sexuality in the film, Marta replies uncertainly: "My sexuality . . . uh—what?" For the protest march, she then starts by overloading herself with three placards. Later, she tries awkwardly to copy her fellow demonstrators to get the right pose for the "die-in"—publicly pretending to be dead—but fails to realize that she ought to stop talking. What does Marta want? What are her demands? Marta herself imagines that she is the outreach officer of the movement, even when it becomes clear that she has distributed her shopping cart full of flyers to a hotel that is already full of ACT UP activists. Her campaign to encourage outrage over the *Peter Pan* musical with Cathy Rigby—"Peter Pan is a white slaver; he exploits fairies. . . . For decades Peter Pan has been played by women, why can't Peter Pan be a woman?"—meets with puzzlement even from her otherwise supportive fellow protesters, although she does attract great admiration for managing to get a "Silence = Death" sticker into Doris Day's garden.[4] In the finale of the short film, we return to the key scene in which Marta jumps up and down on a traffic island, chanting, "We will never be silent again." Finally, someone manages to interrupt her from off camera. "What?" Marta yells. Only then, to her great bewilderment, does she notice the blank side of her placard. She had been holding it the wrong way round all along.

A demand that is only legible to the person making it—and maybe also to those standing behind her—is a striking picture of the unintelligibility of practices, as we have described it here. I argued that it is possible to follow patterns that are generally unrecognizable, but that this can only succeed in the interstices of society, which are significantly more isolated than words such as "marginality" or "minority" might suggest. But why must we rely on such precarious connections in order to understand the dynamic of radical change?

There would be no point in trying to place Ebert's installation in the context of a discussion of revolutionary action if we were to dismiss Marta's performance as an ironic series of missteps. But drag, whether as a parody of gender or—in this case—as a parody of militant activism, need not be seen as a caricature in this sense. It can also be understood as a pastiche, as a celebration of a model.[5] This perspective partly overlaps with the notion of a "camp aesthetic." In her article "Camp Materialism," Juliane Rebentisch characterizes such a position as follows: "Just as it is inadequate to read the relation to the useless, decayed thing as ironic, so would it be equally insufficient to characterize the camp relation to the fallible diva in terms of parody and mockery. The camp relation to its objects of choice is, to the contrary, one of siding with failure and decay."[6]

Matt Ebert speaks of his own creation with similar empathy: "The powerless hero who changes the world. Only doesn't quite know it yet . . . what? This is my favorite film about ACT UP (and the activist spirit) because there is a little Marta in every ACT UPer. Marta, herself an enigma, was a great leveler of factions."[7] But how can something that is itself a puzzle cause a shift in the lines of division? And in the context of transformation theory, what does it mean if we side with failure?

Taking the side of failure means first of all opting for antiheroism. This is a move that often comes to the fore from the perspective of queer and diaspora politics—borne by the experience of groups who could never hope to win a militant revolutionary civil war. Taking the side of failure means acknowledging one's weakness, yet refusing to halt the struggle. And it means changing the face of that struggle. In line with an exodus model of revolution, reworking everyday practices becomes more crucial than fighting directly against the opponent—not because we have forgotten that there is an opponent, but because we refuse to give up in spite of the opponent's superior strength. Thinkers as different as Michael Walzer and Uri Gordon are recent proponents of "exodus" from within the

Jewish diaspora tradition. Already before the First World War, the German Jewish anarchist Gustav Landauer formulated a far-reaching account of interstitial revolution. His approach stands out for its anti-heroism, too. When an acquaintance asked him about the perspective of one of his major texts, *Call to Socialism*, he answered: "That is quite right: in *Call to Socialism*, the heroic is combined with the unheroic. But if I had to choose—which I don't—which is more important to me, I would say: the unheroic, the very quiet, plain, noiseless beginning of a fair economy. . . . The heroic approach to life grows from a lie."[8]

However, this plea for the unheroic need not lead us to romanticize failure. Simply wanting to fail again and fail better is a position that political movements working urgently against injustices and disasters can hardly afford. Thus, Marta is simultaneously the embodiment of antiheroic "awkwardness" and of the unerring "activist spirit." In a scene in which she sits down on a curbstone in exhaustion, she talks about the motivation for her work: "Well, I think I've been told . . . I think I've been told more than once that my contribution is vital, so as long as there are people out there who need me, I'll be there for them . . . What?" Precisely this absence of a purposefully announced agenda reveals what it can mean to take the side of failure "noiselessly": occupying the space of failure with something that changes its quality. Where "failure" was, there is now "taking a side," solidarity, or enduring praxis. Persisting in spite of a lack of recognition would then not simply mean remaining invisible but also not giving up on the invisible or letting it remain empty. This precarious abundance carries the promise of changed structures, where joining forces openly and taking an undisguised position would be possible. It is Marta's most puzzling statements that show this most vividly. Her Peter Pan campaign is essentially no more incomprehensible than the official demands of the ACT UP activists were in the United States of the eighties. For broad swathes of the public, it was unimaginable that people should ask for legal and medicinal measures that would, in the face of an epidemic, facilitate a self-determined, enlightened, and safe life in promiscuity and beyond the boundaries of gender. Leo Bersani encapsulated this power imbalance very fittingly when he wrote in 1987 that the movement had nothing on its side but a moral argument that did not even count as a moral argument.[9] Given the pressure to let the hostile opinions of the majority encroach on one's own self image, Marta does well to distribute her flyers to her own people. This act of care is also the beginning of a "fair economy." In fact, a large part of the work of ACT UP did consist of counteracting the recriminations being voiced within parts of the gay movement, which presented AIDS, if not as a punishment, then as an inevitable result of an "irresponsible" way of life.[10]

This work in the interstices marks the starting point from which we will establish a picture of change within the conceptual framework developed here so far, by means of a performative theory of structuration. In the following, I will start by summarizing how the social theory developed in the first half of the book already demonstrates that interstitial praxis is a necessary condition for transformation. From this, a weak picture of interstitial change emerges. I will then go on to discuss the topic of the second half of the book, and ask which theoretical motifs would have to be added in order to lay the foundations of a strong theory of interstitial change—that is, one in which the work in the interstices would actually be sufficient for overarching structural change.

For in spite of all the emphasis on stability, a dual understanding of transformation has already emerged. On the level of practices, it is the overlaps that allow innovation; on the level of structures, it is the interlocking of processes of erosion and aggregation. Since practices are open to interpretation and the way in which they are carried out can often be placed under many schemas, it is possible to transfer both material resources and practical knowledge from one praxis into another. Where two practices overlap to the extent that they can, in some way, be followed simultaneously, they ultimately merge and form a new pattern. The fact that these connections on the level of practices take place locally is already enough to make this *interstitial* change: because they happen locally, they are never immediately intelligible in a more general context. In addition, change is not derived here from particular central mechanisms, but ascends from specific concrete contexts.

For this to go beyond innovation among practices and alter societal structures, the new praxis has to find space to perpetuate its rules and resources for long enough that it comes to articulate itself as a structure. Clearly, this is only possible if it can join with existing anchor practices without being limited by opposing chains of practices. It is often the erosion of established structures that creates the opportunity for a practice to fill a gap. Where the material disappears that was involved in the carrying out of a praxis, that praxis either has to find a different, equivalent path by overlaying itself on other practices, or must come to a halt. Processes of erosion can also set in from the side of the rules, because, for instance, altered anchorings mean that the internal rules of a praxis have become questionable, or because schemas have become unclear through increasing numbers of deviations. Structures will only be dissolved if such breakdowns do not remain isolated, and if the gaps that appear cannot be closed immediately. Shifts in alignments and anchorings, as well as the increased ambivalence of practices that have become unmoored, then create conditions allowing practices that were once interstitial to replicate themselves continually. Thus, through performative aggregation, new structures gradually become sedimented.

By paying attention to the interstices, we have discovered a crucial factor of social change. There can be no new practice that does not arise from the overlapping of existing patterns; there can be no new structures that were not rehearsed somewhere in the interstices.

However, this means that the "theory" of interstitial change shrinks, reduced to proving a necessary condition. Already such a deflated version would certainly have implications at the level of analysis, as well as consequences for the way in which revolutionary praxis sees itself. Historians would be obliged to seek the hidden preliminary stages of new structural articulation; activists would be well advised to keep postrevolutionary practices at hand "underground" until the day when they break through. But the actual question would have to be addressed elsewhere: how the gaps in the structures emerge that give way to the interstitial, and which mechanisms carry them over to form the new core of social structures.

In the dialectical understanding of history, this work is carried out by contradictions that manifest themselves in crises. With the addition of the interstitial dimension, the dialectical perspective would first of all gain depth of focus. It could then perceive not only the escalation of central contradictions but also the multiple subterranean disparities of a social realm no longer understood as a self-contained totality.

This expanded field of vision also shifts our perspective on the dynamic of transformation. In dialectical conceptions, innovation emerges through a process in which opposing structures enter a state of crisis, the resolution of which brings forth progress. This picture can be called negativist, in the sense that the contradiction or the collision takes precedence. First of all, something is not working—and only then does a solution emerge. This means that critique itself can also remain negativist: it is enough to point out clearly that something is not working and is undermining its own aims. If we trust that the crisis yields the elements of its solution, then articulating the crisis in this way would be revolutionary enough. On the one hand, the interstitial approach shares dialectical criticism's insistence on the existing situation. Where else should the solution come from? On the other hand, the interstitial approach also allows us to admit that the contradiction does not already include "everything" that is needed. In order to overcome a crisis, to replace the tendency toward erosion with some kind of new shape, something still needs to be brought into the situation in question. We cannot rely on the idea that the society we desire has been ripening gradually in the middle of the old one. For the interstitial position, crises remain an important factor, but they are an aspect, not a cause, of change.

Crises, after all, might just as well lead to paralysis. In order for a contradiction to have an effect, alternative practices must be available, having been rehearsed tenaciously in interstitial practice. Moreover, a contradiction is often only visible at all from perspectives which are eccentric enough that they will not risk the ground under their feet if they admit to a central dysfunctionality. Critique gains its force from a sense for other patterns that might be more workable, against which the existing conditions measure up badly. In short, every productive negative is dependent on an invisible positive, in which it is rooted.

But not only utopian, postrevolutionary patterns of action are dependent on previous training—so are the practices of power struggle itself. Marta demonstrates this particularly well. In order to storm a building, she must first take off her shoes. To participate in the die-in, she must first learn to be silent. And before the demo, she must first find a placard. This shows that practices depend on a plethora of preconditions, which are all too often simply taken for granted in concepts of political action or revolutionary struggle.

Nevertheless, the role of the interstices remains supplementary here. In order for real change to happen, they would have to succeed in articulating themselves on the dominant level. Interstitial patterns do not transfer themselves automatically, just as Marta's protest sign does not directly speak of the paradox of having to say the unsayable out loud. Within this weak theory of interstitial change, at the current stage in our argument, we can only show that practical training and anticipation are a necessary condition for successful transformation.

Meanwhile, a strong or complete theory of interstitial social change would have to show how micropolitics, anticipatory everyday actions, prefigurative practices themselves take on the crucial role. As far as crises are necessary, interstitial practices would themselves have to conjure them up, so that change is not only prepared, but actually achieved "on a small scale." The key claim, according to such a view, would be that interstitial praxis is not only necessary but sufficient to bring about structural upheaval. In such a strong model of interstitial revolution, instead of understanding the relationship between small-scale change and the big revolution, we need to recognize that everyday change actually is the revolution.

It is here that we can turn back to Gustav Landauer. The most prominent communist-anarchist agitator in the German Empire is perhaps the most persistent proponent so far of such an interstitial theory of revolution. His scattered works—he was an essayist, a novelist, a philosopher, a professional speaker, and a commentator on current affairs—combine to form a tireless critique of the "scientific" Marxism of his time. He finds the eschatological undertone of the dogmatic philosophy of history particularly suspect, and polemicizes against the textbook vision of the transition to socialism: "Superstition

(whatever it calls itself) believes in a miracle; materialism and mechanism pre-
sume that this miracle will take place: that great things come without any
great effort and full-grown socialism emerges not from socialism's early childhood but from capitalism's monstrous miscarriage, but this miracle will not
come, and soon people will lose their belief in it."[11]

The idea that we should not wait for the dialectically maturing revolution but
begin with the "childhood" of socialism is the leitmotiv of Landauer's work.[12] A
different economy and new forms of sociality should be practiced in day-to-day
life if we want them to gain acceptance: "We do not start with the end, but with
the beginning. Nothing has happened yet for socialism, nothing has yet been done
for it: so what is it that you're fighting for and letting yourselves be killed for?"[13]
Francis Beal's text, quoted in the introduction ("Dying for the revolution is a one
shot deal"), resonates here, as well as the idea that we must reverse the usual order
of end and means. Landauer uses a plethora of formulations for this anti-
instrumental and counterchronological reversal. "We say: don't put the cart
before the horse! We are not waiting for the revolution so that socialism can begin;
instead we are starting to make socialism a reality so that the big change will
come."[14]

Thus, in contrast with the Leninist concept of the avant-garde, here the revolutionaries are not supposed to set out a party line according to their analysis of
society, and then organize the masses accordingly. They should simply put what
they are striving for into practice and see it as part of a prolonged process of change.
Indeed, Landauer believes that those who "go on ahead" in this way have a cata-
lyzing effect that works its way back through the whole of society: "What we call
socialism is a joyful life in a fair economy. People today do not know, they do not
experience it with the true knowledge of being there and touching it, with the
knowledge that brings with it envy and desire and imitation, they do not know
what that is: a joyful, beautiful life. We have to show them. . . . We have go on
ahead, we have to get moving and through our movement we have to get the
masses to move."[15]

Landauer's emphasis on setting an example through socialist cooperation rests
on Kropotkin's variant of the "propaganda of action." In contrast with the later
terrorist interpretation of this idea, in which spectacular murders of those in
power were supposed to awaken awareness of the anarchist cause, here the point
is to encourage people to imitate the positive content of revolutionary hope. This
could be reformulated to say that praxis should speak for itself. Instead of adver-
tising it through rhetorical struggles and agitation, we should instead establish it
as an example and make it possible for others to follow. The isolated interstices
would become the enzyme for large-scale change—they would be all it took to

bring it about. With Landauer, we are dealing with a much more far-reaching conception of "interstitial labor," since it functions as the pivotal point for a strong theory of interstitial change and is regarded as sufficient for a revolution.

Landauer's theory of why change could succeed in this way is much more complex than can be conveyed by the quotations from pamphlets presented here. It unites a proto-deconstructivist understanding of social institutions with a mutualist social psychology and a collective notion of the subject. Nevertheless, this conception never quite avoids the problem that is instantly thrown up by its catchier variant: Why should that work? Wouldn't it make much more sense to assume that these isolated attempts will fail?

If we try to transfer the strong theory of interstitial change into the terminology developed here so far, this doubt is initially reinforced further. In the distinctions between transient, sedimented, and petrified structures—that is, in the difference between those patterns that are only visible occasionally and those that are generally recognized or that even come to form the very foundations of recognition—isn't a power imbalance already inscribed that clearly decides the outcome? How is it possible at all that a praxis that is in any case unrecognizable should bring the general rules of action to a halt and take their place? Even if Landauer, with his general skepticism toward revolutionary success, repeatedly makes clear that he is not a naïve optimist, on this basis we could reach the conclusion that there will seldom—or, indeed, never—be a case in which the small form wins against the great whole, unless the prevailing structures are already so eroded that it is no longer a case of "winning." Then, in turn, interstitial praxis would again only be a necessary condition for change and not a sufficient one.

In the previous part, we explained how continued praxis accumulates into structures by referring back to the concept of performativity. Since every praxis orientates itself according to those that preceded it, repetitions of a practice mean that its previous instantiations form an increasingly strong rule. Thus, we could say that this preceding praxis is retrospectively tied together more firmly than it was before. The "performative" element here is the effect of taking up a particular practice in such a way that it becomes structural. Now, though, we have to ask precisely the opposite question, and consider how a relatively isolated interstitial praxis can assert itself against aggregated praxis. We are essentially on the lookout for the reverse effect: does performativity also work "backward"?

The most detailed points of reference for how overarching structures can be disaggregated by intervening praxis are offered by the work of Judith Butler. In one of the few places in her work where she relates her thoughts about performative critique directly to the campaigns of ACT UP, she provides a powerful description of the confusion that can be created by acts like Marta's:

For instance, when Act Up (the lesbian and gay activist group) first started performing Die-ins on the streets of New York, it was extremely dramatic. There had been street theatre, a tradition of demonstrations, and the tradition from the civil disobedience side of the civil rights movement of going limp and making policemen take you away: playing dead. Those precedents or conventions were taken up in the Die-in, where people "die" all at once. They went down on the street, all at once, and white lines were drawn around the bodies, as if they were police lines, marking the place of the dead. It was a shocking symbolisation. It was legible insofar as it was drawing on conventions that had been produced within previous protest cultures, but it was a renovation. It was a new adumbration of a certain kind of civil disobedience. And it was extremely graphic. It made people stop and have to read what was happening. There was confusion. People didn't know at first, why these people were playing dead. Were they actually dying, were they actually people with AIDS? Maybe they were, maybe they weren't. Maybe they were HIV positive, maybe they weren't. There were no ready answers to those questions. The act posed a set of questions without giving you the tools to read off the answers.[16]

In her recapitulation of how die-ins work, Butler traces the ways in which this praxis was learned and transferred, becoming a moving mixture of legibility and unrecognizability. In its very disorientation, the audience is moved by the scene and forced to ask certain questions. It experiences a crisis provoked by the unintelligible praxis itself. In a movement that is sometimes reduced retrospectively to a minority interest group, we find an example of the structure with which all revolutionary action wrestles: the wish to articulate a praxis that is impossible in the framework of existing structures. The seemingly muddled demonstrator Marta perfectly acts out this dilemma. She makes the performatively self-fulfilling announcement that she will never be silent again, but her demand is not directly legible from her appearance or from her placard: it remains turned away from the viewer. Still, it opens up a blank space, inviting questions that were not present before.

Butler's leitmotiv of performative critique is generally discussed using the vocabulary of subversion, and is applied more often to disruptions to and interventions in prevailing orders than to actual victories over them. The next chapters will begin to show, by a relatively detailed process of interpretation, that this typical categorization of Butler's work is an unnecessary deradicalization. Performative critique—contrary to the approaches of both Butler's followers and her critics—can be used as a model for effective change. However, the prevailing impression of playful variability instead of fundamental transformation is also owing to Butler's tendency not to thematize the conditions for the success of subversive acts, or rather to delegate these to contingent processes of repetition. Her interpretation of the street theater scene also demonstrates this. Although she attributes sufficiently far-reaching power to the unintelligible praxis to dismantle established structures, she overlooks—or perhaps passes over—the constructive elements in the situation she describes. Herself a veteran of a queer guerrilla theater group, she nevertheless reconstructs a hegemonic viewer-perspective. More than that, although she names a crucial variation in the way in which the activists adopt the die-in as a praxis, she does not make full use of the context she invokes. The chalk lines that mark the scene of a crime suggests that the dead are victims not of fate but of murder. Dying, mostly experienced as a private trauma within particular communities, is not simply repeated publicly. In the process of making it public, it becomes a political offense, for which the perpetrators can be held accountable.

This reinterpretation was key to the militant impulse of ACT UP. It is also exemplified by the common slogan "The government has blood on its hands," which is captured in the Marta video when the camera pans over the walls of houses marked with red handprints.[17] The metaphor of bloody hands does not lack a certain irony, given that the government, or rather the "arm of the law," was in fact panicking in its efforts to avoid getting any potentially infectious blood on its hands. When the police decided, as a result of this, to appear at the National AIDS Demo at the White House in Washington wearing yellow household gloves, they earned themselves the following chant: "Your gloves don't match your shoes! You'll see it on the news!"[18] That puts us once again deep in the context of a humor that was internal to the movement, and that in itself should not be underestimated as a constructive resource. Still, the wit is only comprehensible if our analysis also enters the interstices and includes a reconstruction of interstitial praxis. In other words, we have to take account of Marta's affinity group.

In the following chapters, the traces of structural and collective conditions that only make isolated, "ghostly" appearances in Butler's work will be revised and expanded. As a result, reversed performativity can be shown to "unravel" structures. Revolutionary contexts are not only characterized by a *lapsus* in the process of repetition. If there were nothing more than an "iterability lottery" at play in social change, social theory would remain entirely uninformative for an analysis of society. But we can say at least a bit more about the structure of revolutionary situations: they are metaleptic. They enable a breakthrough praxis to bring down structures and replace them. Thus, interstitial practice assumes a genuinely revolutionary force, rather than just a supplementary one.

The strong and the weak variants of interstitial change can then be related to each other as follows: in every "here and now," as Landauer evokes it, there is an opportunity for interstitial labor. But only in contexts structured in a specific way, only "now and then," is there also a possibility of drawing a sufficient dynamic of transformation from that interstitial praxis.

In the next three chapters, I will demonstrate in more detail how Butler's conception can be reshaped so as to bring out the conditions for performative critique. This means that the deconstructivist position moves along a particular axis—that of the satisfying of conditions—toward historical materialism. Revolutionary potential is contained not in the interplay of signifiers, but in specific interfaces of material practices and structures. However, my explanation of how this change happens still means turning the dialectical laws of movement inside out, even if, this time, it is not the Bastille that is stormed from the inside, but the proverbial closet.

7
Disaggregation

Performative Critique and the Laughter of Mimesis

A t the end of the previous part of this book, we distinguished between different degrees of aggregation among structures, in order to defend against the criticism that structuration theory underplays the rigidity of many social structures.[1] This differentiation also allows us to respond to certain reservations about Judith Butler's work, as expressed by Andreas Reckwitz, for instance. Reckwitz draws attention to what he sees as a long-standing tendency of praxis theorists "to extract at least some of their general premises about the way in which praxis functions from very specific, particular, locally and temporally situated social practices, and then simply to generalize their statements about these cases."[2] According to his diagnosis, Butler renders in absolute terms a specific high-modern culture belonging to the aesthetic avant-garde, involving practices that reward transgression and celebrate the proliferation of identities. The historical source of this specific type of practice is revealed, for Reckwitz, in her reference to a text by Joan Rivière from 1929.[3] The theory of performativity is simply aesthetic modernism writ large. Now, it should have become clear already that for me, if we are going to talk about anchoring contextualization, the discussion about forms of protest in "Marta's affinity group" is a more productive source for Butler's work than the artistic milieu of the Kleinian Rivière in interwar England. But to respond on the level of social theory: performativity does not celebrate excessive variability. It is tied to petrified anchor structures and regulated by alignments, and is more about the perpetuation of complex arrangements of power than about self-stylization.[4]

However, this seems to make the theoretical framework all the more vulnerable to another prominent accusation. Under the fitting title "Da Capo senza

Fine," Slavoj Žižek has voiced the suspicion that Butler's theory of the subversive possibilities of our gender order only distracts attention from the fact that "actually," in terms of the mode of production and of the symbolically unquestionable gender difference, nothing is changing at all.[5]

Ultimately, this accusation rests on similar grounds to Reckwitz's claim that transgression is being generalized: it relies on leveling the difference between "normal" performative variation and moments of performative critique. But "performativity backward" is more than just a bit more variation in the same forward-performativity. In response to the "perpetuum mobile" accusations, I would therefore like to show that Butler's method allows us to theorize not only a certain nonconformity toward structural parameters but also the drastic transformation of those parameters under specific conditions. Performative critique then becomes a model for interstitial structural upheaval, and not just for occasional subversion.

In actual fact, Butler does not answer the question of the conditions under which interstitial deviation can, "now and then," dissolve the petrified anchor structure. Rather than blaming her approach for its specificity to certain milieus, it seems necessary instead to analyze the context of her examples more thoroughly—precisely in order to gain a better view of the aspects that must come together so that interstitial structural change can take place.

PERFORMATIVITY BACKWARD

We have already made use of the notion of performativity to trace the aggregation of practices into structures, which in turn work as a template for continued mimetic praxis. Since structures depend on their instantiations, which take them up and continue them recursively, these instantiations can also work backward on the structures and create variation. However, it seems to me that performative critique must still be differentiated from these movements of destabilization. For it could be said that in performative critique, performativity works in reverse. Performative critique refers to the specific effect of those practices that do not just subtly change the structures on which they are based, but actually *dis*aggregate them and become the starting point for a new configuration that is substantially different. The relationship to the original structure therefore works in the opposite direction from the performative structuration described in the previous part: the relevant praxis has an "explosive" effect on the conditions from which it arose.

Butler offers a prime example of this process: the change to gender norms that can be brought about, according to her analysis, by a drag performance. This mechanism will first be reconstructed here through a close reading of the final chapter of *Gender Trouble*, and then expanded in stages. However, we will continue to take account of Reckwitz's intervention. To avoid the serious danger of falsely generalizing certain characteristics of practices "in themselves," the investigation in the next two chapters will be focused throughout on the contextual conditions that enable and limit the potential of interstitial praxis to work in such a transformative way—we will keep coming back to Marta.

Butler once confessed in an interview that her gender theory was inspired by the experience of how her parents and grandparents—the latter owned a cinema in Butler's hometown of Cleveland—imitated successive film-stars of their generation.[6] The drag analysis in *Gender Trouble*, which aims to sound out the subversive potential of certain gender performances, also starts from the big screen—the production of heterosexual glamour by a lesbian diva. Thus, Butler prefaces her observations in the final chapter of *Gender Trouble* with the following remark by the film critic Parker Tyler: "Garbo 'got in drag' whenever she took some heavy glamour part, whenever she melted in or out of a man's arms. . . . It is all impersonation, whether the sex underneath is true or not."[7] The chapter itself is divided by the two-part title: "Bodily Inscriptions, Performative Subversions." The actual drag analysis can be found in the second section. There, Butler tries to establish drag in two ways as an analogy. Firstly, from a critical-phenomenological perspective, the outstanding point that she makes in her book is that any gender identity is developed in a way that corresponds to a drag performance. The expansion of the drag diagnosis to the femininity of a woman such as Greta Garbo, which already appears in the epigraph, is converted into a general *tu quoque*. Gender identity is always, according to Butler, the effect of various gestures and elements of "impersonation."

Secondly, as heralded in the conclusion of *Gender Trouble* and clearly shown in Butler's subsequent work, drag also becomes emblematic for critique itself. For Butler, following Foucault, critique does not mean the justified questioning of statements or social conditions.[8] Its task shifts, as a result of Butler's strong emphasis on the internalization of power, to become an act of desubjectivation, a process of distancing oneself from learned practices through other forms of action. It is therefore both less and more than critique in the more familiar sense. Less, because it does not back up its claim to validity, and more, because if it succeeds it does not only identify shortcomings but already changes something.[9] The transition from the notion of critique to the understanding of transformation that I envisage here is therefore already prepared by Butler, and we should be able to conceptualize it analogously to the parody of gender.

In fact, Butler handles her account in such a way that the performative nature of gender only becomes clear due to the change in perspective brought about in the face of drag. Overcoming a particular concept of gender, the model of expressive identity, should be the performative effect of a specific act of portrayal. And in fact, the traditional idea is not only destabilized but replaced by a counteroffer, although Butler, as will be discussed later, mostly reflects on and generalizes the destabilization. If drag is therefore supposed to demonstrate and carry out the critique of gender, the question now arises of how it does so, that is, how it enacts the performative mechanism.

Up to this point in *Gender Trouble*, Butler has spent most of her time analyzing the unquestionable nature of the structurally anchored two-gender system. Crucially, she focuses on how the regulation of sexuality interlocks with the regulation of the boundaries between the genders, summarizing her ideas in the model of the "heterosexual matrix." This rests on the notion that gendered bodies, social gender roles, sexual desire, and sexual praxis are each placed in a relation to one another so that they are forced into two-pole coherence. Here Butler argues that it is not simply the case that external regulation only allows two patterns of combination—those of a heterosexual two-gender system—and that the others are punished as exceptions. Instead, the elements themselves are already imagined in such a way that exceptions are unthinkable (a male gender role *is* the social behavior of a male body and the object of female desire and so on).[10] Exceptions are thus not "odd mixtures" but an absolute absurdity, and any social practice that they maintained would remain "unintelligible."[11] Precisely by ignoring the alternatives in this way, "coherent" gender identities then take on the appearance of simply following an "internal law" and of automatically (or naturally) finding their particular expression. With this analysis, then, not much has yet been said about how gender identity "actually" emerges, as opposed to which structural paths it follows.

THE SPECIFICS OF PERFORMATIVE CRITIQUE: DRAG

For Butler, the drag queen becomes a kind of chief witness for the gender order. She articulates the secret recipe for the creation of all forms of gender identity, because she rehearses a takeover that is not supposed to be possible within this order. When a woman in an everyday situation produces "femininity" through various sexually coded gestures and ways of behaving, this does not become noticeable in itself. It is only when a drag queen uses the same methods, going against our usual habits of seeing, that these methods become visible at all, rather than being taken for granted as the background of any interaction with a "woman." Butler interprets this change in perspective as follows: "In the place of the law of heterosexual coherence we see sex and gender denaturalized by means of a performance which avows their distinctness and dramatizes the cultural mechanism of their fabricated unity."[12]

Thus, Butler refuses to offer an alternative, conventional resolution to the scene being presented. In a traditional logic of original and imitation, the "takeover" could also be dismissed as a bad copy. She insists instead that the realization that there is something "copyable" about gendered behavior already resists that traditional logic of originality. Even if we declare a case to be a failed transfer, we will have to accept that there is such a thing as successful transfer, and if gender could at all be decided based on the success of a transfer, then it is already no longer the expression of an "inner" truth or a natural disposition. What is then revealed by the drag performance according to Butler is both the imitative structure of gender in itself and the contingency of every existing variant of it: "*In imitating gender, drag implicitly reveals the imitative structure of gender itself—as well as its contingency.*"[13] It is not a supposed "true gender" that has priority, but the performance being presented. It is performance that, as repeated praxis, brings forth the very image of a gender identity. What seemed to be the inaccessible inner cause of gender-specific behavior therefore becomes the precariously fabricated effect of that continually repeated behavior. For Butler, this leads to a new, "performative" understanding of gender: "Gender identity might be reconceived as a personal/cultural history of received meanings subject to a set of imitative practices which refer laterally to other imitations and which, jointly, construct the illusion of a primary and interior gendered self or parody the mechanism of that construction."[14]

Thus, when a set of practices combine—in aggregation—either to lend emphasis to the significance of gender or instead to parody the mechanisms by which gender is constructed, the question nevertheless emerges of which practices are capable of ensuring the latter critical effect. When, we could ask, is a drag queen a drag queen, in the sense that she provokes a change of perspective regarding gender identity? And where it has just become clear that parody itself is a mode of critique, on the very next page Butler draws distinctions in the phenomenology of drag and interprets it not as parody—as the mockery of an original—but as pastiche, an imitative homage to an ideal. The actual parodistic effect of this homage is then toward originality itself, or the exclusive claim on originality by the model.[15] But how does performance come to be turned around in this way? Already at the outset, drag was related to Greta Garbo's acting skill, so the criterion cannot simply be that femininity is being performed by a male body. Where, then, does the critical-transformative power of parody come from?

One requirement for the critical effect with which Butler is concerned is certainly that of persistently nonidentical repetition. Both Garbo's appearance and that of the emblematic drag queen may be read as femininity—if they were simply unintelligible, they could not have any effect—but at the same time, they introduce a distinction within femininity itself. Butler argues that any iteration fails to approach its model. As described in the previous part of this book, each imitative repetition assembles its reference practices anew into a structure. It therefore does not fulfill every last one of some series of existing instructions. However, it seems rather overdramatic and one-sided to stylize this inexact replication as constant "failure." For Butler, this description emerges because, at the structural level, she applies a notion of norms that creates a one-sided emphasis on the symbolic or schematic side of praxis. On the level of concrete norm instantiations she has the materiality and embodiedness of "performances" clearly in view, but precisely because of this she tends to see structural specifications being implemented in an "impure" fashion: the implementation is hindered by the inertia of material. Failure arises, for Butler, from the necessary tension between norm and performance. At best, it can draw attention to the fact that the power of the norm is reliant on its instantiations: norms are constructed and stabilized recursively through the perpetual attempts of the instantiations to approach them. Different approaches could therefore produce different norms.

However, if the resources themselves, as Giddens and Sewell suggest, become part of the structure, if the arrangements of objects do not represent the material that has been brought to the norm, but are instead the medium of the structure, then any discrepancy between particular practices and the structure that carries them cannot be described formally as an inevitable gap between ideal and reality—the structure itself is nowhere near abstract enough to serve as a sharply outlined measure—but can always only be defined substantially through those aspects of the praxis that prove, in the light of the structure, to be different from expectations, whether it is the femininity that is created with the resources of a "male body," or whether it is the clumsiness of a militant activist. We can only discover more about the genesis of these aspects if we abandon the perspective of "one-way" performativity in favor of a picture of crisscrossing structures and practices.

Reformulating Butler's motif in these terms, we could say that the success of critical performance relies on the effect of an occurrence that ought to be unintelligible. The artist and queer theorist Renate Lorenz has suggested a comparable reading of drag that classes it as "radical drag" when its praxis can be seen as one "which thematizes dichotomies,. . . while at the same time refusing to endorse them, and which sketches bodies that cannot be addressed within such categories."[16] Here, too, the crucial work seems to be achieved by the occurrence of something that should be impossible. If we remind ourselves that what stands in its way, as an unspoken "ground of hard facts," ensures that it remains unquestionable through the lack of any alternative, we can clearly see why a counterexample can become so effective. The drag scene could then be read as one in which the structure just described as the "heterosexual matrix" is confronted with an uncategorizable counterexample—with the male body producing femininity. According to my differentiation between different states of aggregation in the social realm, we could then say in summary that the interstitial praxis of drag challenges the gender-specific anchor structure in such a way that it has to articulate itself. The specific contour of expectations only becomes clear in the moment in which these expectations are disappointed. However, in Butler's example of critical success, the movement of repetition that undermines authority is already accompanied by the deviation that creates an alternative: with the praxis of drag, there is already a counteroffer in the room, suggesting how gender identity could be interpreted differently—performatively, à la drag, even in contexts where it so far appeared to be unproblematic or "natural."

PERFORMATIVE CRITIQUE IN GENERAL:
INTRACTABLE PRAXIS

Butler herself has continued to work with the mechanism in which structures are shattered by instantiations that are, from their perspective, "impossible." She transfers it to a whole series of other moments of subversive performativity, which sometimes also receive further theoretical metareflection.[17] While her arguments in *Excitable Speech* locate performative critique primarily at the semantic level of resignification,[18] in the essay "What Is Critique?" and also in some of her more recent texts, variants can be found that take a praxis-theoretical approach to the transfer of the initial example.[19]

Here it sometimes emerges that the deviance of critical praxis need not be drawn from the error-prone iteration of one and the same structure. Certainly, the "detour through structure" is inevitable in Butler's theoretical framework (as well as in the praxeological approach), meaning that a pattern of action cannot simply be created without precedent. But if practices do not appear "from thin air," this does not mean that the only alternative is difference arising from repetition itself (especially since this actually seems to resemble the thin-air version quite strongly): instead, there is the discrepancy that emerges when practices are simultaneously involved in several structures. Butler never quite gives up her model of a relatively monolithic normative order, but in her interpretation of Antigone, she coins the phrase "promiscuous obedience," which tends to predicate performative critique on the idea that various structures are played off against one another.[20]

Thus, in her general discussion of critical acts, she summarizes her perspective by explaining that the formation of subjects draws on various practices, whereas the crucial question is whether it is situated within a structurally secure frame or in, as she calls it, an "ontologically uncertain position." From such a position, it would in turn be possible to work retroactively on the opposing frame, in a performative, disaggregating manner:

> One might say, it [the subject] is compelled to form itself within practices that are more or less in place. But if that selfforming is done in disobedience to the principles by which one is formed, then virtue becomes the practice by which the self forms itself in desubjugation, which is to say that it risks its deformation as a subject, occupying that ontologically insecure position which poses the question anew: who will be a subject here, and what will count as a life, a moment of ethical questioning which requires that we break the habits of judgment in favor of a riskier practice that seeks to yield artistry from constraint.[21]

The risk of "deformation" arises because existing principles use their very exceptions to demonstrate that exceptions cannot be: "fairies" are not real people; queer subculture is not a form of life. But if such positions are still taken up—we might think, for instance, of the striking determination with which Marta holds on to her position as a self-appointed outreach officer—then something shifts in the structure that was so far taken for granted. It is clearly not without alternatives, it could be revised, and the question, as Butler says, is once again raised: "Who will be a subject here, and what will count as a life?" From a certain perspective, it could now be argued that the way in which Butler models critical acts in this essay bears a striking resemblance to liberal conceptions of civil disobedience. For her, it is not the law itself that is transgressed with reference to higher norms (often taken from the spirit of the constitution, in the US context), but a "solid," fortified structure or social pattern of action, which is abandoned in search of a much more transient praxis. In the passage quoted, Butler does evoke the daring and "virtue" of the subject involved, but for the effectiveness of the critical performative, it is still not crucial whether the "unintelligible practices" are intended as targeted acts of resistance or whether they emerge in the course of particular interstitial practices—"in passing," so to speak. Marta, at least, is notoriously evasive when it comes to the question of whether she is following a deliberate agenda or whether she has simply been caught up in something—"My sexuality?. . . Uh . . . what?"

Performative critique takes place, then, if a praxis becomes visible that ought to be unintelligible, and disaggregates the anchor structure that stands in its way. But precisely this reformulation is a good demonstration of how demanding it is, not to say paradoxical. First of all, the antecedent—"if a praxis becomes visible that ought to be unintelligible"—is certainly not unproblematic. Why should something ever manage to assert itself if it is defined by being unable to do so? Why don't those very variants of failure or praxis-overlap—the most interesting ones—always remain "in the dark"? I will turn to this point specifically in the next chapter—that is, to the question of how the antecedent of the performative formula can possibly be fulfilled. But even if we were to accept here that such situations can ever arise, then the conditional would become even more extreme in the second half of the sentence:. . . *if* it "disaggregates the anchor structure that stands in its way." It doesn't have to do that. The repetition of a praxis in an unpredictable context can lead to resignification, but it can just as well fade away, as an outlier, or be overtaken more or less violently by the original context. Drag queens and trans people are much more likely to be subjected to violence and hostility in public spaces than they are to destabilize gender norms in a lasting way. Especially if this example is to be used to explain a general transformation mechanism, the conditions for the success of the performative critique would have to be made more precise than seems to be allowed by the reference to unstable iterability.

SUBVERSIVE LAUGHTER

If we return to Butler's analysis with this skeptical approach, it becomes noticeable how strongly she herself focuses on the contingency of subversive success. Again and again, she interrupts her characterization of drag as parody and gender as performative with relativizations and critical interjections. "Practices of parody can serve to reengage and reconsolidate the very distinction between a privileged and naturalized gender configuration and one that appears as derived, phantasmatic, and mimetic—a failed copy, as it were."[22]

Having shown that effective criticism relies on parodic repetitions, she claims that parody alone certainly need not always be critical. "Parody by itself is not subversive, and there must be a way to understand what makes certain kinds of parodic repetitions effectively disruptive, truly troubling, and which repetitions become domesticated and recirculated as instruments of cultural hegemony."[23] Here, our question about the criteria for the success of subversiveness finds only an amplifying echo: "What performance where will compel a reconsideration of the place and stability of the masculine and the feminine? And what kind of gender performance will enact and reveal the performativity of gender itself in a way that destabilizes the naturalized categories of identity and desire?"[24]

What performance where?—which praxis in which context? The text refuses to answer this; it seems to put it off beyond the end of the book, of which the last sentence once again takes the form of a question: "What other local strategies for engaging the 'unnatural' might lead to the denaturalization of gender as such?"[25] If Butler refuses to identify criteria for the success of critical praxis, that is partly because it is not possible to make general prognoses about the effect of particular acts, precisely because they depend on context. Looking at the acts themselves, we cannot judge whether they are capable of creating a subversive shift: "A typology of actions would clearly not suffice, for parodic displacement, indeed parodic laughter, depends on a context and reception in which subversive confusions can be fostered."[26]

However, once we have stated this dependence on context, we could still reformulate the question and ask about the contextual conditions. Which would be the contexts and modes of reception in which subversive confusion could be maintained? Butler's text does not follow this path further, at least not explicitly—the passages cited are followed by a shift back to phenomenological assertions about gendered bodies "after" the critique has succeeded. In the quotation, however, there is a suggestion of a contextual criterion that also returns at other points: "parodic laughter." Oscillating between skeptical relativizations and the emphatic, sometimes euphoric postulation of a new description of gender, *Gender Trouble* repeatedly has recourse to this liberating laughter, as a particular reaction to the successful performative act. Rather than offering stable criteria for the effectiveness of critique, Butler therefore presents us with a further praxis that becomes the shibboleth of performative success: different acts of laughter. "In this sense, laughter emerges in the realization that all along the original was derived."[27] But who is laughing here? Is this not a first important clue that might allow us to differentiate between contexts? In another formulation, Butler summarizes the effective critical process in such a way that a

certain empty space emerges in the syntax itself: "There is a subversive laughter in the pastiche-effect of parodic practices in which the original, the authen-
tic, and the real are themselves constituted as effects."[28] This could mean that
there is a subversive laughter in the pastiche effect of parodic practices—
practices in which originality, authenticity, reality are created. Or is it in the
laughter that these (the originality and so on) are shown to be purely effects?
Does every performative process of construction contain the germ of the laughter
that would dissolve it? Whose laughter? If we are concerned with the decenter-
ing not only of authors but also of their speech acts, couldn't the laughter then
be given back to the audience, thus introducing collectivity to Butler's theoretical edifice?

8

Constitution

Subcollective Association

In the previous chapter, we uncovered the core of performative critique—that is, the disaggregating effect of an unintelligible praxis on the anchor structure that stands in its way. Although I find this a very promising motif, it seems to present more puzzles than it solves. For instance, the conditions are not clear that would actually cause this performative effect to come into play, and it is still possible that the starting point itself is irredeemably paradoxical. How can a praxis occur in the first place if it is not supposed to be intelligible?[1] We have already stated that it would be too much of a shortcut to derive it from the (by implication necessary) failure of one-track iterability. However, when we combed Butler's own text for contexts that foster subversion, the traces of a different genesis did become visible: there, "in the pastiche effect of parodic practices," laughter made itself heard.[2] From this point of reference, which hovers in Butler's text without being tied to a location, I would like to develop a concept of interstitial constitutive processes. I will accomplish this in two stages. The first connects directly with Butler's drag theme, but situates this in empirical sociology. The second angle is provided by the vocabulary of Hannah Arendt's theory of power, which I will link with the arguments on structure and agency developed in the second part of this book, regarding the way in which structures are formed. For performative critique requires a collective dimension, just as constitutive power needs references to the conditions for seemingly spontaneous action.

SUBCOLLECTIVES

The last chapter ended with Butler's remarkable statement that the performative constructive process engenders laughter that might dissolve it. I interpreted this as a trace of collectivity, omitted in Butler's drag analysis but nevertheless presupposed in her argument. The notion that we should pay more attention to the relational aspects of drag as a praxis than is allowed by Butler's concept of performativity is also found in Renate Lorenz's work, and guides her impressive analysis of a Ron Vawter performance: "In my view however, drag creates something else, something that goes beyond, which cannot be sufficiently grasped through the model of performative repetition. Drag produces . . . a practice that is in no way individual, but always relational."[3] Indeed, large parts of queer-theoretical research into gender can be seen as illuminating the various relational, collective contexts from which specific practices such as drag emerge. Antke Engel synthesizes very fittingly the extent to which these approaches resist Butler's overaccentuation of the hegemonic level:

> In *Bodies That Matter* (1995), Butler emphasizes that the compulsory, violent nature of the heteronormative gender order affects "everyone." . . . Without wishing to deny this violence, we might point out that even people who experience these upheavals still inhabit social spaces, produce representations, form subjectivities, and claim subject status. Calling binary gender into question and especially being transgender or intersex are not only epistemic concepts but also everyday social practices that counter experiences of devaluation, exclusion, or rejection with a range of social and subcultural projects and individual strategies. Corinna Gentschel coined the term "hard-won subjectivity" ["erstrittene Subjektivität"]. . . . This is defined by inclusion in or the creation of collective subcultural contexts and by the production of knowledge that goes against mainstream discourses.[4]

While Butler may emphasize that every order is incomplete and susceptible to errors, her focus on the prevailing structures does seem to forfeit the depth necessary to recognize that these "pores" are "inhabited," as Engel insists. Butler's analysis throws a detailed light on the performance of the drag queen, in terms of its possible effects. But like the beam of a stage spotlight, this description leaves the collective dimension in shadow. This dimension defines the praxis of drag as one that is shared by the audience and the performers.[5]

Engel follows Gentschel in speaking of "collective, subcultural contexts"; these will be condensed here into "subcollective" contexts.[6] This picks up on the interstitial spaces of the previous part, but in such a way that their collective structure is once again emphasized. While the connotations of "subcultural" are too specific—unquestionably relevant to the drag example, but already misleading and anachronistic in the case of Wollstonecraft's prisoners and Dickens's knitters—"subcollective" means that these may be collective contexts, but they are located beneath the articulated, overarching collectivity to which their protagonists simultaneously also belong.

Now, expertise in navigating between differently structured collectives is distributed asymmetrically, in the sense that on the subcollective level, even where particular general structures may be suspended at times, a knowledge of their schemas can nevertheless be assumed—the same is not true in reverse. Uta Schirmer, who has conducted a detailed empirical study of drag kinging, documents this aspect very impressively. The overriding result of her investigation is that the practices being analyzed created a counterpublic by communicating through specific subcultural codes, and remain reliant on that counterpublic.[7] Drag performances, according to her analysis, can always be understood as collective practices, the effect of which is entirely dependent on interaction with the audience within the scene. The key to this interpretation lies in the way in which Schirmer's interview partners assess the tendencies of different audiences to laugh. If the laughter comes in the "wrong" places, in response to risqué dances or parodies of gay people, it becomes clear that this is a "hetero audience," as one of her informants reports:

> They basically just look at the performance level, which they know from film, TV, and other things, and they clap *afterward*, but actually it's about something more, in a way. And for them to see that "something more" at all, we pretty much have to make an announcement beforehand, which shouldn't be with a sledgehammer, because that can easily make the whole thing descend into a kind of freak show, um, we kind of have to give them a bit of a hint: this is going to be something a bit different from what you might be expecting, okay.[8]

In contrast with this clapping and laughter *afterward*, which the drag performer laments, Butler talked of a subversive laughter *in* the pastiche effect of the performance itself as proof of a successful critical performance—in that laughter, it would be possible to recognize the knowledgeable laughter of the scene audience, which, according to Schirmer, not only is a reaction to the praxis of drag, but is constitutive for that praxis. Following the sociologist Amy Robinson, Schirmer speaks of the need for an "in-group clairvoyance," a "literacy" of the audience, which is fed by previous shared experiences.[9] I would refer here to the "knowing by seeing" of the corresponding schemas, through which recognition is granted, which in turn is required so that those who have also mastered the rules of drag *by doing* do not remain unintelligible in their actions.[10]

Now, the notion of praxis does already imply a certain collectivity, as I showed in the first part of this book. Practices always have recourse to social—that is, shared—structures. Practices that do not have any location in which they are repeatable and recognized cannot exist. However, this applies in an even more specific sense to "fleeting" practices that are only based on interstitial structures. Because, unlike the patterns of action that are generally articulated, they are hardly sedimented at all. They are neither the basis for various further articulated practices, nor upheld throughout by supportive alignments. Devoid of underpinning by generally recognized institutions, collective memory, or mainstream discourses, interstitial practices rely more heavily on the actors who carry them. If their subcollective context dissolves, all points of reference for further instantiations are lost. Despite what Butler's text suggests, even the praxis of "grinning" cannot hang in the air with no one to carry it.[11]

POWER THROUGH ASSOCIATION

When Hannah Arendt, in the long final chapter of her book *On Revolution*, laments the vanishing of revolutionary memory, it seems that even though she is talking about a very different praxis from gender parody, she is imagining a similar constellation—patterns of action maintained in subcollectives, unable to outlast the dissolution of the context that maintains them.[12] Arendt introduces the chapter with a quotation from René Char which she uses often—"Notre héritage n'est précédé d'aucun testament." Something of the lost praxis may remain tangible, but without its rules finding a lasting expression. The praxis with which Arendt is concerned here is that of forming revolutionary councils, or soviets. Although this always occurred episodically in modern revolutions, Arendt points out that they were regrettably never institutionalized successfully or turned into a fundamental political principle.

> *Soviets* and *Räte* ... were to make their appearance in every genuine revolution throughout the nineteenth and twentieth centuries. Each time they appeared, they sprang up as the spontaneous organs of the people, not only outside all

revolutionary parties but entirely unexpected by them and their leaders.... They were utterly neglected by statesmen, historians, political theorists, and, most importantly, by the revolutionary tradition itself.[13]

Arendt mourns the transience of the councils, which have in her view a very specific relationship with the way in which action itself is constituted: they embodied the spontaneity or the "ability to begin," and that is what placed them in a paradoxical relationship with stabilization and institutionalization. But her diagnosis also hits on something that is common to all interstitial practices, namely, that they are precariously dependent on being picked up and expanded, if they are not to disappear without a trace when the situation dissolves in which they were able to manifest themselves. In her description, Arendt stages the way in which fleeting moments are assembled and connected with one another, which would have to become a guide for further action, if a structure was to emerge from the praxis of founding councils. However, this description cannot replace the power that emerges only through actual collective association, and also remains dependent on it, according to Arendt: "*Power* corresponds to the human ability not just to act but to act in concert. Power is never the property of an individual; it belongs to a group and remains in existence only so long as the group keeps together."[14]

Thus, the potential for a new beginning emerges from the coordination of those who act, as they assemble and refer to one another. The notion that power emerges when people act together forms one of the central motifs in Arendt's work and underpins her concept of politics. Without question, this very specific understanding of power is primarily suited neither to analyzing personal power relations, nor to examining the structural power that solidifies in resources and institutions. However, it provides the basis for the theorem of "counterpower," or constitutive power,[15] which informs the approach of conflict theory to politics in general and civil disobedience in particular. Arendt herself also conceives of civil disobedience as a power-generating phenomenon. However, here—and also in her remarks about the hopes for a council republic—a crucial distinction emerges between the "radical democratic" view of constitutive power and her own. Although she states firmly that political action is an end in itself,[16] she does not regard the agonal element as playing such a fundamental role that power can only be defined in relation to conflict. Rather, she prioritizes the moment of "founding," the association between those who work together, and warns that "there is nothing more futile than rebellion and liberation unless they are followed by the constitution of the newly won freedom."[17]

Arendt would no doubt prefer that counterpower were formed against rigid institutions, rather than for domination to continue. But crucially, she does not allow the political to be subsumed in that. She would certainly see politics as being even more impressively realized if the fleeting praxis of founding the councils were to become the anchor point for the entire social self-government, rather than simply flaring up episodically in moments of protest. Compared with the concept of power in contemporary political theory, Arendt's concept therefore has a stronger transformational twist.

Before taking on the difficult task of switching back from the political to the social register in discussing the notion of action, I would still like to go into Arendt's actual analysis of the "small political form" of disobedience. She places this firmly on a continuum with revolutionary actions, and not just because of the characteristic of "beginning" that is related to revolutionary action, but due to the potential reach of political intentions: "The civil disobedient shares with the revolutionary the wish 'to change the world,' and the changes he wishes to accomplish can be drastic indeed."[18] Arendt advocates that protest action should be seen as the form of political association that Alexis de Tocqueville had already noticed in North America: "As soon as they have found one another out, they combine. From that moment, they are no longer isolated men but a power seen from afar, whose actions serve for an example and whose language is listened to."[19] From this perspective, the entire liberal discussion about civil disobedience seems to her to start from entirely false, individualist premises and to rest on a misleading paradigm: "The literature on the subject relies to large extent on two famous men in prison—Socrates, in Athens, and Thoreau, in Concord."[20] Arendt contrasts this with her own interpretation, arguing that protesters must always be understood as groups that create potential power through their association.[21]

I have already mentioned that Butler's conception of performative critique actually orients itself more closely toward what we would normally call disobedience or direct action than toward classic forms of critique. In fact, Arendt's reproach that we have failed to recognize the collectivity of the practice in question precisely matches the gap that has already been emerging in Butler's conception, held open by the floating laughter.[22] Although she starts from very different premises, Butler does share with the liberal understanding of civil disobedience the focus on the following two relationships: the relationship of the disobedient subject with the order as a whole, and with itself. Even if these relationships are accentuated and acted out quite differently—in the conflict with the ruling normative regime rather than as an appeal to the majority opinion, in the sense of work on oneself rather than as a relationship with one's own conscience—we could still say that performative critique, rather than a theory of individual famous men in prison, is a theory of the lonely drag queen.

PRAXIS BETWEEN THE WORLD OF THINGS AND THE WORLD OF ACTION

In her own modulations of the concept of performativity, Butler has herself shifted toward adopting the Arendtian element of concerted action and presented a performative reading of the assembly. Just as the drag queen symbolized the idea that all gender is drag, the assembly highlights that the individual is itself assembled, always more than one, more than just there, always already relational: "A new space is created, a new 'between' of bodies, as it were, that lays claim to existing space through the action of a new alliance, and those bodies are seized and animated by those existing spaces in the very acts by which they reclaim and resignify their meanings."[23] Yet for bodies to be legible in that way, even without demands printed neatly on placards, they need to replicate modes of belonging and congregating that are more specific than the plurality of assembly as such. The assembly then becomes more of a metaleptic structure, a passage through which specific prefigurative forms of collectivity can recur.

Much as Arendt demands that we foreground the relationship of protesters with one another, a Butlerian lens makes it questionable how—if at all—the motif of concerted action can be incorporated into the praxeological framework on which this social theory of change is based. For it seems initially that Arendt's implied image of action as a horizontal constitution of power and a spontaneous new beginning is incompatible with the praxeological premises that we have adopted so far. Butler herself points out Arendt's much-criticized tendency to relegate the private realm to the prepolitical,[24] and mentions her lack of appreciation for the material conditions of assembly. "The square and the street are not only the material support for actions, but they themselves are part of any account of bodily public action we might propose."[25] Yet again, materialism is not just about bricks. Can we integrate Arendt's emphasis on collective spontaneity with a more structurally conditioned understanding of agency? Action, I have argued, is always dependent on patterns of action that have already been established; as a repetition, it is precisely the opposite of Arendt's concept of the ability to begin, which she equates with human freedom. Praxeologically speaking, as I indicated in the first and second parts, power can best be understood as the structurally assured ability to act. It does not come "from thin air," but feeds on structures that are aggregated in recursive processes. For Arendt, meanwhile, power is due to concerted action—free-floating, in some ways. Suddenly, a potential for action is there which did not exist before.

However, Arendt does not argue that this process of constituting power lacks any conditions. It is only the presence of a "Mitwelt"—fellow human beings, in a shared web of connections created by previous actions—that makes it possible to act at all, and thus potentially to act together: "To be isolated is to be deprived of the capacity to act. Action and speech need the surrounding presence of others. . . . Fabrication is surrounded by and in constant contact with the world: action and speech are surrounded by and in constant contact with the web of the acts and words of other men."[26] Arendt does not explain the metaphor of the web of acts and words much further. It precedes all individual action and speech, and she sees its "threads" as the actions that were always already configured as stories, which the actors bring into the web. Arendt also says that "the actual 'products' of action" are "narratable stories";[27] here she does not regard action as being directed toward these stories, but instead sees the stories as an unintentional side effect of all action.[28] They therefore remain without an author—the actors carry them out, but do not invent them—and also remain untold; they are "narratable," not narrated stories. Arendt contrasts their solidity with the intangibility of the web of connections. The "Mitwelt" or the "web of connections" thus describes the necessary background of a kind of "addressable" or "articulable" collectivity, in which actions are not subsumed, but find a foothold in an existing fabric. If actions then refer to one another in a concerted manner, it could be said that a more concentrated "Mitwelt" emerges, which Arendt calls power, and, as its counterpart, a "space of appearance": "The space of appearance comes into being wherever men are together in the manner of speech and action. . . . Power is what keeps the public realm, the potential space of appearance between acting and speaking men, in existence. . . . While strength is the natural quality of an individual seen in isolation, power springs up between men when they act together and vanishes the moment they disperse."[29]

Ebert and Landry's video work provides a good example of the creation of such a space of appearance. Focusing on a teenage activist who is presented as an odd loner, it reveals the role of her collective network of supporters. Various talking heads from within the scene declare their solidarity with Marta, describing her actions with great praise—though sometimes with incomprehension. They form, in turn, Marta's point of reference, when she sits down on the sidewalk, seemingly exhausted, and announces in her only comment on the motivation of her work: "Well, I think I've been told . . . I think I've been told more than once that my contribution is vital, so as long as there are people out there who need me, I'll be there for them . . . What?" Like Butler's drag queen, she is taking action from a subcollective cosmos of recognition, though she is acting "in public" in a much more obvious way. Still, Arendt's vocabulary allows us to make a very smooth transition here. The much-criticized distinction that she draws between the public and the private awakens the misleading impression that "public" refers to a place that can be unambiguously located. However, alongside the negative distinction, by equating the public with spaces of appearance, Arendt designs her notion of the public in such a way that it is bound primarily not to particular media, forums, or institutions, but to the collectivity of those who act in concert. For this reason, in his detailed study of Arendt's notion of the public, Hannes Bajohr describes spaces of appearance as "in-between spaces that suddenly emerge."[30] In the context of my discussion of interstitial structures, this could be differentiated further, in the sense that it is not the in-between space but its "appearance" that emerges "suddenly." It is not only when she joins the demonstration that Marta begins to make connections with others. She already knew very well where she belonged. Even practices of politicization in the narrower sense are very much dependent on the relative continuity of particular collective connections in niches within society—that is, subcollectives.

The sociologist Michael Warner goes so far, in his studies of queer counterpublics, as to credit them with a world-making function, in spite of their precarious lack of institutions that might reproduce their form of life.[31] This dimension of "world-making," which is obviously not derived from Arendt's terminology, is further specified by the historian Deborah Gould in her richly informative study *Moving Politics*; in it, she identifies which basic patterns made the activism of ACT UP possible. She draws connections between a wide range of practices, including the structure of affinity groups (which were often also a network of care for the ill and dying), the regular Monday plenaries, ACT UP's sex-positive erotics,[32] the reinterpretation of shame-ridden losses as reason for militant anger, as well as ACT UP's specific humor.[33]

For Hannah Arendt, there is a clear terminological gulf between the "Mitwelt," which is created collectively, and the material "Ding-Welt," even if the world of things acts as a further fundamental condition for the precarious power potentials beyond the collective space of appearance. People live, according to Arendt, in a world of things that have been made, whose lasting presence introduces an element of permanence and reliability to the day-to-day process of living that is precisely not present in the transient actions and words of human beings.

It is this durability which gives the things of the world their relative independence from men who produced and use them, their "objectivity" which makes them withstand, "stand against" and endure, at least for a time, the voracious needs and wants of their living makers and users. From this viewpoint, the things of the world have the function of stabilizing human life, and their objectivity lies in the fact that—in contradiction to the Heraclitean saying that the same man can never enter the same stream—men, their ever-changing nature notwithstanding, can retrieve their sameness, that is, their identity, by being related to the same chair and the same table.[34]

However, given the arguments presented here, it would be possible to claim that all practices are actually "world-making." Through their generally unintentional side effects, they create structures on which action remains dependent. It is not only the things that outlast us which represent the inventory of a world in which action is possible, it is not only stories that precede our actions but also the patterns that are established in action itself, the configurations of resources and schemas.[35] Between things and the authorless narrative threads of the web of connections forming the "Mitwelt," we could therefore inscribe a philosophical vocabulary that takes account of the conditional nature of human action in a more far-reaching way.

STRUCTURES BETWEEN SPONTANEITY AND LASTING APPEARANCE

What I have imagined here as "Arendt's objection" to Butler can therefore also be turned around into a criticism of Arendt from the perspective of performativity theory, which takes Arendt's isolated phenomenon of spontaneous concerted action and embeds it in a continuum of dual structures. The Marta video demonstrates this process magnificently. On the edge of the demonstration, when Marta is able to sift through a pile of abandoned placards and then join the protest equipped with several of them, she literally takes over the resources that are provided by previous praxis, in order to be able to enter into the praxis herself. But the carrying out of a praxis is obviously not just a question of props. In one of the most detailed scenes, we can observe how she adopts the die-in as a form of action. She comes across a situation in which other activists have already sunk down in theatrical death poses on the asphalt. She awkwardly tries to lie down, but sits up repeatedly, in order to mimic the others and find out exactly how

playing dead is supposed to look. As an observing participant, she tries to identify the "rule" of the praxis—learning by seeing. She takes on particular gestures, lies emphatically rigid on her back—and continues to talk incessantly. But
this is not simply the necessary failure of all mimesis, but an intersection with
another practice that Marta has only just acquired. If she has learned one thing
from the placards and as a fledgling outreach officer, it is the slogan "We will
never be silent again." Precisely in this parodic exaggeration, the "recipe" emerges
for a form of action. To describe this form of action as a spontaneous expression of protest would not only be wrong, but would also be denying its origins
in recursively aggregated patterns of praxis.

This need not even kill off the spontaneity on which Arendt places such an
emphasis. For if actions rearticulate structures, as the drag performance does in
Gender Trouble, then, from the perspective of this innovative effect, they can retrospectively be described as a "new beginning." In the mode of the "narratable
story," the connections between Marta and her context provide an ideal example, if we are looking for a starting point from which to narrate how it could come
to something like the queer-theoretical reflection on the connection between
transformation and subversion that is achieved by Butler in *Gender Trouble*. If
we say that new experiences have come about here in the realm of political action,
this is still compatible with analyzing that newness on a praxeological level as a
blend of preexisting patterns of action dependent on many conditions.

Given Arendt's own metaphor of "concerted" action, it is actually even more
fitting if "beginning" is imagined not as the unconditional ability to start an
action from scratch, but instead as the ability of a musician to start playing on
cue. As acting human beings, we are always also joining in.

Thus, on the one hand, the ability to constitute political power through concerted action is dependent on structural conditions that themselves confer the
"power" to enact these forms of praxis. On the other hand, we can take Arendt's
crucial insights about the genesis of the power that concerns her—political power
in the narrower sense—and transfer them to the power that interests us here, that
is, to the consolidation of the power to act, which is dependent on structures.

Interstitial structures, which fill the "in-between spaces" of articulated structures and which Engel and various others have emphatically presented as "inhabited," are consolidated when actors take up one another's practices, when they
share and repeat practices in such a way that no resources remain unused and the
rules of practices are reinforced. When Marta inspects a die-in, finds her way into
it, and receives comments from her comrades, the rules that generate, define, and
evaluate practice in this form of action are simultaneously intensified and
reinforced.

The power-constitutive process offers good points of reference to show how interstitial structures are articulated, expanded, and reinforced in the places where they do not go against the fundamental anchor structures—where they were "only" interstitial, but not radically unintelligible. This recursive aggregation, which recapitulates the process of structuration discussed in the previous part, with a slightly differently arranged vocabulary, may perhaps be limited by opposing alignments, but it does not need to begin by breaking through the boundaries of what is thought impossible.

These are all motifs that were already developed in the chapter on structure formation—and that certainly owe much to Butler. They only become a corrective of Butler here in the sense that they are brought back into her scenario of performative criticism in a smaller form, so to speak, while Butler only examines her scenario in terms of the general structures and the isolated deviation that invades them. If we ask which interstitial structures constitute that deviation—or, in Arendt's terms, lend it a space of appearance—we open up a perspective on the shared practices among the people in Marta's affinity group, who are actually not so invisible to one another.

Translating this acting-together into the intensified interstitial recursivity of practices, we can then once again—going beyond both Butler and Arendt, in a sense—emphasize the defining role of mobilized resources. If we understand action as praxis and not only as "appearing to one another" or "performance," it becomes clear that the materiality that this requires is usually not limited to the bodies that participate. Arendt relegates the way in which we interact with objects, depending on whether these are goods to be consumed or to be used continuously, to the sphere of labor and fabrication, or views them as instruments of violence. But practices such as those of civil disobedience, which unambiguously belong to Arendt's sphere of action in the narrower, genuine sense, involve juggling with props and making use of infrastructures, which in turn have an effect on the contours of the particular space of appearance—as an interstitial space of shared, mutually intelligible practices. A die-in, for instance, requires public places; people can only block the traffic if it flows in the first place, and if the megaphone does not work, it will not be possible to attack the staging of *Peter Pan*. Even if the generalizable aspects of ACT UP activism can be summed up as strategies of performative critique in which the boundaries of unintelligibility are broken down, they were concerned not with recognition per se, but with access to medication, clinics, and research resources, and the abolition of laws that had legalized the firing of employees based even on a suspicion of HIV. It is important not to lose sight of such resources and alignments due to a fascination with a very specific aspect of transformation, a point that was also emphasized in theoretical self-reflection of the movement: "ACT UP lost its incisiveness when it ceased to realize that it had been the combination of mass support, solid documentation, and hard-hitting graphics, and not theatricality alone, that had disrupted scientific and moral logics."[36]

If the overarching question was that of the starting conditions for performative critique, then, alongside a broad field of further factors, one particular condition has emerged as, in a sense, "sufficient." The praxis that appears "new" or even "unintelligible" when measured against the articulated practices has been traced back to a subcollective context invested with the "power" to provide a space of appearance to specific, interstitial patterns of action through mutual uptake. The performance of the drag queen is made possible, as Schirmer's empirical investigations show, by the presence of her affinity group, which constitutes a specific power to act. By laughing at the right moments, the audience stabilizes the praxis.

However, this still tells us very little about the critical power of the performance itself, which is what makes Butler's portrayal so appealing. Here, it is not the performance of drag that changes the notion of gender; rather, it only has an effect at all among those who already have quite different habits of seeing and parameters, who are familiar with drag practices, and who therefore perceive and value their "constructed" aspects. This process of making links back to the subculture, which makes Schirmer's analysis so plausible, appears at first glance to rob Butler's analysis of the aspect that makes it so interesting—the intervention of a local practice into a hegemonic structure.

Thus, since we have now explained how subcollective references enable seemingly unintelligible practices to occur in the first place, we must look again at the conditions allowing them to reach the overarching collective level.

9

Contamination

Overlaying Structures

T o illustrate the process of performative critique, in which an unintelligible praxis disaggregates the anchor structures that exclude it and becomes the starting point for restructuring, Butler uses the example of drag. In her example, it is the heteronormative sexual order that is resignified through the drag performance. Analogously to this, Marta was introduced here, as the main character in the video installation about ACT UP, *Portrait of a Teen Activist*, in order to shift the image of militant political practices into a decidedly antiheroic register.

The central theoretical question of this section is whether and how Butler's theory of performative critique might be substantiated, expanded to include its conditions, and thus reformulated in a less paradoxical way. In the previous chapter, we saw that the first such requirement, in a sense the enabling condition, was the process by which power is constituted subcollectively. However, as long as this constitutive process is limited by the prevailing anchor structures, the actual transformative moment still does not take place. This chapter will therefore introduce an additional and decisive condition for success, in which structures are superimposed on one another, or articulated structures are "contaminated" by interstitial practices.

I will develop this point by unfolding the context of Butler's motif in two ways. First, I will bring to light some of the aspects and arguments of a debate about subversive parody that began already before Butler's contribution, among theorists close to ACT UP. Second, with the material collected there, I will extend the phenomenology of Butler's example hypothetically, to demonstrate the specific transformation that takes place in the course of restructuring disaggregation. This will bring together—though initially only on a microlevel—all the elements necessary to corroborate the metaleptic dynamic of performative critique: an articulated structure contaminated by interstitial praxis, which interlocks with a subcollective process of constitution, is refunctioned and brought into position against the anchor structure, thereby forcing it to articulate itself.

SUBVERSION OR PERVERSION?

It goes without saying that Butler was not the first to discuss the possible effectiveness of particular practices in the sense of a "subversive parody." Performative critique has a particularly clear affinity with Dadaist antiart, and with Situationist performances. As Raymond Geuss has shown in his interpretation of various Dadaist (anti)artworks, it is their blatant lack of meaning that is significant: "Failing to obey given rules, breaking the code, can be a way of bringing to our attention something, for instance, that our forms of 'intelligibility' are more arbitrary than we usually take them to be or that they are severely limited and deficient."[1]

The Brechtian alienation effect also works by taking the things that are normally veiled in order to stage a theater production—social power relations and the actual process of producing the performance—and placing them in the foreground.[2] However, since this book takes a praxis-theoretical approach, I will leave aside the aesthetic discussion of acting practice and view Butler's drag performance not in the sense of a theatrical happening being staged, but instead as one among many relational, collective practices, as described in the previous chapter. These practices could just as well take place in everyday life as on the stage and in the auditorium.

In fact, there has been a vigorous discussion of critical parody, with many parallels to Butler's formulations. In his essay "Is the Rectum a Grave?," published in 1987 at the height of the AIDS crisis and three years before *Gender Trouble*, the activist and literary theorist Leo Bersani offers a good insight into the ubiquitousness of the motif:

> It has frequently been suggested in recent years that such things as the gay-macho style, the butch-fem lesbian couple, and gay and lesbian sado-masochism, far from expressing unqualified and uncontrollable complicities with a brutal and misogynous ideal of masculinity, or with the heterosexual couple permanently locked into a power structure of male sexual and social mastery over female sexual and

social passivity, or, finally, with fascism, are in fact subversive parodies of the very formations and behaviors they appear to ape.[3]

Having introduced a spectrum of potentially parodic figures, Bersani himself initially concentrates on the accoutrements of hypermasculinity, as adopted in the gay leather scene. His arguments were indeed preceded by a broad discussion surrounding the parody motif that has become prominent through Butler. The contribution of the London film critic Richard Dyer is particularly striking. Already in 1980—similarly to Gayle Rubin, Monique Wittig, and later Butler[4]—Dyer had described gender roles as being derived from the order of (compulsory) heterosexuality. In a collection on contemporary communist cultural politics, he published an article in which he describes how the eroticization of masculine paraphernalia in openly homosexual contexts weakens the dominant definition of masculinity:

> Gender roles are crucially defined in terms of heterosexuality—"men" as a social category are people who screw "women." By taking the signs of masculinity and eroticizing them in a blatantly homosexual context, much mischief is done to the security with which "men" are defined in society, and by which their power is secured. If that bearded, muscular beer-drinker turns out to be a pansy, however are you going to know the "real" men any more? From this too stem the play, exaggeration and parody of much contemporary gay masculinization.[5]

The left-wing sociologist and gay activist Jeffrey Weeks even went so far as to use Situationist vocabulary to proclaim these acts of appropriation "semiotic guerrilla warfare" against the heteropatriarchal order.[6] Bersani himself, however, reacts against this belief in the effects of performative critique avant la lettre with the following laconic observation: "It is difficult to know how 'much mischief' can be done by a style that straight men see—if indeed they see it at all—from a car window as they drive down Folsom Street."[7] He concedes that in the eyes of a heterosexual observer, the norms of masculine representation could at some point fall into a state of crisis if that observer, as imagined earlier, were to drive along the gay leather promenade of San Francisco and see how tokens of the utmost masculinity combine with gay and feminine gestures. However, this crisis would remain temporary if the observer were then to reassert his superiority, or rather the symbolic framework for that superiority, by deciphering the outlandish appropriation of such masculinity as a necessarily unfulfilled yearning for precisely that position which the "real" heterosexual macho (the observer himself?) occupies: "The very real potential for subversive confusion in the joining of female sexuality and the signifiers of machismo is dissipated once the heterosexual recognizes in the gay-macho style a *yearning* toward machismo, a yearning that, very conveniently for the heterosexual, makes of the leather queen's forbidding armor and warlike manners a *per*version rather than a *sub*version of real maleness."[8]

Bersani is not accusing these practices of being complicit with the prevailing order because they have failed as subversion. His point is that they should also not be glorified outright and recast as targeted resistance, rather than erotic forms of expression.[9] With his intervention, Bersani shows that the context in which these practices are perceived defines, in two ways, "what" they are. The spatial setting is crucial—where do the deviant repetitions meet with which audience? Do such meetings even take place? In addition, the horizon of the spectators plays a role. Which structures constrain them? Do they see the alternatives to their own practice as alternatives, or as failed attempts at their own practice?

However, Bersani also turns to a situation that he is more willing to accept as a successful parody, namely, that of "campy talk" at a dinner party.

> The male gay parody of a certain femininity, which, as others have argued, may itself be an elaborate social construct, is both a way of giving vent to the hostility toward women that probably afflicts every male (and which male heterosexuals have of course expressed in infinitely nastier and more effective ways) and could also paradoxically be thought of as helping to deconstruct that image for women themselves. A certain type of homosexual camp speaks the truth of that femininity as mindless, asexual, and hysterically bitchy, thereby provoking, it would seem to me, *a violently antimimetic reaction* in any female spectator.[10]

Thus, while Butler tended to the ugly side of drag, which caricatures femininity, by dissolving it into pastiche in order to reach a liberating metaeffect (the critical insight into the performative constructedness of all femininity), Bersani focuses on the very ambivalence of misogynist gestures as a critique of the norms of femininity that are generated by patriarchy. When femininity is exaggerated as silly, asexual, and bitchy, it provokes in the female spectator a strongly antimimetic reaction. Generalizing this position would certainly give rise to counterexamples,[11] but Bersani's sharp perception of the context-dependency of examples once again allows us to trace the particular conditions in which the critical performative can succeed. It is significant that in this drag situation, too, there is an awareness of the constructed nature of femininity—"which, as others have argued, may itself be an elaborate social construct." Even if this is not quite presented as a result of imitative practices, it does seem that these practices call it to mind. The exchange occurs in a more specific setting than some abstract public place—a dinner party assumes a certain familiarity between the participants. Women and gay men are present, but the hypothetical guests also cannot know one another all that well—it is unlikely that a fully fledged fag hag would be overcome by a sudden antimimetic reaction;[12] lesbians close to the male gay scene, meanwhile, would probably already have found their own way to disidentify themselves with the femininity being parodied here.

Bersani therefore starts by reinforcing the doubts that also concern Butler, doubts about the effectiveness of subversive parody or performative critique. He draws attention to the sobering case of ineffective drag practices, but also discusses a variant that does have a certain effect, at least in a negative sense: the disidentification of a woman with the distorted image of femininity. Does this simply mean that we have chosen a different example, or have we learned something more general about the factors determining the success of performative critique?

BLENDING THE SCENARIOS AND SYNCHRONOUS GENEALOGY

It seems to me that the question of transformative potential can be illuminated if we draw together the points of view examined so far, connecting Butler's free-floating change of perspective with the subcollectives of the previous chapter and with Bersani's public settings.

From the discussion so far, we now have three prototypical ways in which spectators might react. First, there is "the macho in the car" (A), who regards the performance as nothing more than a failed attempt to occupy a position in the sexual order that he himself dominates. Then there is "the woman at the dinner party" (B), who finds that drag reveals a repellent femininity, from which she immediately seeks to distance herself. And finally, there is the "in-group clairvoyant" (C), who understands drag as drag and situates it in the framework of subcultural codes. We could now construct a situation in which these subjects did not remain among themselves in hermetic contexts, but were brought together— such a milieu could be found in the street scenes of the Marta video, or indeed in the performance situation that Butler evidently has in mind. Even if the spectators are no longer distributed between the car, the dinner party, and the queer bar, they are still differentiated by their structural positions. In many ways, the heteronormative anchor structure places A at the top of the hierarchy; B is in an ambivalent situation that may allow the articulation of her practices, but that brings crucial alignments against her; and finally, C is located in precarious, inter-stitial practices outside the basic structure.[13] The simultaneous perspectives emerging from this structuring can then be reconstructed as follows.

In a space that is not entirely dominated by A and by the alignments that keep the heteronormative anchor structure fixed in place, the performance of the drag queen cannot immediately be "neutralized." As such, there is at least a tempo-rary moment of confusion, as Bersani admits. The praxis that ought to be "impos-sible," in which a body perceived as male appears to be combined with female behavior, can nevertheless still be connected back with the anchor structure in many ways. As Bersani puts it, it then represents only a perversion, not a subver-sion. Still, this inevitably means that the foundations that are supposedly self-evident at least begin to articulate themselves. As we already demonstrated in the reading of Butler in chapter 7, when a transfer is perceived to have failed, this already brings the idea into view that gender is transferable in principle. For bet-ter or for worse, even the "God hates gays" placards of the Christian fundamen-talist counterdemonstration with which Marta gets entangled announce that there is such a thing as "gays."

B, who is trapped in a femininity anchored in heteronormativity, may, as Ber-sani concedes in passing, herself already experience this femininity rather as an articulated structure, and not as an unproblematic one. Perhaps a perspective also emerges for her in the moment of the drag performance, as Butler seems to envis-age, allowing her to see femininity through the praxis of drag as being made rather than given. The crucial catalyst that leads the structure to be evacuated is then the off-putting content. The realization that she does not want to be like that can admittedly only come into play if she knows that she does not *have* to be like that. The drag queen offers an alternative that is ambivalent, because at first it is repellent.

The disidentifying effect, which could already be called performative, is anal-ogous with the critical effect of genealogy, as defined by Foucault. Martin Saar summarizes the genealogy as a "critique of how we became this way, of power, of the self," which is achieved through a historical narrative in standard examples of critical genealogy, such as Foucault's *Discipline and Punish* and Friedrich Nietzsche's *On the Genealogy of Morals*. This historical narrative must succeed in connecting with the position of the recipients so as to enable them to make drastic readjustments in their practical and normative orientation: "The audience sets the authors of genealogies the following task: 'Tell me the story of how my view of myself came to be, and how my relationship with myself came to be. Tell it as a story of power, and do so in such a way that when I hear it, I no longer want to be the way I thought I had to be, and so that I also understand that I don't have to be like that.' "[14] However, such a history of how we became this way, proving contingency and horrifying its readers, can also be brought together dramatically with the parodic capturing of practices that have become self-evident.[15] The drag queen, too, who exhibits the "constructed" aspects of femininity, shows the spectator a "history of the power of the self."[16] Her performance fans out the whole arsenal of gestures and practices that can be aggregated and combined into "natural" femininity; rather than the history of how we became this way, it reveals the building plans of how we are made. The mode of critique that Butler offers could therefore also be understood as a synchronous genealogy—as performative critique that stages rather than historicizing.

Butler herself seems to follow the motif of genealogy in her praxeological reading of Foucault's notion of desubjectivation. However, the individualistic tendency of that reading, which has already been criticized, expands to such an extent that Butler finally stylizes a subject that risks itself or its own intelligibility on ontologically uncertain terrain as being "virtuous."[17] It seems to me that this puts us even further from the answer to the question posed already in *Gender Trouble*, as to those contexts "in which subversive confusions can be fostered."[18] In other words, who would then be left and still be able to laugh?

At this point, then, I do not want to merge performative critique with synchronous genealogy,[19] but merely to indicate a parallel between an element of performative critique and the workings of genealogy, namely, the practical disidentification or mimetic distancing made possible by the shattering of a structure that has become self-evident.

STRUCTURAL TURNAROUND AND REARTICULATION

If subversive confusion is really to be maintained, there must also be people present for whom the deviant practice taking place is not unintelligible at all, but recognizable, though in a way that is incompatible with the publicly articulated structures. They do not find themselves confronted with a monstrous mixture of the sexes, like A, or with a repulsive variant of femininity, like B, but instead with a familiar praxis of drag, like Schirmer's audience of insiders. Along with the performer, they form an interstitial space of appearance. However, when this is experienced in a context that is (partly) open to the public, the experience of reception is changed. This could give rise to annoyance and create distance—"who is laughing so hysterically at the wrong time? And why are there people here that I wouldn't want to meet on a dark night?" Drag in front of a mixed audience is already no longer the same praxis as it would be in a basement bar only frequented by people from the subculture. It is in this milieu that C can also be imagined as a mediating "clairvoyant." It is no coincidence that a spectator who is informed about feminism, doesn't generally identify with (heteronormative) femininity, and is knowledgeable about the gay scene would be perfectly suited to this role.[20] For she is the one who could see drag not only in terms of its "drag side," so to speak, but also in terms of the "femininity variant" with which B is disidentifying herself. Interstitial praxis therefore "hijacks" the articulated structure, or rather the latter seems to be refunctioned according to the interstitial praxis.

If my schematic setup has not only constructed three different perspectives but also overlaid them on one another, this is not simply an arbitrary assumption as part of an illustrative thought experiment. People like C did act in solidarity with a gay scene in the throes of politicization, and they did begin to identify with it, owing to the specific historical constellation that actually emerged in the AIDS activism of the 1980s in Western Europe and the United States, fostered by particular divisions within feminism. In order to trace the alignments that in turn define this overlaying, it would obviously be necessary to conduct a full sociohistorical analysis, but even my cursory array of factors enabling militant queer disobedience should provide a good glimpse of what frames Butler's more free-floating focus. The chances of success of the exodus as a transfer of praxis that overturns established structures nevertheless cannot be derived directly from the power balance. The critical performative brings a contextual logic of its own into play, a logic that might precisely overcome the existing power balance. But this logic is not contingent all the way down. It hinges on there being a particular kind of articulated structure: one that could be refunctioned in the sense of interstitial praxis, such that it turns against its former anchoring ground.

In the drag situation described in this way, a specific dynamic can now perpetuate itself: if the interpretations are even partly transferred—perhaps through laughter at particular points—then B has the additional possibility of shifting into the perspective and praxis of C. Once she has disidentified herself with a conventional notion of femininity, she can approach gender as a performance and, while rejecting the variant of femininity performed by the drag queen, make femininity her own "as drag." For the situation "after" the shattering of the anchor structure reveals a new schema to her—"gender as drag." In addition, perhaps a few fragments of knowledgeability are transferred to those present who are already very familiar with the schema. In this case, they do have access to the crucial resource—the performing body, though untrained. Thus, their bodies can begin to replicate the praxis.

If this were to become perceptible, if B were suddenly to begin behaving in a feminine way "with a difference," then the initial scene would be amplified and A would once again be in the situation of having to "repair" his anchor structure—this time, however, irritated not by a praxis that ought to be "impossible," but by the "redirected" articulation of "femininity," which would suddenly no longer follow the tracks set out by the anchor structure. This would mean that two articulated structures would ultimately confront each other—heteronormative or "natural" gender identity vs. "gender as drag," which would compete for anchoring and for favorable alignments.

It is this potential escalation that would open up the perspective for C and perhaps also for B to see A's behavior, regardless of his own quite different view of himself, as "drag"—reason enough to laugh.

METALEPTIC INTERLOCKING

This minute analysis expands the core understanding of performative critique that has already been formulated by adding the motif of overlapping structures. The first important aspect here is that the interstitial praxis is constituted in such a way that when it "mingles with the audience," it continues to work as a subcollective context that supports an otherwise unintelligible praxis. However, the whole further dynamic depends on the fact that in this context, structures overlap so that interstitial praxis can be said to occur as something other than itself. In Butler's example, the "explosiveness" of drag comes from the fact that it suddenly figures as "femininity." This occurrence of an interstitial praxis under cover of an articulated structure is what I understand here as "contamination."[21]

However, to ensure that a specific contamination is not simply one option among many, the copresence of the interstitial context is indispensable. If the drag performance simply merged with "femininity"—for instance, if it confirmed a general desire to be like Marilyn Monroe—then its transformative potential would be lost. But if this interlocking of structures is kept poised in a state of balance, then the alternative praxis can become the pivotal point from which the contaminated structure changes shape, like a trick image that can be seen in two ways. That is, if the contaminated, articulated structure is hijacked by the interstitial practice, then its resources are in a certain way refunctioned. The fact that the interstitial praxis can be integrated at all already means that the resources present in the articulated structure are a perfect fit. Thus, where a performative takeover can take place, the material is already present, albeit in a different configuration. This condition is often obscured in Butler's own work and does not play a marked role in the case we have just discussed, which follows her example, because the practices in question, as "performances of gender," require only a few relatively easily procured "props" or resources beyond the bodies that participate. However, for instance, when HIV-positive activists who were taking part in double-blind pharmaceutical trials brought their samples to an autonomously organized lab for testing and divided the active medication among all participants, this was a praxis with a much more complex materiality. Nevertheless, it still meant refunctioning a structure, and in this case really did lead to a lasting revolution in the standards of medical tests with terminally ill patients.[22]

At any rate, if an articulated structure is redirected in this way, it runs "openly" against the anchor structure that had kept the interstitial praxis unintelligible, and forces that anchor structure to articulate itself. Even in order to maintain the structural upheaval brought about locally by this double liquefaction, it is necessary to continue the process of interstitial constitution—everything depends on what happens next. Still, this analysis should have shown the extent to which the possibility of radical change relies on the supposedly "small form" of the critical performative.

If Marta is also to be allowed this sort of success scenario, like Butler's drag queen, then we should return once again to her unintelligible demands. After all, the content of her Peter Pan campaign, which still meets with skepticism from her fellow protesters, is not necessarily as empty as the blank side of her placard. "Peter Pan is a white slaver; he exploits fairies. . . . For decades Peter Pan has been played by women, why can't Peter Pan *be* a woman?"—we might be forgiven for thinking that Marta is announcing the two seminal works of queer theory, which also appeared in 1990. The first of these would be Eve Kosofsky Sedgwick's deconstruction of twentieth-century literature and culture, in which she shows that it is fundamentally dependent on the continued erasure of homosexuality:[23] it is only because the love of the loyal fairy Tinker Bell "doesn't count" that Peter Pan's family romance with the human Wendy can have its full effect. And it is when we bid goodbye entirely to the differentiation between biological and performed gender, as Butler demands in *Gender Trouble*, that we finally reach a fluidity of gender that allows the Lost Boys' captain Peter Pan also to *be* a woman.

In this case, a metaleptic overlapping of structures arises in which the theoretical discourse established since provides the articulated structure within which Marta's strange statement, which is declared in the film itself to be downright incomprehensible, "suddenly" becomes legible. In this case, the rearticulating turn is a rather unspectacular one: in the right circumstances, this maneuver could show that crucial ideas from queer theory are in continuity with activist and aesthetic discourses of the previous decade. Thus, my revised and extended version of performative critique essentially rests on the idea of processes of constitution and contamination interlocking with each other. When an interstitial, unintelligible praxis makes itself visible by contaminating existing articulated structures, it articulates and disaggregates the anchor structure that ought to stand in its way, and can itself become a "new" starting point for further praxis. The dynamic concerned can be described as "metaleptic," both in terms of a double transfer and in terms of a reversal of cause and effect.[24] For if unintelligible praxis brings about a restructuring, then this is only so because the "new" forms of praxis already functioned interstitially as the causes of that restructuring. And if the "transfer" of an articulated structure into the form of a new praxis is successful, it is only because another transfer was achieved before that, namely, the hidden insertion of the interstitial praxis into the course of an articulated structure.

The reason this motif is so central to a conception of interstitial change is that it allows us to distill the mechanism of performative critique from its few examples of success, precisely through a detailed analysis of its contexts. The more insight we have into the conditions, the clearer it becomes, on the one hand, that performative critique does not "always" succeed. At the same time, it also emerges that it is not only a specific element of queer gender parody. It can, in many different interstitial processes of transformation, become the moment in which "outlandish" practices take on a defining role for the course of further events, and assert themselves against structural resistance in a manner that is not agonistic. However, as the next and final part of this book will demonstrate, this is almost never achieved in a unique act, but in continuous events that enrich and reinforce one another. To show which rearticulations and which dynamics of repetition are needed so that moments of performative disaggregation are also consolidated on the macrolevel and bring about long-term restructuring, we will use the model of paradigm change.

When it comes to the notion of revolutionary praxis, Marta will continue to play a paradigmatic role in my approach. Her determined, odd, mischievous behavior, which is deeply connected to her fellow protesters—her "interstitial labor," which is sometimes so clumsy and puzzling—nevertheless forms the foundation for radical change.

PART 4

The Execution
of the Marquise and
Metaleptic Paradigm Shifts

The last part revised the motif of performative critique, developing the mechanism whereby a small form resists the balance of power and breaks through against deeply anchored structures. This analysis suggests that "the new," which seemed to have shifted out of reach in terms of praxis and structuration theory, emerges due to a double transfer: from interstitial unintelligibility into hidden articulation, and from there into rearticulation—the moment in which the new also becomes generally recognizable. Seen in this way, performative critique becomes a metaleptic transformation—not only do structures become fluid, they are actually broken down.

Although this underlines the effectiveness of the mechanism, it does not yet tell us anything about how the temporary occurrence of this mechanism relates to the transformation of the social formation as a whole. Is it simply that many small changes become one big change? Or can we define in more specific terms how a qualitative change is measured? In the following chapters, we will establish such terms through the concept of the paradigm shift, understood as a gradual exchange of anchor practices. This is essentially a constellative process—neither elimination nor rupture, but rearrangement.

There is probably no thinker who has interpreted revolution as a change in constellation in such complex and idiosyncratic terms as Walter Benjamin. I will begin by introducing his conception, to the extent that it can be read as an answer to the problem of transition that concerns me here. As will become apparent, Benjamin's motif of the dialectical image follows the same dynamic as the figure of metalepsis. Nevertheless, although the author of *The Arcades Project* was downright obsessive in his concern for concrete historical material, he does not designate any place in his understanding of revolution for a gradual consolidation of practices—this place is kept occupied by the messianic elevation of the singular revolutionary moment.

So if Gustav Landauer and the prefigurative approaches in general propagate the notion of interstitial change without finding an effective mechanism of transformation, reading Benjamin draws attention to the opposite problem. With his model of "pure metalepsis," he misses some of the underground preliminary work, as well as the stabilizing iterations that are required for actual revolutionary agency. It is this requirement that leads me to suggest that we should not only transfer the motif of local structural change into an understanding of comprehensive paradigm change but also keep underpinning it in terms of praxis theory.

The completion of revolution is also up for debate in the literary text that will be discussed in this section. In a story by Isak Dinesen (also known as Karen Blixen), published posthumously in 1977 under the title "The Proud Lady," we find ourselves in the dining room of the executioner Samson, in the second year of the revolutionary calendar, 1794.[1] Two women from the country have come to see him. They have a request regarding the execution of the Marquise Perrenot, due to take place the next day. Samson lets us know that this beheading will be an unusual event: "She will be, I think, my last aristocrat. We have rid ourselves fairly thoroughly of them by now. It was only by hiding away in a corner of her old château all alone that the woman Perrenot escaped the sharp eye of the republic for such a long time."[2] Samson enumerates the misdeeds that the Marquise is supposed to have committed:

> "There never was a harder, a more cruel or miserly old hag in France. She was known in London and Saint Petersburg as a gambler always in luck at the card tables, but she grudged her own servants and serfs the food in their mouths. Why, that was the woman who knocked out the eye of a peasant with her horsewhip because he did not take off his cap quickly enough to her." . . ."And who," said Samson, "shut up one of her maids in a tower room for three years because she had displeased her. . . . Who left her only daughter to starve," he went on, "because, against her designs, the girl married an honest man, a friend of the people."[3]

Speaking for both of them, the older of the two women, Marie-Marthe, confirms these incidents and introduces herself as the very servant girl who was once imprisoned, and the daughter of the farmer who was blinded. However, in her own telling she recontextualizes the events in various ways. The Marquise apparently resorted to these draconian punishments because she was stunned that her daughter Angélique had eloped with the aforementioned "friend of the people," a bourgeois officer, instead of agreeing to an arranged marriage. In her tower room, Marie-Marthe was at least well provided with food and work and learned a new technique of weaving patterned rugs. The Marquise finally freed the servant after hearing that her son-in-law had died, so that Marie-Marthe could go and join Angélique. The two, Marie-Marthe and Angélique, had evidently always been close friends. Rather than renewing the servant contract, Marie-Marthe formed a small household together with Angélique and her only surviving child, her daughter Jocelynde-Jeanne, and the three supported themselves by selling hand-made textiles.

But Angélique died relatively young, and the Marquise then formed a new plan, namely, that the marriage arrangements that were scotched by her daughter's elopement should be transferred to her granddaughter.

> Now Madame began to imagine that the marriage which she had once arranged for her daughter might still be brought about on behalf of her granddaughter. Only to make up for the lack of nobility in the girl's father a much bigger dowry than her daughter's would be needed. It was from this moment that she gave up traveling and gambling and instead set herself to hoard up money. . . . She no longer cared about her own looks, she had no more frocks made and hardly left her own land. It is from this time, Citizen, that all those stories of her greed and avarice date. It was then that she grudged her servants the food in their mouths, and she herself sat down in her big dining room to plain meals.[4]

Marie-Marthe reports that there was already much talk of political change at this time, which the Marquise ignored entirely—" 'When all this nonsense is over again–' she said at every message from Paris."[5] When many neighbors began to go into exile, "she was angry, and said they ought to have their heads cut off."[6]

While Marie-Marthe tells her story, the young Jocelynde-Jeanne sits silently beside her and does not react when Samson comments: "I wish we could drain the Perrenot blood out of you, then you might make a pleasant wife for any good sansculotte."[7] The two women have still not told him the request that brought them there, and Samson declares that he will fulfill it in exchange for a kiss from Jocelynde-Jeanne, regardless of what it is, whereupon the latter presents her petition: "If her face and figure were those of a child, her voice was very clear and sonorous, and although it was low and slow it was controlled and authoritative. . . .'I beg you, Citizen Samson,' she said, 'at the moment when my grandmother has mounted the scaffold, to lay away your hat and say to her: "At your service, Madame la Marquise."'"[8]

I would now like to reject two interpretations of this that might seem plausible, but that would reduce the openness of the twist in the tale to which Dinesen has insistently steered us. I will then present two readings that are perhaps more faithful to the text, which in turn lead us to explore how the characters themselves assess the situation. However, by pointing out that the story allows strikingly divergent interpretations, I do not mean to relativize the various perspectives or show that there is unlimited space for interpretation. In a critical dialogue with Walter Benjamin's materialist hermeneutics, I would instead like to show that Marie-Marthe's perspective emerges from a better analysis of the given circumstances, meaning that it permits an emancipatory openness. Samson, on the other hand, fails to recognize the change in constellations that has already been completed, and therefore drifts into a view that is so rigid regarding revolutionary praxis that it certainly does not contribute to the success of the revolution. (Jocelynde-Jeanne's version will be reserved for the end of this final part.)

But back to the beginning of this spectrum of interpretation—and the question of what the puzzling request is supposed to mean. It does not seem right to interpret the wish for a humble greeting as a cruel joke against the old lady. The story undoubtedly contains enough reasons for the women to be embittered, but given how Samson is presented, it would not be at all necessary to propose this plan to him via such a circuitous route. He seems—and in this he represents the general mood of the Paris guillotine audience, rather than the respectful attitude of the historical executioner Sanson[9]—motivated enough to play any kind of trick on "the old hag."

The opposite interpretation proves to be just as simplistic. Certainly, the story fits well into the motifs of sentimental exile literature, such as the memoirs of Rosalie Lamorlière, who worked in the Paris prison known as the Conciergerie. Addressing a counterrevolutionary audience, Lamorlière wrote after her flight from France about the services she performed for Marie-Antoinette. She describes how she risked her life to make things easier for the former queen in certain ways. In particular, she lamented the fact that Marie-Antoinette was not appropriately looked after during her imprisonment—being required to eat with tin cutlery rather than silver, for example.[10] In line with this, we could infer that the two women in Dinesen's story were "actually" not patriotic citizens at all. All the references and statements implying their patriotism could have been lies; maybe they longed, like the Marquise, for the end of the "nonsense," and would have liked to see their former mistress saved. But then, their actions before the arrest would be incomprehensible. Evidently they did everything in their power to build a different form of life. In particular, the nonhierarchical relationships of Angélique and Marie-Marthe are as different as they possibly could be from the order of estates in the ancien régime. If the women wanted to maintain that regime, they could have returned to the château.

It seems to me, then, that the more naïve interpretation, which takes the narrative voice and the actors at their word, is also the more complex and challenging approach. The women do not want a counterrevolution, but they still want the executioner to bow to the Marquise. But does this mean that the revolution has actually failed? Does it mean that, while Samson is still expecting to chop off the last aristocratic head the next day, at least two people are there to take her place, who still believe that the subservient bow has not yet had its day? Seen like this, the story seems to reiterate the skepticism toward revolution from which this book began, and which we were aiming to counter in praxis-theoretical terms. The habit of bowing, this example might be saying, proves to be more stubborn than the supposed victory in class struggle.

Or does the actual failure lie in the fact that revolutionary energy only knows one solution to the practical relics of the old order—that of the guillotine?[11] In Year II, it was common among the sansculottes who ruled the political discourse at the time to assume that all problems of the Republic would be solved if there were a guillotine on every street corner and if all dandies, wholesalers, and moderates were executed.[12] From a praxis-theoretical perspective on processes of construction, in which *new* patterns of action would be rehearsed, the story could therefore also be read as demonstrating the dilemma which results from the fact that because no resilient alternative practices to bowing had established themselves, the guillotine became the only "solution."

At any rate, at this point in our discussion, the story does not offer any clear measure with which we could weigh whether the revolution failed because its anchoring in the past tragically caught up with it, or whether it succeeded in spite of certain embedded continuities.

Given the concept of praxis developed in the first part of this book, we cannot simply look at the act of bowing to read its meaning. Instead, we would need to analyze its contexts and its anchoring in order to decide whether it speaks for or against the failure of the revolution. Even then, the question returns of how this failure should be measured. Thus, we need a criterion for the radical nature of social change.

Historical materialism has an unambiguous answer to this problem, because it rests on an assumption about what constitutes "the roots" of the social. Here, the crucial criterion for revolutions is whether the mode of production has changed. There is therefore no need to think about the rest of society, since it is either dependent on the form of economic organization or simply unimportant. Alternatives to the economistic notion of revolution rely on a phenomenology of the event to decide whether something can count as a revolution. This in turn makes them very tightly dependent on those war-like scenarios that are at variance with interstitial change—in fact, they often categorically exclude the idea that there could be long-term, "quiet" processes of revolution.

With the image of interstitial change, then, we have already left behind the established set of alternatives. However, this means that it is still necessary to specify the criteria for success. What would be the indications that the request for a bow is part of a lost revolution, or a successful one? What are constellations and how can they be distinguished from one another?

This problem is also at the center of Walter Benjamin's thoughts about the philosophy of history. Although Benjamin stubbornly insists that he is formulating a model of historical materialism, he suspends the basic assumptions of such an approach almost entirely. In place of progress, a catastrophic timeline is introduced, which drives history through "empty time" for as long as it takes until an entirely different mode of reference—"citability"[13]—collects the material that has been discarded on the way into liberating arrangements.[14] This notion of reference material, which reaches out from the past, forms the remnant of that which actual historical materialism sees as "material." Rather than using the term "dialectics" to refer to a dynamic that feeds on objective contradictions in the mode of production and subjective conflicts of interest between the classes, Benjamin ultimately situates dialectics in something which he calls "image" or "constellation": "Image is that wherein what has been comes together in a flash with the now to form a constellation. In other words, image is dialectics at a standstill."[15]

For Benjamin, the revolutionary situation is characterized by the arrival of a particular relation between past and present. He contrasts this relation with the normal continuous ratio, which features both "emptiness" and "continuity." This becomes clear in the metaphor of events running through someone's fingers "like a rosary."[16] The continuity of events—one bead like the last—is what makes time appear "empty." It could be said that there is "nothing" in it that could throw off the course of events. Accordingly, Benjamin's polemic against progress is directed neither against the hope that the future could be better, nor against the materialist assumption that the key to a better future is conveyed along with the conditions that have arisen over time, but against the belief that the past, as we have it in our hands now, has already set us on the right course. "Nothing has so corrupted the German working class as the notion that it was moving with the current."[17]

But what would the alternative be? After all, we cannot simply wish for a different, richer past. Here we see the effects of Benjamin's idea that the "emptiness" of time is itself created by existing power relations. He argues that this dominant perspective is ideally embodied in bourgeois historiography: "The enshrinement or apologia is meant to cover up the revolutionary moments in the occurrence of history. At heart, it seeks the establishment of a continuity. It sets store only by those elements of a work that have already emerged and played a part in its reception. The places where tradition breaks off—hence its peaks and crags, which offer footing to one who would cross over them—it misses."[18]

Here Benjamin's approach closely resembles that of interstitial praxis theory, in that he sees the closed nature of existing circumstances as being due to a perspective that is blind to the minor anomalies and resisting elements, and that actually contributes actively to concealing them. In contrast with that, precisely those elements, the "peaks and crags"—or, as Benjamin says elsewhere, "rags" and "refuse"[19]—become a point of reference for transformation. But in order to have an effect, in order to allow someone to reach beyond the dominant tradition, the places that have not made it into the "reception" must become visible. "For the historical index of the images not only says that they belong to a particular time; it says, above all, that they attain to legibility only at a particular time. . . . Each 'now' is the now of a particular recognizability."[20] But what does Benjamin mean by "legibility"? "Reading" here is a very far-reaching term. It means not only gaining knowledge but also liberating the reference material itself: "A revolutionary chance in the fight for the oppressed past."[21] In fact, Benjamin makes no distinction between the "oppressed past" and those who were oppressed in it.

This is somewhat easier to understand if we return to Dinesen's material. Samson is only able to report accusingly that the Marquise struck out her servant's eye with her whip because a revolution has since taken place and thrown an entirely different light on feudal rule. Instead of continuous exploitation, in which everyone would have remained in their places and the story of the stubborn servant being severely punished would have remained without consequence and without meaning, Samson is now able to make use of this event in judging the cruel mistress, in order to stage the last execution as a definitive break with the ancien régime. The request that he doff his hat as her servant once did runs counter to this picture in such a drastic way because it would not simply mean an embarrassing moment for him. Rather, it would mean a further betrayal of the unwavering resolve of the servant who had already withheld his bow, whose actions would be flattened into the continuity of expressions of humility, rather than being a "peak and crag" that would allow us to get out from it. Seen in this way, the women's request is virtually a dialectical image of counterrevolution.

This also corresponds with the strangely steadfast refusal of the two supposed patriots who have come to Samson to address the *ci-devant* Perrenot de la Lionne with her patriotic name. The revolution that had stepped in to avenge the suffering of Marie-Marthe's father, among others, is now being betrayed—by his daughter and her young friend, of all people. Samson therefore has reason to see the struggle as an open one. He senses that there is what Benjamin calls "a constellation of dangers."[22] In the story, this struggle, once again represented allegorically, is written on Jocelynde's body. That is the field on which the Marquise and Samson fight out their power struggle. Stylistically, this is symbolized several times through the metaphor of her blood—half aristocratic, half patriotic/citizen.[23] The Marquise had done everything to increase the dowry and thus bring her granddaughter back into feudal circulation. But Samson now resorts to a praxis ensuring ultimate victory for republican marriage policies. That, at least, is how he interprets the kiss that he demands in exchange for the wish that he has not yet heard: "Do you know what you are going to do now? You are going to kiss Samson, the man who cut off the heads of the king and queen of France. You may still become the wife of a sansculotte, but no aristocrat will ever kiss those lips which have kissed Samson. Even if all this nonsense of a revolution comes to an end."[24]

Evidently, Samson secretly shares the doubts of the Marquise as to whether the revolution might actually turn out to be nothing but passing "nonsense," and it is because of this that he seeks a praxis that would bring the ambivalent Jocelynde unambiguously onto the side of the Republic. Not guessing what he will be required to do in return, he sees his idea as a way of ensuring that the Republic wins the day. The constellation emerging here connects the past moment of the King's execution with the seemingly unrelated kiss in the present. The Marquise may have ignored revolutionary jurisdiction and stubbornly continued to hatch aristocratic wedding plans for her granddaughter, but now those plans will be foiled after all. Samson believes that he can bring together regicide and matchmaking in such a way that the woman concerned is catapulted out of the structures that serve noble reproduction and transported irrevocably onto the side of the sansculottes. This validates and continues her mother's decision to marry a "man of the people," which at the time still seemed "illegible" and "mad." From the point of view of praxis theory, this would mean joining onto certain practices that were previously unintelligible—and repeating them in such a way that they would be aggregated into a structure.

For Benjamin, historical materialism becomes a method of discovery that deliberately draws attention to those moments when previous praxis is adopted, adoptions that otherwise take place unwittingly as part of revolutionary praxis: "The historian . . . grasps the constellation into which his own era has entered, along with a very specific earlier one. Thus, he establishes a conception of the present as now-time shot through with splinters of messianic time."[25]

If Benjamin calls the constellation of past and present that bursts continuity a "monad"—"the historical materialist approaches a historical object only where it confronts him as a monad"[26]—then this can be related to the element that is responsible for effective transfer in metalepsis. A "monad"—that is, a "primary element" that is complete in itself—would be the praxis that emerges as a future paradigm precisely in the moment when it shifts from unrecognizability into articulation and does not simply begin to outline itself, but hijacks and refunctions an existing dominant structure. In terms of performativity theory, this monad is not an image, but simply the effect created when a praxis is taken up and continued. However, in order not only to ensure radical change in formal terms but also to substantially safeguard the revolutionary content, it might be necessary to freeze the process in a way that, measured against the processual unfolding of practice, seems slightly artificial. This allows us to judge the revolutionary moment. Is it really the case that the oppressed past is being articulated in this image, and not just the wishful thinking of a covetous hangman? Is it a "messianic" tableau pointing to a liberated future, or just an arbitrary refunctioning—a "fashion," as Benjamin says, which would of course also include past or subcultural elements influencing the dominant style?

No matter how much he tries to bring together his method with revolutionary praxis, Benjamin holds fast to the monadic picture, meaning that he remains dependent on the historian's "lonely" efforts at construction. The historian's dialectical view and his judgment "in the battle for the oppressed past" keep the perspective focused steadily on liberation. Such an anchoring could also be expanded and adopted for collectives whose practices are informed in hidden ways by revolutionary tradition. The alternative that guides revolutions would then not have to be wrestled only from the past in cerebral salvage work, but could also be taken from subaltern forms inhabiting the present.

Based on this observation, we could distill a competing dialectical image from Dinesen's story. Marie-Marthe seems to be more sure than Samson that the question of whether the constellation could "tip back" into the feudal past has been decided. She draws this conclusion on the basis of everyday practices and economic relations, rather than culmination points in the struggle for power. The Marquise is defeated by the household set up by her daughter, and the women gain financial independence; the Marquise is isolated already before her arrest and fails in all her stubborn plans for restitution: this points to a change that is complete and can no longer be reversed. In assessing the danger of the moment, Samson had in any case overestimated the powers of his opponent. Marie-Marthe corrects him, pointing out that the Marquise neither starved her daughter nor had her son-in-law stabbed. If we seriously accept that Samson's analysis is wrong, his fixing of the constellation loses precisely the revolutionary index that it would need in order to represent a dialectical image in Benjamin's sense. It is Year II of the revolutionary calendar; by connecting the regicide with a kiss, Samson does not respond to an unintelligible, buried moment in history, but repeats an act in which he is on the winning side. In the middle of the revolution, we could say that this makes time become empty and continuous again, instead of bringing further possibilities for emancipation into view.

If, like Marie-Marthe, we assume that, between the bow that the Marquise forced out of Marie-Marthe's father and the bow that the women want to see enacted before her the next day, there is a successful paradigm shift, then the two practices are no longer arranged in the same grouping, similar as they may be, but belong to structures that are entirely different in their anchoring. For example, as citizens of a sovereign people, the women could request that the practices of mercilessness with which the Marquise tormented her servants should not be continued against enemies of the Republic. Even if they were simply repeating the praxis of bowing due to an internalized compulsion to repeat the past (however that might be proved), we could nevertheless also describe this praxis as one of generosity toward one's enemies. What it "is" depends not on how it was meant, but on how it then goes on. From this point of view, if the women's request were upheld, it would in fact mean that the humiliation of Marie-Marthe's father would *not* be repeated. Dinesen's story would then form a monad that could help to replace the fixation on total enforcement with a sensitivity for the changed constellation.

Benjamin himself secures the reach of his dialectical images by ensuring that they are always concerned with the notion of history itself, or of coextensive grand concepts such as "progress," "the past," and "class struggle." Thus, they always form the culmination of "the whole." However, the price of this is that everyday and unconscious practices fall by the wayside. When he conjures up class struggle, Benjamin already sounds forced at times; beyond Robespierre's classical references, it is really only the historical-materialist observers who seem to realize the dialectical image, and not the historical actors themselves.

Thereby, the constellative understanding of revolution threatens to uncouple itself from revolutionary praxis.

Can the constellative criterion for change also be maintained if constellations do not rely on such rare points of culmination? Or if the possible perspectives even turn out to multiply in the struggle, because it has not already been decided at the start that the historical continuum will be exploded in order to liberate a unanimous subject from history itself? Can constellations be scattered across the breadth of practices that Marie-Marthe has in mind, without disintegrating as a criterion for radical change?

I would like to follow up on Benjamin's fundamental idea with less messianism and more exodus. In order to substantiate the idea that metaleptic changes in constellation are a criterion for successful revolutions, we need not only to identify the pivotal point but also to define the completion of the change, which can sometimes be protracted. The existing conditions—the structures in which the actors find themselves—must be formed in such a way that practices taken from other contexts can be articulated in them. The revolutionaries have to take up previous practice in such a way that they can not only see their initial situation differently in the light of these "messianic" practices but also refunction it gradually—precisely because praxis that is continued differently transforms the configuration of existing structures.

The first of the following chapters will underpin the concept of constellations in praxis-theoretical terms, through the notion of paradigms. Here, I make use of a particular reading of Thomas S. Kuhn's book *The Structure of Scientific Revolutions*. This may be a surprising point of reference, given that paradigm shift is generally understood as a radical break between two incommensurable worlds, in line with Richard Rorty's adoption of Kuhn's motif. This cannot be compatible either with a processual theory of praxis or with one that emphasizes the resilience of socially rehearsed patterns. In contrast to the emphasis on incommensurability, I make use of Margaret Masterman's interpretation of paradigms, which proposes a pragmatist alternative. Her arguments, especially when it comes to how a paradigm is adopted, take up the thread again at precisely the point where the motif of performative critique broke off in the previous part of this book, with the still very precarious articulation of a praxis that was formerly interstitial. The core metaleptic moment can then be embedded in Kuhn's conception of the crisis of a field, and Masterman's idea that new paradigms are gradually reinforced, beginning from temporary "tricks." The reanchoring of articulated social praxis in previously unintelligible practices that were only maintained interstitially eventually forms the criterion for the revolutionary, even if this is not what the paradigm-applying scientist or the unheroic activist might have had in mind.

From the abstract terms of the theory of science, my approach then moves again to historical material, in order to test out interstitial transformation theory, using the term "revolution" itself as an example. In fact, the debates between historians reflect both the economistic and the phenemological, event-focused paradigm. Bringing together two newer (but already classic) interpretations of how the French Revolution turned the political culture of France upside down and made something like "revolution" thinkable in the first place, I sketch out the contours of an interstitial historiography. The two works on which this is based are Lynn Hunt's study of French provincial towns during the revolution, and William R. Sewell's interpretation of the storming of the Bastille. What is crucial here is that Sewell's focus on the supposed culmination of events in the center can be relativized in view of the interstitial preconditions that tend to be ignored—no event without the path through the periphery, no dialectic without the metaleptic possibility of recourse to the scattered interstices.

In the third and final chapter of this part, we will explore the full meaning of the term "metalepsis," which has already been used here. As a Greek loanword and a rhetorical figure, we can understand this concept in such a way that it already includes both culminating constellation change and gradual cumulative transfer. Against the fully unfolded backdrop of this core term, we can finally turn around the ending of Dinesen's story once again. If we anchor the metaleptic perspective in Jocelynde's final statement, then an image emerges that places her not at the end but at one of the starting points of a human emancipation that has yet to arrive.

10

Paradigm Shifts as a Gradual Replacement of Anchoring Practices

I n order to understand revolutions as a change in constellations, without reducing them to hyperbolic moments of culmination, this chapter will adopt Thomas S. Kuhn's understanding of scientific paradigm shifts for performative praxis theory. In one way, the reference to Kuhn makes sense; it is common in postfoundationalist social theories. At the same time, Kuhn might seem to be a proponent of total and immediate transformations, criticized by Alasdair MacIntyre for conceiving of transformative processes as complete breaks between incommensurable theories or traditions.[1] In the following, I will not only reject this interpretation but also show that with Kuhn—with a particular Kuhn—the motif of performative critique that was revised in the previous part can be further enriched.

To this end, I base my approach on a more precise version of the Kuhnian notion of paradigm, an interpretation that has ironically hardly found any supporters other than Kuhn himself.[2] Margaret Masterman was a pupil of Wittgenstein who firmly objected to the usual holistic interpretation of the term "paradigm," in an essay published in 1965, when *The Structure of Scientific Revolutions* was receiving its first wave of responses from theorists of science. In "The Nature of a Paradigm," she instead suggests understanding paradigms as specific "tricks" or temporary practices, an interpretation that Kuhn adopts when he defines "paradigms" as "exemplary" in his later work.[3]

First of all, I will sketch out the way in which Kuhn conceives of the structure of scientific revolutions in *Structure*, already working against the image of a leap from one theory into another incommensurable one. It should also become obvious how great the overlap is between these processes and the dynamic that I have described as metaleptic. Next, I will examine the term "paradigm" afresh, translating Masterman's theses on the adoption of paradigms back into my own context of performative praxis theory. The transition to a new, formerly interstitial anchor structure and the accompanying rearticulation of other structures thus finally become a criterion for whether the change in question deserves to be called "radical," which precisely does not mean that it has to be understood as total.

PARADIGM SHIFTS ACCORDING TO KUHN

One crucial innovation introduced by Kuhn to the description of science is the definition of normal science. Contrary to what he (like many practicing natural scientists) sees as an idealization of the everyday business of science—namely, the descriptions of continuous tests of falsifiability in Karl Popper's theory of science—he observes that for long phases, science is not focused on innovation or discoveries at all.[4] Instead, it is concerned with solving puzzles that can in principle be relied upon to be solvable, and to which the rough answers are already clear, so that it is only necessary to find the precise route to the solution. Within this normal scientific framework, it is then possible to trace an increase in knowledge, of which the progress according to Kuhn is often falsely extended backward across different approaches, in scientific historiography—an effect of the fact that textbooks and overviews are always written from the standpoint of the current paradigm and only throw selective light on a few previous stages of the field, which have now been superseded, and which can be integrated into the relevant line of development.

Kuhn outlines the course of scientific revolutions in several phases. Within "normal science," which concentrates on "puzzle-solving" and the articulation of theories, we keep coming across stubborn problems and incomprehensible results. These "anomalies" initially only contradict expectations, but never immediately become refutations of a theory. However, for various reasons, they can become "pressing anomalies." That may be the case if they undermine the practical applicability of a branch of research, or if they actually contradict the core of a given paradigm. If a larger group of researchers then concentrates on solving precisely this problem, even elevating it to the central question of the field, then the perception of the anomaly can sharpen into the perception of a crisis in the prevailing paradigm.

Crises are accompanied by a muddying of the paradigm—it is no longer clear what we can build on, and variations are tested out more frequently.[5] However, it is in no way certain that a crisis will mean the end of a paradigm. Typically, the anomaly is somehow made to disappear within the framework of the old paradigm after all, or the problem is simply postponed ("set aside for future generations to solve").[6] However, it is also possible that a new paradigm is discovered, so that the crisis is solved through a paradigm shift. The function of the crisis is to create an enabling framework for the paradigm shift: it increases the willingness of researchers to be receptive. However, even in the crisis, the old paradigm will not break apart or be given up unless a promising new candidate is at hand. Otherwise, according to Kuhn, we would be giving up science entirely. ("To reject one paradigm without simultaneously substituting another is to reject science itself.")[7] The "discovery" that finally shows the way out of the crisis is therefore relativized for Kuhn, in the sense that it is not new in content but in status. "The solution to each of them had been at least partially anticipated during a period when there was no crisis in the corresponding science; and in the absence of crisis those anticipations had been ignored."[8] Even in science as described by Kuhn, the solutions are usually already there for a long time, but they elude perception *as solutions.*[9] But according to Kuhn, the anomaly itself can constitute the core of the new solution: "Sometimes the shape of the new paradigm is foreshadowed in the structure that extraordinary research has given to the anomaly."[10]

This description essentially follows the dynamic with which I have characterized performative critique: the "new" praxis is already present in an interstitial form; it may already have entered an articulated structure under cover, but it only comes into effect when it succeeds, through an interstitial constitutive process, in continuing that structure openly.

Kuhn places greater emphasis on the fact that if innovation is to be accepted, there must be an awareness of the existing crisis, an awareness that the usual praxis no longer works. In performative critique, this is covered by the disaggregation of anchor structures, though it remains unclear whether this is a result or precondition of the emergence of unintelligible praxis. However, if we regard the process of performative critique as being iterative anyway, then there is no chicken-and-egg problem here, but simply a crisis dynamic that gradually becomes more extreme.[11] The more stubborn the anomaly, the more the prevailing praxis is undermined; the more the prevailing praxis is undermined, the greater the readiness to take up completely new forms—perhaps the very forms that emerge in the anomaly. In Kuhn's own vocabulary, this is summarized as follows:

> If, therefore, these epistemological counterinstances are to constitute more than a minor irritant, that will be because they help to permit the emergence of a new and different analysis of science within which they are no longer a source of

trouble. Furthermore . . . these anomalies will then no longer seem to be simply facts. From within a new theory of scientific knowledge, they may instead seem very much like tautologies, statements of situations that could not conceivably have been otherwise.[12]

Paradigm shifts could thus also be reformulated as transitions in which a previously unintelligible, interstitial praxis becomes the starting point for a new anchor structure.

This metaleptic temporality of the paradigm shift also fits together with the fact that—according to Kuhn—it often extends across a long period of time and can essentially not be dated. Kuhn himself takes the side of the event-skeptics: "No wonder historians have had difficulty in dating precisely this extended process that their vocabulary impels them to view as an isolated event."[13]

STRETCHING OUT THE REVERSIBLE IMAGE

At one point, in order to illustrate the transition that a supporter of the old paradigm would have to go through after the new one has articulated itself as described, Kuhn also uses (with some clear caveats) the analogy with a reversible figure that can be seen in two different ways, as a rabbit and as a duck, for instance.[14] It is this illustration which fuels the interpretation that scientific revolutions are a shift between incommensurable worlds.[15] After all, the reversible image includes neither intermediate steps nor compromises: it is either entirely a duck or entirely a rabbit.[16]

This is how Richard Rorty understands cultural change in terms of an event, for instance, taking the logic for this from a version of the structure of scientific revolutions that has been stripped of its structural elements. First of all, he extends Kuhn's model of scientific paradigms into a general description of different worldviews. Rorty doubts whether a categorical difference between scientific and political differences in worldviews exists: "What could show that the Bellarmine-Galileo issue 'differs in kind' from the issue between, say Kerensky and Lenin, or that between the Royal Academy (circa 1910) and Bloomsbury?"[17] Transferring Kuhn back into the political in this way is at least justified in the sense that Kuhn himself claims to have used the term "revolution" explicitly in order to emphasize analogies between general history and the history of science.[18]

In any case, the crucial question is whether the structure of scientific revolutions works as a convincing model in social theory. Rorty interprets the distinction made by Kuhn between normal science and revolutionary science as a difference between discourses deemed rational and irrational. He argues that the vocabulary of rational discourse forms such a tight, inferentialist network of justifications that it is entirely incommensurable with another vocabulary. Unlike Kerensky and Lenin, speakers of different vocabularies have no common ground at all. This drastic distance can now be bridged, if we adopt the holistic assumption that no sentence can be comprehensible without the whole language also being intelligible. This would mean that innovative, new ways of speaking, however they emerge (Rorty gives us no information about this), become Trojan horses for an entirely new vocabulary. At the beginning, they cannot be estimated using familiar measures—after all, they are incommensurable—but if they are not rejected as madness, and are instead accepted and disseminated, they form the pivotal point for a whole worldview. This means that Rorty's antifoundationalist claim that the social has no roots actually leads to a picture in which one particular move can bring everything else along with it. But in this case, this is not because the social is thought of as being structured in such a way that particular core areas within it define the rest, but because of the holistic basic assumptions making its construction so watertight that if it could be dismantled at all, it could only be dismantled as a whole.

Newer historiography of the French Revolution also concentrates on the changes in political culture and rhetoric that are regarded as the most momentous result of the years after 1789. Here, the emphasis is often placed on political culture in a narrower sense;[19] at other times, the transformation of general cultural or even psychodynamic formations becomes the focal point.[20] However, in contrast with Rorty's clean break, here we see that the nature of such "revolutionary" achievements remains particularly protracted and also extremely fragile. In addition—and despite the fact that historians of the revolution remain substantially dependent on linguistic sources—the avant-garde position of particular formulations and ways of speaking is not necessarily confirmed. It is often chains of practices, ambiguous stagings, and material arrangements that gradually lead to the point where actors get to know new concepts and express them. As I hope to show in the next chapter, a praxis-theoretical understanding of the social corresponds much better to these analyses than holistic pragmatism.

In my initial thoughts about terminology, I will follow Masterman in showing the extent to which we can also distill quite a different, more processual, and less holistic reading from Kuhn's *Structure*, and equip "innovations" with a revealing and significant prehistory.

Kuhn himself uses the analogy with reversible images not for paradigm shifts in the field of research, but for the demand that these shifts make on a person who has seen neither the urgency of the anomaly nor the crisis. For such a researcher, it must be possible to shift perspective by learning to see something as self-evident that hugely disrupted her expectations of probability. Kuhn then laconically admits that this kind of "conversion" is particularly unusual, and that fields are more likely to change because newcomers and marginal figures outlive those who stubbornly deny the field's crisis. Yet the resistance of the seemingly incorrigible does not simply prove their irrationality but also demonstrates, as Kuhn emphasizes, this belief in the ability of a paradigm to solve problems, a belief that is after all responsible for the success of normal science at other times.[21]

It seems that the example of the Marquise is an opportunity to study all the ways in which people can resist a paradigm shift: the flight of her daughter fundamentally threatens the way in which she reproduces her world, so she tries first of all to explain it as a result of madness. Even the servant girl who did not prevent her daughter from leaving is accused of having lost her reason and imprisoned.[22] But since this event cannot simply be erased, the Marquise then begins the painstaking endeavor to correct the problem, by making sure that the planned marriage at least takes place properly in the next generation—for which she has to make substantial reparative measures in the form of an increased dowry. However, the revolution itself gets in the way of this, and the Marquise would rather die than share Samson's attitude to the choice of partner, which would mean accepting that the only proper decision is to share one's life with "an honest man, a friend of the people": the new paradigm.

Thus, it is only from a very particular standpoint that a sudden switch in gestalt can be seen as a model for paradigm shift. Now, it would be possible to object that the conception of interstitial change itself actually suggests a transformation in gestalt, since the interstices expand in such a way that they at some point become the keystone of the new order. However, the crucial difference is the fact that this takes place in a diachronic process. Through this, the reversible image is stretched out for restructuring. Instead of the other side of the new picture becoming entirely invisible in the transformation, reconstructing such processes offers an insight into the way in which we have reached the given arrangement, which in its new interstices always remains connected with "the old."

In order to show more clearly that paradigm shifts consist of a redistribution of crucial structures and not a fantastical conversion of the Marquise to Samson's worldview,[23] we still have to explain in more detail how a paradigm is adopted and what exactly a paradigm is in the first place.

PARADIGM SHIFTS ACCORDING TO MASTERMAN

Already in 1965, Margaret Masterman was astonished to find that most of those who interpreted Kuhn's work—and philosophers in particular—"assume without question either that a paradigm is a 'basic theory' or that it is a 'general metaphysical viewpoint'; whereas I think it is in fact quite easy to show that, in its primary sense, it cannot be either of these."[24]

Instead, the future founder of the Cambridge Language Research Unit begins her essay by listing twenty-one ways in which the term "paradigm" is used in *Structure*, which she then groups into three primary meanings—worldviews, sociologically observable standard approaches by scientists, and artifacts that bring solutions.[25] Here, we must first of all keep hold of the fact that none of the three senses is identical with "theory." A worldview is much more general and comprehensive than a scientific theory, while the established approaches of scientists and their technical constructions are located on quite a different, nondiscursive level. In this vein, Masterman summarizes her reading of Kuhn as follows:

> He never, in fact, equates "paradigm," in any of its main senses, with "scientific theory." For his metaparadigm is something far wider than, and ideologically prior to, theory: i.e. a whole Weltanschauung. His sociological paradigm, as we have seen, is also prior to theory, and other than theory, since it is something concrete and observable: i.e. a set of habits. And his construct-paradigm is less than a theory, since it can be something as little theoretic as a single piece of apparatus: i.e. anything which can cause actual puzzle-solving to occur.[26]

It is the last two meanings of paradigm that Masterman sees as definitive for an understanding of paradigm shifts, and that she shows to be recursively dependent on each other.[27] The point about paradigms is that they have to exist already before theories are formed—they ought to explain the transition itself.[28] Masterman, who has newly emerging sciences more clearly in mind than Kuhn does, emphasizes that his specific contribution was to illuminate this process: "Thus, by assigning the central place, in real science, to a concrete achievement rather than to an abstract theory, Kuhn, alone among philosophers of science, puts himself in a position to dispel the worry which so besets the working scientist confronted for the first time with professional philosophy-of-science, 'How can I be using a theory which isn't there?' "[29]

Nevertheless, she believes that Kuhn did not analyze the mechanism of this specific kind of "bootstrapping" in enough detail. The description of normal science in sociological categories (that is, using the second meaning of paradigm as observable habits) is, for her, accurate but insufficient, if we place ourselves in the position of those who make the essential contributions, without which an approach that can later be seen as being orientated toward a prototypical achievement would never have become a prototype. So what is it that originally causes someone to use a new paradigm as a frame of reference? "But how does the scientist himself, in a new science, first find out that what he is following is going to become a concrete scientific achievement, unless he already knows that he is following a paradigm? There is clearly a circularity here: first we define a paradigm as an already finished achievement; and then, from another point of view, describe the achievement as building up round some already existent paradigm."[30]

So when we ask how a paradigm works, we have to rely on its third sense as its fundamental meaning, and it is necessary to explain the specific mechanism that brings a paradigm into the world in the first place: "Thus the real problem, in getting a philosophy of new science, is to describe philosophically the original trick, or device, on which the sociological paradigm (i.e. the set of habits) is itself founded."[31]

Masterman then develops her view of paradigms as "constructs" in two steps. First, she describes the role that the paradigm plays at the beginning, namely, that of a trick which promises to remain useful and which can therefore have a foundational effect:

> What, in actual fact, is this "paradigm," this entity?... "just going on as we are now"; that is, with some trick, or embryonic technique, or picture, and an insight that this is applicable in this field. And it is this trick, plus this insight, which together constitute the paradigm.... All those things which, taken together, will later become "the concrete established scientific achievement" ... nearly always come along after the initial practical trick-which-works-sufficiently-for-the-choice-of-it-to-embody-a-potential-insight, that is, after the first tryout of the paradigm.[32]

She goes on to ask what sort of mechanism the paradigm must actually be, or which characteristics it has to have, in order to play this role. Here, she shows that a "puzzle-solving trick" is always first of all a "crude concrete analogy." Whether it is a model made of building blocks or a new metaphor or a particular gesture, some kind of temporary measure proves to be "the initial practical trick-which-works-sufficiently-for-the-choice-of-it-to-embody-a-potential-insight." As to whether a paradigm really comes out of this that could then be observed as the basic pattern of the field, this depends on whether the analogy in question can be extended or transferred further. In contrast with theoretically grounded normal science, this process particularly recalls iterability. Masterman endeavors to capture it as follows:

> Within normal science (says Kuhn, on this reading) paradigms are capable of expansion and development in two quite different ways. They develop, in the end, by mathematical or other rule-governed inference—which alone enables true puzzles to be solved. But they also develop, initially, by intuitive "articulation" (or "family resemblance," or, "direct modelling," or "replication," in an extended sense—any or all of these). This second process also is a form of inference in a wider sense of "inference"—in that sense in which "inference" is literally any kind of permission to pass from one unit or sequence of units or states of affairs to another unit or sequence of units or states of affairs—but it is intuitive; it does not go by rules.[33]

Masterman talks of crude analogies as being doubly concrete. On the one hand, they are concrete as specific, material models, while on the other, that which acts as a model and which can be transferred further becomes concrete as it continues to be applied to scientific material.[34] This application has retroactive repercussions that are then gradually theorized, formalized, and put into mathematical terms. However, the actual transfer takes the lead, in a way that cannot be codified, as a replication based on family resemblance. When Masterman says here that this transfer—measured by the standards of sound theorizing in the natural sciences—takes place without rules, this still allows us, in my view, to see it as obeying rules from a praxis-theoretical standpoint. In fact, it follows the sort of rules that—even after Wittgenstein's critique of rule-following—can still be identified in the continuation of praxis: praxis-generating competence, praxis-defining recognition, and praxis-evaluating knowledgeability. This transfer is "intuitive" in the sense that it has unconscious and spontaneous elements, but it can certainly be broken down more specifically into progressing "by doing," "by seeing," and "by talking."

By distinguishing between practical replication and theoretical conclusions, Masterman also succeeds in pinpointing the incommensurable element. It would then not be the theories that are incommensurable with one another, since it is those very theories that explain and translate the approach. Instead, it is the crude initial analogies that would be incommensurable: "How, for instance, can you compare, 'Man, the paragon of animals,' to 'Man, that wolf?' "[35]

REPLICATION AND RECURSIVENESS

The aspects that Masterman raises in order to conceptualize the acceptance of paradigms can be brought in to explain the process that must take place if performative critique, understood in terms of praxis theory, is to have an effect that not only is destabilizing but also extends into actual restructuring. It must be possible to see "unintelligible" or "anomalous" praxis in such a way that at least some actors will consider it as a trick that might be effective. In the first place, the praxis cannot be entirely without carriers; otherwise it could not occur. But there must be some initial transfer of the praxis to show that it can be extended at all. Masterman may refer to the paradigm as a "construct" or "artifact," but in order for it to become a paradigm in her sense, it must also be practically effective in a certain way, namely, when used as an analogy. What seems like madness to the Marquise—marriage for love—must be seen by somebody, at least, as a praxis with a possible future. It must be recognized not only by the priest who marries the eloped couple but also by other couples who see it as an approach that can be replicated.

What is interesting now is the way in which Masterman describes how things continue from there. For the new praxis not only has to grow in breadth but also has to sink down deeper and become an anchor praxis, if it is really to bring about a paradigm shift. In order to articulate itself at all as a structure, the praxis must be repeated and continued. Those who see it in the light of success take possession of a new schema. "Intuitive articulation" "or 'family resemblance,' or, 'direct modelling,' or 'replication,' in an extended sense—any or all of these"[36]—leads to the point where, in the field of given practices, regroupings take place. Practices are assembled as structures in a different way, and in imitations or continuations of the new practice, these structures are perpetuated and reinforced.

Here the crucial question emerges as to the extent to which the replication or the formation of analogies can be continued. Paradigms, Masterman also says at one point, are like metaphors in poetry—they are productive but at a certain point they can become overstretched. By experimenting with how much can be solved by an "initial trick," for how many further contexts the new praxis can be used as a model, it becomes clear how "deep" it can reach. Depending on how far the analogy can be extended, we come to know whether it can anchor broad regions of praxis in itself, or whether it remains limited to a very specific context.

In this context, "replication" or the creation of "family resemblances" is a process working in two directions. Not only is an original model extended ever further, but in all such transfers there is a slight shift in the definition of the model's use. Thus, we are dealing not only with a process of ever-greater generalization, but with a generalization that remains malleable at its core.[37] Just as the shape of structures emerges performatively from the way in which those structures are continued, when a praxis is a possible candidate for a paradigm, we only gradually find out what is actually paradigmatic about it, and always in new terms.

In the scientific realm, and certainly in the social realm, the boundaries of generalizability are contested quite differently than, for instance, the boundaries of a metaphor. The Marquise, with her contacts in exile, will be executed so that she cannot continue to pursue family politics through her granddaughter. Samson invents practices resembling branding in order to ensure that bourgeois marriage triumphs. Jocelynde evades this "inexact matching," by obliging the executioner of the royals to bow before the last countess.

The conflict over the enforcement and limitation of revolutionary practice is demonstrated by many highly significant everyday practices. In the summer of 1793, for instance, arguments raged over how the introduction of the compulsory tricolor cockade in the previous year should be interpreted. This fabric rosette was an early Jacobin symbol. When Louis XVI appeared on July 17 in front of the people wearing a tricolor cockade, this put a seal on the permanent change in the balance of power following the storming of the Bastille. Three years later, there was a debate over whether the new dress code also applied to women. The Société des Citoyennes Républicaines Révolutionnaires under Claire Lacombe fought hard for the law to be extended, keeping the city on tenterhooks for the whole summer and sparking physical fights between opponents and supporters of the patriotic dress code. They succeeded in establishing the general obligation to wear the cockade, so that Marie-Marthe and Jocelynde-Jeanne would have risked punishment if they were to go out without it. At the same time, the triumph of the cockade was also the last political success of the female Jacobins. One month later, all women's clubs were banned, including the Société des Citoyennes Républicaines Révolutionnaires, which was the most prominent. Pierre-Gaspard Chaumette, leader of the Paris commune and a tireless supporter of the revolutionary cult of reason, articulates the limits that were placed on the rearticulation of political culture as soon as women began to enter into it. Alongside less effective suggestions, such as the idea that only simple wooden shoes should now be worn, he felt that patriotic women should stay at home, in order to allow men to attend political gatherings: "Since when is it permitted to give up one's sex?. . . Is it to men that nature confided domestic cares? Has she given us breasts to feed our children?"[38]

Seen from this vantage point, the fight over the cockade could also be understood in more abstract terms as part of a conflict over the limits demarcating the republican—and therefore sovereign—people. This level of abstraction would then allow us to make out more far-reaching family resemblances. This "inexact matching" is still a question of family resemblances, as can be reconstructed in the sense of the anchoring relationship (cf. chapter 3): what Masterman calls intuitive inference can succeed by mimetically taking up the schemas, by subordinating further practices to the praxis-internal norms of the paradigm, or by exploiting the praxis-generating know-how that is incorporated with the paradigm (cf. chapter 1).

Depending on how we interpret the paradigm that is to be replicated, the diagnosis of how far it has caught on will be different. Still, there will always be a countertest allowing us to estimate whether a paradigm shift has taken place at all. For in the structures of the ancien régime, the entire content of the struggle over the cockade and the place of women would have remained groundless and unintelligible. Political representation was not up for debate in any way as something transferable, at least not beyond the two bodies of the king. Marie-Marthe's mother most likely nursed two infants at once, as a wet nurse, while the Marquise did not nurse any—but nobody would have imagined that this had anything to do with how many breasts they had.

In this sense, already the description of the initial situation in Dinesen's story— that two citizens can bring a request to the state executioner regarding the treatment and public punishment of their former mistress—assumes that since the time when she punished a stubborn farmer, not only have a few structures changed, but their underlying constellation has shifted. "Before," the harshness of the punishment might perhaps have been an anomaly, but not the expected bow. But now, it is specifically the idea of Samson bowing that is a scandal. In the light of the new, revolutionary paradigm, this formerly unremarkable gesture is a deviation bordering on madness. If Samson had been more certain of the revolution's success, he would have been able to join the two women in seeing the provocative "counterpractice" as a litmus test of that success. Rigidly clinging to a more definitive criterion, he instead insists that the matchmaking practices of the "old hag" should be continued toward Jocelynde.

11

The Revolutionary Emergence of the Concept of Revolution

In this book, the term "revolution" is refigured on the basis of a social theory of radical change. We have defined radical change as the gradual exchange of anchor practices, in a dynamic that can be described as performative paradigm change. But can this terminology actually be used to describe revolutions? How does it fit into the field that knows how to deal with historical material—how can it be integrated into the work of historians and their own discussions of methods? After an overview of the main methodological axes in revolutionary historiography, two studies in social history will be discussed here—William R. Sewell's interpretation of the storming of the Bastille in terms of an event theory, and Lynn Hunt's main praxeological work, *Politics, Culture, and Class in the French Revolution*. These samples allow us at least to outline how historical processes can be reconstructed plausibly through the motif of performative paradigm shift. In addition, the metaleptic perspective allows us to integrate the conflicting explanatory models used in the two approaches—whether the term "revolution" was established in the central event or in peripheral processes of translation—into a common framework.

PROCESS OR EVENT?

The question of whether a process of transformation deserves to be called "radical" could be answered in a very satisfying way if we knew what it was that functioned as a "root." This would give us a useable criterion to define what would have to be altered so that we could talk of real change, as Marx argues in *The*

Poverty of Philosophy: "The social relations are intimately attached to the pro-ductive forces. In acquiring new productive forces men change their mode of production, and in changing their mode of production, their manner of gaining a living, they change all their social relations."[1]

This assumption also formed the backdrop of the heated debate among his-torians about the social interpretation of the French Revolution. For the more detailed their examination of the sources became, the less the dynamic of the revolution fitted into a Marxist model of bourgeois revolution.[2] Even in the class-focused historiography of Albert Soboul, undoubtedly one of the greatest interpreters of the French Revolution in the twentieth century, the implied revolutionary subject already became more complex.[3] As a motor of change, the bourgeoisie faded entirely into the background, in contrast with the sanscu-lottes, who drove the dynamic, and whom Soboul described not as a proto-proletarian class, but rather as a disparate group held together by their demeanor and political style, including "urban consumers," "small traders," "craftspeople and apprentices," and "independent small producers."[4] Theda Skocpol aug-mented this picture by adding the crucial role of farmers in the revolution, and the effects of the ailing feudal state that could not keep up with international military competition. She elevated the latter into a far more significant condi-tion of the revolution than the supposed tension between increased economic efficiency and the feudal economy, which could be found to a much greater extent in unrevolutionary Prussia.[5] While these findings could still more or less be integrated into the overarching line of development of historical material-ism, so long as their effect would be to help the bourgeois-capitalist order achieve its breakthrough, even that was ultimately called into question by revisionist historians. They claimed that the revolution actually had a very obstructive effect on capitalist development in France, and if anyone profited, it was the land-owning class, of which one can hardly say that it was pushed to the top by the revolution.[6]

Historians investigate their subject in a more basic, phenomenological way than social theorists—revolutions can be analyzed as events, even if they do not fit into a particular scheme of overarching development. Despite what their lib-eral readers and Marxist opponents implied,[7] the revisionists rarely meant to claim that no revolution took place. They just wanted to separate it from a particular root.

Precisely in the impulse to render the revolution as an event, revolutionary historiography overlapped from the seventies onward with another philosophi-cal strand of historical thinking, particularly in France.[8] The development of that strand can be described as a conflict between a focus on structure and a focus on events. The primacy of structure was represented in two waves. The Annales School around Fernand Braudel, Lucien Febvre, and Marc Bloch followed Durkheim's social theory in flying the flag for historical research into extremely long-term processes and persistent mentalities, against what it pejoratively called "event-historiography." They shaped the intellectual climate for several decades, until in the sixties once again a younger generation of theorists departed with renewed verve from the supposed voluntarism of Sartre to embrace a structuralist approach. In different disciplines, different variants of Ferdinand de Saussure's extremely fruitful approach became paradigmatic—as is shown by the influence of Levi-Strauss on ethnology, Jacques Lacan on psychoanalysis, and Bourdieu on social science, and with certain restrictions also Althusser's interpretations of Marx, and Foucault's early work.

However, in order to go beyond a crude dichotomy, it should be mentioned here that those very thinkers who held on to their diachronic perspective in the midst of the structuralist influences developed interesting suggestions for significantly weaker conceptions of event—suggestions that did not give up the term, but caught it in the net of structural analysis. Thus, for example, Althusser states in *Reading Capital*: "What makes such and such an event historical is not the fact that it is an event, but precisely its insertion into forms which are themselves historical . . . into forms which . . . are perfectly definable and knowable."[9] In a very similar way, Foucault makes use of the staccato list that is so typical of his writing to underline a perspective in which structure and event are treated not as competing categories, but as categories depending on each other: "But what's crucial is that historians do not examine an event without placing it in a defined series, without seeking to understand the regularity of phenomena and the limits on the probability of their emergence, without interrogating variations, inflections, and the shape of the graph, without trying to determine the conditions on which these depended."[10] However, at least at a theoretical level, such attempts at a synthesis remain rare.

Instead, at roughly the same time as the protests in 1968, which were always called "the May *events*" in France, a poststructuralist emphasis on events set in. Liberated not only from any dependence on structure but also from teleology, from dialectics, and even from a reliance on actors, this category took on a key position in the work of thinkers like Gilles Deleuze and Jean-François Lyotard as "pure difference" or "traumatic encounter."[11] For Jacques Derrida and Alain Badiou—as disparate as their work may be in other regards—the event became absolute, with reference to late Heidegger, while actors could only respond to it from a retrospective, passive-recognizing position.[12] Unlike the performative, Derrida outright declares that events are inexpressible, "pure" happening. Thus, in *L'université sans condition*, he explains that "where there is a performative, an event worthy of the name cannot arrive."[13]

Rejecting *this* understanding of events certainly does not seem to mean that the category of event should be rejected altogether. However, as I hope to show with reference to a much more sober concept of event, the moment we declare something that occurs to be an event, this almost inevitably brings with it the tendency to invest it with an immanent causal power cut off from its context. Events are those moments that are described as if they took their meaning and their power from themselves, and not from a cascade of conditioning factors and favorable connections, in which practices are taken up and continued. Just as the dual notion of structure works on the ontological level against the absolute status of certain forms of praxis by drawing attention to their continued course, a performative understanding of transformation should avoid consigning the theorization of social change to the "black box" of an inflated notion of events.

Being able to view revolutions in the context of their own logic and not having to force the broad field of social practices to fit together with economistic assumptions have led to an interpretation of the French Revolution becoming canonical in the last decades that once again—but differently from Marx—sees it as a political revolution. It is the change in political culture that is regarded as significant. In a somewhat paradoxical way, this produces the argument that the revolution was revolutionary because it invented the revolution as a political form—and with it "the political" in its modern sense.[14] The two social historians discussed in this chapter also argue for this interpretation, but in fact point out above all the structural conditions for such a "cultural transformation." Accordingly, William Sewell's essay is titled "Inventing Revolution at the Bastille." He is specifically concerned with the connection between violent mass uprisings and popular sovereignty that was brought together in the modern notion of revolution, through the storming of the Bastille: "It was by this process that the modern concept of revolution definitively entered French political culture, effecting a hitherto undreamed of but henceforth enduring articulation of popular violence to popular sovereignty."[15] Ten years earlier, Lynn Hunt's influential monograph *Politics, Culture, and Class* explored the "unexpected invention of revolutionary politics."[16] Hunt's study combines meticulous quantitative sociohistorical research into the background, status, and interests of revolutionary protagonists across France with culturalist analyses of the "general patterns of thought and action" articulated in revolutionary discourses. The integration of the two approaches becomes programmatic, in what could also be called a structural duality: on the one hand, Hunt identifies new practices and their structural characteristics, and on the other, she investigates which actors carry them into which contexts. Later, this perspective will be woven together with Sewell's analysis of the Bastille events, in order to show how culmination and cumulation must be interlinked in interstitial change. At the same time, I will argue against Sewell's core thesis. For he combines his defense of the notion of event with a more far-reaching claim: that *only* events and no cumulation of individual local changes can ever bring about radical change. In contrast with this, although I would agree that we can distinguish between culminating and cumulative processes, I would still like to hold fast to the view that the more eventful dynamic of culmination can only ever actually change the structural framework thanks to prolonged cumulative processes composed of small transformative moments. The "path through the periphery" that Hunt proposes ultimately decides whether what happens in the center is simply a series of occurrences, or comes to be seen retrospectively as events.[17] Sufficient cumulation of small changes can suffice to change "everything," but no event can ever make a revolution alone.

CULMINATION AT THE BASTILLE

William R. Sewell defines events as "sequences of occurrences that result in transformations of structures."[18] This would mean that every performatively disaggregating praxis that I discussed in the previous part could be elevated into an event. However, alongside the criterion of changing structures, which is part of the definition, Sewell brings in a requirement as to the scale of what is happening. He argues that events have to yield meaningful consequences, that it should be possible to say about them that they change "the course of history," which Sewell characterizes in rather ad hoc terms as follows: "Lumpiness, rather than smoothness, is the normal texture of historical temporality."[19]

My general reservation about the notion of events is that it almost always leads inevitably to an overly absolute approach, obscuring the diverse forms of transformative process rather than encapsulating them. The term "event" often allows us to avoid explaining the transition rather than analyzing it. With Sewell, we do gain an insight into the dynamic and conditions of the change in question, but this insight—as I hope to show—can certainly still be refined in places, using the terminology of performative praxis theory.

If Sewell evaluates the storming of the Bastille as having established the modern notion of revolution, he still does not simply allow this new invention to coincide with the act itself. Rather, he demonstrates impressively that it is only gradually, in the face of drastically changed power relations, that a particular understanding of what happened on July 14 is reached among the speakers of the National Assembly. What was at first understood as an unfortunate excess on the part of a bloodthirsty mob gradually came to be seen quite differently, as a manifestation of the people's sovereignty. This sovereignty was legitimized precisely by the fact that the freedom being demanded was achieved by a crowd representing the whole people:

> The seemingly miraculous victory of the National Assembly caused its orators to reassess their initial opinion that the taking of the Bastille was a lamentable disorder and to accept the Parisians' own characterization of it as an act of legitimate resistance against despotism and a valid expression of the nation's will. They did so somewhat tentatively on July 16, but more firmly on July 20 and 23. By the 20th, the evolution of the balance of political forces had not only made it unthinkable for the Assembly's majority to criticize the violence of July 14, but made it imperative for them to embrace the violence as a foundation of their own authority. It was by this process that the modern concept of revolution definitively entered French political culture, effecting a hitherto undreamed of but henceforth enduring articulation of popular violence to popular sovereignty.[20]

What Sewell regards as the "result" of the storming of the Bastille therefore consists in a restructuring of the political schemas of interpretation, orientated toward a notion of revolution based on a connection between popular uprising and popular sovereignty. In the vocabulary of performative praxis theory, we could say that he dates this rearticulation to the point in time when appealing to the events at the Bastille became a new anchor structure in the National Assembly. From the end of July, it is not only unthinkable that any delegate would cast doubt on the legitimacy of this popular uprising, but even conservative and moderate speakers (here Sewell cites Malouet in detail) must henceforth anchor their own authority in the storming of the Bastille.[21]

Why did the National Assembly change its opinion of these events so drastically? Why do we still associate revolutions with this uprising, even today? Sewell analyzes the events of July in four stages: dislocation, initial break from routine, rearticulation, and authoritative sanction. I would like to approach this from the middle, so to speak, and explore the break from routine and the rearticulation. Here, it is important to remember first of all that Sewell does not let events be conflated with a particular historical act. As we have already seen, he views them as a sequence: "In spite of the punctualist connotations of the term, historical events are never instantaneous happenings: they always have a duration, a period that elapses between the initial rupture and the subsequent structural transformation. During this period, the usual articulations between different structures become profoundly dislocated."[22]

Thus, events begin with an initial break from routine that is then not neutralized by what happens afterward, but instead reinforced.[23] They then lead to a phase of increased activity and interpretation, which contributes to a deepening of the break, and which is reproduced through cascade effects. Sewell attributes the particular productivity of this phase, in which the actual rearticulation or joining of structures is supposed to take place, to the idea that times of great uncertainty are also always times of the greatest creativity. This assumption is anything but self-evident. Particularly against the background of his theory of action, which ultimately resembles that of Giddens, and connects the practical ability to act with structural preconditions, the opposite would be far more plausible: structures that have gone off the rails lead to paralysis and impotence or reduce the actors' repertoire to a few basic patterns of action that are particularly well anchored.[24] It seems more promising to pay precise attention to which breaking points and intersections emerge from a specific "dislocation." Sewell gestures toward this analytical perspective at one point when he tries to explain the multiplication of breaks, without building on it further: "Because structures are articulated to other structures, initially localized ruptures always have the potential of bringing about a cascading series of further ruptures that will result in structural transformations."[25] The fact that structures are connected up in some way is the condition enabling certain "domino effects" in the interruption of structures. In contrast with this, Sewell's analysis is much more rigorous when he interprets the historical events, but he does not grant it the status of terminology, precisely because he is trying to establish the notion of events as a more independent category.

However, the motif of performative paradigm shift offers us a better understanding of the material he presents. It also produces a clearer picture of what it can mean when metaleptic transfers take place in the course of revolutionary praxis. Sewell's description of the storming of the Bastille shows not only the extent to which its meanings depend on the interpretations that come afterward but also how a particular interpretation is laid out or prepared in the events themselves.

Storming prisons was not unusual, but belonged throughout the eighteenth century to the standard repertoire of social unrest.[26] In military terms, the occupation of the Hôtel des Invalides, which enabled the people to arm themselves, was far more crucial than the discovery of further munitions in the Bastille.

However, through the taking of the Bastille, a building whose walls were already a particularly clear manifestation of despotism, very specific points of reference emerged for the redefinition of political praxis. But why is it that the storming of this building not only flattened the power of the absolutist state apparatus but also created a new understanding of the people?

What makes the storming of the Bastille an event is the fact that it went down in history not as a mob uprising but as a manifestation of the will of the nation. The term that describes both "people" and "*the* people"—*le peuple*—allows such a reversal, but the fact that it took place was due to the specific details of what people did at the Bastille.

Sewell demonstrates that the rebels made use of particular practices that refunctioned the resources of sovereignty. Thus, the heads of Launay and Flesselles (the commander of the troops defending the Bastille, and a city official loyal to the king) were paraded on pikes after they were beheaded by the people—a form of representation generally reserved for the sovereign power of the monarch. The rebels also processed through the city after the handover of the Bastille, which again led to their being recognized as sovereign subjects of the events.

For Sewell, it is paradoxical that during an event, great creativity is accompanied by recourse to highly ritualized, preexisting patterns of behavior. He attributes this to the exceptional emotional state of mass frenzy.[27] However, it seems to me that intense emotionality in itself, like the lack of orientation mentioned earlier, can lead to creative paralysis and a breakdown of ritual patterns, just as much as it can cause them to flourish. Lynn Hunt, meanwhile, argues that the intensification of ritual forms is due to the fact that it is easy to follow them and they have a structuring power, meaning that they play a key role not only in the heated moments when the fortress is stormed but also constantly throughout the years of the revolution:

> In the rushing forward of revolutionary events, it was difficult to locate the legitimacy of any government. To "have" power in this situation meant to have some kind of control, however brief, over the articulation and deployment of outward manifestations of the new nation. Speakers in clubs and assemblies tried to claim the right to speak for the nation, but individual voices were often easily overwhelmed. More enduring, because more collective and reproducible, were the symbols and rituals of revolution; liberty trees and liberty caps, female figures of liberty and the Republic, and ritual occasions as diverse as festivals, school contests, elections, and club meetings. The ritual forms were as important as the specific political content. Political symbols and rituals were not metaphors of power; they were the means and ends of power itself.[28]

The fact that people "spontaneously" reach for ritual forms, as in the staging of sovereignty at the Bastille, can also be explained by their collective reproducibility. From the performative perspective on transformation, Sewell ultimately identified the very "ingredients" that create a situation of contaminated structures, thanks to which it is possible to transfer all the auspices of sovereign nations to a group of marauders. Because they succeed in repeating the practices of sovereignty, they enter into a schema previously only accessible to them as an oscillating possibility, if at all—the schema of "the people." The ritual is not an expression of an ecstatic mood, but a praxis that itself already—consciously or not—forms a particular interpretation of what is going on. Sewell's interpretation of the storming of the Bastille as a break from routine and a rearticulation corresponds to the workings of performative critique, in which structures of interstitial praxis are contaminated and then reconstituted.

Strictly speaking, at this point Sewell has only allowed us to reconstruct the transformation in the way in which the deputies of the National Assembly talked, and not, as he implies, the transformation of "French political culture" as a whole.[29] Performatively altered practices can only be reinforced when they are taken up and continued in follow-up actions that aggregate structures according to the "new" practices. Here, this is a particularly multilayered issue, since the resources for continued practices of popular sovereignty have many preconditions. In a certain way, the National Assembly, which aligns itself with violently demonstrable popular sovereignty, is not only an authority that interprets or verifies the events, but is itself a complex resource of the structure that is articulating itself. Sewell's criterion for the conclusion of an event—sanctioning by an authority—seems unclear. After all, in revolutions, the open question is precisely who counts as an authority.

We must therefore examine the structural preconditions and the stabilizing of performative transformation in more detail and ultimately extend them beyond Sewell's depiction.

CUMULATION BY WAY OF THE PERIPHERY

In many ways, Sewell offers a clear alternative to the treatment of events as mysterious monoliths. For him, events result from smaller fractures and cannot be traced back, contrary to his own talk of an "initial break," to a single starting point:[30] "A single, isolated rupture rarely has the effect of transforming structures because standard procedures and sanctions can usually repair the torn fabric of social practice. Ruptures spiral into transformative historical events when a sequence of interrelated ruptures disarticulates the previous structural network, makes repair difficult, and makes a novel rearticulation possible."[31]

The precondition for transformation is therefore, according to Sewell, a situation in which the structures have already shifted. He calls it "dislocation of structures," as opposed to the general "articulation of structures"—evoking the difference between dislocated and functioning joints in the human body. For the actors, a high degree of instability and uncertainty arises from this situation, in which structures have been derailed. The conflicting claims on representation by the absolutist monarchy and the National Assembly, alongside the subsistence crisis following the bad harvest of 1788, stand for this structural disorientation. Sewell expands the diagnosis of crisis, approaching Hannah Arendt's claim that revolutions only take place when power is already lying in the street.[32] "It was because sovereignty was up for grabs that the taking of the Bastille could be interpreted as a direct and sublime expression of the nation's will."[33] However, thanks to Sewell's thorough reconstruction, the example of the Bastille shows that it only actually emerged that sovereignty must have been "up for grabs" after it had been successfully refunctioned. Perhaps this never would have been known if particular practices had not actually rehearsed the takeover.

When Sewell switches to and fro between declaring that the emergence of anomalies is the condition for an event and claiming that it is an event in itself, he actually demonstrates precisely the extent to which the practices culminating in the event are inseparable from the cumulation of many small moments involving breaks from routine and the redirection of structures. Even if sovereignty really is up for grabs, it cannot be suspended in a single act—or even resignified.

In the vocabulary of performative paradigm change, we can transfer this oscillation between small breaks and the actual event to the gradual formation of a new paradigm that was already present in the preexisting anomalies. Through the Bastille, popular sovereignty is articulated in such a way that it suddenly no longer increases the crisis of representation, but presents itself as the solution to that crisis, in a changed framework. However, this only identifies the potential innovation and does not yet complete the actual change. In order to explain it, quite a different story would still be required, rather than that of episodic structural change through the articulation of interstitial praxis. We have to find an equivalent for the process of gradual replication, which is how Margaret Masterman described the adoption of new paradigms.

The results of Lynn Hunt's investigation can be understood precisely as demonstrating such a process. In the light of her sources and analyses, it becomes clear just how reductive it is to make a suggestive connection between a memorable event and a familiar result. According to Hunt, the change in French political culture was certainly not decided only in the capital, despite all centralism: "Most of the new practices got their official stamp of approval in Paris.... Nevertheless, the new political culture was not dominated by Paris. Revolutionary values and symbols were powerful, because so many people in so many different places began to act on them in concert with the aim of restructuring social and political life."[34] Hunt substantiates this finding by counting up the voting records and the membership of associations in all the *departements*. In a certain way, these sources show that the capital is not even unambiguously the capital of the revolution, and that the fate of the revolution is crucially indebted to mobilization in the provinces:

> In general the left was strongest in the periphery (except in the south-east). This geographical pattern is telling: it shows that the Jacobin deputies got most support from the periphery, not from the center of the country. Paris itself was fickle in its allegiance to the left, and the regions closest to Paris were usually staunchly right wing. The deputies who rallied most enthusiastically around the new rhetoric, rituals, and images came out of places far removed from Parisian sophistication.[35]

Lynn Hunt's search for the most crucial carriers of praxis also demonstrates just how much work was necessary to actually establish the new political culture of the revolution. In a certain way, her investigation of the town parliaments in mid-sized towns and of the Jacobin clubs remains inconclusive—it is not possible to identify a specific class or profession that made a particular contribution to the revolution. However, one characteristic that marked out active representatives of the new politics everywhere was the fact that they were, as Hunt says, "mediators" or "outsiders," who drove the transfer of new practices from the margins into the contexts to which they themselves were not entirely confined.[36] It is therefore particularly those who are not too deeply anchored in previous praxis who pick up on a new "possibly functional trick" and perpetuate it. Without the amplification caused by such figures, the events in Paris would not have brought about a rearticulation of political culture. Ultimately, Hunt describes the coming together of practices to form a revolution in vocabulary that Sewell would tend to dismiss as fruitless "small and undramatic changes."[37]

> The power of the revolutionary state did not expand because its leaders manipulated the ideology of democracy and the practices of bureaucracy to their benefit; power expanded at every level as people of various stations invented and

learned new political "microtechniques." Taking minutes, sitting in a club
meeting, reading a republican poem, wearing a cockade, sewing a banner, singing a song, filling out a form, making a patriotic donation, electing an official—
all these actions converged to produce a republican citizenry and a legitimate
government.[38]

Social change, in which the structures of society are really transformed starting
from everyday practices, is achieved when such "microtechniques" are accumulated. At the same time, beyond Hunt's work, we must remain aware of the fact
that already with the claim that these are cumulative processes, a generalization emerges that reaches beyond the microlevel. Only from more fundamental
anchor practices can all these tasks be classified as part of the same process at
all—we have to group them from the point of view of a particular paradigm.
"Taking minutes, sitting in a club meeting, reading a republican poem, wearing
a cockade, sewing a banner, singing a song, filling out a form, making a patriotic donation, electing an official" are all practices in which popular sovereignty is perpetuated through family resemblance or "inexact matching." If the
practices to which we refer emphatically as "events" can often be described better as models than as the causes of a changed historical framework or as arrangements of structures, then we could also, in a deflated, praxeological understanding, describe them as paradigms. In the sense of Masterman's notion of paradigm
as doubly concrete, all these practices ensure that the question of what "popular
sovereignty" actually consists of remains malleable—once again, the event dissolves into the performative process of perpetuation.

CAPTURING PROCESSES OF TRANSFORMATION

Sewell himself admits that the phase that he accentuates as an event—what
occurred in public in Paris, starting with the dismissal of the popular finance
minister Jacques Necker by the king on July 11, 1789, and lasting until the aforementioned state of the discussion in the strengthened National Assembly on
July 23—is not inherently defined in this way, but arises from his own research
interests. Identifying events therefore always involves hermeneutic circularity.
First of all, a particular change in structures is identified—here the articulation
of the modern notion of revolution—and then the crucial phase of transformation is located and investigated as an event. Given the difficulties arising from
the claim that the isolated sequence really effected the change in question, we

could of course distance ourselves from the somewhat hyperbolic idea that the event can be made responsible for the change observed in the framework. In order to capture the change in the whole framework, it would make sense also to take a tour through the periphery, tracing the "sequences of occurrences" that could actually have brought about the structural change.

The notion of event itself would then be freed from the suggestion of sufficient causality and would simply isolate a particular sequence that deserves the title of event due to a specific dynamic in which change speeds up or culminates.

However, if the notion of event is relativized like this, in favor of a processual concept of social change, the question of closure seems to take on fresh urgency. When would the change actually be complete?

As a criterion showing that an event can end, Sewell offers its closure by means of "authoritative sanction."[39] However, this raises the difficult question as to whose authority should seal the transformation. It seems doubtful whether the National Assembly should be the decisive voice here, since by this time it derived its own authority from the July events. Once again, it is unclear whether and to what extent it can be seen as "French political culture in general." The Marquise, at least, did not recognize this. Sewell does concede that the last word has actually still not been spoken; the same view is put forward by Lynn Hunt in her fittingly titled essay "The World We Have Gained: The Future of the French Revolution."[40] This seems even more justified if we consider that Sewell wrote an essay eleven years earlier in which he is determined to show that *the* decisive event of the French Revolution was the night of August 4[41]—the change in emphasis to the storming of the Bastille is thanks to the shift in interest in revolutionary historiography from the social to the political. Of course, this does not refute his analysis, but it draws further attention to the fact that an event whose beginning is lost in disparate moments of dislocation and whose end has still not been reached may be captured appropriately in processual terms but cannot be assigned an endpoint.

Thus, if events intrude into the present, the perspective seems to be reversed. We are actually talking about processes that, from the perspective of a history of the present,[42] are very significant to our current arrangement of structures. Essentially, we could say of events what Foucault says of the models that have flourished historically, writing in *Discipline and Punish*: "It is precisely these models that, before providing a solution, themselves pose problems; the problem of their existence and the problem of their diffusion."[43] At this point, I would now go one step further and offer the following suggestion: events can best be understood as this type of model. We refer to them, especially in historical depictions, because they make something clear on a small scale—as a model—that is characteristic for the rearrangement brought about by a protracted and multi-layered process, which has brought us to the point where we are.

This does *not* mean that events are only narrative constructs, or that they have not had any effect at all. The storming of the Bastille did take place and did unquestionably have real historical effects, probably even more than the actions of a provincial schoolmaster, or a noble who abandoned his privileges. But only when they combined did these things bring about a "change in political culture." On its own, as *the* event, the Bastille is not the solution that explains how a new political culture came to exist and take root. It makes sense to use the familiar events at the Bastille as an illustration of that new political culture, rather than undertaking the painstaking work of traveling from one provincial archive to another, locating badly catalogued sources, and talking about politicians in small towns whose names will immediately be forgotten by the reader. But if we do not only want to exemplify the paradigm shift but also to explain it, connecting together these metaleptic moments of transfer is essential.

Thus, when it comes to the axis of process vs. event, if the point is that revolution may be understood and explained in terms of a process, but metaleptic moments of culmination can be identified that match the usual understanding of event, then the historiographical question of the social vs. the political approach arises afresh. For the moments of constitution and refounding, which are so strongly emphasized by the "political" school of revolutionary historiography, cannot lay claim to any independence. (This recalls the differently focused Marxist dismissal of "political revolutions.") They depend on preconditions, both in material terms and in terms of the theory of action, which can only be captured by a wide-ranging social theory of praxis. Changes in political culture are social revolutions to the extent that there is no political culture whose anchor structures do not also mark out the course of broad sections of everyday life. Contrary to the Marxist interpretation, however, it is certainly possible to imagine that political revolutions can do without a specific paradigm shift in the mode of production. If we are interested in economic change, then we have all the more reason to let go of the model that orientates itself according to an absolute phenomenology of the French Revolution as an event. The mode of production is much more likely to change in arduous processes of cumulation than in moments of culmination. It is when Marie-Marthe leaves the tower in which she learned to weave that an economic change in structure becomes visible, rather than when the Marquise is executed.

12

Metaleptic Dynamics

I n this book, we have gone in search of a very specific form of social change. A change emerging from the interstices of the existing order. A change that could be understood as a process, rather than as an abrupt event. As a driver of this change, we looked closely at performative critique. I argued that there should at least be a possibility that this change would be radical. Furthermore, the interstitial conception of change was meant to respond to a few of the dilemmas in which the term "revolution" seems to be entangled once we reject both the idea that history is teleological, and the notion that actors have a Promethean ability to act without precedent.[1] This interstitial understanding of revolution was spelled out as a performative praxis theory of radical change. Its crucial mechanism was already defined in passing as metalepsis, without much discussion. I would like to conclude by establishing this term in more depth, because it promises to cut through the thicket of adjectives specifying my theory of change—interstitial, processual, performative, and radical. In that sense, I use the term "metalepsis" for purely rhetorical reasons, in that it is only supposed to solve a problem of presentation at this point.[2]

This evidently means that the term itself must be presented. I will start by discussing its meaning in ancient Greek, where it can be translated as "participation" and "exchange," and where it comes to describe the three loosely connected stylistic phenomena referred to as "metalepsis" in rhetoric.[3] Two of these are special forms of metonymy, while the third is a doubly encoded play on words.[4] Each of these stages offers an opportunity to revisit the motifs that have arisen so far, and to find a term for the dynamic shared by performative critique and paradigm shifts.

μετάληψις

Like many Greek words, μετάληψις ("metalepsis") is a compound. It combines the common prefix "meta-" with the noun form of the verb "lambano" (λάμβάνω). In its basic form, "meta" is a preposition meaning "in the midst of" or "among," always implying a group of similar elements. "Lambano" means "I take" or "I grasp," and becomes an abstract noun in "lepsis," shifting away from the physical movement of "grabbing" and toward the more abstract senses of "taking" (as in words such as "partaking" or "undertaking"). It can then be extended to denote "capture" and "confiscation," but also "acceptance."

"Metalepsis" therefore connects "being in the midst" with "taking away." It describes the action in which an object is taken from the middle of a group of (similar) objects. The process need not mean taking *away*; it might also suggest "taking part" and thus imply "enjoyment," or "enjoying together with others."

Alongside "taking out" and "taking part," "exchanging" also emerges as a further meaning of "metalepsis," which in fact becomes particularly salient. In Aristotle's *On Rhetoric*, the word appears in this sense and describes the "exchange of greater for less [evil]."[5] It is easy to imagine that when something is being taken from a lot of related things, a mix-up or mistake might occur: when we take one thing instead of another, this might mean ending up with something unexpected.

With the help of this understanding of metalepsis, we now have an excellent way to capture the situation that I had outlined for performative critique. It was defined in the broadest terms as an overlapping of structures. Structures, as I showed in the second part, can be described as aggregated practices. Aggregated practice forms structures because it accumulates resources and praxis-generating rules, but also because it serves as orientation for observing participants. These participants adjust their own praxis according to the available schemas. Depending on the weighting with which actors assemble practices to make rules, and allow them to become effective through repetition, the existing constellation of structures starts to be reconfigured.

Now, for performative critique to take place, a specific situation is necessary. The practices grouped as a structure have to overlap with another chain of practices, which may be much more transient and only apparent to a few participants. The first, generally recognizable and articulated structure can then be described as "contaminated." Practices are mixed in among its instances that may be similar enough to find a place there, but that can also be seen in another light, playing into an entirely different structure. In the third part, I discussed in detail how the repercussions of drag performance on the gender order, which Butler analyzes, are dependent on the fact that the praxis of drag first of all succeeds in appearing as an example of *femininity* (and not simply as a monstrosity or as a form of gender confined to a subculture). It can be slotted into the generally familiar "rule and resource set" (Giddens). However, this makes two things possible: Firstly, that when the supposedly familiar structure is accessed, something suddenly emerges as an anomaly that calls it into question, and that unsettles the criteria of the grouping in some ways. And secondly, connections can be made that would drastically refunction the structure in question. Because when it is the instance with an interstitial side that is chosen as the gateway for connecting practices, its schema can confirm itself through what has been articulated previously. No longer is the drag queen also female in some ways, but instead: "All gender is drag."

In the switch that takes place here, the "mistake" is certainly no coincidence—it is based on actual similarity. Not a "lapsus" (as in error-prone iterability), but *metalepsis*. Because the resources of the practices match one another sufficiently, because there really is some similarity, an interstitial structure can contaminate an articulated structure. But this means not only that it creates a slight variation of that structure, but that it creates the necessary conditions for a more radical maneuver, in which precisely *this* instance is taken as paradigmatic—meta*lepsis*.

LONG-DISTANCE METONYMY

Metalepsis has also been employed in a range of different ways as a rhetorical category. It is not one of the central established figures in rhetoric, but has taken on more than one different meaning. It seems to me that these can all be viewed as forms of a double or "roundabout" transfer, with three distinct variants, which I will present individually. The first two are complicated forms of metonymy, and only the third form once again captures the full interplay that I sketched out according to the Greek meaning of the word.

In contrast with simple metonymy, in which neighboring terms are exchanged, the first tropological definition of metalepsis does not describe a situation in which one phrase is replaced by another, but refers to the way in which this relationship is established in a longer chain of derivation. For instance, the English renaissance rhetorician Henry Peacham defines it as follows: "Metalepsis, when we goe by degrees to that which is shewed."[6] Because in this form metalepsis always goes through several such steps of transfer, bridging a large semantic distance, it

can also be described as "long-distance metonymy." A canonical example is
Vergil's use of "ears [of corn]" to represent years, which can only be decoded
through several intermediate steps (such as ears—corn—harvest—summers
—years).[7]

As a figure of rhetoric requiring us to insert intermediate steps, metalepsis in
this sense could, for instance, be projected onto the relationship between Hunt's
interpretation of revolution and Sewell's, as discussed earlier: we have to take a
"long-distance metonymic" view with Hunt and complete various intermediate
steps through the periphery in order to explain how the process of redefining
political culture took place, of which Sewell's storming of the Bastille is an
abridged version.

A trope of gradual transfer, metalepsis as long-distance metonymy is particularly suited to capturing the dynamic of gradual, interstitial processes of
transformation.

In an extremely allegorical manner, such a process is also expressed in Dinesen's story. Imprisoned in the tower of the château of Mauntfalcon, the servant
Marie-Marthe learns the skills that will make her a successful businesswoman
after she is freed. The gulf between a feudal tower room and a flourishing textile
shop is filled, through the transfer of long-distance metonymy, by an unbroken
chain of praxis. It is no coincidence that this example relates to the transition from
feudal to capitalist production. The emergence of capitalism is generally described
as the slow development of an economic system that gradually takes in broader
and broader social realms. For instance, Michael Mann has provided a sociohistorical description of this development as a process of interstitial emergence.[8]

The correspondence would therefore be in the fact that ears and years can be
seen as "the same thing" when we have gone through several expansions (ears—
corn—harvesting the corn—summer—year), along a continuous line of derivation. When it comes to "interstitial emergence," we could draw a similar line: the
skills that were already acquired under feudal rule, when released into an independent household, enable a simple business, which, if it flourishes, can lead to
manufacturing, to a factory, and to the global textile industry.

Long-distance metonymy does not feature the characteristic turning point.
Still, this more continuous dynamic—"when we goe by degrees"—is a crucial
complement to the metaleptic exchange described earlier. The metaleptic process
will seem different to the actors depending on the structures constraining them.
From an interstitial perspective, the transfer is not abrupt, but is a gradual shift
in context and an expansion. Subcollective constitution of power has to be added
to the situation of contaminated structures; one needs people involved who
already practice the formation of analogies from the starting point of interstitial

praxis. Margaret Masterman formulated the praxis-theoretical puzzle as to the origin of new orders as a puzzle of science theory: "How can I be using a theory which isn't there?"[9] The answer was that it is not necessary to have an entire theory in order to continue a praxis, but only to have a paradigm candidate: "Some trick, or embryonic technique, or picture, *and an insight that this is applicable in this field.*"[10] However, someone has to demonstrate this trick and that is, as I have emphasized, never just the drag queen alone, but always her affinity group too. Someone already has to be experienced in carrying out a gradual transfer to another context, by continuing an interstitial praxis, so that for someone else, something entirely unexpected can emerge.

CONFUSING CAUSE AND EFFECT

The second variant of metalepsis can also be read as metonymy along a roundabout path, namely, the description of an expression through its reason or its result. Melanchthon defines metalepsis in his tropology as taking place "where a name for something comes not from something similar, but from the cause or the effect."[11] Butler uses the term "metalepsis" in this sense several times in her work, in affirming that the formation of the subject, understood as subjection to interpellation, has a paradoxical structure in which the cause (the subjection of the subject) already assumes the effect (the subject).[12]

Anarchist and feminist conceptions of revolution can be characterized in this "Melanchthonian" sense as metaleptic. For they build on a reversal of the relationship between means and end in classic understandings of revolution. The revolution does not emerge—perhaps as a seizing of power in class struggle—between the present and the future, to bring about the better future, but instead, anticipating a better future in the interstices of the present becomes a mode of transformation in itself. In fact, even Marx assumed that the new must already be present before the revolution—"The organisation of the revolutionary elements as a class supposes the existence of all the productive forces which can be engendered in the bosom of the old society."[13] However, for him this does not result in a relationship of inversion, since the interdependence between these forces of production and other areas of society[14] means that they have to develop before the communist future arrives. The position proposed here is distinct from that, in that it dissolves the distinction between objective factors (such as the development of the forces of production) and subjective factors (the ability to act) and declares the latter to be equally the subject and the object of the revolution. This step need not lead in the direction of voluntarism if we name structural, material conditions for "metaleptic" moments of turnaround. In their way, Buber and Landauer already had a stronger sense of the conditional nature of revolutionary praxis—even if this praxis is ultimately understood to be dependent on itself, so that in their case a metaleptic symmetry ensues between causes and effects. Socialist praxis based on solidarity requires socialist praxis based on solidarity. What must be the effect of the revolution would have to precede it. And if it does not, then the dilemma would arise that Buber called "tragic," namely, that the means of the revolution bring about precisely the opposite of its aims. "Their tragedy is that as regards their *positive* goal they will always result in the exact opposite of what the most honest and passionate revolutionaries strive for, unless and until this [deep social reform] has so far taken shape *before* the revolution that the revolutionary act has only to wrest the space for it in which it can develop unimpeded."[15]

I have tried to show which distinctions in praxis theory allow us to envisage this figure without being held up by a paradox. The crucial steps consisted first of all in expanding the repertoire of practices that might be available, making use of the greatest possible heterogeneity. This added interstitial forms to the repertoire. It was then necessary to show that practices can be transferred in the first place, because it is possible to enter into their rules gradually by doing, seeing, and talking.

The precondition for the new must therefore not always already be the new itself and thus remain paradoxical, but can also be found in the old, which was so far not visible, or not visible at this point. Popular sovereignty may have been articulated by adopting monarchical rituals of victory, but this does not mean that it was not new. Instead, it makes newness a metaleptic figure: whenever it occurs, it is clear that it was already "actually" present "somewhere."

But in order not to fall prey to a form of voluntarism, as mentioned earlier, in which all the cards could always be shuffled again, I have tried to describe in terms of structural theory the paths along which practices repeat themselves. For only under very particular circumstances do they open up the possibility for such rearrangements, as we will see again now.

A MEDIOCRE JOKE

The third and most familiar version of metalepsis, however, is not metonymy but a special form of synonymy that often appears in wordplay, namely, "the replacement of a word with several meanings with a synonym matching a part of the meaning which does not relate to the given context."[16] This means that terms that are homonyms are replaced by a synonym that does not fit in the context in question. Quintilian identified metalepsis as a rhetorical figure in this sense, defining it as a transition from one trope to another—it leads us from one play on words to another that is necessary in order to understand the first. He illustrates this with a very convoluted example, but the pattern of the example consists in making fun of someone by first playing on their name along the lines of nominative determinism, and then replacing that with a more disparaging synonym, as if people were to mock the Marquise, hidden in her castle, with her middle name of Leonne (lioness), by calling her a "house cat." As this example might suggest, Quintilian came to the conclusion that metalepsis was not only a rare but also a rather inferior stylistic device, which was better avoided.

When it comes to the device of double transfer—or transfer from one trope to another—there are of course also more sophisticated examples. Marx, for instance, describes the arduous, grueling course of the proletarian revolutions of the nineteenth century as a process that advances "until a situation is created which makes all turning back impossible, and the conditions themselves cry out: *Hic Rhodus, hic salta! Here is the rose, here dance.*"[17]

Depending on how we count, we could tot up a threefold or fourfold metalepsis here. First of all, the whole formulation from "Hic Rhodus" to "here dance" is taken from the prologue to Hegel's *Philosophy of Right* (transfer 1).[18] Hegel took the saying from one of Aesop's fables (transfer 2) and translated it quite differently into German, not as "Here is Rhodes, jump here!" but as "here is the rose, dance here!" He reached this point metaleptically, by shifting Rhodus to rhodon (meaning "rose" in Greek—transfer 3) and then translating it as "rose" (transfer 4). In Aesop's own version, too, we only find ourselves in Rhodes in a figurative sense—the addressee is a show-off bragging about how far he jumped in a pentathlon in Rhodes, until a bystander challenges him to jump here and now (transfer 5). Here Hegel means to argue against those who wax lyrical about the future, arguing that we should see that which is "rational in itself" embodied in the existing state (transfer 6). On the one hand, Marx retains this perspective, insisting on the real conditions of building socialism, in contrast with utopian socialism (transfer 7), but he still turns the tables on Hegel in the sense that reason is not yet being realized here and now, but can only be realized through revolution across society (transfer 8).

Measured against this grand display of transfers, the basic form of Quintilian metalepsis is very simple: only a double transfer or the use of one trope in order to imply another.

To return from the rhetorical figure to defining how practices relate to each other, we can locate the process of "taking literally, but in reverse" in the refunctioning of a structure through ambivalent practices. A good example of this can be found in one of the central dynamics of the French Revolution itself. The abolition of privileges in the night of August 4 is regarded as the crucial moment that elevates the revolution to the level of a *social* transformation, and is generally attributed to the rural uprisings that were raging in summer 1789, fueled by a kind of mass panic about a supposed destruction of the harvest by the nobility. In his famous study of this "Great Fear," George Lefebvre analyzes the structural conditions of the events in question, demonstrating the central significance of the *baillages*, which were ironically convened by the king himself. In these local committees, the electors for the National Assembly were supposed to be decided in spring 1789. At the same time, however, the rural population was also asked to make lists of complaints. These *cahiers de doléance* represent one of the most important sources for historians of the revolution, although in fact what is especially striking is their restraint and the absence of more radical demands. The revolutionary consequences of the *baillages* are rooted above all in the process by which they were drawn up, which in turn is directly connected with the wave of dissent that was then ultimately to lead to many demands being met—through the National Assembly, by that point.[19] For once the farmers were assembled, the conditions were created for violent uprisings against feudal levies, which had flared up repeatedly in the past. The unrest that drew such attention in summer 1789 in Paris thus mainly began already in the spring. Lefebvre uses reports from royal officials to show that there was a very specific shift in the *baillages* in many places. For the farmers assumed that simply by writing down certain demands, they had secured agreement with their cause. The escalating violence during the Great Fear is then already a reaction, as they felt they had been cheated out of something they had been promised. For instance, one report is as follows: "'What is really tiresome,' wrote Desmé de Dubuisson, lieutenant-general of Saumur *baillage* during the elections, 'is that these assemblies believed themselves invested with some sovereign authority and that when they came to an end, the peasants went home with the idea that henceforward they were free from tithes, hunting prohibition and the payment of feudal dues.'"[20]

An assembly orchestrated by the royal administration can therefore be "contaminated" by a series of rebellious gatherings, and a mere survey of opinions can be turned into a transfer of sovereignty. If such metaleptic transfers then occur in many places at the same time, as they did in summer 1789, and build on one another as a reinforcing model, that can culminate in a consolidation of the structural turnaround, and we can be faced not only with a successful example of performative critique, but with a paradigm shift.

But to return to the fictional story of revolution in Dinesen's tale, we can find another possible point of transformation there, too—though this is not an actual point of culmination, but a metaleptic moment, a context from which a change in constellations can be projected.

We already referred to two different patterns of interpretation for the process of change, which Dinesen herself puts in the mouths of her characters (and precisely the woodenness of that demonstrates the fact that these are collective perspectives and not individual viewpoints). Samson presents the story as an active struggle between two political groups, and sees the execution of the Marquise, who seems to be the last of her kind, as a sort of climax. In Marie-Marthe's narrative, the much more significant point is the failure of the Marquise's marriage policy when her daughter runs away. What happens after that seems to be decided less by the "news from Paris" than by the financial independence of the household that defects from the chateau. This is also shown by the fact that the Marquise herself, from her quite different standpoint, cannot avoid paying attention to the new constellation. She reserves the right to dismiss the events altogether as "nonsense." Nevertheless, the changed alignments gradually force her, if not to give up this interpretation—for nothing can force her to do *that*—then at least to see the greatest possible narrowing of the space within which she can act in an intelligible manner, based on the assumption that her praxis will be recognized according to the old anchor practices. Marie-Marthe reports that the Marquise answered the question of whether it wasn't too hard for her to carry water for herself by saying that she would always see it as an honor to serve a Peronnet. It is only in her conduct toward herself that she can continue feudal praxis undisturbed. Although this means that she does not need to agree in any way with the interpretation of her executioner, even from her perspective it is no longer possible to deny that "something" has happened. Regardless of which categories she would use to interpret what has taken place, and given the possibility that she is free to refuse any acknowledgment whatsoever—perhaps the two petitioners want to offer a merciful validation of this option—from the praxis-theoretical point of view of the observer, we could say in turn that the old anchor praxis of feudal obedience has itself become an interstitial structure. Angélique's "fit of madness," on the other hand, has now become the ordinary way to choose a partner. Somewhere in the course of this process of transformation, a prison was also stormed—and it begins to be clear that it is only through its intersections with the emancipation from many other imprisonments that this movement grows into a revolution. Retrospectively, we can therefore make use of the criterion of the replacement of anchor practices to identify successful change.

Meanwhile, real undecidability emerges in the social realm in the moments where, with a new paradigm, the possibility for radically changed praxis presents itself, but it is unclear whether this will be picked up and continued. Dinesen's story can be read in a third way as a reversible image that is entirely open. For if we do not look at the axis of class struggle, or the struggle between the estates, but at the patriarchal axis, different groupings emerge. In terms of their attitude to Jocelynde, the Marquise and the executioner fall into exactly the same pattern.[21] When it comes to this fundamental structure, there is no change dividing them, let alone a paradigm shift. However, Jocelynde-Jeanne's metaleptic adoption of her grandmother's imperious tone, when addressing the man who wishes to free her from the matchmaking plans of that grandmother, could now perhaps embody precisely that "initial practical trick-which-works-sufficiently-for-the-choice-of-it-to-embody-a-potential-insight," which represents the first manifestation of a new paradigm—depending on what happens next. Just as in the storming of the Bastille, monarchical rituals led to the rebels shifting into practices of sovereignty, here the voice of the tyrannical grandmother not only orchestrates her own execution but also, in the same move, brings the competing matchmaker into a situation that topples his division between friends and enemies of the Republic: he will have to bow to the Marquise. Where he thought he had decided that the future of Jocelynde-Jeanne would be at the side of a sansculottes, she herself compromises precisely the status of the most clear-cut sansculottes, namely, Samson himself. In these complicated transfers, however, something is revealed that would have been unthinkable from within the patriarchal structures both before and after the revolution: that the young woman leaves behind the power of ancestors and executioners equally, that she can live together with her older friend autonomously and in solidarity, and that she even grants a certain amount of recognition to the needs of her enemies.

Conclusion

"The Difficulties of the Plains" and the Revolutionary Tradition

The difficulties of the mountains lie behind us
Before us lie the difficulties of the plains.

—Bertolt Brecht, "A Realization"

Now that radical social change has been defined as interstitial and metaleptic, how are we to imagine a revolution? A social theory of transformation in general does not yet define which more specific form should be called a "revolution." However, we can already begin to trace how the usual ways of understanding revolution are refigured in my approach to transformation theory.

Against the commonplace understanding of revolution based on the phenomenology of the French Revolution, my approach emphasizes duration. Revolutions are long processes. Even intense moments of culmination gain their effectiveness from practices that are laboriously rehearsed over time, and from the coming together of structures that are anchored in specific ways. The uproar of the barricades is not only set against these lengthy efforts but also contrasted with Landauer's "noiselessness": Revolutionary praxis as labor in the interstices, as a reproduction of transient alternative praxis, as a virtuoso transfer of resources into other patterns of action. This draws attention to other settings for radical change, such as those that we visited in our literary examples: prison cells, conspiratorial knitting circles, affinity groups, a hangman's dining room.

In the Marxist view of revolution, the drawn-out, quiet development of the productive forces and the step-by-step association between workers certainly correspond with this concept of processuality, contrasted here with the paradigm of the event. However, the metaleptic theory of revolution regards this processuality as being far less inexorable than classic dialectical theory would have it. Both the movement and the direction of history are uncoupled from all grand fundamental tendencies, and instead depend on the precarious course taken by practices, as they are reproduced and transferred. The interstitial dynamization of the social, arising from the in-between spaces, also liberates revolutions from the hyperbolic notion of a single, central contradiction. Changes in constellation can take place not only gradually but also in a kaleidoscopic manner, through the regrouping of diverse points of intersection.

Many anarchist perspectives also argue for this decentralizing approach, often proposing that revolutions are local processes anticipating the future. However, while performative praxis theory also insists on rehearsal, it rejects the voluntarist tendencies accompanying this idea of prefiguration. "The new" must not only be constructed as something that was long present in the interstices—it also has to push through against the existing situation. This ability to push through is a question not only of power relations but also of structural circumstances. Has the course been set in such a way that we can articulate the disruptive anomalies, so that they themselves become the basis for re-structuring? The shape of change is decided not only by the form of these promising exceptions but also by the conjuncture of the structures in which they occur.

Feminist theory has often reflected on its own entanglement in existing power relations, observing how we long for new beginnings, and how they persist in eluding us. This precludes false analogies between revolution and territorial war. In revolutions, it is not one side that conquers and subjugates another—and this is not only because continuing subjugation would contradict revolutionary ideals. Instead, immense efforts are made to rehearse practices on what seems to be the "side of failure," which can become a new basis. When we fight in a revolution, this is different from fighting a war: the subject and the object of the change are one and the same. The women's movement did not ultimately aim to eliminate opponents, but to change the constellation so that the same victimizations did not have to be repeated all over again. With the motif of performative paradigm shift, this is not seen as an exception, but is elevated to form a revolutionary rule.

The understanding of transformation suggested in *Praxis and Revolution* therefore has repercussions for the term "revolution," as formulated on the basis of other social theories. However, this still does not tell us how to gain an understanding of revolution entirely on the basis of the present theory—that is, within the framework of metalepsis.

Should we simply describe all processes of radical change as revolutions? In everyday usage, the term is often overstretched in this way. Since the term "revolution" was originally shaped by factual observations about the movements of the stars, we could name all radical change in this way—or at least, all radical change in the social realm. After all, there are also conservative, even fascist revolutions.

However, this would force the term to become uncoupled from the practical contexts in which it is used, and would no longer correspond with the assumptions of metaleptic praxis theory. If we say "revolution," we usually mean more than just any radical change. We mean something pointing toward the future; we mean something that is actively being pushed forward, at least by someone; we mean that there is at least a hope that things will not only change, but improve; we mean that certain paradigmatic instances such as the French Revolution resonate in this naming. All these aspects should take effect here, in defining revolution more precisely. However, they do not function as independent characteristics, but are taken up from previous practices. For even the term "revolution" itself cannot be defined other than "metaleptically," from a specific, densely woven context. And this definition is visible in the way in which traditions are grouped and structured. In abstract terms, this criterion seems tautological: revolutions, we would then claim, are those instances of radical social change that are anchored in the revolutionary tradition. Revolutions must be composed in such a way that we can recognize moments in them that are already regarded as revolutionary. They have to feed on practices anchored in practices that we—that is, a specifically situated subcollective that is nevertheless able to transfer its practices further—would recognize as revolutionary based on our own praxis.

Anchoring was described in more detail in the first part of this book as a relationship of a series of practices to a fundamental "anchor praxis." This relationship is one not of identity, but of mimetic constitution. This means that when the rules of the anchor practice continue to be repeated in the instances that are anchored in it, we can see an approximation in terms of shape, a similarity. This relationship does not form a purely coincidental proximity, but decides what is going on in the praxis being approximated—it is constitutive for the meaning of that praxis. Continuing the legacy of the French Revolution in the broadly Hegelian fashion of normative reconstruction rests on an anchoring in the praxis-evaluating rules, which are progressively extended. All sociality is to be measured against the ideals of liberty, equality, and fraternity. Other interpretations, which identify the French Revolution as the original moment of "the political," tend instead to raise the praxis-generating rules into a general characteristic. Everything revolutionary must perpetuate the know-how that allows us to generate constitutive power. Meanwhile, understandings of revolution focused on events seem to latch onto the schema, that is, the rule defining the French Revolution as a practice, and to elevate this to a criterion: something needs to be stormed.

My approach brings all three facets of practical normativity equally into play. Through this, we gain a new level of specificity, while the single point of reference recedes into a broader spectrum of practices. Practices are revolutionary if they can be measured against revolutionary norms, if they embody revolutionary competence, and if they can be defined as moments of revolution. The broadening of the points of reference, as well as the fact that the third criterion ("if they can be defined as moments of revolution") is much less narrow than it would be in a one-sided schema-oriented event-based model, has been shown in detail in the course of this book. If radical social change takes place interstitially and metaleptically, then it is not only the intense moments of culmination but also the lengthy processes that are transformative—or, if all other criteria are met, revolutionary. Thus, we leave behind the fixation on the climactic moment in the term "revolution." The important part is still ahead of us: "The difficulties of the plains."

The four stages of my argumentation, from praxis, to structure, to performativity and paradigm, were interwoven with the fictional presentation of very concrete practices. With an exception that is metaleptically significant, they were all situated in the context of the French Revolution—more than that, they proved to be anchored in it. Maria's ménage referred quite explicitly to the praxis-evaluating rules of the French Revolution. Not only did Maria, Jemima, and Darnford aim to fight for liberty from patriarchal control and authority, they also pursued the project of an egalitarian household without financial dependency and exploitation. Finally, fraternity was to serve as a template to emancipate love relationships from the model of marriage, and refunction them as an institution that would lead to a fraternal world. The specific know-how revealed in the figure of the knitter, who unwaveringly fixed her gaze on the murderous Marquis, turned out not to be an isolated moment of resistance when we looked at it more closely, but was in fact an instance of a praxis anticipating structures that would ultimately make it possible to call the Marquis's peers to account. And in the negotiation between the Jacobin executioner and the two citizens who came to see him, the very form of the revolution was at stake. Was it to be sealed by the extermination of its last opponent, or by the realization that the places that were once the centers of power had long been sidelined by new forms of relation?

Since these three literary scenarios of revolution are composed in concrete terms, none of them lacks the multidimensionality and materiality of the practical, in spite of the different emphasis in each. They are concrete replications of a paradigm that only begins to be visible through them. But as a paradigm in Masterman's sense, the point where generalization begins is also not an abstract one. The criteria for revolutions are to be established not in an ever-thinner definition, but in a continuing process in which practices are taken up and aggregated. Paradigms are formed, here too, in a process of double concretion, in which the starting points remain malleable. They remain malleable not only when they are filled with practices but also as they are shaped by grouping and by forming connections.

The examples, arranged in a series like this, also relate to one another instructively, complementing and correcting one another. The knitters demonstrate what Jemima tries repeatedly to show her romantic comrades at the institution: existing structures are not just rigid, but are maintained by force. The knitters concentrate on taking over the law courts; Maria is herself convicted. The moment in which the Reign of Terror takes on a life of its own, which seems of secondary importance to the knitters, measured against the fury built up over the generations, against rape and exploitation, is up for debate when we come to the "proud lady." Which gestures can we find to ensure that the violence of the past is not turned back against the perpetrators, but left behind? The women propose a puzzling mitigation of the punishment, which at least lets them try to prevent revolutionary jurisdiction from being enforced all too automatically. These two patriots could have come straight out of Maria's plans. They succeeded in founding a financially independent female household that broke the bounds of social status. They seem to have found a stable form for some of the solidarity that culminated for a short time in the ménage before disintegrating, succumbing in various ways to patriarchal and bourgeois habits.

Could the libertine Darnford have looked to M. Defarge in order to recognize that he should have reliably supported Maria, as a "frightfully grand woman"? Could Maria have learned from Marta that the axioms of bourgeois sexual morality could be turned upside down entirely, and that she should see Jemima not as a fallen woman but as a precursor of her own freedom, too? No. Given how these characters are written, that is precisely what they could not have done. Still, it is telling that we wish they could have done it—and that this wish crystallizes into a particular judgment, gained through interstitial reconstruction. We could describe this judgment, in Hannah Arendt's sense, as emerging when we consult as many different positions as possible. Sending our imagination "on its travels" in this way, as Arendt formulates it along with Kant, precisely does not mean that we really know what the figures we consult are feeling. But it is the best means of visualizing the fact that the world or the revolution can be portrayed from the point of view of the asylum, the Faubourg Saint-Antoine, or the dining room of the executioner. If this does not merely provide an arbitrary panorama of perspectives, this is because Arendt, in her theory of judgment, also theorizes our anchoring in our own context. When we reconstruct other perspectives, we begin from particular terms. To these terms, we add things that seem to exemplify particular judgments. Arendt also envisages this exemplary status in terms of figures, as when she identifies bravery with Achilles.[1] Like Masterman, however, she sees such paradigms as being malleable. The definition of bravery can change in the replication of the paradigm—for example, if we see it as being better embodied by the rather confused Marta, when she occupies a traffic island. The transfer is therefore not a leveling adoption of the world through the initial perspective: As we discover the world, we also break out of our perspective. Just as metalepsis as a rhetorical device goes through two forms of wordplay to the point of solution, the normative contextualism proposed here allows us to transcend the context through a doubling in the immanent movement. The judgment remains anchored in its own initial context. But as the reference material is decoded, measured, and rehearsed from there, groupings emerge against which the original context can change its own criteria.

Radical social change is a process of transformation, in the course of which anchor practices are exchanged. Where the practices that were once interstitial and that are later paradigmatic can be identified as being anchored in the norms that define, evaluate, and generate revolutionary praxis, a revolution is taking place. In order for revolutions to be defined as such, they cannot be measured by whether it really got better afterward—still, this question clearly has to be asked of them continually. Nevertheless, in terms of the definition, the crucial point is merely that revolutions are anchored in practices aiming for improvement. When the ménage makes plans to move to France, when the knitters keep a record of privileged wrongdoers, when the protesters organize die-ins and the women rebel against matchmaking—all of them place their hopes in the idea that things will get better.

However, as discussed in the introduction, the aim of this book was not to establish a normative basis for social change, but to develop a notion of revolution that could tackle the dilemmas of outbreak, transition, and stabilization.

The question of how revolutions break out seemed to be made more difficult by ideological blindness, rigid routines, and subjectivation in conformity with domination. In an interstitial model, this question does not relate to a particular point in time. Instead, it is necessary to recognize anomalies and take up and continue those that lead beyond the existing circumstances with a revolutionary index. While orthodox Marxist theories of revolution assume that in a highly capitalist society everything is already prepared for the transition to a rational communist mode of production—which is what raises the question of why revolution still does not break out—praxis theory tends toward skepticism. As Landauer would say, not much has yet been done for the revolution. Revolutionary praxis still has to be rehearsed and to gain in recognition. Rather than an anomaly, it has to prove to be a "trick that works." The focus on practices also helps in the search for revolutionary starting points—as sparse as these may be on the plains—ensuring that we do not simply declare certain groups automatically to be an avant-garde, while others are dismissed. If the notion of praxis means that the revolutionary ability to act becomes itself the subject and the object of revolution, it is certainly possible that the reversible figures of pro- and counterrevolutionary constellations crisscross the boundaries of classes, groups, milieus, and individuals. Beginning, then, would mean decoding revolutionary practices everywhere, continuing them, and fighting to be able to spread them further. It would at the same time mean recognizing that we are not at the beginning, but that we've actually been working in the interstices to bring about a transition that was already an aim for the revolutionary enthusiasts of the eighteenth century, the inhabitants of Saint-Antoine, ACT UP, and petitioners pleading with executioners, each in their own way.

The crucial paradox of the transition—namely, that the new would already have to be there to be possible at all—is solved with the figure of double transfer in metalepsis. Yes, it was already there, but it was not yet intelligible. Yes, it is new—but only as a paradigm, not as a praxis. However, this only untangles a theoretical contradiction and does not say much about how the transition should actually be carried out. Metalepsis sticks to formal terms in describing its conditions for success: structures must exist that can be contaminated by interstitial practices, in order to lead to a crisis in the existing anchoring basis. The prevailing conditions must further the replication of previously unintelligible praxis, letting it become a new paradigm. Whether it is the organization of the means of production that is being refunctioned here and newly established or the ecosystem of the planet, the apparatus of a political party or a spontaneous meeting of councils,[2] ways of relating to one another or to ourselves, that is not explained by the model—though it does give us a clue that we should not try to answer this question without looking in detail at the existing arrangements and anchorings of praxis. Performative theory of praxis reminds us that in such analyses, we should concentrate particularly on anomalies and on tendencies toward erosion and aggregation that are intensified by those anomalies. Paying attention to contradictions, as we have learned from dialectics, does not become obsolete. However, the perception of contradictions is itself mediated interstitially. It requires specific practices that allow us in the first place to see and feel societal structures in the mode of an untenable crisis. Thus, the epistemological function of interstitial praxis is that it forms a kind of platform for spotting contradictions. As we have seen, this means first of all that specific practices convey alternative experiences that are the starting point from which contradictions in existing circumstances can be articulated—as, for instance, when Maria reaches the decision that in spite of its bigoted insistence on morality, bourgeois marriage is ultimately an exploitative relationship resembling enforced prostitution. She can only make this diagnosis once she is in a form of relationship defined by egalitarian and romantic fraternity. Secondly, however, interstitial praxis can also become a platform for spotting contradictions in the sense that it underpins the militant praxis that fuels antagonisms within society. M. Defarge's words of encouragement from the background on that evening in the proto-Jacobin quarter are a good example of this—in the image of interstitial change, reproductive work in the revolutionary interstices is always already a part of the actual transition.

The dilemma of stabilization, in a metaleptic, processual conception, is a question of how revolutionary practices sink in and spread. Where this succeeds, the same premise that presented an obstacle at the beginning—the inertia of practice—benefits the model. Once patterns of praxis become an anchor for a changed constellation of structures, they can no longer change so easily. The fact that structures can be reanchored, that the vehicles for transformation are always the existing, refunctioned structures, has a protective function. Many rules and much material can remain in the same place, while a few aspects change in the way that practices are grouped, taken up, and continued—and yet, afterward everything is different.

Thus, an interstitial and metaleptic position is undoubtedly concerned with "winning," with actually reaching a qualitatively different state of affairs after the revolution. It does not merely want to stage an intervention, nor does it perpetuate the pathos of revolt and declare the revolution to be an end in itself, something that Bini Adamczak criticizes as "the revolution fetish."[3] At the same time, it can never aim to win "across the board," without anything being left over.[4] This is not because of abstract reservations toward the violence that might be inherent in the universal, but because of the principles on which the metaleptic position is constructed. If normativity always remains tied to certain anchor practices, paradigms have a point where they become overstretched, and remain reliant on disparities. But the interstices are also still needed for other reasons, because this is the only way of ensuring that further change and improvement are impossible—and in fact the only way of enabling the distanced perspective from which the new paradigm can prove itself to be altogether justified.

Even the old practices, the residue of the ancien régime, need not only act as counterrevolutionary forces. When they become fluid, or when they solidify in a new way after being reanchored, their quality can change too. The anomaly that they represent in relation to the new paradigm need not necessarily copy the old antagonism. With its skepticism on the question of whether "French principles" were desirable in all realms of life,[5] the patriarchal court that wrongly convicted Maria would be a good counterpoint alongside the victorious Jacobin tribunals, which were all too automatic in meting out punishment. And if not perhaps the Marquis himself, then at least the festivities of the masked ball could represent a more joyful postrevolutionary form of sociability than that which is evidently envisaged by Samson, who makes no distinction between kissing and branding. In the Marta video, the camera work itself already makes the uniformed police who march against the demonstrators seem rather like a harmless, homosocial fetish club—and perhaps we would trust them more than Marta to sort out the traffic laws. The Marquise, finally, who maintains her vanished form of life alone in a corner of her castle with iron discipline, offers a good example of "degrowth"—if anyone wants to keep hold of antiegalitarian privileges, then that is the way to do it.

Recognizing this does not mean that we cannot fight against all of them as tyrannical rulers, as long as they act as such. After all, apart from conceptualizing the forces preventing change, this is the other theoretical advantage of praxis theory. Not only does it not identify any specific group as the revolutionary subject; it instead checks the paradigm-possibilities of any praxis that seems strange. But it does more: it does not declare anyone to be lost to the revolution because of their connection to a certain group, nor does it see anyone as an archenemy. It is not about individual people. It is particular practices that must end, and links between practices that must be broken. Praxis is the realm where the subject and the object of revolution coincide—that which must be changed, and that which makes change happen.

Notes

PREFACE TO THE AMERICAN EDITION

1. For a theorization of "messiness," see Katrin Pahl, *Sex Changes with Kleist* (Evanson, IL: Northwestern University Press, 2019), 23–35.

2. Julia Lurie, "They Built a Utopian Sanctuary in a Minneapolis Hotel. Then They Got Evicted," *Mother Jones*, June 12, 2020, www.motherjones.com/crime-justice/2020/06/minneapolis-sheraton-george-floyd-protests/.

3. Avi Lewis and Opal Tometi, *A Message from the Future II: The Years of Repair*, Canada, 2020, www.youtube.com/watch?v=2m8YACFJlMg.

4. As will have become obvious by now, much as my book aims to peripheralize the French Revolution, it does nothing to recenter theorizing around Haiti. For a decolonial political theory based on the Haitian Revolution, see Jeanette Ehrmann, *Tropen der Revolution: Die Haitianische Revolution und die Dekolonisierung des Politischen* (Berlin: Suhrkamp, 2021).

5. Audre Lorde, *Sister Outsider* (Berkeley: Crossing, 1984), 140.

6. Kehinde Andrews, *Back to Black: Retelling Black Radicalism for the 21st Century* (London: Zed, 2018), xxvii.

7. Alexis P. Gumbs, China Martens, and Mai'a Williams, *Revolutionary Mothering* (Oakland: PM, 2016), 29, 22.

8. adrienne maree brown, *Emergent Strategy: Shaping Change, Changing Worlds* (Chico: AK, 2017), 116.

9. Vicky Osterweil, *In Defense of Looting: A Riotous History of Uncivil Action* (New York: Bold Type, 2020), 13–14.

10. Eva von Redecker, *Revolution für das Leben: Philosophie der neuen Protestformen* (Frankfurt: Fischer, 2020).

11. I offer an account of alt right and fascist tendencies in Eva von Redecker, "Ownership's Shadow: Neoauthoritarianism as Defense of Phantom Possession," *Critical Times* 3, no. 1 (2020): 33–67.

INTRODUCTION

1. Karl Griewank, *Der neuzeitliche Revolutionsbegriff: Entstehung und Entwicklung* (Frankfurt: Europ. Verl.-Anstalt, 1969), 144.

2. Charles Tilly, *The Contentious French: Four Centuries of Popular Struggle* (Cambridge, MA: Harvard University Press, 1986).

3. William H. Sewell Jr., "Historical Events as Transformations of Structures: Inventing Revolution at the Bastille," *Theory and Society* 25, no. 6 (1996): 841–881.

4. Lynn Hunt, "The Rhetorics of Revolution in France," *History Workshop* 15 (1983): 78–95.

5. Hannah Arendt, *The Life of the Mind* (New York: Harcourt Brace, 1981), 207; Karl Marx, "The Eighteenth Brumaire of Louis Bonaparte" (1852), in *Later Political Writings*, ed. Terell Carver (Cambridge: Cambridge University Press, 1996), 31–127, 32.

6. See Jon Elster, *Making Sense of Marx* (Cambridge: Cambridge University Press, 1985), 428ff.

7. Karl Marx, "A Contribution to the Critique of Hegel's Philosophy of Right. Introduction" (1843–1844), in *Early Writings* (London: Penguin, 1996), 243–257, 252; Rahel Jaeggi, *Critique of Forms of Life* (Cambridge, MA: Harvard University Press, 2019), 42.

8. See Rahel Jaeggi, "Crisis, Contradiction, and the Task of a Critical Theory," in *Feminism, Capitalism, and Critique: Essays in Honor of Nancy Fraser*, ed. B. Bargu and C. Bottici (Basingstoke, UK: Palgrave Macmillan, 2017), 209–224.

9. Theda Skocpol, *States and Social Revolutions* (Cambridge: Cambridge University Press, 1979); Alfred Cobban, *The Social Interpretation of the French Revolution* (1964; Cambridge: Cambridge University Press, 1999).

10. See Eric J. Hobsbawm, *The Age of Revolution: Europe, 1789–1848* (London: Weidenfeldt and Nicolson, 1962).

11. See Hobsbawm, *The Age of Revolution*.

12. See Raymond Geuss, "Dialectics and the Revolutionary Impulse," in *The Cambridge Companion to Critical Theory*, ed. F. Rush (Cambridge: Cambridge University Press, 2006), 103–138.

13. See Bini Adamczak, *Yesterday's Tomorrow: On the Loneliness of Communist Specters and the Reconstruction of the Future* (Cambridge, MA: MIT Press, 2021).

14. See Edmund Burke, *Reflections on the Revolution in France* (1790; Middlesex, UK: Penguin, 1982); Friedrich von Gentz, *The Origin and Principles of the American Revolution, Compared with the Origin and Principles of the French Revolution* (1800; Indianapolis: Liberty Fund, 2010).

15. Rosa Luxemburg, "Organizational Questions of the Russian Social Democracy" (1904), in *The Rosa Luxemburg Reader*, ed. Kevin Hudin and Kevin B. Anderson (New York: Monthly Review Press, 1971), 248–264, 264.

16. Martin Buber, *Paths in Utopia* (1949; Syracuse: Syracuse University Press, 1996), 44, emphasis in original.

17. Alain Badiou, *The Communist Hypothesis* (London: Verso, 2015); Slavoj Žižek, "Afterword: Lenin's Choice," in *Revolution at the Gates* (London: Verso, 2002), 165–336.

18. Axel Honneth, *The Idea of Socialism: Towards a Renewal* (New York: John Wiley and Sons, 2016).

19. Axel Honneth, "Rejoinder," *Critical Horizons* 16, no. 2 (2015): 204–226.

20. Geuss, "Dialectics and the Revolutionary Impulse," 136.

21. Wendy Brown, "Feminism Unbound," in *Edgework* (New Jersey: Princeton University Press, 2005), 115; see also Wendy Brown, "Resisting Left Melancholy," *Boundary 2* 26, no. 3 (1999): 19–27.

22. Brown, "Feminism Unbound," 114.

23. Wendy Brown et al., "Redoing the Demos? An Interview with Wendy Brown," *Theory, Culture, and Society*, 2017, www.theoryculturesociety.org/interview-wendy-brown/.

24. Hannah Arendt, *On Revolution* (1963; London: Penguin, 1990), 232.

25. Judith Mohrmann, *Affekt und Revolution: Politisches Handeln nach Arendt und Kant* (Frankfurt: Campus, 2015).

26. Walter Benjamin, *Selected Writings*, vol. 4, ed. Howard Eiland and Michael W. Jennings (Cambridge, MA: Harvard University Press, 2006), 402.

27. Hauke Brunkhorst, *Critical Theory of Legal Revolutions: Evolutionary Perspectives* (London: Bloomsbury, 2014).

28. Christoph Menke, *Critique of Rights* (Cambridge: Polity, 2020), 226.

29. René Char, *Feuillets d'Hypnos* (Paris: Gallimard, 1946), 8.

30. Hannah Arendt, "Walter Benjamin," in *Men in Dark Times* (1955; New York: Harcourt Brace, 1983), 205–206.

31. Frances Beal, "Double Jeopardy: To Be Black and Female," in *Black Women's Manifesto*, ed. G. Lynch (New York: Third World Women's Alliance, 1969), 32.

32. Alexis P. Gumbs, China Martens, and Mai'a Williams, *Revolutionary Mothering* (Oakland: PM, 2016).

33. Cited according to Ilse Lenz, ed., *Die neue Frauenbewegung in Deutschland: Abschied vom kleinen Unterschied: Eine Quellensammlung* (Wiesbaden: VS, 2008), 61–62 (quotation trans. LD, no capitals in original).

34. Daniel Loick, "21 Theses on the Politics of Forms of Life," *Theory and Event* 20, no. 3 (2017): 788–803.

35. Juliet Mitchell, "Women: The Longest Revolution," *New Left Review* 1, no. 40 (1966): 11–37.

36. Paolo Virno, *Exodus* (Vienna: Turia + Kant, 2002); John Holloway, *Crack Capitalism* (London: Pluto, 2010).

37. Stefano Harney and Fred Moten, *The Undercommons: Fugitive Planning and Black Study* (Wivenhoe: Minor Compositions, 2013).

38. Uri Gordon, *Anarchy Alive* (London: Pluto, 2013).

39. Iwona Janicka, *Theorizing Contemporary Anarchism: Solidarity, Mimesis and Radical Social Change* (London: Bloomsbury, 2017).

40. José Muñoz, *Cruising Utopia: The Then and There of Queer Futurity* (New York: NYU Press, 2009); Jack Halberstam, *In a Queer Time and Place: Transgender Bodies, Subcultural Lives* (New York: NYU Press, 2005).

41. Isabell Lorey, *Figuren des Immunen: Elemente einer politischen Theorie* (Berlin: diaphanes, 2011).

42. Thomas S. Kuhn, *The Structure of Scientific Revolutions* (1962; Chicago: University of Chicago Press, 2012); Judith Butler, *Gender Trouble: Feminism and the Subversion of Identity* (1990; New York: Routledge, 1999).

43. Margaret Masterman, "The Nature of a Paradigm," in *Criticism and the Growth of Knowledge*, ed. I. Lakatos and A. Musgrave (Cambridge: Cambridge University Press, 1965), 231–378.

44. Marx, "Brumaire," 115.

45. Rahel Jaeggi, *Fortschritt und Regression* (Berlin: Suhrkamp, 2020).

46. Amy Allen, *The End of Progress: Decolonizing the Normative Foundations of Critical Theory* (New York: Columbia University Press, 2016).

47. See Linda M. G. Zerilli, *A Democratic Theory of Judgment* (Chicago: University of Chicago Press, 2016); and Eva von Redecker, *Gravitation zum Guten: Hannah Arendts Moralphilosophie* (Berlin: Lukas, 2013).

PART I. MARIA'S *MÉNAGE*

1. Mary Wollstonecraft, *Mary* and *The Wrongs of Woman* (1798; Oxford: Oxford University Press, 2009).

2. Mary Wollstonecraft, "A Vindication of the Rights of Women," in *A Vindication of the Rights of Men* and *A Vindication of the Rights of Women* (1792; Cambridge: Cambridge University Press, 1995), 65–303.

3. Wollstonecraft, *Mary* and *The Wrongs of Woman*, 108.

4. Michel Foucault, "Of Other Spaces" (1984), *Diacritics* 16 (1986): 24. Foucault's text on heterotopias dates back to the manuscript of a lecture from 1967 and was only published shortly before his death in 1984, in unedited form, in the French journal *Architecture-Mouvement-Continuité*.

5. The genre of the "Jacobin novel" refers to fiction written between 1780 and 1805 by radical British authors, in which the ideals of the French Revolution are defended. The term was coined by the literary critic Gary Kelly; the paradigmatic example of the style is William Godwin's three-volume work *Things as They Are; or, The Adventures of Caleb Williams*. See Gary Kelly, *The English Jacobin Novel* (Oxford: Clarendon, 1976).

6. This is also notable insofar as a particular image of feminist history often gives the impression that the trailblazers of the first wave were liberal reformers who were aiming to secure guarantees of rights from the state, while it was only the radical feminists of the second wave who set about envisioning the revolutionary restructuring of everyday practices and forms of relationship: see, e.g., Germaine Greer, *The Female Eunuch* (London: Paladin, 1970), 3. Victoria Browne endeavors to counter this by proposing a concept of "nonlinear" feminist historiography; Victoria Browne, *Feminism, Time, and Nonlinear History* (London: Palgrave Macmillan, 2014).

7. Wollstonecraft, *Mary* and *The Wrongs of Woman*, 137.

8. Lucian Hölscher, "Utopie," in *Geschichtliche Grundbegriffe: Historisches Lexikon zur politisch-sozialen Sprache in Deutschland*, ed. R. Koselleck (Stuttgart: Klett-Cotta, 1990), 768–769.

9. Michel Foucault, *The History of Sexuality*, vol. 1, *The Will to Knowledge* (1976; Harmondsworth, UK: Penguin, 1990), 92.

10. Foucault, 95–96.

11. Wollstonecraft, *Mary* and *The Wrongs of Woman*, 176.

12. Despite the implications of my interpretation here, it would in fact be possible to read this as a "happy ending," at least on the individual level, since Maria then vomits, which could mean that she does not die of the laudanum.

13. Wollstonecraft, *Mary* and *The Wrongs of Woman*, 103.

14. For a detailed analysis of the rhetorical use of analogies by Wollstonecraft and her contemporaries, see Penelope Deutscher, "Analogy of Analogy: Animals and Slaves in Mary Wollstonecraft's Defense of Women's Rights," in *Reproduction, Race and Gender in Philosophy and the Early Life Sciences*, ed. S. Lettow (Albany: SUNY Press, 2014), 187–215. On Wollstonecraft's abolitionist perspective, see Moira Ferguson, "Mary Wollstonecraft and the Problematic of Slavery," *Feminist Review* 42 (1992): 82–102.

15. Foucault, "Of Other Spaces," 25.

16. Michel Foucault, *Discipline and Punish: The Birth of the Prison* (1975; New York: Vintage, 1995). In a more succinct and absolute form, the argument that closed institutions—in this case, homes for girls—show the "true face" of society can also be found in Ulrike Meinhof's preface to her play *Bambule*: Ulrike Meinhof, *Bambule* (Berlin: Wagenbach, 1971).

17. "The Panopticon, on the other hand, must be understood as a generalizable model of functioning; a way of defining power relations in terms of the everyday life of men." Foucault, *Discipline and Punish*, 205.

18. Foucault, 198.

19. See Wollstonecraft, *Mary* and *The Wrongs of Woman*, 105.

20. Foucault, *Discipline and Punish*, 120.

I. THE RULES OF PRAXIS

1. Of course, even supposedly "pure" contemplation can in turn be reconstructed as a specific practice. In this sense, Hannah Arendt endeavors in her late work to describe the *vita contemplativa* in terms of activities: see Hannah Arendt, *The Life of the Mind* (New York: Harcourt Brace, 1981).

2. Karl Marx, *Selected Works*, vol. 1 (1845; Moscow: Progress, 1969), 13.

3. Jorge Larrain, *A Reconstruction of Historical Materialism* (London: Allen and Unwin, 1986), 92ff.

4. Jean-Paul Sartre, *Critique of Dialectical Reason*, vol. 1 (1960; London: Verso, 2004), 266.

5. Louis Althusser, "Ideology and Ideological State Apparatuses," in *Lenin and Philosophy* (New York: Monthly Review Press, 1971), 114.

6. Martin Heidegger, *Being and Time* (1927; Oxford: Blackwell, 1962), 241.

7. Foucault gave rise to wide-ranging speculation when he professed in his last interview that Heidegger was the most essential philosopher for him and an influence on his entire thinking. The relationship between Foucault's work and Heidegger's ontological project will not be pursued further here; for an impressively systematic analysis, see Robert Nichols, *The World of Freedom: Heidegger, Foucault, and the Politics of Historical Ontology* (Stanford University Press: Stanford, 2014).

8. Charles Taylor, "Lichtung or Lebensform: Parallels Between Heidegger and Wittgenstein," in *Philosophical Arguments* (Cambridge, MA: Harvard University Press, 1995), 75, 69.

9. Detailed arguments against such interpretations, as well as more specific accounts of the individual dimensions of the priority of praxis, will be developed later on, when the concept of praxis is explained further (see chapter 2).

10. René Descartes, *Meditations on First Philosophy* (1641; Cambridge: Cambridge University Press, 2017), 27.

11. Already very early on, Sherry B. Ortner produced a superb overview ("Theory in Anthropology Since the Sixties," *Comparative Studies in Society and History* 26, no. 1 [1984]: 126–166). See also Theodore R. Schatzki, Karin Knorr Cetina, and Elke von Savigny, eds., *The Practice Turn in Contemporary Theory* (London: Psychology Press, 2001), 10ff.; Andreas Reckwitz, "Towards a Theory of Social Practices: A Development in Cultural Theorizing," *European Journal for Social Theory* 5, no. 2 (2002): 243–263; Hilmar Schäfer, *Die Instabilität der Praxis: Reproduktion und Transformation des Sozialen in der Praxistheorie* (Weilerswist: Velbrück Wissenschaft, 2014), 13ff.

12. See Reckwitz, "Towards a Theory of Social Practices."

13. See Schatzki, Cetina, and von Savigny, *The Practice Turn*.

14. Michel de Certeau, *The Practice of Everyday Life* (1980; Berkeley: University of California Press, 1988).

15. Bruno Latour, *Reassembling the Social: An Introduction to Actor-Network Theory* (Oxford: Oxford University Press, 2005).

16. Harold Garfinkel, *Studies in Ethnomethodology* (Englewood Cliffs, NJ: Prentice-Hall, 1967).

17. Pierre Bourdieu, *The Logic of Practice* (1980; Stanford: Stanford University Press, 1990).

18. Alasdair MacIntyre, *After Virtue* (Notre Dame: University of Notre Dame Press, 1981), 24–25.

19. Bourdieu, *Logic of Practice*.

20. Andreas Reckwitz, "Grundelemente einer Theorie sozialer Praktiken: Eine sozialtheoretische Perspektive," *Zeitschrift für Soziologie* 32, no. 4 (2003): 290. Some references here are to this later German version of Reckwitz's article ("Towards a Theory of Social Practices"), which differs from the English (quotation trans. LD).

21. Reckwitz, "Towards a Theory of Social Practices," 249.

22. Jaeggi, *Critique of Forms of Life*, 67, 75.

23. Jaeggi, 61.

24. Reckwitz, "Grundelemente," 293 (quotation trans. LD).

25. The "homo oeconomicus" is the utility-maximizing actor of rational-choice theory, with its methodical individualism and thin notion of rationality, which praxis theory seeks to invalidate through the concept of a normatively saturated and collectively shared pattern of agency. Meanwhile, praxis theory also remains distinct from the approach to normativity developed by writers such as Max Weber or Talcott Parsons, according to which social actions are coordinated through explicable normative rules of behavior. "Homo sociologicus" therefore refers to the limited concept of an actor "programmed" by social values or roles.

26.   Mary Wollstonecraft, *Mary* and *The Wrongs of Woman* (1798; Oxford: Oxford University Press, 2009), 149.

27.   Wollstonecraft, 148.

28.   Alexis Shotwell provides a very useful discussion of the various dimensions of implicit knowledge. She distinguishes not only between knowledge that can, in principle, be explained and implicit knowledge that can genuinely not be verbalized, but also between different manifestations of the latter category as understanding that is either somatic, practical ("know-how"), or emotional: Alexis Shotwell, *Knowing Otherwise: Race, Gender, and Implicit Understanding* (University Park: Pennsylvania State University Press, 2011), xi.

29.   MacIntyre, *After Virtue*, 24.

30.   Certeau, *Practice of Everyday Life*, xiv–xv.

31.   Pierre Bourdieu, *Outline of a Theory of Practice* (1972; Cambridge: Cambridge University Press, 1977), 17.

32.   Bourdieu, 17.

33.   In the next section, I will reconstruct Anthony Giddens's concept of structure and explore the Wittgensteinian understanding of rules, on which Giddens's approach is based, in more detail. Like many other praxis theorists, Giddens addresses the normativity of practices starting from Wittgenstein's discussions of following rules. This means that the question of the "implicit" is, in a sense, approached from the other end, that is, beginning from the rule as a concept. Rather than emphasizing that practices are set apart by the way in which their normativity stretches far into nonexplicable realms of practical knowledge or know-know, the argument is that we first realize that there is such a thing as practical knowledge not because swimming, cycling, and riding cannot be learned from an armchair, but because the supposed opposite case, the idea that there could be a rule that guides actions in a fully explicit manner, turns out to be untenable when examined more closely. The search for a criterion for the existence of a correspondingly stringent and unambiguous following of rules would only lead us, in the end, back to observing the continuation or repetition of practices. Wittgenstein sees this "weakness" of the rule not as a deficit or a dilemma for praxis, but rather as its characteristic element. For that is exactly how the following of a rule is expressed: in implicit, practical knowledge of how to continue ("how to go on"), which is only ever expressed in subsequent practices: see Ludwig Wittgenstein, *Philosophical Investigations/Philosophische Untersuchungen* (1953; Oxford: Blackwell, 2004), §§82–83, §§143ff.

34.   It has become common to follow Searle in distinguishing between constitutive and regulative rules: John R. Searle, "How to Derive 'Ought' from 'Is,'" *Philosophical Review* 73, no. 1 (1964): 55; John R. Searle, *Speech Acts* (Cambridge: Cambridge University Press, 1969), 33. Constitutive rules contain definitions. They determine when something in the social realm has validity—and the collective acceptance and recognition of these rules by social actors then create what Searle (following Elizabeth Anscombe) calls institutional circumstances. These rules are themselves not prescriptive, but only form the setting in which Searle's "regulative" rules then come into force. My provisional distinction between praxis-defining and praxis-evaluating rules corresponds to some extent with this terminology. Nevertheless, for praxis theory, a collectively recognized definition does not yet constitute a praxis. It still needs what I call here "praxis-generating" rules. Corrado Roversi has, however, suggested introducing mimetic rules as a subtype of Searle's constitutive rules, which seems an interesting way of bridging the gap: Corrado Roversi, "Mimetic Constitutive Rules," *Phenomenology and Mind* 2 (2012): 144–151.

35.   See also Jaeggi, *Critique of Forms of Life*, 344: "Forms of life are not something voluntary, a club that one can choose to join or not."

36.   "A being, with a visage that would have suited one possessed by a devil, crossed the path, and seized Maria by the arm.... 'Who are you? what are you?' for the form was scarcely human. 'If you are

made of flesh and blood,' his ghastly eyes glared on her, 'do not stop me!' " Wollstonecraft, *Mary and The Wrongs of Woman*, 166.

37. Jaeggi, *Critique of Forms of Life*, 79.

38. Wollstonecraft, *Mary and The Wrongs of Woman*, 171.

39. Wollstonecraft, 174.

40. The justified question of how something that supposedly remains implicit can be learned in a stable manner and shared by different actors, which has been posed by Stephen Turner, can be answered more easily when we consider the fact that actors do share practices and always relate to existing patterns of action through interaction and imitation. Actors do not enter the social realm like players coming to a table where an unfamiliar game is being played, but instead always orientate themselves according to countless practices in which they participate before they can reflect on them at all. In addition, a praxis theory like the one outlined here always has built into it the element that Turner himself suggests as a solution and alternative to praxis theory, namely, that we should assume people adopt habits through imitation: see Stephen Turner, *The Social Theory of Practices: Tradition, Tacit Knowledge, and Presuppositions* (Chicago: University of Chicago Press, 1994), 121.

41. Wollstonecraft, *Mary and The Wrongs of Woman*, 67.

42. Jaeggi, *Critique of Forms of Life*, 56.

43. Reckwitz, "Grundelemente," 292 (quotation trans. LD).

44. Jacques Derrida, "Signature Event Context" (1972), in *Limited Ink* (Evanston, IL: Northwestern University Press, 1988), 7.

45. There is nevertheless no doubt that a characteristic and central element of praxis theory is its capacity to show how decisive the routinized portion of our actions is, which would fall outside the focus of a narrower, more rationalistic theory of action: see Anthony Giddens, *The Constitution of Society: Outline of the Theory of Structuration* (Cambridge: Polity, 1984), xxiii, 20, 72; Reckwitz, "Grundelemente," 293; Jaeggi, *Critique of Forms of Life*, 96.

46. Hans Joas and Wolfgang Knöbl, *Sozialtheorie: Zwanzig einführende Vorlesungen: Aktualisierte Ausgabe* (Frankfurt: Suhrkamp, 2004), 406.

47. Giddens, *The Constitution of Society*, 35.

2. THE MATERIALITY OF PRAXIS

1. See David Bloor, "Wittgenstein and the Priority of Practice," in *The Practice Turn in Contemporary Theory*, ed. Theodore R. Schatzki, Karin Knorr Cetina, and Elke von Savigny (London: Psychology Press, 2001), 103.

2. Edmund Burke, *Reflections on the Revolution in France* (1790; Middlesex, UK: Penguin, 1982).

3. "The French revolution challenged almost every human feeling, and every human passion, to the most vehement resistance, and could therefore only force its way by violence and crimes"; "The French in their giddiness no longer acknowledged the prescriptions of the clearest right, nor the prescriptions of nature. They were so proud as to think they could bend impossibility itself, under the arm of their violence, and so daring that they thought the clearest right must yield to the maxims of their arbitrary will. The resistance of which they complained, was with perfect certainty to be foreseen; it lay in the unalterable laws of human feelings, and human passions; it was just, it was necessary; it was impossible to believe that it would not take place." Friedrich von Gentz, *The Origin and Principles of the American Revolution, Compared with the Origin and Principles of the French Revolution* (1800; Indianapolis: Liberty Fund, 2010), 85, 88.

4. Elizabeth Shove, Mika Pantzar, and Matt Watson, *The Dynamics of Social Practice: Everyday Life and How It Changes* (London: Sage, 2012), 1.

5. William H. Sewell Jr., *The Logics of History: Social Theory and Social Transformation* (Chicago: University of Chicago Press, 2005), 225ff.

6. A detailed investigation of the dynamic potential of praxis theories was also recently undertaken by Hilmar Schäfer. He compares different theories and suggests that social praxis should be understood "as a repetition in which recurrence and change are paradoxically combined." Hilmar Schäfer, *Die Instabilität der Praxis: Reproduktion und Transformation des Sozialen in der Praxistheorie* (Weilerswist: Velbrück Wissenschaft, 2014), 12 (quotation trans. LD). Beyond this conclusion, which remains tied to the motif of iterability, my work aims also to reconstruct radical social change in praxeological terms.

7. Shove, Pantzar, and Watson, *The Dynamics*, 22.

8. Shove, Pantzar, and Watson, 23.

9. Shove, Pantzar, and Watson, 24.

10. Karl Marx, *Capital*, vol. 1 (1867; London: Penguin, 1990), 132.

11. Martin Heidegger, *Being and Time* (1927; Oxford: Blackwell, 1962), 99.

12. "As if the 'reflected' society existed somewhere else and was made of some other stuff. [The things] are in large part the stuff out of which socialness is made." Bruno Latour, "When Things Strike Back: A Possible Contribution of 'Science Studies' to the Social Sciences," *British Journal of Sociology* 51, no. 1 (2000): 113.

13. Michel Foucault, *Discipline and Punish: The Birth of the Prison* (1975; New York: Vintage, 1995), 238.

14. In "science studies," which deals with a world of things that includes highly complex devices providing information and insights, such a posthumanist variant of praxis theory has established itself. See Latour, "When Things Strike Back"; Joseph Rouse, *How Scientific Practices Matter: Reclaiming Philosophical Naturalism* (Chicago: University of Chicago Press, 2002); Andrew Pickering, *The Mangle of Practice: Time, Agency, and Science* (Chicago: University of Chicago Press, 1995). Karen Barad converts this position into a so-called "agential realism," which extends a performative concept of the ability to act far beyond (self-)conscious actors or agents: "On an agential realist account, agency is cut loose from its traditional humanist orbit. Agency is not aligned with human intentionality or subjectivity.... Agency is a matter of intra-acting; it is an enactment, not something that someone or something has." Karen Barad, "Posthumanist Performativity: Towards an Understanding of How Matter Comes to Matter," *Signs* 28, no. 3 (2003): 826–827. Foucault's notion of praxis can also be understood in a more strongly posthumanist sense than I have highlighted here, as Frieder Vogelmann demonstrates, taking his cue from Rouse. See Frieder Vogelmann, "Foucaults Praktiken," *Coincidentia: Zeitschrift für europäische Geistesgeschichte* 3, no. 2 (2012): 275–299.

15. Here my reconstruction is artificially limited to the definition of praxis. Both Giddens and Sewell always also define structures at the same time as being a combination of rules/schemas and resources. Since the question of the transition from recursive praxis to social structures is discussed in other chapters of this book, structure is not a key concern here. This exclusive approach seems exegetically justified to me, since both authors repeatedly pledge allegiance to the praxistheoretical premise that practices are to be seen as socioontological basic elements. Giddens even goes so far as to claim that the linguistic turn could be better understood as a "pragmatic turn." Anthony Giddens, *The Constitution of Society: Outline of the Theory of Structuration* (Cambridge: Polity, 1984), xxii, 2.

16. Sewell, *The Logics of History*, 132.

17. In the English-speaking debate, this difference has come to be expressed terminologically in the phrases "power over" and "power to." Jeffrey Isaac has been particularly vehement in demanding that personal power relations be referred back to structural power relations—the fact that

someone has power over someone else is ultimately always a result of what she or he is able to do within the social hierarchy. See Jeffrey C. Isaac, "Beyond the Three Faces of Power: A Realist Critique," in *Rethinking Power*, ed. T. E. Wartenberg (Albany: SUNY Press, 1992), 32–55. I develop this point further in chapter 3.

18. See Dominique Godineau, *The Women of Paris and Their French Revolution* (Berkeley: University of California Press 1998), 8.

19. The connections between practices are discussed in detail in chapter 3.

20. Sewell, *The Logics of History*, 131.

21. Cited in Godineau, *The Women of Paris*, 8.

22. "In a way, laundresses represented for women what shoemakers represented for men: they were a professional group with sansculotte tendencies." Godineau, 8.

23. Sewell, *The Logics of History*, 135.

24. Sewell, 137.

25. It is in Sally Haslanger's reception of Sewell that the form-content analogy really becomes explicit. See Sally Haslanger, *Resisting Reality: Social Construction and Social Critique* (Oxford: Oxford University Press, 2012), 464.

26. Mary Wollstonecraft, *Mary* and *The Wrongs of Woman* (1798; Oxford: Oxford University Press, 2009), 101.

27. Karl Marx, *Grundrisse: Foundations of the Critique of Political Economy* (1857–1858; London: Penguin, 1993), 158.

28. In his "crisis experiments," Harold Garfinkel offers particularly striking evidence that even small deviations from routine scripts unsettle social interactions profoundly. See, e.g., Harold Garfinkel, *Studies in Ethnomethodology* (Englewood Cliffs, NJ: Prentice-Hall, 1967), 221.

29. Wollstonecraft, *Mary* and *The Wrongs of Woman*, 71.

30. Tobias Matzner has discussed the doubt that appears frequently in Wittgenstein's work as to the mental health of those who leave behind the shared common ground in their praxis, pointing out that it would be better to see it as a specific form of exclusion from a group resulting from the experience of radically different practices. See Tobias Matzner, "The Interdependence of Normalcy and Exclusion—Some Political Thoughts Inspired by *On Certainty*," unpublished lecture manuscript (2011).

31. Alasdair MacIntyre demonstrates this in an essay that has become classic: "But any action will fall under a number of descriptions, some nonintentional. Thus, to the question, 'What is he doing?' the answer might be 'digging,' 'planting lettuce seedlings,' 'making sure that they will have an adequate source of vitamin C,' 'doing as his wife told him,' 'taking his prescribed twenty-minute exercise,' 'filling in time till the bars open,' 'earning money,' 'overstraining his heart,' 'using the wrong tool for the job.' The correctness of any one of these is compatible with the correctness of all or any of the others." Alasdair MacIntyre, "Ideology, Social Science, and Revolution," *Comparative Politics* 5, no. 3 (1973): 323–324.

32. Wollstonecraft, *Mary* and *The Wrongs of Woman*, 137.

33. See Wollstonecraft, 145.

34. Alongside Rahel Jaeggi, Terry Pinkard represents a Hegelian teleological understanding of praxis: Terry Pinkard, *Hegel's Naturalism* (Oxford: Oxford University Press, 2013), 98. In the social-ontological debate, Seumas Miller has developed a teleological notion of praxis and particularly of institutions: see Seumas Miller, *Social Action: A Teleological Account* (Cambridge: Cambridge University Press, 2001), 13–14, 193–194. An intermediate position is occupied here by Theodore R. Schatzki, who argues that practices have a structure with "teleological leanings," meaning that particular aims are suggested by each praxis. See Theodore R. Schatzki, *The Site of the Social: A Philosophical Account of the Constitution of Social Life and Change* (University Park: Pennsylvania State University Press, 2002), 80.

35. Rahel Jaeggi, *Critique of Forms of Life* (Cambridge, MA: Harvard University Press, 2019), 59.

36. "The purpose of the conversation in the grocery store is not just to make a successful purchase but also to flirt with the shop assistant, and the activity as a whole may serve as a distraction from work. . . . Strictly speaking, one would have to say in such cases that a single practice is not determined in several ways but that one and the same sequence of actions simultaneously constitutes several practices—flirting as well as shopping." Jaeggi, 59–60.

37. Pierre Bourdieu, *The Logic of Practice* (1980; Stanford: Stanford University Press, 1990), 54.

38. Bini Adamczak suggests that we should focus our endeavors on forms of relationship, both in revolutionary action and in the theory of revolution: Bini Adamczak, *Beziehungsweise Revolution: 1917, 1968 und kommende* (Berlin: Suhrkamp, 2017). In defining my own praxis-theoretical terms, I sympathize with her project; indeed, my approach could be a way of spelling out this focus.

39. As exemplified by Isaac and Schuck in the context of critical realism, when attempting to connect a nomological concept of structure with the innovative abilities of actors: see Isaac, "Beyond the Three Faces of Power"; Hartwig Schuck, "Macht und Herrschaft: Eine realistische Analyse," in *Anonyme Herrschaft: Zur Struktur moderner Machtverhältnisse*, ed. I. Elbe, S. Ellmers, and J. Eufinger (Münster: Westfälisches Dampfboot, 2012), 35–81.

40. This aspect of *The Wrongs of Woman* gives the book a narrative structure characterized by multiple mirrorings; the summary here, which passes over the subplots, cannot hope to do it any justice.

41. In this, the characters follow a pattern that Lynn Hunt has shown to be the "family romance" of the French Revolution on the level of the political imaginary, namely, the replacement of patriarchal relationships with intrafilial ones: see Lynn Hunt, *The Family Romance of the French Revolution* (London: Routledge, 1992), 53ff.

42. As the previous chapter should have shown, this distinction is not stable. The reception of events—those of the French Revolution in particular—can in itself be analyzed and historicized as a praxis.

43. Wollstonecraft, *Mary* and *The Wrongs of Woman*, 173.

44. Wollstonecraft, 75–76.

3. THE CONNECTIONS BETWEEN PRACTICES

1. Ann Swidler, "What Anchors Cultural Practices?," in *The Practice Turn in Contemporary Theory*, ed. Theodore R. Schatzki, Karin Knorr Cetina, and Elke von Savigny (London: Psychology Press, 2001), 90.

2. Pierre Bourdieu, *The Logic of Practice* (1980; Stanford: Stanford University Press, 1990), 139.

3. Bourdieu, 54.

4. As a reaction against the notion of national statehood as a "container" and an equivalent of society, a number of theorists in sociology have shifted the concept of structure into the center of their analyses. A particularly pioneering role is played here by the historical sociological work of Michael Mann, whose vehement criticism of the notion of society found particular resonance with Anthony Giddens. Giddens goes so far as to describe the closed notion of society as a result of "noxious presumptions." Anthony Giddens, *The Constitution of Society: Outline of the Theory of Structuration* (Cambridge: Polity, 1984), 163.

   To ensure that structure does not in turn come to imply a closed system, it is either held open via the poststructuralist claim that all processes of signification are open-ended, or transferred into a perpetual recursive interrelation with individual practices. A variant of the latter option, which became prominent in Giddens's theory of structuration, is proposed in the next chapter.

5. In principle, this concept does not exclude the possibility that one extreme constellation or the other (arbitrary juxtaposition or inseparable connected whole) might occur. However, this would not be a sociotheoretical assumption, but only an individual result of a diagnosis that would have to be conducted again for each new case.

6. In the so-called "power debates," US sociologists started from basic behavioralist assumptions in order to define a notion of power that could be operationalized in empirical studies. Initially, the central concern was purely personal power exerted in conflicts ("power over"): see Robert A. Dahl, "A Critique of the Ruling Elite Model," *American Political Science Review* 52 (1958): 463–469. This definition was enriched by the "second face" of "agenda-setting," meaning the authority to decide which conflicts were to be conducted in the first place: Peter Bachrach and Morton Baratz, "The Two Faces of Power," *American Political Science Review* 56 (1962): 942–952. Steven Lukes then began to leave the behavioralist framework behind and include as a third dimension of power the concealed exertion of power, which manifests itself not in conflicts but, for example, in the manipulation of interests: Steven Lukes, *Power: A Radical View* (Houndsmills, UK: Palgrave, 1974), 14–59. Wartenberg, meanwhile, tries to use the situative notion of power to cover all three dimensions, without having to adopt a structural concept of power that would no longer be empirically demonstrable: see Thomas E. Wartenberg, *The Forms of Power: From Domination to Transformation* (Philadelphia: Temple University Press, 1990).

7. Thomas E. Wartenberg, "The Situated Conception of Social Power," *Social Theory and Practice* 14, no. 3 (1988): 330.

8. "An adequate formulation of the concept of power must recognize that the power one agent exercises over another agent in interaction is parasitic upon the powers to act that the agents possess." Jeffrey C. Isaac, "Beyond the Three Faces of Power: A Realist Critique," in *Rethinking Power*, ed. T. E. Wartenberg (Albany: SUNY Press, 1992), 41.

9. "Under the influence of Foucault, many theorists have attempted to move in the direction of a more structural and less strictly intentional understanding of phenomena like power (and coercion). In his discussion of the history of penal systems, Foucault discusses Bentham's project of a 'panopticon.' The 'panopticon' was a way of arranging the space in the prison so that the prisoners felt they were under constant surveillance, even if they were not. Foucault's point is that in such a prison the prisoners are clearly subject to a very distinct coercive 'power,' but this 'power' is not obviously best analysed as a property of the intentional action of any human individual or group of individuals. It is, as it were, the space of the prison itself which is powerful and coercive. . . . The better one understands the prison system, the wider one casts the net in the present and past, the more the very idea of power as related to what any individual wants or intends gets lost." Raymond Geuss, *History and Illusion in Politics* (Cambridge: Cambridge University Press, 2001), 27.

10. Amy Allen, "Power Trouble: Performativity as Critical Theory," *Constellations* 5, no. 4 (1998): 36. Isaac defines power in a similar vein as "the capacity to act possessed by social agents in virtue of the enduring relations in which they participate." Isaac, "Beyond the Three Faces of Power," 48.

11. Joseph Rouse, "Two Concepts of Practices," in Schatzki, Cetina, and von Savigny, *The Practice Turn*, 204. In the process, he falsely accuses Wartenberg of only being able to theorize social power. "A more adequate conception would recognize the *material* mediation of power by its circumstances, such that tools, processes, and physical surroundings more generally all belong to dynamic alignments of dominance, subordination, and resistance" (204). As my discussion of praxis has shown, I find it much more useful to understand the material conditions via the notion of praxis precisely as a part of the social, rather than setting them against the latter with extra italics for emphasis. If we take Wartenberg at his word when he talks of an "entire set of practices," then his alignments are always also a question of material resources.

12. At the end of the eighteenth century, the so-called "coverture" law applied in England, which prescribed that all a woman's property went to her husband in case of marriage, since the married

couple formed a single legal person, represented by the man: see Amy Louise Erickson, *Women and Property in Early Modern England* (1993; London: Routledge, 1995), 99–100.

13.   Mary Wollstonecraft, *Mary* and *The Wrongs of Woman* (1798; Oxford: Oxford University Press, 2009), 137. Interestingly enough, Wartenberg continues to work away at precisely the same institutions in his article and discusses the specific alignments that make marriage in the United States in the second half of the twentieth century an unequal power relationship: see Wartenberg, "The Situated Conception," 336ff.

14.   Rahel Jaeggi has suggested the following praxis-theoretical definition of institutions, which also includes their sociotheoretical role: "Institutions are constituted by social practices and characterized by habit. They represent more or less complex systems of lasting expectations placed on behavior, which establish more or less stable positions of status and which achieve particular public effectiveness and recognition." Rahel Jaeggi, "Was ist eine (gute) Institution?," in *Sozialphilosophie und Kritik*, ed. R. Forst, M. Hartmann, R. Jaeggi, and M. Saar (Frankfurt: Suhrkamp, 2009), 531 (quotation trans. by LD). While she also offers normative criteria of evaluation in the form of "vitality" and "inhabitability," my thinner understanding of institutions as alignments aims merely to capture their role in the power structure.

15.   Wollstonecraft, *Mary* and *The Wrongs of Woman*, 161.

16.   Swidler, "What Anchors Cultural Practices?," 92.

17.   "The first claim is that practices of a particular kind—those that enact constitutive rules that define fundamental social entities—are likely to be central, anchoring whole larger domains of practice and discourse. The second suggestion is that practices may be more firmly anchored when they are at the center of antagonistic social relationships. Third, the establishment of new social practices appears not so much to require the time or repetition that habits require, but rather the visible, public enactment of new patterns so that 'everyone can see' that everyone else has seen that things have changed." Swidler, 95–96.

18.   The notion of paradigms will be discussed in detail in the final part of this book, where it will be brought together with that of the anchor praxis.

19.   Michel Foucault, *Discipline and Punish: The Birth of the Prison* (1975; New York: Vintage, 1995), 233.

20.   See Barbara Schaeffer-Hegel, "Die Freiheit und Gleichheit der Brüder," in *1789/1989: Die Revolution hat nicht stattgefunden*, ed. A. Deuber-Mankowsky, U. Ramming, and E. W. Tielsch (Tübingen: edition discord, 1989), 53ff.

21.   Wollstonecraft, *Mary* and *The Wrongs of Woman*, 148.

22.   Wollstonecraft, 149.

23.   Karl Polanyi, *The Great Transformation: The Political and Economic Origins of Our Time* (1949; Boston: Beacon, 2001), 80.

24.   Foucault, *Discipline and Punish*, 296.

PART 2. JACOBIN KNITTERS

1.   Karl Marx, "The Eighteenth Brumaire of Louis Bonaparte" (1852), in *Later Political Writings*, ed. Terell Carver (Cambridge: Cambridge University Press, 1996), 31–127, 32.

2.   Cf. Gregory Claeys, *The French Revolution Debate in Britain: The Origin of Modern Politics* (London: Palgrave Macmillan, 2007).

3.   Lynn A. Hunt, *Politics, Culture, and Class in the French Revolution* (Oakland: University of California Press, 1984).

4.   Charles Dickens, *A Tale of Two Cities* (1859; Oxford: Oxford University Press, 2008), 106–107.

5.   Dickens, 106–107.

6.   Jeffrey C. Isaac, "Beyond the Three Faces of Power: A Realist Critique," in *Rethinking Power*, ed. T. E. Wartenberg (Albany: SUNY Press, 1992).

7.   Dickens, *A Tale of Two Cities*, 223.

8.   Karl Marx, *The Poverty of Philosophy* (1847; New York: Cosimo, 2008), 181–184.

9.   Friedrich Engels and Karl Marx, *The Communist Manifesto* (1848; London: Penguin, 2002), 229–230.

10.   Marx, *Poverty of Philosophy*, 187–189.

11.   Marx, "Brumaire," 117. Here Marx flatly equates the ability to represent oneself on the national stage with the political ability to act; this has been criticized in detail in subaltern studies. Cf., e.g., Vinayak Chaturvedi, ed., *Mapping Subaltern Studies and the Postcolonial* (London: Verso, 2000).

12.   As in, e.g., G. A. Cohen, *Karl Marx's Theory of History: A Defence* (1978; Oxford: Oxford University Press, 2000), 55.

13.   Marx, "Brumaire," 34.

14.   Martin Buber, *Paths in Utopia* (1949; Syracuse: Syracuse University Press, 1996), 44.

15.   Marx, "Brumaire," 33–34.

16.   Hauke Brunkhorst, "Kommentar," in *Der achtzehnte Brumaire des Louis Bonaparte*, by Karl Marx (Frankfurt: Suhrkamp, 2007), 191.

17.   Marx, 32.

18.   Marx, 32.

19.   Marx, 33.

20.   Marx, 32.

21.   Marx, 35.

22.   Marx, 35.

4. THE DUALITY OF SOCIAL STRUCTURES

1.   Douglas V. Porpora, "Four Concepts of Social Structure," *Journal for the Theory of Social Behaviour* 20, no. 1 (1989): 202; see also Alex Callinicos, "Anthony Giddens: A Contemporary Critique," *Theory and Society* 14, no. 2 (1985): 133–166.

2.   Anthony Giddens, *The Constitution of Society: Outline of the Theory of Structuration* (Cambridge: Polity, 1984), xx.

3.   Giddens, xxvi.

4.   Giddens, 25.

5.   Giddens, 19.

6.   Giddens, 25 et passim.

7.   Giddens, xxiii.

8.   Giddens, 20.

9.   Stanley Cavell, "The Ordinary as the Uneventful" (1984), in *The Cavell Reader*, ed. Steven Mulhall (Cambridge, MA: Blackwell, 1996), 253.

10.   Giddens, *The Constitution of Society*, xxv.

11.   Giddens, 2. "Human social activities . . . are recursive. That is to say, they are not brought into being by social actors but continually recreated by them via the very means whereby they express themselves as actors. In and through their activities agents reproduce the conditions that make these actions possible."

12.   Giddens, 8.

13.   Giddens, 43.

14. See also William H. Sewell Jr., *Logics of History: Social Theory and Social Transformation* (Chicago: University of Chicago Press, 2005), 127–128; Andreas Reckwitz, *Struktur: Zur sozialwissenschaftlichen Analyse von Regeln und Regelmäßigkeiten* (Opladen: Westdeutscher, 1997), 104.

15. Giddens, *The Constitution of Society*, xxii.

16. Giddens does say more about structures, but he still presents practices as the actual socio-ontological fundamental building blocks. For him the "linguistic turn" could be better described as a "pragmatic turn." Giddens, xxii, 2.

17. Ludwig Wittgenstein, *Philosophical Investigations/Philosophische Untersuchungen* (1953; Oxford: Blackwell, 2004), §§82–83; §§143ff.

18. Giddens, *The Constitution of Society*, 21.

19. Cf. David Bloor, "Wittgenstein and the Priority of Practice," in *The Practice Turn in Contemporary Theory*, ed. T. R. Schatzki, K. Knorr Cetina, and E. von Savigny, 103–114 (London: Psychology, 2001), 104.

20. Giddens, *The Constitution of Society*, 21.

21. Giddens, 22–23.

22. Giddens, 15, 258.

23. An accusation that actually applies much more to Schatzki than to Giddens. Schatzki, meanwhile, accuses Giddens of failing to draw all the constructivist conclusions from the rule-following argument. Cf. Theodore R. Schatzki, "Practice and Actions: A Wittgensteinian Critique of Bourdieu and Giddens," *Philosophy of the Social Sciences* 27, no. 3 (1997): 283–308.

24. Giddens, *The Constitution of Society*, 17.

25. Sewell, *Logics of History*, 136.

26. Sewell either does not take later Giddens's Wittgensteinianism into account, or discards the Wittgensteinian critique of rule-following, as is shown in his complaint that the content of Giddens's rules remains too vague. Sewell, *Logics of History*, 130.

27. See also Giddens, *The Constitution of Society*, 18: "Rules cannot be conceptualized apart from resources, which refer to the modes whereby transformative relations are actually incorporated into the production and reproduction of social practices."

28. Porpora, "Four Concepts of Social Structure," 195.

29. Charles Dickens, *A Tale of Two Cities* (1859; Oxford: Oxford University Press, 2008), 106–107.

30. Porpora, "Four Concepts of Social Structure," 205.

31. Giddens, *The Constitution of Society*, 19.

32. The following quotation illustrates Mann's impressive aims: "State, culture, and economy are all important structuring networks; but they almost never coincide. There is no one master concept or basic unit of 'society.' It may seem an odd position for a sociologist to adopt; but if I could, I would abolish the concept of 'society' altogether." Cf. Michael Mann, *The Sources of Social Power*, vol. 1 (Cambridge: Cambridge University Press, 1986), 2. From the point of view of structuration theory, the problematic element of Mann's approach is of course the fact that he claims to have found the four factors that have a transhistorical structuring effect (ideology, economy, military, politics).

33. Dickens, *A Tale of Two Cities*, 106–107.

34. See also chapter 11. During the "Great Fear," farmers across France were convinced that the king's troops would destroy their harvest while it was still in the fields. They mobilized to defend themselves, and used this mobilization in many places to protest against rent or against feudal obligations, setting fire to some local seats of nobility in the process. The unrest had much more far-reaching effects than only allowing the farmers to threaten their rent-collectors—in histories of the revolution, the decision of the National Assembly on August 4, 1789, to abolish noble privileges is attributed directly to the impression made by the farmers' rebellion.

35. Dickens, *A Tale of Two Cities*, 223.

36. Karl Polanyi, *The Great Transformation: The Political and Economic Origins of Our Time* (1949; Boston: Beacon, 2001), 61.

37. Porpora, "Four Concepts of Social Structure," 209.

5. RECOGNITION AND PERFORMATIVE STRUCTURATION

1. Andreas Reckwitz, *Struktur: Zur sozialwissenschaftlichen Analyse von Regeln und Regelmäßigkeiten* (Opladen: Westdeutscher, 1997), 34–35; see also Jürgen Habermas, *Theory of Communicative Action*, vol. 1, *Reason and the Rationalization of Society* (Boston: Beacon, 1984), 102–141.

2. Anthony Giddens, *The Constitution of Society: Outline of the Theory of Structuration* (Cambridge: Polity, 1984), 283. Although at one point he also emphasizes the logical priority of power over subjectivity (15), Giddens's use of the term "power" is very various, if not inconsistent. At another point he equates power with domination (258). However, there are also passages in which he locates power exclusively on the resource side of structures (15), exactly as Sewell later suggests. Then, elsewhere, power is—as I assume here—coextensive with the ability to act (14).

3. Judith Butler, *Undoing Gender* (New York: Routledge, 2004), 48.

4. The same already went for the status of the gendered body in *Gender Trouble*: "That the gendered body is performative suggests that it has no ontological status apart from the various acts which constitute its reality." Judith Butler, *Gender Trouble: Feminism and the Subversion of Identity* (1990; New York: Routledge, 1999), 185.

5. Giddens, *The Constitution of Society*, 17.

6. In the first chapter, I distinguished between three different types of rules that are brought to bear in practices. Praxis-generating rules describe the incorporated know-how that actually enables actors to follow a praxis, praxis-defining rules are the shared schemas that make practices intelligible, and praxis-internal rules are the evaluation criteria and regulations that are set out explicitly with practices.

7. Pierre Bourdieu, *The Logic of Practice* (1980; Stanford: Stanford University Press, 1990), 158.

8. Pierre Bourdieu, *Outline of a Theory of Practice* (1972; Cambridge: Cambridge University Press, 1977), 22–32.

9. Bourdieu, 79.

10. Reckwitz, *Struktur*, 181–182.

11. Giddens, *The Constitution of Society*, 157.

12. Butler, unlike Paul Ricoeur, does not subdivide different meanings of "recognition." Paul Ricoeur, *The Course of Recognition* (Cambridge, MA: Harvard University Press, 2005). Estelle Ferrarese distinguished in Butler's work between positive and subjugating recognition, though both of these first require what I call here "basic recognition" or intelligibility. Estelle Ferrarese, "Judith Butler's 'Not Particularly Postmodern Insight' of Recognition," *Philosophy and Social Criticism* 37, no. 7: 767.

13. See J. L. Austin, *How to Do Things with Words* (Cambridge, MA: Harvard University Press, 1962), 13.

14. Contrary to many claims, Austin does not argue that every illocutionary act is performative. Performative speech acts are a possible variant of the pragmatic, illocutionary aspects of a statement.

15. In contrast with this, Austin describes the perlocutionary dimension as the purely contingent effects of a speech act in the world. Austin, *How to Do Things with Words*, 100–101. The fact that Defarge throws the coin back could be described as the perlocutionary effect of the praise and the "gift," which are interpreted as being cynical. Butler's critique of Austin and the "interposition" of the

condition of iterability could therefore also be encapsulated by saying that she deconstructs the difference between the illocutionary and the perlocutionary aspects. Judith Butler, *Excitable Speech: A Politics of the Performative* (New York: Routledge, 1997), 361.

16. Jacques Derrida, "Signature Event Context" (1972), in *Limited Ink* (Evanston, IL: Northwestern University Press, 1988), 1–25, 15.

17. In fact, Dickens responds to the failure of the law in great detail in his novel—before his imprisonment in the Bastille, Dr. Manette tried hard without success to bring the then young Marquis and his brother to account for the rape and murder of a farm girl. As the plot would have it, the knitting wine-seller turns out to be the sister of the victim.

18. See Charles Taylor, "Theories of Meaning," in *Philosophical Papers 1* (Cambridge: Cambridge University Press, 1985), 248–292, 280.

19. Butler, *Gender Trouble*, 41.

20. Ludwig Wittgenstein, *Philosophical Investigations/Philosophische Untersuchungen* (1953; Oxford: Blackwell, 2004), §198.

21. Klaus Puhl, "Die List der Regel: Zur Retroaktiven Konstruktion sozialer Praxis," in *Institutionen und Regelfolgen*, ed. U. Baltzer and G. Schönrich (Paderborn: Mentis, 2002), 91 (quotation trans. LD).

22. If we take Wittgenstein's rule-following argument seriously, we would of course have to argue against the categorical difference between regularity and rules. However, my concern here is to make the transition between them plausible in a way that might also be convincing to non-Wittgensteinians and above all produce a fuller social theory that retains a certain explanatory force.

6. STRUCTURES IN THREE STATES OF AGGREGATE

1. Margaret Archer, "Morphogenesis Versus Structuration," *British Journal of Sociology* 33, no. 4 (1982): 161–162.

2. Ludwig Wittgenstein, *On Certainty* (Oxford: Blackwell, 1969), 15e.

3. Wittgenstein, 33e.

4. Charles Dickens, *A Tale of Two Cities* (1859; Oxford: Oxford University Press, 2008), 107.

5. Dickens, 107.

6. Ranajit Guha, *Dominance Without Hegemony: History and Power in Colonial India* (Cambridge, MA: Harvard University Press, 1998).

7. Gayatri Chakravorty Spivak, "Can the Subaltern Speak?," in *Marxism and the Interpretation of Culture*, ed. C. Nelson and L. Grossberg (Chicago: University of Illinois Press, 1988), 271–313.

8. Dickens, *A Tale of Two Cities*, 178–179.

9. Jean-Paul Sartre, *Critique of Dialectical Reason*, vol. 1 (1960; London: Verso, 2004), 266.

10. This refers to an edict of August 29, 1792, which ordered that all church bells should be melted down into cannon balls.

11. Dickens, *A Tale of Two Cities*, 179.

PART 3. MARTA'S INVISIBLE AFFINITY GROUP

1. See Deborah B. Gould, *Moving Politics: Emotion and ACT UP's Fight Against AIDS* (Chicago: University of Chicago Press, 2009), 263, 350.

2. Matt Ebert and Ryan Landry, *Marta: Portrait of a Teenage Activist* (Atlanta, 1990), http://vimeo
.com/59859368.

3. Douglas Crimp, "How to Have Promiscuity in an Epidemic" (1987), in *Mourning and Melancholia: Essays on AIDS and Queer Politics*, ed. D. Crimp (Cambridge, MA: MIT Press, 2002), 21.

4. The "Silence = Death" emblem became the logo of the movement. The slogan was written in white capitals in Gill Sans under a pink triangle against a black background. For a more detailed analysis, see Douglas Crimp, *AIDS|DEMO|GRAPHICS* (Seattle: Bay Press, 1990), 14.

5. Judith Butler, *Gender Trouble: Feminism and the Subversion of Identity* (1990; New York: Routledge, 1999), 189.

6. Juliane Rebentisch, "Camp Materialism," *Criticism: A Quarterly for Literature and the Arts* 56, no. 2 (2014): 243.

7. See comment on Ebert and Landry, *Marta*: http://vimeo.com/59859368.

8. Gustav Landauer, *Sein Lebensgang in Briefen*, ed. Martin Buber (Frankfurt: Rütten und Loening, 1929), 376 (quotation trans. LD).

9. Leo Bersani, "Is the Rectum a Grave?," in *AIDS: Cultural Analysis, Cultural Activism*, ed. D. Crimp (Cambridge, MA: MIT Press, 1987), 205.

10. On this, see in particular the text in which Crimp argues among other things for the claim that "it is our promiscuity that will save us," because only with sexual awareness and imagination can safer sex practices be established. Crimp, "How to Have Promiscuity," 64.

11. Gustav Landauer, *Beginnen* (1924; Wetzlar: Büchse der Pandora, 1977), 87–88 (quotations trans. LD).

12. See Eva von Redecker, "Topischer Sozialismus: Zur Exodus-Konzeption bei Gustav Landauer und Martin Buber," *WestEnd: Neue Zeitschrift für Sozialforschung* 11, no. 1 (2014): 93–108.

13. Landauer, *Beginnen*, 94.

14. Landauer, 92.

15. Landauer, 109.

16. Judith Butler, Peter Osborne, and Lynne Segal, "Gender as Performance: An Interview with Judith Butler," *Radical Philosophy* 67 (1994): 32–39.

17. See Crimp, *AIDS|DEMO|GRAPHICS*, 80–81.

18. See Crimp, 33.

7. DISAGGREGATION

1. See Margaret Archer, "Morphogenesis Versus Structuration," *British Journal of Sociology* 33, no. 4 (1982): 455–483.

2. Andreas Reckwitz, "Die Reproduktion und die Subversion sozialer Praktiken," in *Doing Culture: Neue Positionen zum Verhältnis von Kultur und sozialer Praxis*, ed. K. Hörning and J. Reuter (Bielefeld: transcript, 2004), 49 (quotation trans. LD).

3. "If practices, in Butler's portrayal, cannot depend on an internalized core, but represent nothing more than physical performances, and if these contain a quasi-natural tendency to multiply identities, to change unpredictably, to deviate, then this means that a culturally and historically highly specific type of praxis is being described. Butler only reveals where this model comes from historically in a short passage in which she refers to Joan Rivière's article 'Womanliness as a Masquerade,' from 1929. Joan Rivière's article is more than a neutral analysis of gendered behavior, it is instead a programmatic manifesto for a very specific and ultimately very influential cultural movement in Western culture: the aesthetic avantgardes." Reckwitz, "Die Reproduktion und die Subversion," 48 (quotation trans. LD).

4. In fact, this objection could also be rejected simply based on Butler's work, since she also gives prominence to irreparable upheavals and unliveable lives. Her discussion of Rivière does not serve as proof of subversive masquerades in gender relations, but to back up the extremely structuralist claim that it is the taboo status of homoerotic object relations that motivates the learning of gender roles that Rivière describes: "It may, however, be less her own masculine identity than the masculine heterosexual desire that is its signature that she seeks both to deny and enact by becoming the object she forbids herself to love. This is the predicament produced by a matrix that accounts for all desire for women by subjects of whatever sex or gender as originating in a masculine, heterosexual position." Judith Butler, *Gender Trouble: Feminism and the Subversion of Identity* (1990; New York: Routledge, 1999), 72.

5. Slavoj Žižek, "Da Capo senza Fine," in *Contingency, Hegemony, Universality: Contemporary Dialogues on the Left*, ed. J. Butler, E. Laclau, and S. Žižek (London: Verso, 2000), 213–262.

6. See Marie Mandy's film, *Judith Butler: Philosophin der Gender* (France, 2006).

7. Cited after Esther Newton, *Mother Camp: Female Impersonators in America* (Chicago: University of Chicago Press, 1972), 108.

8. See Michel Foucault, "What Is Critique?," in *The Politics of Truth*, ed. S. Lotringer and L. Hochroth (New York: Semiotext[e], 1997), 41–82; Judith Butler, "What Is Critique?: An Essay on Foucault's Virtue," 2001, https://transversal.at/transversal/0806/butler/en.

9. The intrinsic connection with transformation can to some extent also be claimed by immanent critique of ideology; see Rahel Jaeggi, "Rethinking Ideology," in *New Waves in Political Philosophy*, ed. B. de Bruin and C. F. Zurn, 63–86 (New York: Palgrave Macmillan, 2009); in contrast, Richard Rorty's pragmatic criticism relies on effective intervention rather than argumentative delegitimization, putting the focus only on the linguistic side of language games, making it seem less useful than Butler's model for the purposes of a theory of social change; see Richard Rorty, "Feminism and Pragmatism" (1994), in *Truth and Progress: Philosophical Papers* (Cambridge: Cambridge University Press, 1998), 202–227.

   Meanwhile, the unresolved claim to validity in Butler's model—that is, the difficulty of saying whether the new is really also better—would count as a strength in the eyes of antinormativistic theorists. Those theorists see the role of criticism as being directed at the opening up of new, additional realms, not at the replacement of one order through another, and they reject every attempt at justification which goes further than that as a generator of further exclusions. This position cannot be swept aside with a simple reference to circularity, because it is not antinormative throughout, but is aimed only at a specific attribution of status to these norms: see, e.g., Antke Engel, "Unter Verzicht auf Autorisierung: Foucaults Begriff der Akzeptanz und der Status des Wissens in queerer Theorie und Bewegung," in *Ordnungen des Denkens: Debatten um Wissenschaftstheorie und Erkenntniskritik*, ed. R. Langner, T. Luks, A. Schlimm, G. Straube, and D. Tomaschke (Berlin: LIT, 2007), 269–286; Antke Engel, "Tender Tensions—Antagonistic Struggles—Becoming-Bird: Queer Political Interventions Into Neoliberal Hegemony," in *Hegemony and Heteronormativity: Revisiting "The Political" in Queer Politics*, ed. M. Castro Varela, N. Dhawan, and A. Engel (Farnham, UK: Ashgate, 2011), 63–90; Patricia Purtschert, "Judith Butler: Macht der Kontingenz—Begriff der Kritik," in *Philosophinnen des 20. Jahrhunderts*, ed. R. Munz (Darmstadt: Wissenschaftliche Buchgesellschaft, 2004), 181–202; see also Judith Butler, "Reply from Judith Butler to Mills and Jenkins," *differences* 18, no. 2 (2007): 180–195.

10. "This conception of gender presupposes not only a causal relation among sex, gender, and desire, but suggests as well that desire reflects or expresses gender and that gender reflects or expresses desire. The metaphysical unity of the three is assumed to be truly known and expressed in a differentiating desire for an oppositional gender—that is, in a form of oppositional heterosexuality. Whether as a naturalistic paradigm which establishes a causal continuity among sex, gender, and

desire, or as an authentic-expressive paradigm in which a true self is said to be revealed simultaneously or successively in sex, gender, and desire." Butler, *Gender Trouble*, 31.

11. Butler, 22.

12. Butler, 188.

13. Butler, 187 (emphasis in original).

14. Butler, 188.

15. Butler, 189.

16. Renate Lorenz, *Queer Art: A Freak Theory* (Bielefeld: transcript, 2012), 54.

17. Further key examples of this motif, which is certainly not generalized at random, are the lesbian phallus and the adoption of "queer" as a description of oneself in *Bodies That Matter*, various cases of answering back to hate speech in *Excitable Speech*, and the assumption of sovereignty with which Antigone protests against Creon in *Antigone's Claim*. Judith Butler, *Bodies That Matter: On the Discursive Limits of "Sex"* (New York: Routledge, 1993), 84ff., 226; Judith Butler, *The Psychic Life of Power: Theories in Subjection* (Stanford: Stanford University Press, 1997), 22.

18. Butler, *The Psychic Life of Power*. Hilmar Schäfer demonstrates that at this point Butler already exceeds the linguistic understanding of iterability in a self-critical way, moving toward a social approach. See Hilmar Schäfer, *Die Instabilität der Praxis: Reproduktion und Transformation des Sozialen in der Praxistheorie* (Weilerswist: Velbrück Wissenschaft, 2014), 239. However, this once again brings only the authorization of the speakers into view, which in the best case covers just one part of social structures.

19. Butler, "What Is Critique?"; Judith Butler, *Undoing Gender* (New York: Routledge, 2004), 40–44.

20. Judith Butler, *Antigone's Claim: Kinship Between Life and Death* (New York: Columbia University Press, 2000), 57.

21. Butler, "What Is Critique?"

22. Butler, *Gender Trouble*, 200.

23. Butler, 189.

24. Butler, 189.

25. Butler, 203.

26. Butler, 189.

27. Butler, 189.

28. Butler, 200.

8. CONSTITUTION

1. Tobias Matzner responds convincingly to the question of how something becomes intelligible, connecting Arendt and Wittgenstein without "inserting" Butler: see Tobias Matzner, *Vita variabilis: Handelnde und ihre Welt nach Hannah Arendt und Ludwig Wittgenstein* (Würzburg: Königshausen und Neumann, 2013), 182–186.

2. See Judith Butler, *Gender Trouble: Feminism and the Subversion of Identity* (1990; New York: Routledge, 1999), 200.

3. Renate Lorenz, *Queer Art: A Freak Theory* (Bielefeld: transcript, 2012), 61.

4. Antke Engel, "Akzeptanzschwierigkeiten? Dimensionen und Strategien queerer Politik," in *Kunst der Kritik*, ed. B. Mennel, S. Nowotny, and G. Raunig (Vienna: Turia + Kant, 2010), 68 (quotation trans. LD).

5. Here I do not mean that the division into performers and audience is constitutive, but that collectivity is decisive—there must be a context in which the praxis-defining rules are shared and

therefore recognized. In contrast, Judith Mohrmann proposes that the constitutive marker of political situations is a theatrical division into actors and spectators, which I play down here in terms of performativity theory (and, as regards the theatrical aspect, in terms of performance aesthetics); see Judith Mohrmann, *Affekt und Revolution: Politisches Handeln nach Arendt und Kant* (Frankfurt: Campus, 2015).

6.   Corinna Gentschel, "Erstrittene Subjektivität: Die Diskurse der Transsexualität," *Das Argument* 243, no. 6 (2001): 281–283.

7.   Uta Schirmer, *Geschlecht anders gestalten: Drag Kinging, geschichtliche Selbstverhältnisse und Wirklichkeiten* (Bielefeld: transcript, 2010), 185.

8.   Tino, cited in Uta Schirmer, *Geschlecht anders gestalten: Drag Kinging, geschichtliche Selbstverhältnisse und Wirklichkeiten* (Bielefeld: transcript, 2010), 166 (quotation trans. LD, emphasis Schirmer).

9.   See Amy Robinson, "It Takes One to Know One: Passing and Communities of Interest," *Critical Inquiry* 20, no. 4 (1994): 715–736.

10.   As explained in part 1, chapter 3, these distinctions between the different types of rules that take effect in practices are always relative. The ability to see a praxis in a specific way can in itself be understood as a praxis that would require a certain "knowing by doing."

11.   Of course, I am simplifying grossly at this point by leaving *imagined* relationality aside. However, in previous work, I have tried to show in response to Teresa de Lauretis's theory of perverse desire that even fantasy scenarios that guide our desires can be traced back to subcollective relational contexts. See Eva von Redecker, "Marx's Concept of Needs in the Guise of Queer Desire," in *Global Justice and Desire: Queering the Economy*, ed. N. Dhawan, A. Engel, C. Holzhey, and V. Woltersdorff (London: Routledge, 2015), 23–38; and Teresa de Lauretis, *The Practice of Love: Lesbian Sexuality and Perverse Desire* (Bloomington: Indiana University Press, 1994).

12.   Hannah Arendt, *On Revolution* (1963; London: Penguin, 1990), 215.

13.   Arendt, 249.

14.   Hannah Arendt, *On Violence* (New York: Harcourt Brace, 1969), 44.

15.   On counterpower, see Miguel Abensour, *Democracy Against the State: Marx and the Machiavellian Moment* (Cambridge: Polity, 2011); and Robin Celikates, "Die Demokratisierung der Demokratie: Etienne Balibar über die Dialektik von konstituierender und konstituierter Macht," in *Das Politische denken: Zeitgenössische Positionen*, ed. U. Bröckling and R. Feustel (Berlin: transcript, 2010), 59–76; on constitutive power, see Etienne Balibar, "(De)Constructing the Human as Human Institution: A Reflection on the Coherence of Hannah Arendt's Practical Philosophy," *Social Research* 74, no. 3 (2007): 727–738.

16.   Hannah Arendt, *The Human Condition* (1958; Chicago: University of Chicago Press, 1998), 206.

17.   Arendt, *On Revolution*, 142.

18.   Hannah Arendt, *Crises of the Republic* (Middlesex, UK: Penguin, 1969), 77.

19.   Cited in Arendt, 95 (emphasis Arendt's).

20.   Arendt, 51.

21.   Arendt, 76, 98.

22.   Amy Allen has also emphasized the problem that Butler cannot theorize collectivity; however, she tries to solve this by introducing points of reference that are normatively binding, and not by accentuating different levels of collectivity: see Amy Allen, "Power Trouble: Performativity as Critical Theory," *Constellations* 5, no. 4 (1998): 456–471, 466.

23.   Judith Butler, *Notes Towards a Performative Theory of Assembly* (Cambridge, MA: Harvard University Press, 2015), 85.

24.   Butler, 75.

25.   Butler, 72.

26. Arendt, *The Human Condition*, 188.

27. Arendt, 184.

28. Adriana Cavarero introduces her theory of narrative identity, which builds on Arendt's work, by describing a story in which someone stumbles through the snow at night in order to take care of a frozen spring, and the next morning is astonished to see through the window that his footsteps in the snow form a shape—that of a stork. This beautifully expresses the relationship of action to stories, as its unintended product. See Adriana Cavarero, *Relating Narratives: Storytelling and Selfhood* (1997; New York: Routledge, 2000), 3.

29. Arendt, *The Human Condition*, 199–200.

30. Hannes Bajohr, *Dimensionen der Öffentlichkeit: Politik und Erkenntnis bei Hannah Arendt* (Berlin: Lukas, 2011), 61 (quotation trans. LD).

31. Michael Warner and Lauren Berlant, "Sex in Public," *Critical Inquiry* 24, no. 2 (1998): 561.

32. See Deborah B. Gould, *Moving Politics: Emotion and ACT UP's Fight Against AIDS* (Chicago: University of Chicago Press, 2009), 194: "Given the prevailing climate of sexual fear in the late 1980s—in both gay and straight worlds—ACT UP's celebration of queer sexuality was a political act. Indeed, many ACT UP members experienced their bodies as the battleground on which the AIDS war was being fought, both in terms of HIV and its related illnesses, and in terms of sexual freedom."

33. Gould, 178: "ACT UP was a place to fight the AIDS crisis, and it was always more than that as well. It was a place to elaborate critiques of the status quo, to imagine alternative worlds, to express anger, to defy authority, to form sexual and other intimacies, to practice non-hierarchical governance and self-determination, to argue with one another, to refashion identities, to experience new feelings, to be changed."

34. Arendt, *The Human Condition*, 137.

35. As Rahel Jaeggi emphasizes, Arendt's notion of the "Dingwelt" does actually reach far enough to encompass everything that is "created," including that which does not come from production but from action, such as institutions. See Rahel Jaeggi, *Welt und Person: Zum anthropologischen Hintergrund der Gesellschaftskritik bei Hannah Arendt* (Berlin: Lukas, 1997), 53.

36. Cindy Patton, *Globalizing AIDS* (Minneapolis: University of Minnesota Press, 2002), 22.

9. CONTAMINATION

1. Raymond Geuss, "The Radioactive Wolf, Pieing, and the Goddess Fashion," in *Reality and Its Dreams* (Cambridge, MA: Harvard University Press, 2016), 226–252.

2. While Katrin Sieg allows the alienation effect and drag performance to become one and the same thing (Kathrin Sieg, *Ethnic Drag: Performing Race, Nation, Sexuality in West Germany* [Michigan: University of Michigan Press, 2002]), Renate Lorenz echoes the criticism that Stefan Brecht (Bertolt Brecht's son) expresses in his text *Queer Theatre*, toward the distanced mode of acting that is intended in Brecht's epic theater (Stefan Brecht, *Queer Theatre [Diaries, Letters and Essays]* [Frankfurt: Suhrkamp, 1978]). Its didactic nature rests on the notion that the performers themselves are aware of the boundary between their portrayal and the thing being portrayed—an assumption that not only performativity theory but also the new performance theater dispute. Brecht jr. was one of the first to analyze this new theater in detail. Renate Lorenz, *Queer Art: A Freak Theory* (Bielefeld: transcript, 2012), 69.

3. Leo Bersani, "Is the Rectum a Grave?," in *AIDS: Cultural Analysis, Cultural Activism*, ed. Douglas Crimp (Cambridge, MA: MIT Press, 1987), 206–207.

4.   Gayle Rubin, "The Traffic in Women: Notes on the 'Political Economy' of Sex," in *Toward an Anthropology of Woman*, ed. R. R. Reiter (New York: Monthly Review Press, 1975), 157–210; Monique Wittig, "The Straight Mind," *Feminist Issues* 1, no. 1 (1980): 103–112.

5.   Richard Dyer, "Getting Over the Rainbow: Identity and Pleasure in Gay Cultural Politics," in *Silver Linings: Some Strategies for the Eighties: Contributions to the Communist University of London*, ed. G. Bridges and R. Brunt (London: Lawrence and Wishart, 1981), 60–61.

6.   Jeffrey Weeks, *Sexuality and Its Discontents: Meanings, Myths and Modern Sexualities* (London: Routledge, 1985), 191.

7.   Bersani, "Is the Rectum a Grave?," 207.

8.   Bersani, 208 (emphasis Bersani's).

9.   The actual aim of Bersani's essay is to counter argumentative maneuvers that he regards as sex-negative attempts to justify sexuality as something other than itself—that is, for example, as subversion.

10. Bersani, "Is the Rectum a Grave?," 207 (emphasis EvR's).

11. Especially as Bersani himself is of the opinion that "campy talk" has subversive qualities due to the fact that it is not eroticized (Bersani, 206).

12. Terms such as "fag hag," "Dorothy," "fruit fly," or "fairy godmother" are used particularly in North America to describe heterosexual women who prefer the company of gay men. The term has undergone a similar resignification from insult to self-descriptor as the term "queer." See Dawne Moon, "Insult and Inclusion: The Term *Fag Hag* and Gay Male 'Community,'" *Social Forces* 74, no. 2 (1995): 487–510.

13. This schematic approach serves a purpose that is itself mainly illustrative. If at all, it would apply to the 1980s in the United States, and therefore orientates itself toward the context in which *Gender Trouble* and *Marta* were produced. I am not concerned here with analyzing the actual demographic composition of ACT UP in comparison with the broader public, which would clearly require a more detailed and intersectional investigation.

14. Martin Saar, "Genealogische Kritik," in *Was ist Kritik?*, ed. R. Jaeggi and T. Wesche (Frankfurt: Suhrkamp, 2009), 252 (quotation trans. LD).

15. Already with regard to Nietzsche and Foucault's approach, Saar makes use of theatrical metaphors: "These other images of our origins necessarily contain something violent, even something artificial. For these scenes have been artificially cut and garishly lit, in order to show something which hitherto remained in the shadows of habits, traditions and legitimizing narratives." Saar, "Genealogische Kritik," 256 (quotation trans. LD).

16. Saar, 251 (quotation trans. LD).

17. Butler, "What Is Critique?"; see also chapter 7.

18. Judith Butler, *Gender Trouble: Feminism and the Subversion of Identity* (1990; New York: Routledge, 1999), 189.

19. That is, I would also argue against allowing diachronic, narrative genealogy itself to merge with this notion of genealogy. Where its opponents accuse genealogy of cryptonormativity (which its proponents deny), I would advocate precisely this "cryptonormativity" as its constructive core. This is based on the view that any description evaluates its material in some way, by reconstructing it in terms of thick normative concepts. The normativity of genealogy is justified if and when it both does justice to the measures of appropriate description and finds resonance. Thus, I do not simply understand genealogies as fictions with a rhetorical intention (for a "realistic" understanding of genealogy, see Raymond Geuss, "Nietzsche and Genealogy," *European Journal of Philosophy* 2, no. 3 [1994]: 274–292). Similarly to interstitial practices that articulate themselves, the proof that something is "true" about a genealogy can be found if it weakens the more common views it attacks. So, if Foucault's description of the prison system seems plausible to us, *even though* it does not correspond to the normative evaluation that we previously adopted regarding this topic, then this speaks

for the validity of its (inseparably normative and descriptive) perspective. If, on the other hand, it were to become clear that Foucault's selection of documents was arbitrary and his interpretation slapdash, we would hardly tend to take on his normative skepticism toward disciplinary processes. The pressure for justification only arises urgently at all if we assume that measures of value float free of the realm of objects and that they can be brought to bear while remaining detached.

20. "Femininity, which I understood never to have belonged to me anyway, was clearly belonging elsewhere, and I was happier to be the audience to it, have always been very happier to be its audience than I ever was or would be being the embodiment of it. (This does not mean, by the way, that I am therefore disembodied, as some rather mean-spirited critics have said or implied.)" Judith Butler, *Undoing Gender* (New York: Routledge, 2004), 213.

21. Various articulated structures could obviously function as carriers. Even the example discussed here would have led to a different discussion if I had not decided at the outset that I would ignore the setting in an unforgivable fashion, along with the fact that these are aesthetic practices. For a discussion in this direction, see, e.g., Richard Dyer, *Only Entertainment* (London: Routledge, 1992).

22. See Paula A. Treichler, *How to Have Theory in an Epidemic: Cultural Chronicles of AIDS* (Durham: Duke University Press, 1999), 296.

23. Eve Kosofsky Sedgwick, *Epistemology of the Closet* (Berkeley: University of California Press, 1990).

24. In chapter 12, I recapitulate the rhetorical definitions of "metalepsis" in more detail.

PART 4. THE EXECUTION OF THE MARQUISE

1. Samson is based on the Parisian executioner Charles Henri Sanson, who occupied this inherited position from 1778 to 1795 and whose diary entries, edited by his son and successor Henri, are an important source for revolutionary historiography. Henri Sanson and Charles Henri Sanson, *Memoirs of the Sansons, 1685–1847*, 2 vols., ed. H. Sanson (London: Chatto and Windus, 1876).

2. Isak Dinesen, "The Proud Lady," in *Carnival: Entertainments and Posthumous Tales* (Chicago: University of Chicago Press, 1977), 270–271. This statement is historically incorrect on several levels. In 1794, or "Year II," it is true that *ci-devant noblesse* was barely executed any longer, but that is only because the focus of persecution had shifted to internal "conspiracies." In fact, many French aristocrats survived the revolution in their castles, without having to hide in a corner. See Cobban, *The Social Interpretation of the French Revolution* (1964; Cambridge: Cambridge University Press, 1999), 87. On the other hand, the term "aristocrat" had been rhetorically extended so far that it could refer to all those whose status, style of clothes, or statements cast doubt on their patriotism. See Albert Soboul, *The Sans-Culottes* (1968; Princeton: Princeton University Press, 1980), 7. However, the logic of the final purge being constantly postponed fits the dynamic of revolutionary internal politics very well. Furet even tries to show this to be the inevitable effect of the patriotic ideal of unity, which can only be mobilized in relation to its negative counterimage, the aristocratic plot: François Furet, *Interpreting the French Revolution* (1978; Cambridge: Cambridge University Press, 1981), 61ff.

3. Dinesen, "The Proud Lady," 268–269.

4. Dinesen, 274–275.

5. Dinesen, 278.

6. Dinesen, 278.

7. Dinesen, 270.

8. Dinesen, 282–283.

9. See, e.g., Sanson, *Memoirs*, 2:84–89.

10.   See Georges Pernoud and Sabine Flaissier, eds., *Die Französische Revolution in Augenzeugenberichten* (1959; Munich: dtv, 1976), 248.

11.   This differentiation between "defeat" and "failure" was developed by Bini Adamczak in relation to the Russian Revolution. While revolutions can be defeated by their enemies, their failure is measured by internal aberrations, which do not cost them power, but the fulfillment of their own revolutionary demands. See Bini Adamczak, *Yesterday's Tomorrow: On the Loneliness of Communist Specters and the Reconstruction of the Future* (Cambridge, MA: MIT Press, 2021).

12.   Soboul, *The Sans-Culottes*, 18.

13.   See Hannah Arendt, *Men in Dark Times* (1955; New York: Harcourt Brace, 1983), 202–203.

14.   "Of course only a redeemed mankind is granted the fullness of its past—which is to say, only for a redeemed mankind has its past become citable in all its moments." Walter Benjamin, "On the Concept of History," in *Selected Writings*, vol. 4, *1938–1940*, ed. H. Eiland and M. W. Jennings (Cambridge, MA: Harvard University Press, 2006), 390.

15.   Walter Benjamin, *The Arcades Project* (1927–1940; Cambridge, MA: Harvard University Press, 1999), 462.

16.   Benjamin, "Concept of History," 397.

17.   Benjamin, 393. Benjamin, *Arcades Project*, 460: "It may be considered one of the methodological objectives of this work to demonstrate a historical materialism which has annihilated within itself the idea of progress. Just here, historical materialism has every reason to distinguish itself sharply from bourgeois habits of thought. Its founding concept is not progress but actualization." Benjamin, "Concept of History," 394–395: "The concept of mankind's historical progress cannot be sundered from the concept of its progression through a homogeneous, empty time. A critique of the concept of such a progression must underlie any criticism of the concept of progress itself."

18.   Benjamin, *Arcades Project*, 474.

19.   Benjamin, 460.

20.   Benjamin, 462–463.

21.   Benjamin, "Concept of History," 396.

22.   "For the destructive momentum in materialist historiography is to be conceived as the reaction to a constellation of dangers, which threatens both the burden of tradition and those who receive it. It is this constellation of dangers which the materialist presentation of history comes to engage." Benjamin, *Arcades Project*, 475.

23.   "'I happened to attend your grandam's trial. . . . You are like her, a sad thing in such a pretty little republican. I wish we could drain the Perrenot blood out of you, then you might make a pleasant wife for any good sansculotte.'" Dinesen, "The Proud Lady," 270. "At another time [Angélique] sighed: 'Good Marie-Marthe, look, she is growing so pale and frail, as if somebody would want to drain the Kerjean blood out of my girl's veins.' And that, Citizen, was why I begged you not to say that you wanted to drain the Perrenot blood out of her. For what would there be left of the poor girl?' Dinesen, "The Proud Lady," 276.

24.   Dinesen, 281–282.

25.   Benjamin, "Concept of History," 397.

26.   Benjamin, 396.

10. PARADIGM SHIFTS

1.   Alasdair MacIntyre, "Epistemological Crises, Dramatic Narrative and the Philosophy of Science," *Monist* 60, no. 4 (1977): 453–472. Of course, MacIntyre is above all concerned with the question of continuity in change in relation to the question of the rationality of the transition, which is more

urgent for him. However, he has exactly the same criteria for this as those used by Kuhn, namely, the norms of the search for truth, which are internal to tradition. See Alasdair MacIntyre, *Whose Justice? Which Rationality?* (Eastborne: Duckworth, 1988), 388. Because MacIntyre equates Kuhn's paradigms with comprehensive worldviews, he misses the fact that Kuhn explicitly discusses the extent to which overarching norms of scholarship outlive the paradigm shift and guide it. See Thomas S. Kuhn, *The Structure of Scientific Revolutions* (Chicago: University of Chicago Press, 2012), 166–167.

2. See Ian Hacking, "Introductory Essay," in Kuhn, *The Structure of Scientific Revolutions*, vii–xxvii.

3. Thomas S. Kuhn, "Postscript" (1969), in *The Structure of Scientific Revolutions*, 173–208.

4. Kuhn, *The Structure of Scientific Revolutions*, 52.

5. Kuhn, 84.

6. Kuhn, 84.

7. Kuhn, 79.

8. Kuhn, 75.

9. See also Kuhn, *The Structure of Scientific Revolutions*, 80: "Every problem that normal science sees as a puzzle can be seen, from another viewpoint, as a counter-instance and thus as a source of crisis.... Furthermore, even the existence of crisis does not by itself transform a puzzle into a counter-instance. There is no such sharp dividing line. Instead, by proliferating versions of the paradigm, crisis loosens the rules of normal puzzle-solving in ways that ultimately permit a new paradigm to emerge."

10. Kuhn, *The Structure of Scientific Revolutions*, 89. See also Kuhn, *The Structure of Scientific Revolutions*, 86, 142: "Often a new paradigm emerges, at least in embryo, before a crisis has developed far or been explicitly recognized"; and: "It follows that concepts like that of an element can scarcely be invented independent of context. Furthermore, given the context, they rarely require invention, because they are already at hand."

11. On the solution to supposed chicken-and-egg regresses, see Richard Raatzsch, "Henne oder Ei?," *Deutsche Zeitschrift für Philosophie* 49, no. 4 (2001): 567–570.

12. Kuhn, *The Structure of Scientific Revolutions*, 82.

13. Kuhn, 7.

14. Kuhn, 85.

15. Andrew Pickering, *The Mangle of Practice: Time, Agency, and Science* (Chicago: University of Chicago Press, 1995).

16. At one point, Kuhn talks much more cautiously about incommensurability: "Therefore, at times of revolution, when the normal-scientific tradition changes, the scientist's perception of his environment must be re-educated—in some familiar situations he must learn to see a new gestalt. After he has done so the world of his research will seem, here and there, incommensurable with the one he had inhabited before. That is another reason why schools guided by different paradigms are always slightly at cross-purposes." Kuhn, *The Structure of Scientific Revolutions*, 112.

17. Richard Rorty, *Philosophy and the Mirror of Nature*, thirtieth anniversary ed. (1979; Princeton: Princeton University Press, 2009), 331.

18. Kuhn, *The Structure of Scientific Revolutions*, 92–93.

19. François Furet, *Interpreting the French Revolution* (1978; Cambridge: Cambridge University Press, 1981); Claude Lefort, "Penser la révolution dans la Révolution française," *Annales* 35, no. 2 (1980): 334–352; Lynn Hunt, *Politics, Culture, and Class in the French Revolution* (Berkeley: University of California Press, 1984).

20. Roger Chartier, *The Cultural Origins of the French Revolution* (Durham: Duke University Press, 1991); Lynn Hunt, *The Family Romance of the French Revolution* (London: Routledge, 1992).

21. Kuhn, *The Structure of Scientific Revolutions*, 151.

22.   Isak Dinesen, "The Proud Lady," in *Carnival: Entertainments and Posthumous Tales* (Chicago: University of Chicago Press, 1977), 272.

23.   This extreme comparison is not supposed to exclude the possibility of such individual transformation. However, it would normally take the form of a muddying of the old paradigm and a diagnosis of crisis, as Kuhn describes it for the core of the field.

24.   Margaret Masterman, "The Nature of a Paradigm," in *Criticism and the Growth of Knowledge*, ed. I. Lakatos and A. Musgrave (Cambridge: Cambridge University Press, 1965), 59–90, 61.

25.   Masterman, "The Nature of a Paradigm," 65: "Preliminary attempts to answer this query by textual criticism make clear that Kuhn's twenty-one senses of 'paradigm' fall into three main groups. For when he equates 'paradigm' with a set of beliefs (p. 4), with a myth (p. 2), with a successful metaphysical speculation (p. 17), with a standard (p. 102), with a new way of seeing (pp. 117–21), with an organizing principle governing perception itself (p. 120), with a map (p. 108), and with something which determines a large area of reality (p. 128), it is clearly a metaphysical notion or entity, rather than a scientific one, which he has in his mind. I shall therefore call paradigms of this philosophical sort metaphysical paradigms or metaparadigms; and these are the only kind of paradigm to which, to my knowledge, Kuhn's philosophical critics have referred. Kuhn's second main sense of 'paradigm,' however, which is given by another group of uses, is a sociological sense. Thus he defines 'paradigm' as a universally recognized scientific achievement (p. x), as a concrete scientific achievement (pp. 10–11), as like a set of political institutions (p. 91), and as like also to an accepted judicial decision (p. 23). I shall call paradigms of this sociological sort sociological paradigms. Finally, Kuhn uses 'paradigm' in a more concrete way still, as an actual textbook; or classic work (p. 10), as supplying tools (pp. 37 and 76), as actual instrumentation (pp. 59 and 60); more linguistically, as a grammatical paradigm (p. 23), illustratively, as an analogy (e.g. on p. 14); and more psychologically, as a gestalt-figure and as an anomalous pack of cards (pp. 63 and 85). I shall call paradigms of this last sort artefact paradigms or construct paradigms."

26.   Masterman, 66.

27.   Kuhn's own adoption of this point of view can serve as a lesson in the adoption of knowledge—he mentions that "someone" has been kind enough to list twenty-two (*sic!*) ways of using the term "paradigm," and then presents a reformulation of the term "paradigm," which integrates all aspects of Masterman's analysis in a somewhat less detailed form. See Kuhn, "Postscript," 181ff.

28.   Kuhn himself says, referring to Wittgenstein, that paradigms are "prior to rules." Kuhn, *The Structure of Scientific Revolutions*, 42ff.

29.   Masterman, "The Nature of a Paradigm," 66.

30.   Masterman, 69.

31.   Masterman, 70.

32.   Masterman, 69.

33.   Masterman, 85.

34.   Masterman, 85. "Kuhn's paradigm's 'way of seeing,' however, really is different from this—and not only because, as asserted earlier, his paradigm already exists when the theory is not there. It is different because his paradigm is a concrete 'picture' of something, A, which is used analogically to describe a concrete something else, B. (That is, the trick which, as I said earlier, starts off every new science, is that a known construct, an artefact, becomes a 'research vehicle,' and at the same moment, if successful, it becomes a paradigm, by being used to apply to new material, and in a non-obvious way.) It thus has two kinds of concreteness, not one: the concreteness which it brought with it through being a 'picture' of A, and the second concreteness which it has now acquired, through becoming applied to B." Masterman, "The Nature of a Paradigm," 77–78.

35.   Masterman, 80.

36.   Masterman, 85.

37. Masterman, 78.

38. Cited in Joan Wallach Scott, "French Feminists and the Rights of 'Man,'" *History Workshop* 28 (1989): 3.

II. THE REVOLUTIONARY EMERGENCE OF THE CONCEPT

1. Karl Marx, *The Poverty of Philosophy* (1847; New York: Cosimo, 2008), 119.

2. Jean Jaurès, *Histoire socialiste de la Révolution française* (1904; Paris: Éditions Sociales, 1968); Eric J. Hobsbawm, *The Age of Revolution: Europe, 1789–1848* (London: Weidenfeldt and Nicolson, 1962).

3. Albert Soboul, "Classes and Class Struggles During the French Revolution," *Science and Society* 17, no. 5 (1953): 238–257.

4. Albert Soboul, *The Sans-Culottes* (1968; Princeton: Princeton University Press, 1980), 42.

5. Theda Skocpol, "Cultural Idioms and Political Ideologies in the Revolutionary Reconstruction of State Power: A Rejoinder to Sewell," *Journal of Modern History* 57, no. 1 (1985): 86–96.

6. Cobban, *The Social Interpretation of the French Revolution* (1964; Cambridge: Cambridge University Press, 1999).

7. Georges Lefebvre, "Le mythe de la Révolution française," *Annales historiques de la Révolution française* 259 (1985): 1–7.

8. See the detailed discussion in Martin Jay, "Historicism and the Event," in *Against the Grain: Jewish Intellectuals in Hard Times*, ed. E. Mendelssohn, S. Hoffman, and R. I. Cohen (Oxford: Berghahn, 2013), 143–168.

9. Louis Althusser, *For Marx* (1965; London: Verso, 2005), 126.

10. Michel Foucault, "The Order of Discourse" (1970), in *Archives of Infamy*, ed. N. Luxor (Minneapolis: University of Minnesota Press, 2019), 141–174.

11. Gilles Deleuze, *The Logic of Sense*, ed. C. V. Boundas (New York: Columbia University Press, 1990), 8; Jean-François Lyotard, "March 23," in *Political Writings* (Minneapolis: University of Minnesota Press, 1993), 64.

12. This of course implies that far fewer things can be accorded the status of events. For Heidegger, it is only the breaks between different "fundamental metaphysical positions," which he defines according to the classic epochal breaks between classical, medieval, and modern times. See Martin Heidegger, "The Age of the World Picture" (1938), in *Off the Beaten Track* (Cambridge: Cambridge University Press, 2002), 78–79.

13. Jacques Derrida, *Without Alibi* (Stanford: Stanford University Press, 2002), 234.

14. See Claude Lefort, "Penser la révolution dans la Révolution française," *Annales* 35, no. 2 (1980): 334–352.

15. William H. Sewell Jr., *Logics of History: Social Theory and Social Transformation* (Chicago: University of Chicago Press, 2005), 244.

16. Lynn A. Hunt, *Politics, Culture, and Class in the French Revolution* (Oakland: University of California Press, 1984), 3. In a bit more detail, her conclusions about the political results of the revolution are as follows: "In my view, the social and economic changes brought about by the revolution were not revolutionary. Nobles were able to return to their titles and to much of their land. Although considerable amounts of land changed hands during the revolution, the structure of landholding remained much the same.... Industrial capitalism still grew at a snail's pace. In the realm of politics, in contrast, everything changed. Thousands of men and even many women gained first hand experience in the political arena: they talked, read, and listened in new ways; they voted, they joined

new organizations; and they marched for their political goals. Revolution became a tradition, and republicanism an enduring option" (221).

17.　Hunt, 132, 152.

18.　Sewell, *Logics of History*, 227.

19.　Sewell, 226.

20.　Sewell, 244.

21.　Sewell, 243.

22.　Sewell, 229.

23.　Sewell, 227.

24.　Giddens uses the example of imprisonment in concentration camps to show that the break with all reliable everyday routines makes the ability to act disintegrate completely, as an illustration of his general thesis that structures make action possible. Although the theoretical point is correct, this is a strange and cynical way of substantiating it—the problem with imprisonment in the camps was not "only" the destruction of daily routines, but the practices that replaced them. Anthony Giddens, *The Constitution of Society: Outline of the Theory of Structuration* (Cambridge: Polity, 1984), 61ff. For a much more enlightening approach to this question, see Hannah Arendt's discussion of how very specific measures deeply undermined the core ability of the prisoners to act. Hannah Arendt, *Elemente und Ursprünge totaler Herrschaft* (1955; Munich: Piper, 1986), 927ff.

25.　Sewell, *Logics of History*, 228.

26.　Charles Tilly, *The Contentious French: Four Centuries of Popular Struggle* (Cambridge, MA: Harvard University Press, 1986).

27.　Sewell, *Logics of History*, 252.

28.　Hunt, *Politics, Culture, and Class*, 53–54.

29.　Theda Skocpol voices well-founded reservations against an analogous generalization that Sewell made in his earlier essay on the night of August 4, declaring it the turning point in the ascendency of Enlightenment ideology. See William H. Sewell Jr., "Ideologies and Social Revolutions: Reflections on the French Case," *Journal of Modern History* 57, no. 1 (1985): 57–85; Skocpol, "Cultural Idioms," 88.

30.　Sewell, *Logics of History*, 260.

31.　Sewell, 228.

32.　Hannah Arendt, *Crises of the Republic* (Middlesex, UK: Penguin, 1969), 206.

33.　Sewell, *Logics of History*, 145.

34.　Hunt, *Politics, Culture, and Class*, 124.

35.　Hunt, 132–133.

36.　Hunt, 215–216.

37.　Sewell, *Logics of History*, 226.

38.　Hunt, *Politics, Culture, and Class*, 72.

39.　Sewell, *Logics of History*, 257.

40.　Lynn Hunt, "The World We Have Gained: The Future of the French Revolution," *American Historical Review* 108, no. 1 (2003): 1–19.

41.　Sewell, "Ideologies and Social Revolutions."

42.　Michel Foucault, *Discipline and Punish: The Birth of the Prison* (1975; New York: Vintage, 1995), 31.

43.　Foucault, *Discipline and Punish*, 120.

12. METALEPTIC DYNAMICS

1.　After all, even Prometheus did not invent fire, but stole it from the gods.

2.　Thus, I only want to draw an analogy between the position of practices in situations of social change and the position of concepts when metalepsis is used as a stylistic device. I am not concerned with developing any more far-reaching claim about the way in which the social might be structured in rhetorical patterns of order—on the contrary, I argued in part 2 that it is ordered in connections between practices and their aggregates, structures. I do not mean to suggest that social change is a question of change in meaning. Indeed, in my analogy it is precisely not the meanings of practices that change metaleptically, but practices themselves. In any case, we cannot isolate the meaning of practices from their materiality and the way in which they are carried out, as is shown in chapter 2.

3. I am indebted to Raymond Geuss for his explanation of the Greek terms.

4. See Gert Ueding, ed., *Historisches Wörterbuch der Rhetorik*, 10 vols. (Tübingen: Niemeyer, 2001), 5:1087. I do not discuss the narratological adoption of the term "metalepsis" by Genette to refer to the device of transgressing the boundaries between narrative levels. Gérard Genette, *Métalepse: De la figure á la fiction* (Paris: Editions de Seuil, 2004), 77.

5. "τίθημι γὰρ καὶ τὴν τῶν κακῶν ἢ φαινομένων κακῶν ἀπαλλαγὴν ἢ ἀντὶ μείζονος ἐλάττονος μετάληψιν ἐν ἀγαθοῖς" (*Rhetoric*, 1369b25)—"I place removal of evils or apparent evils or exchange of greater for less [evil] among the goods; for they are somehow preferable, and [so is] removal of pains or what appears so; and exchange of lesser for greater similarly among pleasures." Aristotle, *On Rhetoric: A Theory of Civic Discourse*, trans. George A. Kennedy (Oxford: Oxford University Press, 2007), 86. Although this occurs in the book on rhetoric, at this point metalepsis is being discussed not as a stylistic device but as an example of how the word was actually used. Here, Aristotle is discussing the preconditions for speaking, in terms of ethics and the theory of decision-making.

6. Cited in Ueding, *Historisches Wörterbuch der Rhetorik*, 1094.

7. The sentence in question comes from the *Eclogues* (1.69): "post aliquot mea regna videns mirabor aristas." This could be rendered as, "After a few ears of corn I will be astonished to see my realm." Although the line is now usually translated differently (see Virgil, *The Eclogues*, trans. Guy Lee [London: Penguin, 1980, 34–35]), it is a standard example of metalepsis: see Ruurd Nauta, "The Concept of 'Metalepsis': From Rhetoric to the Theory of Allusion and to Narratology," in *Über die Grenze: Metalepse in Text- und Bildmedien des Altertums*, ed. Ute E. Eisen and Peter von Möllendorff (Berlin: de Gruyter, 2013), 472.

8. Michael Mann, *The Sources of Social Power*, vol. 3, *Global Empires and Revolution, 1890–1945* (Cambridge: Cambridge University Press, 2012), 7, 16.

9. Margaret Masterman, "The Nature of a Paradigm," in *Criticism and the Growth of Knowledge*, ed. I. Lakatos and A. Musgrave (Cambridge: Cambridge University Press, 1965), 59–90, 66.

10. Masterman, 69.

11. Cited in Ueding, *Historisches Wörterbuch der Rhetorik*, 1091–1092 (quotation trans. LD).

12. Judith Butler, *Gender Trouble: Feminism and the Subversion of Identity* (1990; New York: Routledge, 1999), xiv, 189; Butler, *Excitable Speech: A Politics of the Performative* (New York: Routledge, 1997), 45, 49–50; Butler, *The Psychic Life of Power: Theories in Subjection* (Stanford: Stanford University Press, 1997), 16.

13. Karl Marx, *The Poverty of Philosophy* (1847; New York: Cosimo, 2008), 190.

14. In *The Poverty of Philosophy*, from which this quotation is taken, Marx himself quite clearly propounds what later became the dogmatic school of the "base-superstructure relationship." Of course, other points of emphasis are found elsewhere in his work. I have previously traced the motif of radical needs, which plays a much more metaleptic role in Marx's understanding of transformation. Eva von Redecker, "Marx's Concept of Needs in the Guise of Queer Desire," in *Global Justice and Desire: Queering the Economy*, ed. N. Dhawan, A. Engel, C. Holzhey, and V. Woltersdorff (London: Routledge, 2015), 23–38.

15. Martin Buber, *Paths in Utopia* (1949; Syracuse: Syracuse University Press, 1996), 44.

16. Helmut Glück, *Metzler Lexikon Sprache* (Stuttgart: Metzler, 2005), 406.

17. Karl Marx, "The Eighteenth Brumaire of Louis Bonaparte" (1852), in *Later Political Writings*, ed. Terell Carver (Cambridge: Cambridge University Press, 1996), 31–127, 35.

18. G. W. Friedrich Hegel, *Elements of the Philosophy of Right* (1821; Cambridge: Cambridge University Press, 1991).

19. Thus, Theda Skocpol summarizes: "That process raised hopes for change and brought peasants together in community settings where antiseigneural struggles, especially, had historically been a shared enterprise. The strengthening of collective consciousness and organization associated with the drawing up of the *cahiers* better prepared the peasants to act for the insurrectionary ends of 1789." Theda Skocpol, *States and Social Revolutions* (Cambridge: Cambridge University Press, 1979), 123.

20. Georges Lefebvre, *The Great Fear of 1789: Rural Panic in Revolutionary France* (New York: Pantheon, 1973), 39.

21. This refers to Dinesen's narrative. At the end of the previous chapter, meanwhile, I explicitly emphasized that the mechanisms of oppression and the ideas regarding the sexual order that accompanied the revolution did deviate clearly from those of the ancien régime. However, it seems justified to describe both as patriarchal.

CONCLUSION

1. Hannah Arendt, *Lectures on Kant's Political Philosophy*, ed. R. Beiner (Chicago: University of Chicago Press, 1992), 77.

2. I owe this clarification to very helpful and generous comments from Jodi Dean. Much as I might personally favor spontaneous councils, my metaleptic model could be adapted to Leninist strategy: the party is that articulated structure which allows fleeting insurrectionary moments to be transferred into a new order. Jodi Dean, *Crowds and Party* (London: Verso, 2016).

3. Bini Adamczak, *Beziehungsweise Revolution: 1917, 1968 und kommende* (Berlin: Suhrkamp, 2017), 23ff.

4. Antke Engel, "Tender Tensions—Antagonistic Struggles—Becoming-Bird: Queer Political Interventions Into Neoliberal Hegemony," in *Hegemony and Heteronormativity: Revisiting "The Political" in Queer Politics*, ed. M. Castro Varela, N. Dhawan, and A. Engel (Farnham, UK: Ashgate, 2011), 63–90.

5. Mary Wollstonecraft, *Mary* and *The Wrongs of Woman* (1798; Oxford: Oxford University Press, 2009), 174.

Bibliography

Abensour, Miguel. *Democracy Against the State: Marx and the Machiavellian Moment*. Cambridge: Polity, 2011.

ACT UP New York. Civil Disobedience Training. www.actupny.org//documents/CDdocuments/ACTUP_CivilDisobedience.pdf.

Adamczak, Bini. *Beziehungsweise Revolution: 1917, 1968 und kommende*. Berlin: Suhrkamp, 2017.

——. *Yesterday's Tomorrow: On the Loneliness of Communist Specters and the Reconstruction of the Future*. Cambridge, MA: MIT Press, 2021.

Allen, Amy. *The End of Progress: Decolonizing the Normative Foundations of Critical Theory*. New York: Columbia University Press, 2016.

——. "Power Trouble: Performativity as Critical Theory." *Constellations* 5, no. 4 (1998): 456–471.

Althusser, Louis. *For Marx*. 1965; London: Verso, 2005.

——. "Ideology and Ideological State Apparatuses." In *Lenin and Philosophy*, 85–126. New York: Monthly Review Press, 1971.

Andrews, Kehinde. *Back to Black: Retelling Black Radicalism for the 21st Century*. London: Zed, 2018.

Archer, Margaret. "Morphogenesis Versus Structuration." *British Journal of Sociology* 33, no. 4 (1982): 455–483.

Arendt, Hannah. *Crises of the Republic*. Middlesex, UK: Penguin, 1969.

——. *Elemente und Ursprünge totaler Herrschaft*. 1955; Munich: Piper, 1986.

——. *The Human Condition*. 1958; Chicago: University of Chicago Press, 2018.

——. *Lectures on Kant's Political Philosophy*. Edited by R. Beiner. Chicago: University of Chicago Press, 1992.

——. *The Life of the Mind*. New York: Harcourt Brace, 1981.

——. *Men in Dark Times*. 1955; New York: Harcourt Brace, 1983.

——. *On Revolution*. 1963; London: Penguin, 1990.

——. *On Violence*. New York: Harcourt Brace, 1969.

Aristotle, *On Rhetoric: A Theory of Civic Discourse*. Translated by George A. Kennedy. Oxford: Oxford University Press, 2007.

Arruzza, Cinzia. *Dangerous Liaisons: The Marriages and Divorces of Marxism and Feminism*. Pontypool: Merlin, 2013.

Austin, John L. *How to Do Things with Words*. Cambridge, MA: Harvard University Press, 1962.

Bachrach, Peter, and Morton Baratz. "The Two Faces of Power." *American Political Science Review* 56 (1962): 942–952.

Badiou, Alain. *The Communist Hypothesis*. London: Verso, 2015.

——. "One Divides Itself Into Two." In *Lenin Reloaded*, edited by S. Budgen, S. Kouvelakis, and S. Žižek, 7–17. Durham: Duke University Press, 2007.

——. *Philosophy for Militants*. London: Verso, 2012.

Bajohr, Hannes. *Dimensionen der Öffentlichkeit: Politik und Erkenntnis bei Hannah Arendt*. Berlin: Lukas, 2011.

Balibar, Etienne. "(De)Constructing the Human as Human Institution: A Reflection on the Coherence of Hannah Arendt's Practical Philosophy." *Social Research* 74, no. 3 (2007): 727–738.

Baltzer, Ulrich, and Gerhard Schönrich, eds. *Institutionen und Regelfolgen*. Paderborn: Mentis, 2002.

Barad, Karen. "Posthumanist Performativity: Towards an Understanding of How Matter Comes to Matter." *Signs* 28, no. 3 (2003): 801–831.

Beal, Frances. "Double Jeopardy: To Be Black and Female." In *Black Women's Manifesto*, edited by Gayle Lynch, 19–34. New York: Third World Women's Alliance, 1969.

Bedau, Hugo A. "On Civil Disobedience." *Journal of Philosophy* 58, no. 21 (1961): 653–661.

Bedorf, Thomas, and Kurt Röttgers, eds. *Das Politische und die Politik*. Frankfurt: Suhrkamp, 2010.

Benhabib, Seyla. "Feminismus und Postmoderne: Ein prekäres Bündnis." In *Der Streit um Differenz: Feminismus und Postmoderne in der Gegenwart*, edited by S. Benhabib, J. Butler, D. Cornell, and N. Fraser, 9–30. Frankfurt: Fischer, 1993.

Benjamin, Walter. *The Arcades Project*. 1927–1940; Cambridge, MA: Harvard University Press, 1999.

——. "On the Concept of History." In *Selected Writings*, 4:389–400.

——. *Selected Writings*. Vol. 4, *1938–1940*. Edited by H. Eiland and M. W. Jennings. Cambridge, MA: Harvard University Press, 2006.

Bersani, Leo. "Is the Rectum a Grave?" In *AIDS: Cultural Analysis, Cultural Activism*, edited by Douglas Crimp, 97–222. Cambridge, MA: MIT Press, 1987.

Bloor, David. "Wittgenstein and the Priority of Practice." In *The Practice Turn in Contemporary Theory*, edited by T. R. Schatzki, K. Knorr Cetina, and E. von Savigny, 103–114. London: Psychology, 2001.

Bourdieu, Pierre. *The Logic of Practice*. 1980; Stanford: Stanford University Press, 1990.

——. *Outline of a Theory of Practice*. 1972; Cambridge: Cambridge University Press, 1977.

Brecht, Bertolt. "Episches Theater/Entfremdung" (1937). In *Schriften*, 6:243–244.

——. *Große kommentierte Berliner und Frankfurter Ausgabe*. Vol. 15. 1949; Frankfurt: Suhrkamp, 1993.

——. *Schriften: Werke in sechs Bänden*. Vol. 6. Frankfurt: Suhrkamp, 1997.

——. "Verfremdungseffekte in der chinesischen Schauspielkunst" (1936). In *Schriften: Werke in sechs Bänden. Sechster Band*, 232–242. Frankfurt: Suhrkamp, 1997.

Brecht, Stefan. *Queer Theatre (Diaries, Letters and Essays)*. Frankfurt: Suhrkamp, 1978.

Bridges, Georges, and Rosalind Brunt, eds. *Silver Linings: Some Strategies for the Eighties: Contributions to the Communist University of London*. London: Lawrence and Wishart, 1981.

Bröckling, Ulrich, and Robert Feustel, eds. *Das Politische denken: Zeitgenössische Positionen*. Berlin: transcript, 2010.

brown, adrienne maree. *Emergent Strategy: Shaping Change, Changing Worlds*. Chico: AK, 2017.

Brown, Wendy. *Edgework*. New Jersey: Princeton University Press, 2005.

——. "Feminism Unbound: Revolution, Mourning, Politics." In *Edgework*, 98–136.

——. "Resisting Left Melancholy." *Boundary 2* 26, no. 3 (1999): 19–27.

Brown, Wendy, Samuel Burgum, Sebastian Raza, and Jorge Vasquez. "Redoing the Demos? An Interview with Wendy Brown." *Theory, Culture, and Society*, 2017. www.theoryculturesociety.org/interview -wendy-brown/.

Browne, Victoria. *Feminism, Time, and Nonlinear History*. London: Palgrave Macmillan, 2014.

Brownlee, Kimberley. "Civil Disobedience." In *Stanford Encyclopedia of Philosophy*. Stanford: CSLI, 2009. http://plato.stanford.edu/entries/civil-disobedience/.

Brunkhorst, Hauke. *Critical Theory of Legal Revolutions: Evolutionary Perspectives.* London: Bloomsbury, 2014.

——. "Kommentar." In *Der achtzehnte Brumaire des Louis Bonaparte,* by Karl Marx, 133–328. Frankfurt: Suhrkamp, 2007.

Buber, Martin. "Alte und Neue Gemeinschaft" (1900). *Association for Jewish Studies Review* 1 (1976): 41–56.

——. *Paths in Utopia.* 1949; Syracuse: Syracuse University Press, 1996.

Budgen, Sebastian, Stathis Kouvelakis, and Slavoj Žižek, eds. *Lenin Reloaded.* Durham: Duke University Press, 2007.

Burke, Edmund. *Reflections on the Revolution in France.* 1790; Middlesex, UK: Penguin, 1982.

Butler, Judith. *Antigone's Claim: Kinship Between Life and Death.* New York: Columbia University Press, 2000.

——. *Bodies That Matter: On the Discursive Limits of "Sex."* New York: Routledge, 1993.

——. *Excitable Speech: A Politics of the Performative.* New York: Routledge, 1997.

——. *Gender Trouble: Feminism and the Subversion of Identity.* 1990; New York: Routledge, 1999.

——. *Giving an Account of Oneself.* New York: Fordham University Press, 2005.

——. *Notes Toward a Performative Theory of Assembly.* Cambridge, MA: Harvard University Press, 2015.

——. *The Psychic Life of Power: Theories in Subjection.* Stanford: Stanford University Press, 1997.

——. "Reply from Judith Butler to Mills and Jenkins." *differences* 18, no. 2 (2007): 180–195.

——. *Undoing Gender.* New York: Routledge, 2004.

——. "What Is Critique? An Essay on Foucault's Virtue." 2001. https://transversal.at/transversal/0806/butler/en.

Butler, Judith, Peter Osborne, and Lynne Segal. "Gender as Performance: An Interview with Judith Butler." *Radical Philosophy* 67 (1994): 32–39.

Callinicos, Alex. "Anthony Giddens: A Contemporary Critique." *Theory and Society* 14, no. 2 (1985): 133–166.

Castro Varela, María do Mar, Nikita Dhawan, and Antke Engel, eds. *Hegemony and Heteronormativity: Revisiting "The Political" in Queer Politics.* Farnham, UK: Ashgate, 2011.

Cavarero, Adriana. *Relating Narratives: Storytelling and Selfhood.* 1997; New York: Routledge, 2000.

Cavell, Stanley. "The Ordinary as the Uneventful" (1984). In *The Cavell Reader,* edited by Steven Mulhall, 253–259. Cambridge, MA: Blackwell, 1996.

Celikates, Robin. "Die Demokratisierung der Demokratie: Etienne Balibar über die Dialektik von konstituierender und konstituierter Macht." In *Das Politische denken: Zeitgenössische Positionen,* edited by U. Bröckling and R. Feustel, 59–76. Berlin: transcript, 2010.

——. *Kritik als soziale Praxis: Gesellschaftliche Selbstverständigung und kritische Theorie.* Frankfurt: Campus, 2009.

——. "Ziviler Ungehorsam und radikale Demokratie: Konstituierende vs. Konstituierte Macht?" In *Das Politische und die Politik,* edited by T. Bedorf and K. Röttgers, 274–300. Frankfurt: Suhrkamp, 2010.

——. "Ziviler Ungehorsam—zwischen symbolischer Politik und realer Konfrontation." In *Demonstrationen: Vom Werden normativer Ordnungen,* edited by Frankfurter Kunstverein/Exzellenzcluster "Die Herausbildung normativer Ordnungen," 352–357. Nürnberg: Verlag für moderne Kunst, 2012.

Celikates, Robin, and Rahel Jaeggi. "Verflüssigung der Demokratie: Zwischen Revolution und Institution." Polar 1, no. 1 (2005). www.polar-zeitschrift.de/polar_01.php?id=33.

de Certeau, Michel. *The Practice of Everyday Life.* 1980; Berkeley: University of California Press, 1988.

Char, René. *Feuillets d'Hypnos.* Paris: Gallimard, 1946.

Chartier, Roger. *The Cultural Origins of the French Revolution.* Durham: Duke University Press, 1991.

Chaturvedi, Vinayak, ed. *Mapping Subaltern Studies and the Postcolonial.* London: Verso, 2000.

Claeys, Gregory. *The French Revolution Debate in Britain: The Origin of Modern Politics.* London: Palgrave Macmillan, 2007.

Cohen, G. A. *Karl Marx's Theory of History: A Defence.* 1978; Oxford: Oxford University Press, 2000.

Crimp, Douglas, ed. *AIDS: Cultural Analysis, Cultural Activism*. Cambridge, MA: MIT Press, 1987.

——. *AIDS|DEMO|GRAPHICS*. Seattle: Bay, 1990.

——. "How to Have Promiscuity in an Epidemic" (1987). In *Mourning and Melancholia: Essays on AIDS and Queer Politics*, 43–82. Cambridge, MA: MIT Press, 2002.

Dahl, Robert A. "A Critique of the Ruling Elite Model." *American Political Science Review* 52 (1958): 463–469.

Deleuze, Gilles. *The Logic of Sense*. Edited by C. V. Boundas. New York: Columbia University Press, 1990.

Derrida, Jacques. "Signature Event Context" (1972). In *Limited Ink*, 1–25. Evanston, IL: Northwestern University Press, 1988.

——. *Without Alibi*. Stanford: Stanford University Press, 2002.

Descartes, René. *Meditations on First Philosophy*. 1641; Cambridge: Cambridge University Press, 2017.

Deuber-Mankowski, Astrid. "Kritik der Moderne im Zeichen des Geschlechts." In *1789/1989: Die Revolution hat nicht stattgefunden*, edited by A. Deuber-Mankowski, U. Ramming, and E. W. Tielsch, 87–97. Tübingen: edition discord, 1989.

Deuber-Mankowski, Astrid, Ulrike Ramming, and E. Walesca Tielsch, eds. *1789/1989: Die Revolution hat nicht stattgefunden*. Tübingen: edition discord, 1989.

Deutscher, Penelope. "Analogy of Analogy: Animals and Slaves in Mary Wollstonecraft's Defense of Women's Rights." In *Reproduction, Race and Gender in Philosophy and the Early Life Sciences*, edited by Susanne Lettow, 187–215. Albany: SUNY Press, 2014.

Dhawan, Nikita, Antke Engel, Christoph Holzhey, and Volker Woltersdorff, eds. *Global Justice and Desire: Queering Economy*. London: Routledge, 2015.

Dickens, Charles. *A Tale of Two Cities*. 1859; Oxford: Oxford University Press, 2008.

Dinesen, Isak. "The Proud Lady." In *Carnival: Entertainments and Posthumous Tales*, 267–283. Chicago: University of Chicago Press, 1977.

Distelhorst, Lars, ed. *Staat, Politik, Ethik: Zum Staatsverständnis Judith Butlers*. Baden-Baden: Nomos, 2016.

Dyer, Richard. "Getting Over the Rainbow: Identity and Pleasure in Gay Cultural Politics." In *Silver Linings: Some Strategies for the Eighties: Contributions to the Communist University of London*, edited by G. Bridges and R. Brunt, 53–67. London: Lawrence and Wishart, 1981.

——. *Only Entertainment*. London: Routledge, 1992.

Ehrmann, Jeanette. *Tropen der Revolution: Die Haitianische Revolution und die Dekolonisierung des Politischen*. Berlin: Suhrkamp, 2021.

Elbe, Ingo, Sven Ellmers, and Jan Eufinger, eds. *Anonyme Herrschaft: Zur Struktur moderner Machtverhältnisse*. Münster: Westfälisches Dampfboot, 2012.

Elster, Jon. *Making Sense of Marx*. Cambridge: Cambridge University Press, 1985.

Engel, Antke, "Akzeptanzschwierigkeiten? Dimensionen und Strategien queerer Politik." In *Kunst der Kritik*, edited by B. Mennel, S. Nowotny, and G. Raunig, 65–84. Vienna: Turia + Kant, 2010.

——. "Tender Tensions—Antagonistic Struggles—Becoming-Bird: Queer Political Interventions Into Neoliberal Hegemony." In *Hegemony and Heteronormativity: Revisiting "The Political" in Queer Politics*, edited by M. Castro Varela, N. Dhawan, and A. Engel, 63–90. Farnham, UK: Ashgate, 2011.

——. "Unter Verzicht auf Autorisierung: Foucaults Begriff der Akzeptanz und der Status des Wissens in queerer Theorie und Bewegung." In *Ordnungen des Denkens: Debatten um Wissenschaftstheorie und Erkenntniskritik*, edited by Ronald Langner, Timo Luks, Anette Schlimm, Gregor Straube, and Dirk Tomaschke, 269–286. Berlin: LIT, 2007.

——. "Von gouvernementaler Hegemonie zur postsouveränen Staatlichkeit der Diaspora." In *Staat, Politik, Ethik. Zum Staatsverständnis Judith Butlers*, edited by L. Distelhorst, 41–72. Baden-Baden: Nomos, 2016.

——. *Wider die Eindeutigkeit: Sexualität und Geschlecht im Fokus queerer Politik der Repräsentation*. Frankfurt: Campus, 2003.

Engels, Friedrich, and Karl Marx. *The Communist Manifesto.* 1848; London: Penguin, 2002.

Erickson, Amy Louise. *Women and Property in Early Modern England.* 1993; London: Routledge, 1995.

Ferguson, Moira. "Mary Wollstonecraft and the Problematic of Slavery." *Feminist Review* 42 (1992): 82–102.

Ferrarese, Estelle. "Judith Butler's 'Not Particularly Postmodern Insight' of Recognition." *Philosophy and Social Criticism* 37, no. 7 (2011): 759–774.

Finlayson, Lorna. "On Mountains and Molehills." *Constellations* 21, no. 4 (2014): 483–493.

Forst, Rainer, Martin Hartmann, Rahel Jaeggi, and Martin Saar, eds. *Sozialphilosophie und Kritik.* Frankfurt: Suhrkamp, 2009.

Foucault, Michel. *Discipline and Punish: The Birth of the Prison.* 1975; New York: Vintage, 1995.

——. *The History of Sexuality.* Vol. 1, *The Will to Knowledge.* 1976; Harmondsworth, UK: Penguin, 1990.

——. "Of Other Spaces" (1984). *Diacritics* 16 (1986): 22–27.

——. "The Order of Discourse" (1970). In *Archives of Infamy,* edited by N. Luxor, 141–174. Minneapolis: University of Minnesota Press, 2019.

——. "What Is Critique?" In *The Politics of Truth,* edited by S. Lotringer and L. Hochroth, 41–82. New York: Semiotext(e), 1997.

Furet, François. *Interpreting the French Revolution.* 1978; Cambridge: Cambridge University Press, 1981.

Garfinkel, Harold. *Studies in Ethnomethodology.* Englewood Cliffs, NJ: Prentice-Hall, 1967.

Gentschel, Corinna. "Erstrittene Subjektivität: Die Diskurse der Transsexualität." *Das Argument* 243, no. 6 (2001): 281–283.

Gentz, Friedrich von. *The Origin and Principles of the American Revolution, Compared with the Origin and Principles of the French Revolution.* 1800; Indianapolis: Liberty Fund, 2010.

Geuss, Raymond. "Dialectics and the Revolutionary Impulse." In *The Cambridge Companion to Critical Theory,* edited by Fred Rush, 103–138. Cambridge: Cambridge University Press, 2006.

——. *History and Illusion in Politics.* Cambridge: Cambridge University Press, 2001.

——. "Nietzsche and Genealogy." *European Journal of Philosophy* 2, no. 3 (1994): 274–292.

——. "The Radioactive Wolf, Pieing, and the Goddess Fashion." In *Reality and Its Dreams,* 226–252. Cambridge, MA: Harvard University Press, 2016.

Gibson-Graham, J.-K. *The End of Capitalism (As We Knew It).* Oxford: Blackwell, 1996.

——. *A Postcapitalist Politics.* Oxford: Blackwell, 2006.

Giddens, Anthony. *The Constitution of Society: Outline of the Theory of Structuration.* Cambridge: Polity, 1984.

Glück, Helmut. *Metzler Lexikon Sprache.* Stuttgart: Metzler, 2005.

Godineau, Dominique. *The Women of Paris and Their French Revolution.* Berkeley: University of California Press, 1998.

Gordon, Uri. *Anarchy Alive.* London: Pluto, 2013.

Gould, Deborah B. *Moving Politics: Emotion and ACT UP's Fight Against AIDS.* Chicago: University of Chicago Press, 2009.

Greer, Germaine. *The Female Eunuch.* London: Paladin, 1970.

Griewank, Karl. *Der neuzeitliche Revolutionsbegriff: Entstehung und Entwicklung.* Frankfurt: Europ. Verl.-Anstalt, 1969.

Guha, Ranajit. *Dominance Without Hegemony: History and Power in Colonial India.* Cambridge, MA: Harvard University Press, 1998.

Gumbs, Alexis P., China Martens, and Mai'a Williams. *Revolutionary Mothering.* Oakland: PM, 2016.

Habermas, Jürgen. "Mit dem Pfeil ins Herz der Gegenwart: Zu Foucaults Vorlesung über Kants 'Was ist Aufklärung.'" *Die Tageszeitung,* July 7, 1984.

——. *Die neue Unübersichtlichkeit.* Frankfurt: Suhrkamp, 1985.

——. *Theory of Communicative Action.* Vol. 1, *Reason and the Rationalization of Society.* Boston: Beacon, 1984.

——. "Ziviler Ungehorsam—Testfall für den demokratischen Rechtsstaat." In *Die neue Unübersichtlichkeit*, 79–99. Frankfurt: Suhrkamp, 1985.

Hacking, Ian. "Introductory Essay." In *The Structure of Scientific Revolutions*, by Thomas S. Kuhn, vii–xxvii. Chicago: University of Chicago Press, 2012.

Halberstam, Jack. *In a Queer Time and Place: Transgender Bodies, Subcultural Lives*. New York: NYU Press, 2005.

Halbig, Christoph, Michael Quante, and Ludwig Siep, eds. *Hegels Erbe*. Frankfurt: Suhrkamp, 2004.

Harney, Stefano, and Fred Moten. *The Undercommons, Fugitive Planning and Black Study*. Wivenhoe: Minor Compositions, 2013.

Haslanger, Sally. *Resisting Reality: Social Construction and Social Critique*. Oxford: Oxford University Press, 2012.

Hegel, G. W. Friedrich. *Elements of the Philosophy of Right*. 1821; Cambridge: Cambridge University Press, 1991.

Heidegger, Martin. "The Age of the World Picture" (1938). In *Off the Beaten Track*, 57–85. Cambridge: Cambridge University Press, 2002.

——. *Being and Time*. 1927; Oxford: Blackwell, 1962.

Hobsbawm, Eric J. *The Age of Revolution: Europe, 1789–1848*. London: Weidenfeldt and Nicolson, 1962.

Holloway, John. *Crack Capitalism*. London: Pluto, 2010.

Hölscher, Lucian. "Utopie." In *Geschichtliche Grundbegriffe: Historisches Lexikon zur politisch-sozialen Sprache in Deutschland*, edited by Rainer Koselleck, 768–769. Stuttgart: Klett-Cotta, 1990.

Honneth. Axel. *The Idea of Socialism: Towards a Renewal*. New York: John Wiley and Sons, 2016.

——. "Rejoinder." *Critical Horizons* 16, no. 2 (2015): 204–226.

Hörning, Karl, and Julia Reuter, eds. *Doing Culture: Neue Positionen zum Verhältnis von Kultur und sozialer Praxis*. Bielefeld: transcript, 2004.

Hunt, Lynn. *The Family Romance of the French Revolution*. London: Routledge, 1992.

——. *Politics, Culture, and Class in the French Revolution*. Oakland: University of California Press, 1984.

——. "The Rhetorics of Revolution in France." *History Workshop* 15 (1983): 78–95.

——. "The World We Have Gained: The Future of the French Revolution." *American Historical Review* 108, no. 1 (2003): 1–19.

Isaac, Jeffrey C. "Beyond the Three Faces of Power. A Realist Critique." In *Rethinking Power*, edited by T. E. Wartenberg, 32–55. Albany: SUNY Press, 1992.

Jaeggi, Rahel. "Crisis, Contradiction, and the Task of a Critical Theory." In *Feminism, Capitalism, and Critique: Essays in Honor of Nancy Fraser*, edited by B. Bargu and C. Bottici, 209–224. Basingstoke, UK: Palgrave Macmillan, 2017.

——. *Critique of Forms of Life*. 2014; Cambridge, MA: Harvard University Press, 2019.

——. *Fortschritt und Regression*. Berlin: Suhrkamp, 2020.

——. "Rethinking Ideology." In *New Waves in Political Philosophy*, edited by B. de Bruin and C. F. Zurn, 63–86. New York: Palgrave Macmillan, 2009.

——. "Was ist eine (gute) Institution?" In *Sozialphilosophie und Kritik*, edited by R. Forst, M. Hartmann, R. Jaeggi, and M. Saar, 528–544. Frankfurt: Suhrkamp, 2009.

——. *Welt und Person: Zum anthropologischen Hintergrund der Gesellschaftskritik bei Hannah Arendt*. Berlin: Lukas, 1997.

Jameson, Frederic. *The Seeds of Time*. New York: Columbia University Press, 1994.

Janicka, Iwona. *Theorizing Contemporary Anarchism: Solidarity, Mimesis and Radical Social Change*. London: Bloomsbury, 2017.

Jaurès, Jean. *Histoire Socialiste de la Révolution Française*. 1904; Paris: Éditions Sociales, 1968.

Jay, Martin. "Historicism and the Event." In *Against the Grain: Jewish Intellectuals in Hard Times*, edited by E. Mendelsohn, S. Hoffman, and R. I. Cohen, 143–168. Oxford: Berghahn, 2013.

Joas, Hans, and Wolfgang Knöbl. *Sozialtheorie: Zwanzig einführende Vorlesungen: Aktualisierte Ausgabe.* Frankfurt: Suhrkamp, 2004.

Kelly, Gary. *The English Jacobin Novel.* Oxford: Clarendon, 1976.

Kent, Edward, ed. *Revolution and the Rule of Law.* Englewood Cliffs, NJ: Prentice-Hall, 1971.

King, Martin Luther, Jr. "Letter from Birmingham City Jail" (1963). In *Revolution and the Rule of Law*, edited by Edward Kent, 12–29. Englewood Cliffs, NJ: Prentice-Hall, 1971.

Kley, Christine, Catherine Newark, and Simone Miller, eds. *Philosophie und die Potenziale der Gender Studies: Peripherie und Zentrum im Feld der Theorie.* Bielefeld: transcript, 2012.

Kropotkin, Peter. *Gegenseitige Hilfe in der Tier- und Menschenwelt.* Translated by G. Landauer. Leipzig: Theod. Thomas, 1908.

Kuhn, Thomas S. "Postscript" (1969). In *The Structure of Scientific Revolutions*, 173–208. Chicago: University of Chicago Press, 2012.

——. *The Structure of Scientific Revolutions.* 1962; Chicago: University of Chicago Press, 2012.

Landauer, Gustav. *Auch die Vergangenheit ist Zukunft: Essays zum Anarchismus.* Edited by Siegbert Wolf. Frankfurt: Luchterhand, 1989.

——. *Aufruf zum Sozialismus.* 1908; Frankfurt: Rütten und Loening, 1967.

——. *Beginnen.* 1924; Wetzlar: Büchse der Pandora, 1977.

——. *Briefe aus der Französischen Revolution.* 1919; Hamburg: Rütten und Loening, 1961.

——. *Dichter, Ketzer, Außenseiter: Essays und Reden zu Literatur: Philosophie, Judentum.* Edited by Hanna Delf. Berlin: Akademie, 1997.

——. *Die Revolution.* Edited by Martin Buber. Frankfurt: Rütten und Loening, 1907.

——. *Sein Lebensgang in Briefen.* Edited by Martin Buber. Frankfurt: Rütten und Loening, 1929.

——. *Skepsis und Mystik: Versuche in Anschluß an Mauthners Sprachkritik.* Wetzlar: 1901; Büchse der Pandora, 1970.

——. *Der werdende Mensch: Aufsätze über Leben und Schrifttum.* Edited by Martin Buber. Potsdam: Gustav Kiepenheuer, 1921.

Langner, Ronald, Timo Luks, Anette Schlimm, Gregor Straube, and Dirk Tomaschke, eds. *Ordnungen des Denkens: Debatten um Wissenschaftstheorie und Erkenntniskritik.* Berlin: LIT, 2007.

Larrain, Jorge. *A Reconstruction of Historical Materialism.* London: Allen and Unwin, 1986.

Latour, Bruno. *Reassembling the Social: An Introduction to Actor-Network Theory.* Oxford: Oxford University Press, 2005.

——. "When Things Strike Back: A Possible Contribution of 'Science Studies' to the Social Sciences." *British Journal of Sociology* 51, no. 1 (2000): 107–125.

de Lauretis, Teresa. *The Practice of Love: Lesbian Sexuality and Perverse Desire.* Bloomington: Indiana University Press, 1994.

Lefebvre, Georges. *The Great Fear of 1789: Rural Panic in Revolutionary France.* New York: Pantheon, 1973.

——. "Le mythe de la Révolution française." *Annales historiques de la Révolution française* 259 (1985): 1–7.

Lefort, Claude. "Penser la révolution dans la Révolution française." *Annales* 35, no. 2 (1980): 334–352.

Lenin, Vladimir I. *Staat und Revolution.* 1917; Berlin: Dietz, 1960.

Lenz, Ilse, ed. *Die neue Frauenbewegung in Deutschland: Abschied vom kleinen Unterschied: Eine Quellensammlung.* Wiesbaden: VS, 2008.

Lettow, Susanne, ed. *Reproduction, Race and Gender in Philosophy and the Early Life Sciences.* Albany: SUNY Press, 2014.

Lindner, Urs. *Marx und die Philosophie: Wissenschaftlicher Realismus, ethischer Perfektionismus und kritische Sozialtheorie.* Stuttgart: Schmetterling, 2013.

Loick, Daniel. "21 Theses on the Politics of Forms of Life." *Theory and Event* 20, no. 3 (2017): 788–803.

——. *Kritik der Souveränität.* Frankfurt: Campus, 2012.

Lorde, Audre. *Sister Outsider.* Berkeley: Crossing, 1984.

Lorenz, Renate. *Queer Art: A Freak Theory.* Bielefeld: transcript, 2012.

Lorey, Isabell. *Figuren des Immunen: Elemente einer politischen Theorie.* Berlin: diaphanes, 2011.

Lukes, Steven. *Power: A Radical View.* Houndsmills, UK: Palgrave, 1974.

Lurie, Julia. "They Built a Utopian Sanctuary in a Minneapolis Hotel. Then They Got Evicted." *Mother Jones,* June 12, 2020. www.motherjones.com/crime-justice/2020/06/minneapolis-sheraton-george -floyd-protests/.

Luxemburg, Rosa. "Organizational Questions of the Russian Social Democracy" (1904). In *The Rosa Luxemburg Reader,* edited by K. Hudin and K. B. Anderson, 248–264. New York: Monthly Review Press, 1971.

Lyotard, Jean-François. *Dérive à Partir de Marx et Freud.* Paris: U.G.E., 1973.

——. "March 23." In *Political Writings.* Minneapolis: University of Minnesota Press, 1993.

MacIntyre, Alasdair. *After Virtue.* Notre Dame: University of Notre Dame Press, 1981.

——. "Epistemological Crises, Dramatic Narrative and the Philosophy of Science." *Monist* 60, no. 4 (1977): 453–472.

——. "Ideology, Social Science, and Revolution." *Comparative Politics* 5, no. 3 (1973): 321–342.

——. *Whose Justice? Which Rationality?* Eastborne, UK: Duckworth, 1988.

Mann, Michael, *The Sources of Social Power.* Vol. 1, *A History of Power from the Beginning to AD 1760.* Cambridge: Cambridge University Press, 1986.

——. *The Sources of Social Power.* Vol. 3, *Global Empires and Revolution, 1890–1945.* Cambridge: Cambridge University Press, 2012.

Marcuse, Herbert. "Ethics and Revolution" (1964). In *Revolution and the Rule of Law,* edited by Edward Kent, 46–59. Englewood Cliffs, NJ: Prentice-Hall, 1971.

——. *Triebstruktur und Gesellschaft.* 1955; Frankfurt: Suhrkamp, 1979.

Marx, Karl. *Capital.* Vol. 1. 1867; London: Penguin, 1990.

——. "A Contribution to the Critique of Hegel's Philosophy of Right. Introduction" (1843–1844). In *Early Writings,* 243–257. London: Penguin, 1992.

——. "The Eighteenth Brumaire of Louis Bonaparte" (1852). In *Later Political Writings,* edited by Terell Carver, 31–127. Cambridge: Cambridge University Press, 1996.

——. *Grundrisse: Foundations of the Critique of Political Economy.* 1857–1858; London: Penguin, 1993.

——. "Die moralisierende Kritik und die kritisierende Moral" (1947). In *Marx-Engels Werke,* vol. 4, 331–359. Berlin: Dietz, 1972.

——. *The Poverty of Philosophy.* 1847; New York: Cosimo, 2008.

——. *Selected Works 1.* Moscow: Progress, 1969.

——. "Zur Kritik der politischen Ökonomie" (1859). In *Marx-Engels Werke,* vol. 13, 3–160. Berlin: Dietz, 1961.

Masterman, Margaret. "The Nature of a Paradigm." In *Criticism and the Growth of Knowledge,* edited by I. Lakatos and A. Musgrave, 59–90. Cambridge: Cambridge University Press, 1965.

Matzner, Tobias. "The Interdependence of Normalcy and Exclusion—Some Political Thoughts Inspired by *On Certainty.*" Lecture manuscript (unpublished), 2011.

——. *Vita variabilis: Handelnde und ihre Welt nach Hannah Arendt und Ludwig Wittgenstein.* Würzburg: Königshausen und Neumann, 2013.

Meinhof, Ulrike. *Bambule.* Berlin: Wagenbach, 1971.

Menke, Christoph. *Critique of Rights.* Cambridge: Polity, 2020.

——. *Die Gegenwart der Tragödie: Versuch über Urteil und Spiel.* Frankfurt: Suhrkamp, 2005.

Mennel, Birgit, Stefan Nowotny, and Gerald Raunig, eds. *Kunst der Kritik.* Vienna: Turia + Kant.

Miller, Seumas. *Social Action: A Teleological Account.* Cambridge: Cambridge University Press, 2001.

Mitchell, Juliet. "Women: The Longest Revolution." *New Left Review* 1, no. 40 (1966): 11–37.

Mohrmann, Judith. *Affekt und Revolution: Politisches Handeln nach Arendt und Kant.* Frankfurt: Campus, 2015.

Moon, Dawne. "Insult and Inclusion: The Term *Fag Hag* and Gay Male 'Community.'" *Social Forces* 74, no. 2 (1995): 487–510.

Mulhall, Steven. *The Cavell Reader.* Cambridge, MA: Blackwell, 1996.

Muñoz, José. *Cruising Utopia: The Then and There of Queer Futurity.* New York: NYU Press, 2009.

Munz, Regine, ed. *Philosophinnen des 20. Jahrhunderts.* Darmstadt: Wissenschaftliche Buchgesellschaft, 2004.

Murphy, Jeffrie G., ed. *Civil Disobedience and Violence.* Belmont: Wadsworth, 1971.

Nauta, Ruurd. "The Concept of 'Metalepsis': From Rhetoric to the Theory of Allusion and to Narratology." In *Über die Grenze: Metalepse in Text- und Bildmedien des Altertums,* edited by Ute E. Eisen and Peter von Möllendorff, 469–482. Berlin: de Gruyter, 2013.

Newton, Esther. *Mother Camp: Female Impersonators in America.* Chicago: University of Chicago Press, 1972.

Nichols, Robert. *The World of Freedom: Heidegger, Foucault, and the Politics of Historical Ontology.* Stanford: Stanford University Press, 2014.

Ortner, Sherry B. "Theory in Anthropology since the Sixties." *Comparative Studies in Society and History* 26, no. 1 (1984): 126–166.

Osterweil, Vicky. *In Defense of Looting: A Riotous History of Uncivil Action.* New York: Bold Type, 2020.

Pahl, Katrin. *Sex Changes with Kleist.* Evanston, IL: Northwestern University Press, 2019.

Patton, Cindy. *Globalizing AIDS.* Minneapolis: University of Minnesota Press, 2002.

Pernoud, Georges, and Sabine Flaissier, eds. *Die Französische Revolution in Augenzeugenberichten.* 1959; Munich: dtv, 1976.

Pickering, Andrew. *The Mangle of Practice: Time, Agency, and Science.* Chicago: University of Chicago Press, 1995.

Pinkard, Terry. *Hegel's Naturalism.* Oxford: Oxford University Press, 2013.

Polanyi, Karl. *The Great Transformation: The Political and Economic Origins of Our Time.* 1949; Boston: Beacon, 2001.

Porpora, Douglas V. "Four Concepts of Social Structure." *Journal for the Theory of Social Behaviour* 20, no. 1 (1989): 195–211.

Puhl, Klaus. "Die List der Regel: Zur Retroaktiven Konstruktion sozialer Praxis." In *Institutionen und Regelfolgen,* edited by Ulrich Baltzer and Gerhard Schönrich, 81–101. Paderborn: Mentis, 2002.

Purtschert, Patricia. "Judith Butler: Macht der Kontingenz—Begriff der Kritik." In *Philosophinnen des 20. Jahrhunderts,* edited by Regine Munz, 181–202. Darmstadt: Wissenschaftliche Buchgesellschaft, 2004.

Raatzsch, Richard. "Henne oder Ei?" *Deutsche Zeitschrift für Philosophie* 49, no. 4 (2001): 567–570.

Rebentisch, Juliane. "Camp Materialism." *Criticism: A Quarterly for Literature and the Arts* 56, no. 2 (2014): 235–248.

Reckwitz, Andreas. "Grundelemente einer Theorie sozialer Praktiken: Eine sozialtheoretische Perspektive." *Zeitschrift für Soziologie* 32, no. 4 (2003): 282–301.

———. "Die Reproduktion und die Subversion sozialer Praktiken." In *Doing Culture: Neue Positionen zum Verhältnis von Kultur und sozialer Praxis,* edited by K. Hörning and J. Reuter, 40–53. Bielefeld: transcript, 2004.

———. *Struktur: Zur sozialwissenschaftlichen Analyse von Regeln und Regelmäßigkeiten.* Opladen: Westdeutscher, 1997.

———. "Towards a Theory of Social Practices: A Development in Cultural Theorizing." *European Journal for Social Theory* 5, no. 2 (2002): 243–263.

Redecker, Eva von. "Feministische Strategie und Revolution." In *Philosophie und die Potenziale der Gender Studies: Peripherie und Zentrum im Feld der Theorie,* edited by Christine Kley, Catherine Newark, and Simone Miller, 17–36. Bielefeld: transcript, 2012.

———. *Gravitation zum Guten: Hannah Arendts Moralphilosophie.* Berlin: Lukas, 2013.

——. "Marx's Concept of Needs in the Guise of Queer Desire." In *Global Justice and Desire: Queering the Economy*, edited by N. Dhawan, A. Engel, C. Holzhey, and V. Woltersdorff, 23–38. London: Routledge, 2015.

——. "Ownership's Shadow: Neoauthoritarianism as Defense of Phantom Possession." *Critical Times* 3, no. 1 (2020): 33–67.

——. *Revolution für das Leben: Philosophie der neuen Protestformen*. Frankfurt: Fischer, 2020.

——. "Topischer Sozialismus: Zur Exodus-Konzeption bei Gustav Landauer und Martin Buber." *West-End: Neue Zeitschrift für Sozialforschung* 11, no. 1 (2014): 93–108.

——. *Zur Aktualität von Judith Butler*. Wiesbaden: Verlag für Sozialwissenschaft, 2011.

Ricoeur, Paul. *The Course of Recognition*. Cambridge, MA: Harvard University Press, 2005.

Robinson, Amy. "It Takes One to Know One: Passing and Communities of Interest." *Critical Inquiry* 20, no. 4 (1994): 715–736.

Rorty, Richard. "Feminism and Pragmatism" (1994). In *Truth and Progress*, 202–227.

——. *Philosophy and the Mirror of Nature*. Thirtieth anniversary ed. Princeton: Princeton University Press, 2009. Originally published in 1979.

——. *Truth and Progress: Philosophical Papers*. Cambridge: Cambridge University Press, 1998.

Rouse, Joseph. *How Scientific Practices Matter: Reclaiming Philosophical Naturalism*. Chicago: University of Chicago Press, 2002.

——. "Two Concepts of Practices." In *The Practice Turn in Contemporary Theory*, edited by T. R. Schatzki, K. Knorr Cetina, and E. von Savigny, 198–208. London: Psychology Press, 2001.

Roversi, Corrado. "Mimetic Constitutive Rules." *Phenomenology and Mind* 2 (2012): 144–151.

Rubin, Gayle. "The Traffic in Women: Notes on the 'Political Economy' of Sex." In *Toward an Anthropology of Woman*, edited by Rayna R. Reiter, 157–210. New York: Monthly Review Press, 1975.

Saar, Martin. "Genealogische Kritik." In *Was ist Kritik?*, edited by R. Jaeggi and T. Wesche, 247–265. Frankfurt: Suhrkamp, 2009.

Saint-Pierre, Bernardin de. *Paul et Virginie*. 1788; Paris: Librio, 2004.

Sanson, Henri, and Charles Henri Sanson. *Memoirs of the Sansons, 1685–1847*. 2 vols. Edited by H. Sanson. London: Chatto and Windus, 1876.

Sartre, Jean-Paul. *Critique of Dialectical Reason*. Vol. 1. 1960; London: Verso, 2004.

Schaeffer-Hegel, Barbara. "Die Freiheit und Gleichheit der Brüder." In *1789/1989: Die Revolution hat nicht stattgefunden*, edited by A. Deuber-Mankowsky, U. Ramming, and E. W. Tielsch, 51–64. Tübingen: edition discord, 1989.

Schäfer, Hilmar. *Die Instabilität der Praxis: Reproduktion und Transformation des Sozialen in der Praxistheorie*. Weilerswist: Velbrück Wissenschaft, 2014.

Schatzki, Theodore R. "Practice and Actions: A Wittgensteinian Critique of Bourdieu and Giddens." *Philosophy of the Social Sciences* 27, no. 3 (1997): 283–308.

——. *The Site of the Social: A Philosophical Account of the Constitution of Social Life and Change*. University Park: Pennsylvania State University Press, 2002.

Schatzki, Theodore R., Karin Knorr Cetina, and Elke von Savigny, eds. *The Practice Turn in Contemporary Theory*. London: Psychology Press, 2001.

Schirmer, Uta. *Geschlecht anders gestalten: Drag Kinging, geschichtliche Selbstverhältnisse und Wirklichkeiten*. Bielefeld: transcript, 2010.

Schmidt, Christian, ed. *Können wir der Geschichte entkommen?* Frankfurt: Campus, 2013.

Schuck, Hartwig. "Macht und Herrschaft: Eine realistische Analyse." In *Anonyme Herrschaft. Zur Struktur moderner Machtverhältnisse*, edited by I. Elbe, S. Ellmers, and J. Eufinger, 35–81. Münster: Westfälisches Dampfboot, 2012.

Scott, Joan Wallach. "French Feminists and the Rights of 'Man.'" *History Workshop* 28 (1989): 1–21.

Searle, John R. "How to Derive 'Ought' from 'Is.'" *Philosophical Review* 73, no. 1 (1964): 43–58.

——. *Speech Acts*. Cambridge: Cambridge University Press, 1969.

Sedgwick, Eve Kosofsky. *Epistemology of the Closet*. Berkeley: University of California Press, 1990.

Sewell, William H., Jr. "Historical Events as Transformations of Structures: Inventing Revolution at the Bastille." *Theory and Society* 25, no. 6 (1996): 841–881.

——. "Ideologies and Social Revolutions: Reflections on the French Case." *Journal of Modern History* 57, no. 1 (1985): 57–85.

——. *Logics of History: Social Theory and Social Transformation*. Chicago: University of Chicago Press, 2005.

Shotwell, Alexis. *Knowing Otherwise: Race, Gender, and Implicit Understanding*. University Park: Pennsylvania State University Press, 2011.

Shove, Elizabeth, Mika Pantzar, and Matt Watson. *The Dynamics of Social Practice: Everyday Life and How It Changes*. London: Sage, 2012.

Sieg, Kathrin, *Ethnic Drag: Performing Race, Nation, Sexuality in West Germany*. Ann Arbor: University of Michigan Press, 2002.

Skocpol, Theda. "Cultural Idioms and Political Ideologies in the Revolutionary Reconstruction of State Power: A Rejoinder to Sewell." *Journal of Modern History* 57, no. 1 (1985): 86–96.

——. *States and Social Revolutions*. Cambridge: Cambridge University Press, 1979.

Soboul, Albert. "Classes and Class Struggles During the French Revolution." *Science and Society* 17, no. 5 (1953): 238–257.

——. *The Sans-Culottes*. 1968; Princeton: Princeton University Press, 1980.

Spivak, Gayatri Chakravorty. "Can the Subaltern Speak?" In *Marxism and the Interpretation of Culture*, edited by Cary Nelson and Lawrence Grossberg, 271–313. Chicago: University of Illinois Press, 1988.

Springer, Kimberly. *Living for the Revolution: Black Feminist Organizations, 1968–1980*. Durham: Duke University Press, 2005.

Swidler, Ann. "What Anchors Cultural Practices?" In *The Practice Turn in Contemporary Theory*, edited by T. R. Schatzki, K. Knorr Cetina, and E. von Savigny, 83–101. London: Psychology Press, 2001.

Taylor, Charles. "Lichtung or Lebensform: Parallels Between Heidegger and Wittgenstein." In *Philosophical Arguments*, 61–78.

——. *Negative Freiheit? Zur Kritik des neuzeitlichen Individualismus*. Frankfurt: Suhrkamp, 1992.

——. *Philosophical Arguments*. Cambridge, MA: Harvard University Press, 1995.

——. "Theories of Meaning." In *Philosophical Papers*, vol. 1, 248–292. Cambridge: Cambridge University Press, 1985.

Tilly, Charles. *The Contentious French: Four Centuries of Popular Struggle*. Cambridge, MA: Harvard University Press, 1986.

——. "Getting It Together in Burgundy." *Theory and Society* 4, no. 4 (1977): 479–504.

Treichler, Paula A. *How to Have Theory in an Epidemic: Cultural Chronicles of AIDS*. Durham: Duke University Press, 1999.

Turner, Stephen. *The Social Theory of Practices: Tradition, Tacit Knowledge, and Presuppositions*. Chicago: University of Chicago Press, 1994.

Ueding, Gert, ed. *Historisches Wörterbuch der Rhetorik*. 10 vols, Tübingen: Niemeyer, 2001.

Virgil, *The Eclogues*. Translated by Guy Lee. London: Penguin, 1980.

Virno, Paolo. *Exodus*. Vienna: Turia + Kant, 2002.

Vogelmann, Frieder. "Foucaults Praktiken." *Coincidentia: Zeitschrift für europäische Geistesgeschichte* 3, no. 2 (2012): 275–299.

Warner, Michael, and Lauren Berlant. "Sex in Public." *Critical Inquiry* 24, no. 2 (1998): 547–566.

Wartenberg, Thomas E. *The Forms of Power: From Domination to Transformation*. Philadelphia: Temple University Press, 1990.

——, ed. *Rethinking Power*. Albany: SUNY Press, 1992.

——. "The Situated Conception of Social Power." *Social Theory and Practice* 14, no. 3 (1988): 317–343.

White, Hayden. *Metahistory: Die historische Einbildungskraft im 19. Jahrhundert.* Frankfurt: Suhrkamp, 1991.

Wittgenstein, Ludwig. *On Certainty.* Oxford: Blackwell, 1969.

———. *Philosophical Investigations/Philosophische Untersuchungen.* 1953; Oxford: Blackwell, 2004.

———. *Tractatus logico-philosophicus.* 1922; Frankfurt: Suhrkamp, 1960.

Wittig, Monique. "The Straight Mind." *Feminist Issues* 1, no. 1 (1980): 103–112.

Wollstonecraft, Mary. *Mary* and *The Wrongs of Woman.* 1798; Oxford: Oxford University Press, 2009.

———. "A Vindication of the Rights of Women." In *A Vindication of the Rights of Men* and *A Vindication of the Rights of Women*, 65–303. 1792; Cambridge: Cambridge University Press, 1995.

Wright, Eric Olin. *Envisioning Real Utopias.* London: Verso, 2010.

Zerilli, Linda M. G. *A Democratic Theory of Judgment.* Chicago: University of Chicago Press, 2016.

Žižek, Slavoj. "Afterword: Lenin's Choice." In *Revolution at the Gates*, 165–336. London: Verso, 2002.

———. "Da Capo senza Fine." In *Contingency, Hegemony, Universality: Contemporary Dialogues on the Left*, edited by J. Butler, E. Laclau, and S. Žižek, 213–262. London: Verso, 2000.

FILMS

Ebert, Matt, and Ryan Landry, *Marta: Portrait of a Teenage Activist.* USA, 1990. http://vimeo.com/59859368.

Lewis, Avi, and Opal Tometi. *A Message from the Future II: The Years of Repair.* Canada, 2020. www.youtube.com/watch?v=2m8YACFJlMg.

Mandy, Marie. *Judith Butler, Philosophin der Gender.* France, 2006. www.youtube.com/watch?v=PlCmB—sT4.

Index

NEW DIRECTIONS IN CRITICAL THEORY

....

Amy Allen, General Editor